Lecture Notes in Computer Science

Commenced Publication in 1973
Founding and Former Series Editors:
Gerhard Goos, Juris Hartmanis, and Jan van Leeuwen

Editorial Board

Reihaneh Safavi-Naini   Moti Yung (Eds.)

Digital Rights Management

Technologies, Issues
Challenges and Systems

First International Conference, DRMTICS 2005
Sydney, Australia, October 31 – November 2, 2005
Revised Selected Papers

 Springer

Volume Editors

Reihaneh Safavi-Naini
University of Wollongong, School of IT and CS
Northfields Avenue, Wollongong 2522, Australia
E-mail: rei@uow.edu.au

Moti Yung
RSA Laboratories
and
Columbia University, Department of Computer Science
450 Computer Science Building, New York, NY 10027, USA
E-mail: moti@cs.columbia.edu

Library of Congress Control Number: 2006928038

CR Subject Classification (1998): E.3, D.4.6, F.2.1, C.2, J.1, C.3, K.4.4, K.6.5

LNCS Sublibrary: SL 4 – Security and Cryptology

ISSN   0302-9743
ISBN-10   3-540-35998-2 Springer Berlin Heidelberg New York
ISBN-13   978-3-540-35998-2 Springer Berlin Heidelberg New York

Springer is a part of Springer Science+Business Media

springer.com

© Springer-Verlag Berlin Heidelberg 2006
Printed in Germany

Typesetting: Camera-ready by author, data conversion by Scientific Publishing Services, Chennai, India
Printed on acid-free paper   SPIN: 11787952   06/3142   5 4 3 2 1 0

Preface

The First International Conference on Digital Rights Management: Technology, Issues, Challenges and Systems (DRMTICS – pronounced 'dramatics'), took place in Sydney, Australia on 31st October - 2nd November, 2005. It was organized by the Centre for Information Security of the University of Wollongong and in cooperation with the International Association of Cryptologic Research (IACR) and IEEE Computer Society's Task Force on Information Assurance.

DRMTICS is an international conference series that covers the area of digital rights management, including research advancements of an applied and theoretical nature. The goal is to have a broad coverage of the field and related issues and subjects as the area evolves. Since the Internet and the computing infrastructure has turned into a marketplace for content where information goods of various kinds are exchanged, this area is expected to grow and be part of the ongoing evolution of the information society. The DRM area is a unique blend of many diverse disciplines that include mathematics and cryptography, legal and social aspects, signal processing and watermarking, game theory, information theory, software and systems design and business analysis, and DRMTICS attempts to cover as much ground as possible, and to cover new results that will further spur new investigations on the foundations and practices of DRM. We hope that this first conference marks the beginning of a fruitful and useful series of future conferences.

This year, the conference received 57 submissions out of which 26 were accepted for presentation after a rigorous refereeing process. In addition to the regular program, the program also included invited talks and a panel discussion. Renato Ianella gave an invited talk describing "A Brief History of Right Expression Languages," Moni Naor gave a talk entitled "Humans, Computers and Cryptography," and Karen Gettens gave a talk on "DRM– the Legal Issues." The panel was chaired by Bill Caelli and was entitled "Is Reliable and Trusted DRM Enforcement Realistic or Even Possible?"

We wish to thank all the authors of submitted papers for providing the content of this year's workshop; their high quality submissions made the task of selecting a program hard. We would also like to thank the program committee members as well as the external reviewers, who helped in the refereeing process. We wish to thank our sponsors: Smart Internet Technology CRC, Motorola, DigiSensory Technologies, The Telecommunications and Information Technology Research Institute of the University of Wollongong, Research Network for a Secure Australia, Infosys and Markany. We further wish to thank the attendees, speakers and the participants, as well as Susan Branch, Debbie Farrelly, Harikrishna Vasanta, Wenming Lu, Liang Lu, Rungrat Wiangsripanawan, Siamak Fayyaz-Shahandashti, Angela Piper and Martin Surminem, who helped with the organization of the conference.

Last but not least, we would like to thank Wanqing Li and Nicholas Sheppard, general co-chairs of the conference, for their relentless effort in organizing the event and paying attention to every detail, which made DRMTICS a good drama, but one without unnecessary, unexpected dramatic moments! Without the help of the above bodies and individuals this inaugural conference would not have been a possibility.

November 2005   Rei Safavi-Naini
                                                                    Moti Yung

Organization

General Chairs

Wanqing Li   University of Wollongong, Australia
Nicholas Sheppard   University of Wollongong, Australia

Program Chairs

Rei Safavi-Naini   University of Wollongong, Australia
Moti Yung   Columbia University and RSA Security, USA

Program Committee

Feng Bao	Institute for Infocomm Research, Singapore
Stefan Bechtold	Max Planck Institute for Collective Goods, Germany
Jong Uk Choi	MarkAny, Korea
Christian S. Collberg	University of Arizona, USA
Ingemar Cox	University of London, UK
Ezzy Dabbish	Motorola Labs, USA
Jana Dittmann	University of Magdeburg, Germany
Yevgeniy Dodis	New York University, USA
Brian Fitzgerald	Queensland University of Technology, Australia
Susanne Guth	ODRL Initiative, Austria
Greg Heileman	University of New Mexico, USA
HweeHwa Pang	Singapore Management University, Singapore
Hideki Imai	University of Tokyo, Japan
Sushil Jajodia	George Mason University, USA
Ton Kalker	Hewlett-Packard Labs, USA
Stefan Katzenbeisser	Technical University of Munich, Germany
Aggelos Kiayias	University of Connecticut, USA
Kwangjo Kim	Information and Communication University, Korea
Kaoru Kurosawa	Ibaraki University, Japan
Jeff Lotspiech	IBM Almaden, USA
Stefan Nusser	IBM Almaden, USA
Josef Pieprzyk	Macquarie University, Australia
Bin Zhu	Microsoft Research Asia, China

External Reviewers

Yongdong Wu	Christopher Peikert	Dinesh Dhanekula
Yuichi Kaji	Prashant Puniya	Pramod Jamkhedkar
Takao Nishizeki	Kevin Kloker	Fabricio Ourique
Tomoyuki Asano	David Kravitz	Angela Piper
Katsunari Yoshioka	Tom Messerges	Wenming Lu
Goichiro Hanaoka	Kohich Kamijoh	Nicholas Sheppard
Carl Bosley	Deepa Kundur	Harikrishna Vasanta
Nelly Fazio	Jong W. Kim	

Sponsoring Institutions

DigiSensory Technologies, Australia
Infosys, India
MarkAny, Korea
Motorola, USA
Research Network for a Secure Australia, Australia
Smart Internet CRC, Australia
Telecommunications and Information Technology Research Institute, University
of Wollongong, Australia

Table of Contents

Software Issues

Fingerprinting and Image Authentication

Supporting Cryptographic Technology

A Novel Framework for Multiple Creatorship Protection of Digital Movies

Yu-Quan Zhang and Sabu Emmanuel

School of Computer Engineering,
Nanyang Technological University
{zh0004an, asemmanuel}@ntu.edu.sg

Abstract. A digital movie can be created jointly under the cooperation of many creators. It is then necessary to provide protection to the creatorship of each participating creator. In this paper, we propose a framework for providing the creatorship protection of multiple creators involved in creating the object-based digital movie. The proposed framework makes use of digital watermarking techniques and cryptographic protocols to achieve the creatorship protection purpose. Object-based movie may consist of several audio and video objects, which may be created by different creators. The proposed framework embeds different watermarks in different video/audio objects in such a way that each creator can show the joint-creatorship of the movie; as well as each creator can prove his/her creatorship of video/audio object he/she created.

1 Introduction

Nowadays, digital rights management (DRM) issue is discussed more and more since a large amount of digital assets involving media such as text, audio, video etc. are being created. The parties involved in the digital asset creation and transaction are creators, owners, distributors and consumers. Creators have creator rights, owners have owner rights, distributors have distributor rights and consumers have consumer rights. DRM refers to a set of technologies and approaches that establish a trust relationship among the parties involved in a digital asset creation and transaction [16]. Cryptographic techniques and watermarking techniques are important tools in DRM. Cryptographic techniques provide confidentiality, authentication, data integrity, and non-repudiation functions. Watermarking techniques are usually preferred for copyright ownership declaration, creator/authorship declaration, copyright violation detection, copyright violation deterrence, copy control, media authentication, and media data integrity functions. Our proposed framework employs both cryptographic and watermarking techniques to protect the creatorship of multiple creators involved in the creation of object-based digital movie.

The creator has creatorship of digital assets. Many digital media are very complex and almost impossible to be created by single creator. For example, in an image creation, some creators may be good at drawing the plants; some may be good at drawing animals and some may be good at drawing human beings; or in another way, some may do well in sketching the skeleton of the images and others may be good at coloring. Therefore, to create a good complex image, which contains lots of contents

R. Safavi-Naini and M. Yung (Eds.): DRMTICS 2005, LNCS 3919, pp. 1–12, 2006.

inside, the whole creation process needs the cooperation of many creators. Another example, in a cartoon movie, different cartoon characters may be created by different video creators and the associated audio dialogues may be dubbed by many audio dubbers. In addition the background music including special effects and foreground music may be created by many creators. Therefore creating a complex cartoon movie may involve many creators from video and audio domains.

In the case of joint creation of digital media by multiple creators, there are some concerns for each of the participating creators. Firstly, it is possible that a creator disowns his/her object at a later stage due to the malpractices (copying from someone else's work etc.) he/she has done during the creation. This disowning may cause unnecessary hardships for the good creators. Secondly, a creator may pose as the sole creator and sell the product to a buyer. These concerns arise mainly due to the mistrust among the creators. Our proposed framework intends to build the trust relationship among the creators involved in joint creations.

There are different kinds of digital media such as image, video, movie etc. In this paper, we focus on the creatorship protection of multiple creators of object-based digital movies. The digital graphics (cartoon) movies may be an example. The creation process of an object-based movie consists of video creation process and audio creation/dubbing process. In the video creation process, each video creator works on one or more video objects and then they refine their creations through several iterations. Usually the audio dubbing is carried out after the video creation process. The background and foreground musics are created by audio creators and are then dubbed along with the dialogs of characters into the movie. The audio dubbing also employs iterative procedures to refine the audio part of the movie.

We in this paper propose a novel framework to address the creatorship concerns of multiple creators of object-based movies (such as digital graphics/cartoon movies). We make use of watermarking techniques and cryptographic protocols for the framework. The watermarking scheme that the framework employs has certain requirements such as robustness, imperceptibility, asymmetric and non-invertibility. So that it can perform well under the complex joint creation situation to achieve the creatorship protection purpose. Cryptographic protocols require the use of digital signature algorithms.

The remainder of the paper is structured as follows: Section 2 discusses related watermarking and cryptographic schemes. Our proposed framework is presented in Section 3. Section 4 lists some application of our framework. Section 5 presents discussion and Section 6 concludes the paper.

2 Related Watermarking and Cryptographic Schemes

So far, there are quite few watermarking schemes considering the joint-creatorship protection problem. Guo and Georganas [8] introduce a digital image watermarking scheme for joint-ownership verification. The scheme that they used embeds a combined watermark of the creators' individual watermarks and a jointly created watermark, and then verifies the partial ownership and full ownership by setting different levels of thresholds in the detector. This scheme is not suitable for protecting the creatorship of multiple creators in a joint creation environment. It does not provide the protection during the creation process, and each creator cannot specify which video/audio object is created by him/her. For joint-creatorship protection, the scheme needs to provide the protection during the creation process, so it can take care of the two concerns we mentioned in the introduction, which may occur in the creation process. At the same time, single creator should have the ability to show which video/audio object was created by him/her. Our framework gives a solution to this type of problem for object-based movie creation.

Our framework employs both watermarking scheme and cryptographic protocol. The watermarking scheme is mainly used for creatorship protection and the cryptographic protocol is mainly used for digital signature purpose. Some research work on watermarking and digital signature scheme are reviewed below.

There have been many researches done in watermarking area [1][2]. The work by Cox et. al. [3] is spread spectrum based watermark, which is robust and invisible. Being robust watermark, it would be hard for the attackers to make undetectable or remove the watermark. The watermarking techniques proposed in [4] and [5] are asymmetric. The asymmetric watermarks make use of another key for embedding other than the detection key. Thus it would be hard for the watermark verifier to perform watermarking but can detect the watermark. Craver et.al. [6], Qiao and Nahrstedt [7], give a non-invertible watermarking scheme. In order to prove the rightful owner unambiguously, the watermarking scheme should be non-invertible.

Many audio and speech watermarking schemes have been proposed. The dialog in the movie can be seen as speech; the background music and foreground music can be seen as audio. Bassia et. al. [9] applies a straightforward time-domain spread-spectrum watermarking method to audio signals. An audio watermarking technique based on correlation detection is introduced in [13], where high-frequency chaotic watermarks are multiplicatively embedded in the low frequencies of the DFT domain.Wu et.al. [10] propose a low complexity speech-Watermarking scheme as an effective way to detect malicious content alterations while tolerating content preserving operations. The proposed scheme is based on the modified odd/even modulation scheme with exponential scale quantization and a localized frequency-masking model while assuring no mismatch between quantization steps used in watermark embedding and detection. Cheng et. al. [12] propose a speech watermarking technique in which maximum possible watermark signal energy is added to the speech signal satisfying the constraint that the added signal is not audible. Additional watermark energy is embedded into the portions of the speech that have white spectrum, fricative sounds and rapidly changing plosives sounds.

There are many digital signature schemes available such as RSA [14], Digital Signature Algorithm (DSA) and Elliptic Curve Digital Signature Algorithm (ECDSA). Recent years, some new schemes have been proposed. Elkamchouchi et. al. [11] have developed a digital signature scheme with appendix and message recovery in the real and Gaussian integers' domains. The proposed scheme employs the idea of combining the integer factorization, and the Generalized Discrete Logarithm problems. Chang et. al. [15] have proposed a secure digital signature scheme, where neither one-way hash functions nor message redundancy schemes are employed. We can apply any digital signature scheme in our framework as far as it can perform the digital signature safely.

3 Our Proposed Framework

In our proposed framework, a digital movie creation has two stages: video creation process and audio creation/dubbing process. Fig. 1 gives the flowchart of the whole digital movie creation process.

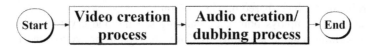

Fig. 1. The digital movie creation process

***Brief Description*:** In the proposed framework the movie creation begins with a video creation process. First, each video creator creates his/her video object. The created video object is then watermarked and signed by the creator and transmitted over the network to other participating video creators. On receiving every others signed watermarked video objects, each video creator then assembles a local video part of the movie by combining every others watermarked video objects and own watermarked video object. The video creators then carry out refinement iterations on their video objects until all the video creators are satisfied with the video part of the movie. The video creators can create their video objects in their own local machine as shown in Fig. 2 and they exchange their creations through the network to every other creators.

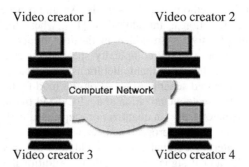

Fig. 2. Hardware infrastructure of the video creation process

Once the video part of the movie is completed, the audio creation/dubbing process begins. Some audio components such as background and foreground music may be created beforehand by some audio creators. Dubbing of all the audio components such as background music, foreground music and the dialogs of characters on to the movie usually will be done in real time while the video is playing. Different audio components can be recorded on different tracks and can be treated as different audio objects. For example, the background music can be one audio object, the dialogs of each character can be considered as individual audio objects. Each audio creator also gets a signed watermarked copy of every audio object. The audio dubbing is also done in

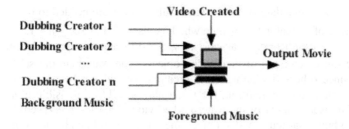

Fig. 3. Hardware infrastructure of audio creation process

iterative manner until all the creators are satisfied with the audio part. And the dubbing is usually done in single computer as shown in Fig 3.

Let N_v be the number of video creators, N_a be the number of audio creators and $N = N_v + N_a$ be the total number of creators jointly creating an object-based movie. Let there be J iterations to complete the video creation process and J_a iterations to complete the audio creation process.

Notation: The notation $Sign_i\{m\}$ denotes the digitally signed message m signed by the ith creator using his/her private key. This signed message can be verified by everyone using the corresponding public key. The verification of signed message will result in message m, thus anyone can obtain the message from $Sign_i\{m\}$.

The video creation process and audio creation process are discussed in detail below.

3.1 The Video Creation Process

The video is created in an iterative manner. The iteration steps focus on the video objects (VOs) created by the video creators. Let vo_{ij} be the video object created or modified by the ith creator in the jth iteration and vo_{ij}^w be the watermarked vo_{ij} using w_i. Each VO is made up of several consecutive video object planes (VOPs). Let vop_{ijn} be the nth VOP of vo_{ij} and vop_{ijn}^w be the watermarked vop_{ijn} using w_i.

First iteration
Let there be N_v video creators and each video creator creates one VO each.
Step 1: Each video creator creates his/her own VO. For example, the ith creator creates vo_{i1} in the first iteration. Then embeds his/ her watermark w_i using his/her watermark embedding key Kw_{iv} into his/her creation vo_{i1} to obtain vo_{i1}^w. The watermarking technique employed is asymmetric and hence the corresponding asymmetric detection key is Kw_{iv}^*. The watermarking is carried out VOP wise, i.e. the watermark w_i is embedded into each VOP using the watermark embedding key Kw_i. Thus watermarked n^{th} VOP of vo_{i1} would be denoted as vop_{i1n}^w.

Each video creator then makes a digitally signed version (using the private key of the creator) of their watermarked creation and transmits them to all other video creators. For example, the ith creator transmits $Sign_i\{VO_{i1}^w\}$ to all other creators. The creator then stores his/her video object vo_{i1}, watermark w_i, embedding key Kw_{iv} and detection key Kw_{iv}^* in a database DB_i. These information are needed to be presented to a judge in case of a creatorship dispute which is discussed in Section 4.1.

Discussion: We use different watermarks w_i for different creators and hence help to declare the full creatorship of their video objects. The watermarking scheme should be robust since others (including other creators) should not be able to remove the embedded watermark. In addition, the watermark should be invisible in such a way that the high visual quality of the watermarked video object is preserved. In order for the buyer to buy a particular video object, the buyer should be able to verify the existence of the watermark in that object without the capability to remove or embed the watermark, which requires the watermarking technique to be asymmetric as well. The transmitted digitally signed watermarked video objects prevent the creators from disowning their own video objects at a later stage. In the case that certain creator tries to disown the creatorship, the rest creators can show the signed version of the person's video object to prove the person's creatorship.

Step 2: On receiving the signed watermarked objects from other creators, the video creator first stores them locally. The creator then verifies all the signed watermarked objects from all other creators, using the public keys of the corresponding signatures and obtains the respective watermarked objects. If there is no signature detected, the video creator will ask for the retransmission of that particular video object. After the successful signature verification, every creator possesses his/her original video object and the watermarked video objects of all creators (vo_{i1}^w for all i's). All creators then assemble the watermarked objects individually, and then discuss on how the video objects should be modified. Fig. 4 gives the flowchart of first iteration. Fig. 5 illustrates the nth frame of the video after the first iteration.

Discussion: The received signed watermarked objects, own object vo_{i1} , own watermark w_i , embedding key Kw_{iv} and detection key Kw_{iv}^* are stored locally for checking-malpractices by other creators during later iterations and also for reference in dispute resolution which is discussed in Section 4.1.

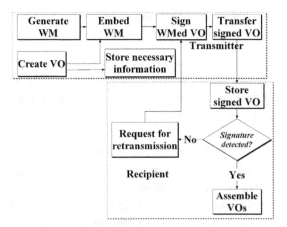

Fig. 4. First Iteration of video creation process

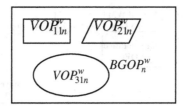

Fig. 5. The nth frame after first iteration

Refinement iterations

Step 3: After all the video creators agree on how to modify the video objects, the original creator will only modify the VOPs that need to be modified, and just rewatermark those modified VOPs. Each creator then makes a digitally signed version (using the private key of the creator) of their modified watermarked VOPs and then transmits them to all other video creators. For example the ith creator transmits $Sign_i$ {all watermarked modified VOPs} to all other video creators. The video creator then stores his/her modified VOPs into database DB_i for solving the creatorship dispute.
Discussion: Normally, the creator does not need to modify all the VOPs of the video object in the second iteration and following iterations. So, they will also transmit only the watermarked modified VOPs of the video object to the rest of the creators. This will reduce the size of data transmission and storage requirement in the database.

Step 4: On receiving the signed watermarked modified VOPs from other video creators, the creator first stores them locally. The creator then verifies all the signed watermarked VOPs from all other video creators using the public keys of the corresponding signatures and obtains the respective watermarked VOPs. If no correct signature is detected, the creator will ask for the retransmission of that object. Every video creator after the successful signature verification possesses the watermarked modifications of all creators. Then, each creator uses all the modified VOPs to replace the corresponding VOPs in the corresponding stored watermarked video object. After that, all video creators assemble the watermarked objects and again discuss how to modify the video objects. The iteration is shown in Fig 6.

Step 5: Iterations (step 3 and 4) are carried out until J^{th} iteration, i.e. the final video is obtained. Fig. 7 describes the nth frame of the final video.
Discussion: Since all the creators have the watermarked video objects of the whole video, sometimes it is possible that a single creator or a group of creators may cheat another creator by putting a second watermark on the person's video object. This action would cause both watermark to be detected from the same video object. In order to defeat this kind of attack, the watermarking technique should be non-invertible which would identify the original creator unambiguously even though two watermarks are detected from the same video object, which is illustrated in Section 4.1.

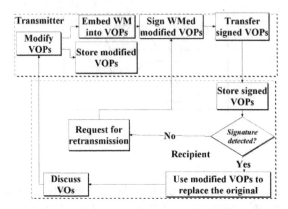

Fig. 6. Refinement iterations of video creation process

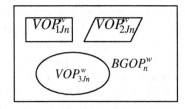

Fig. 7. The nth frame of the final video after J^{th} iteration

3.2   The Audio Creation/Dubbing Process

After the video creation process, a complete video with all the watermarks and without any audio is produced. The subsequent audio dubbing process will add all the audio tracks to the video to complete the whole movie. The audio tracks can be dialogs of characters, background music (including special effects such as thunder, car engine sounds etc.) and foreground music. The background and foreground music tracks may be created beforehand but dubbed along with the dialogs on to the movie. In audio creation process, different audio tracks will be considered as different audio objects. For easiness of discussion, we consider only one background music object (BO) created by one creator, one foreground music object (FO) created by another creator and several audio dubbers dubbing the dialog objects (DOs) of characters in the movie.

The audio creation/dubbing process is also conducted in an iterative manner. But for the easiness of explanation, we assume that the background and foreground music are perfect so they will not be modified during the iteration process. The audio creation/dubbing is usually carried out in one single computer.

First iteration
Let there be N_a audio creators and each audio creator creates one Audio Object (AO) each. For dialog of characters, each character's voice will be treated as one dialog object DO_n, which is dubbed by i^{th} creator in the 1st iteration. Then, the audio object

created by the ith creator will be watermarked with a watermark embedding key Kw_{i_a} which is only known to him/her (the corresponding detection key is $Kw_{i_a}^*$). Let FO_i be the foreground music object created by i^{th} creator and BO_i be the background music object created by i^{th} creator. FO_i and BO_i are also watermarked with watermark embedding key Kw_{i_a} to obtain FO_i^w and BO_i^w. The watermarking scheme employed here needs to be asymmetric.

Then, the watermarked audio objects will be signed by their respective audio creators. Each audio creator then make copies of their signed watermarked audio object which are then passed to all the other creators. All the audio creators store the received audio objects and multiplex the watermarked audio objects together with the watermarked video objects. At this stage, the first draft of audio dubbing is produced. The first iteration is illustrated in Fig. 8.

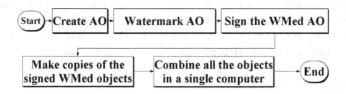

Fig. 8. The first iteration in the audio creation process

Discussion: The watermarking scheme used here must be robust, imperceptible, asymmetric and non-invertible. First, to protect the audio creator's creatorship, the watermarking scheme must be robust so the attackers cannot remove the watermark easily. Second, the human audible system is quite sensitive to the audio, so the watermarking scheme must be imperceptible to keep a good quality of audio. Third, the buyer of the movie may use the watermark to identify the creator of certain audio object, so the watermarking scheme is required to be asymmetric. Fourth, sometimes, attackers may put another watermark on a watermarked audio object. In the detection process, usually two watermarks will be detected; the non-invertibility will help to resolve this problem. For any audio object, if it is found to be illegal in a later time, the creator cannot disown his/her creatorship since all the other creators have his/her signed object.

Refinement iterations
The first draft of the audio dubbing may not satisfy all the people. This requires the audio creators to do some modification on the audio objects. So, the audio creators will modify the parts which are not good enough and rewatermark that part. After the watermarking, the modified parts will be signed by the audio creators and passed to all the audio creators. Then again all the audio creators multiplex the audio and video objects for further evaluation. This process may repeat several times until all the creators (video creators and audio creators) are satisfied with the audio objects. The process is shown in Fig. 9.

Until now, the movie creation process is completed.

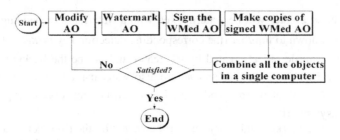

Fig. 9. Refinement iterations of audio creation process

4 Applications of the Proposed Framework

In this section, we will give some applications of the proposed framework. Section 4.1 tells how our framework works for creatorship dispute resolution, and Section 4.2 is for movie purchasing situation under the framework. These situations are discussed in detail below and our framework can successfully handle the two situations.

4.1 Rightful Creatorship Dispute Resolution

In the event of creatorship dispute among creators, the judge asks for the watermarks W_i, watermark detection key Kw_i^* and the video/audio object of dispute in the final watermarked movie from the disputing creators. The judge then verifies the existence of watermarks in the disputed video/audio object of the watermarked movie. If there is more than one watermark found in the same video/audio object, the judge uses non-invertible property (which needs to use the embedding key Kw_i) of the watermark to prove the rightful creator. For resolving the rightful creatorship dispute, the asymmetric property of the watermarking technique is not useful, thus the original unwatermarked object is necessary for using the non-invertibility property to prove the rightful creator. However, for creatorship verification by buyer, the asymmetric property is useful.

4.2 Movie Purchasing Situation

When a buyer wants to buy the entire jointly created movie, the buyer can approach all the creators for purchase of the jointly created movie. In the event that the buyer is interested in only part of the jointly created movie, such as certain video object(s), the buyer can use the watermark detection key to identify the creators of the video objects that he/she is interested in and then contact those creators to purchase their video objects individually.

5 Discussion

The watermarking scheme used in the creatorship protection for multiple creators has the following requirements. First, the watermarking scheme should be robust for the reason that others (including other creators) should not be able to remove the placed watermark. Second, the watermark should be imperceptible in order to have a high quality of video or audio object. Third, It is possible that a conniving creator(s) can place a second watermark on the creation of the creator whom conniving creator(s) wants to get rid of creatorship and claim for the creatorship of that part. In order to safe guard against such attacks the watermarking scheme used must be non-invertible. Fourth, The buyer of the jointly created movie should be able to verify the existence of the watermark (without the capability to remove it or embed it), which requires the watermarking technique to be asymmetric as well. Each creator should watermark his/her video/audio object completely. This will help to identify the creator of the video/audio object. Thus the watermarking technique employed in the framework should have the following properties: robust, invisible, asymmetric and non-invertible. It is possible that a creator disowns his/her video object at a later stage due to the malpractices (copying from someone else's work etc.) he/she has done during the creation. In order to defeat this problem, the framework employs cryptographic protocols in the video and audio creation process.

6 Conclusion

We proposed a novel watermarking framework that solves the creatorship protection problem in the creation of multiple creators, object-based digital movie. The framework employs the watermarking and digital signature scheme and is applied during the video creation and audio creation/dubbing process. The framework successfully handles the creatorship dispute problem among creators. At the same time, the single creator cannot disown his/her creatorship of the object he created. By applying the framework, the creator also has the capability to prove the creatorship of his/her video/audio object to a buyer.

References

1. F. Hartung and M. Kutter, "Multimedia Watermarking Techniques," to appear in Proceedings of the IEEE, Special Issue on Identification and Protection of Multimedia Information 87, June 1999
2. J. J. Eggers, J. K. Su, and B. Girod, "Asymmetric Watermarking Schemes," in Tagungsband Des GI Workshops Sicherheit in Mediendaten, Berlin, Germany, Sept. 2000, pp. 107-123
3. I. J. Cox, J. Killian, F. T. Leighton, and T. Shamoon, "Secure Spread Spectrum Watermarking for Multimedia," IEEE Transactions on Image Processing, vol. 6, no. 12, Dec. 1997, pp. 1673-1687
4. B. Pfitzmann and M. Schunfer, "Asymmetric fingerprinting", in Advances in CryptologyEUROCRYPT 1996, LNCS 1070, SpringerVerlag, 1996, pp. 84-95
5. T. Y. Kim, H. Choi, K. Lee and T. Kim "An Asymmetric Watermarking System With Many Embedding Watermarks Corresponding to One Detection Watermark", IEEE Signal Processing Letters, Vol. 11, No. 3, March 2004
6. S. Craver, N. Memon, B. Yeo, and M. Yeung. "Can Invisible Watermarks Resolve Rightful Ownerships?" Technical Report RC 20509, IBM Research Division, July 1996

7. L. Qiao and K. Nahrstedt "Watermarking Schemes and Protocols For Protecting Rightful Ownership And Customer's Rights", ICLASS and National Science Foundation Career Grant CCR-96-23867

8. H. Guo and N. D. Georganas, "Digital image watermarking for joint ownership," in ACM Multimedia 2002, 362-371, Dec 2002

9. P. Bassia and I. Pitas, "Robust audio watermarking in the time domain," in Proc. European Signal Processing DCDonf. (EUSIPCO 98), Rhodes, Greece, Sept. 1998

10. Wu C.P. and Jay Kuo C.C., "Fragile Speech Watermarking based on Exponential Scale Quantization for Tamper Detection", 2002 IEEE Internotional Conference on Acoustics, Speech and Signal Processing, (Orlando, Florida), May 2002.

11. H. Elkamchouchi, K. Elshenawy and Heba. A. Shaban, "New digital signature schemes in the real and gaussian integers' domains", in 21st National Radio Science Conference (NRSC2004) (NTI) March, 2004

12. Cheng Q. and Sorensen J., "Spread Spectrum Signaling for Speech Watermarking", IEEE 2001 International Conference on Acoustics, Speech and Signal Processing

13. Tefas. A., Giannoula. A., Nikolaidis. N. and Pitas. I., "Enhanced transform-Domain Correlation-Based Audio Watermarking", IEEE International Conference on Acoustics, Speech, and Signal Processing, 2005. Proceedings. (ICASSP '05). Volume 2, Mar 18-23, 2005 Page(s):1049 - 1052

14. R.L. Rivest, A. Shamir, and L.M. Adleman, "A Method for Obtaining Digital signatures and public-key cryptosystems", Communications of the ACM (2) 21 (1978), 120-126

15. C-C Chang and Y-F Chang, "Signing a Digital Signature Without Using One-Way Hash Functions and Message Redundancy Schemes", IEEE Communications Letters, Vol. 8, No.8, August 2004

16. S. Emmanuel and M. S. Kankanhalli, "Digital Rights Management Issues for Video" in Multimedia Security Handbook, Chapter 26, pp. 759-787, Editors: B. Furht and D. Kirovski, Publisher: CRC Press, 2005

TIVA: Trusted Integrity Verification Architecture

Mahadevan Gomathisankaran and Akhilesh Tyagi

Electrical and Computer Engineering,
Iowa State University,
Ames, IA 50011
{gmdev, tyagi}@iastate.edu

Abstract. We are moving towards the era of pervasive computing. The embedded computing devices are everywhere and they need to interact in many insecure ways. Verifying the integrity of the software running on these devices in such a scenario is an interesting and difficult problem. The problem is simplified if the verifying entity has access to the original binary image. However, the verifier itself may not be trusted with the intellectual property built into the software. Hence an acceptable and practical solution would not reveal the intellectual property (IP) of the verified software, and yet must verify its integrity. We propose one such novel solution, TIVA, in this paper.

1 Introduction

We are entering the era of pervasive computing where embedded devices have penetrated most spheres of human activity. These embedded devices carry a wide range of data ranging from sensitive personal information to military confidential information. Moreover, these devices need to interact frequently with the insecure world. Hence it is imperative to check frequently whether any malicious tampering of the software on these devices has occurred.

The different scenarios where such verification is beneficial, for example, are as follows.

- The field officer would like to ensure that her GPS has not been tampered with before entering the enemy territory. Note that the tampering adversary here is the GPS device. The military needs to distribute the binary image of the GPS software to the verifier so that the field officer can use the verifier to ascertain the integrity of the GPS software. The military, however, would be increasing the risk of compromising the IP of the GPS software by distributing the binary image to the verifier. Note that the IP adversary is the verifier (and not the device, which is a tampering adversary). The problem then is devising verification engine (verifier) architecture to minimize the risk of exposing the IP of the distributed GPS software.
- An executive would like to ensure that the software and/or data on her PDA has not been tampered with. She could have a verifier installed on her laptop to verify the PDA. There exists a conflict of interest between the software vendor and the PDA user. PDA user (or the laptop version of the verifier) requires the binary image of the PDA software for verification. The software vendor may be at the risk of compromising the IP of her software by distributing it to the PDA owner. Thus the verification architecture should safeguard both the party's interests.

R. Safavi-Naini and M. Yung (Eds.): DRMTICS 2005, LNCS 3919, pp. 13–31, 2006.

– An organization would like to ensure that their routers were not tampered with. This case is pretty similar to the earlier one except that the verification would be performed remotely. The verification architecture should be robust enough to support the remote verification of the systems.

All these scenarios demand IP protection in addition to the mere verification of the software. The existing solutions like *SWATT*([1]) and *Genuinity*([2]) do not address the concern of IP protection and are very restricted to a certain class of devices hence not generally applicable.

Reverse engineering the low level code into a high level programming language is usually the first step in determining the embedded IP of a software. Such reverse engineering can lead to software piracy. Reverse engineering requires disassembling and decompilation of the instruction sequence. Static obfuscation techniques address this issue by hiding the instantiated instruction sequence. These obfuscation techniques embed the correction points for the control flow (the correct instruction sequence) in the image itself. Such instruction sequence obfuscation, however, applies only to the static program image. The instantiated instruction sequence is exposed during an execution.

In the case of verification model, the verifier needs the binary image for verification purpose only and not for execution purpose. In other words, an instantiated control flow path order is not important to the verifier. The verifier mostly needs only the memory address-content correspondence. Thus any obfuscation technique which modifies the static sequence of instructions need not embed the image with correction points. Such an obfuscated image becomes extremely hard to reverse engineer without the execution address sequence. In TIVA we use a permutation function to generate such an obfuscated image in order to provide the IP protection.

TIVA uses challenge-response protocol between the verifier and the embedded device. In order to keep the tampering adversary, the device, honest in its responses, the challenge has to be different (unique) for each verification. TIVA uses a unique permutation function for each verification to calculate a unique checksum or hash. The novelty of TIVA lies in the fact that it can achieve both IP protection and challenge-uniqueness through the use of a permutation function. TIVA uses a trusted hardware element in the embedded device to achieve this. But this trusted hardware is different from TCG or secure processors as it has very minimal hardware overhead.

The main contributions of this paper, TIVA, are

– identifying the need for IP protection for any practical integrity verification model for embedded devices
– providing both IP protection and challenge-uniqueness to every verification instantiation through permutation functions
– a reconfigurable circuit to achieve these permutation functions

The rest of this paper is organized as follows. Section 2 describes the problem and the assumptions under which the solution is valid. Section 3 explains the proposed solution. Section 4 explains the reconfigurable permutation unit which forms the basis to our solution. In Section 5 we put together these elements and explain the overall verification architecture. Section 6 discusses strengths and weaknesses of our proposed verification architecture. Section 8 concludes the paper.

2   The Problem

Integrity verification allows the verifier to assert that the binary image, which includes both code as well as static data, is as expected. Let $\mathcal{E}$ be the device whose binary image needs to be verified, $\mathcal{V}$ be the entity which would like verify the integrity and $\mathcal{D}$ be the entity which distributes the software image I. The interactions between the entities are as follows. Recall that $\mathcal{E}$ is the tampering adversary for the verification. However $\mathcal{V}$ is the DRM adversary against whom we need to protect the software IP. Note that $\mathcal{V}$ is a logical entity that can be physically realized either as a hardware or software unit separate from $\mathcal{E}$ or it could be physically integrated as a software process or hardware unit within $\mathcal{E}$. In the later case, the hardware version of $\mathcal{V}$ would have to be secured against observation and tampering from $\mathcal{E}$. The software process version would have to be obfuscated and hidden within $\mathcal{E}$ along the lines of software watermarking [3] with unique secret handles for instantiating the verification and for observing the outcome.

- *Distribution:* Software vendor $\mathcal{D}$ distributes the image I to verifier $\mathcal{V}$ to verify the integrity of the corresponding software in the device $\mathcal{E}$.
- *IP Protection:* $\mathcal{D}$ trusts the device $\mathcal{E}$ to have sufficient protection mechanism to protect the IP of image I. Note that $\mathcal{E}$ is protecting the IP of I against possible reverse engineering by $\mathcal{V}$. However, a direct distribution of I to verifier $\mathcal{V}$ by software vendor $\mathcal{D}$ increases the risk of IP compromise. $\mathcal{V}$ could have simulation/emulation environment or use other mechanisms to reverse-engineer I. To avoid such a scenario $\mathcal{D}$ would like to ensure that IP of the binary image I is protected despite its distribution to $\mathcal{V}$.
- *Verification:* $\mathcal{V}$ would like to verify the integrity of the binary image I resident in the device $\mathcal{E}$. The verification process should be challenge-response based, i.e. the verifier $\mathcal{V}$ should be able to generate a challenge at random, and based on the response from $\mathcal{E}$ should be able to assert the integrity of the image I. The verification process should be robust enough so that it is able to detect replay and spoofing attacks.

The problem boils down to $\mathcal{V}$ verifying the image of $\mathcal{E}$ with respect to I without revealing its IP under the condition that $\mathcal{E}$ is not tampered with in hardware. The binary image refers to both the code as well as static data.

3   The Solution

The three dimensions of the problem as explained in Section 2 are *distribution, IP protection,* and *verification.* We first present the solution to the problems of verification and IP protection. The distribution problem arises out of this solution.

A straightforward solution to the problem of verification would be to distribute the binary image I to the verifier $\mathcal{V}$. Hence the verifier can read contents of the $\mathcal{E}$ and compare it against the received image. But there are several problems with this simple and seemingly perfect scheme.

First of all the requirement of IP protection is violated by this scheme, as the verifier $\mathcal{V}$ could very well be an attacker who would like to reverse engineer the IP of the image I. Another problem with this scheme is that it is highly inefficient. It will take time proportional to $N * c$, where c is the number of cycles required to read the memory content from the device $\mathcal{E}$ and N is the size of the memory.

Earlier solutions like, *Genuinity* [2] and *SWATT* [1], addressed this problem by having a verification module in the device $\mathcal{E}$. This verification module receives the challenge and provides a response to the verifier $\mathcal{V}$. This verification logic is critically dependent on the following two dimensions.

1. binary image residing in the memory, I.
2. time to perform the verification, $\mathcal{T}$.

In such a verification module architecture, one solution would be to distribute the hash of the binary image to the verifier $\mathcal{V}$, and to ask the verification logic in the device $\mathcal{E}$ to generate the hash as well, followed by a comparison of the two hashes. Any modifications in the binary image I will modify the hash and any modification to the verification logic to misrepresent the hash itself will result in a perceptible change to $\mathcal{T}$. Since only the hash is available to $\mathcal{V}$, no binary image I is provided, the IP protection problem is moot. But the drawback of such an approach is that the hash used in the verification is fixed. Any malicious software running in $\mathcal{E}$ could spoof the verifier by responding with the fixed hash without having to recompute. The time to perform verification could be easily spoofed by the use of timers.

An alternative would be to request the verification module in the device $\mathcal{E}$ to compute the hash of a variable subset of the image I. Since verifier $\mathcal{V}$ can specify the subset at random the response to every challenge has to be uniquely calculated to thwart the replay attack. Similar method is used in AOL [18] and AIM [19]. In this schema though the verifier $\mathcal{V}$ needs to be able to calculate the correct hash for more or less any subset of I (every challenge). It requires the entire binary image I for this ability. But this violates the IP protection requirement of our problem statement.

Yet another solution is to use keyed hash. The verifier $\mathcal{V}$ can generate a random key and request the device $\mathcal{E}$ to generate the hash for that key. This could also avoid the replay attack since the hash value depends on the key and the key is generated at random by the verifier $\mathcal{V}$. But this model also violates the IP protection requirement since the verifier $\mathcal{V}$ requires the image I in order to calculate the hash for a randomly generated key. Another drawback especially applicable to a software based remote verifier is the ease of mimicking the device behavior. An impostor device $\mathcal{E}'$ could replace $\mathcal{E}$ such that both are behaviorally equivalent (say a malicious router). Moreover, $\mathcal{E}'$ could be computationally much more powerful than $\mathcal{E}$, able to easily calculate the hash within $\mathcal{T}$ from the unmodified original image. In reality, though, $\mathcal{E}'$ could be executing a modified malicious image. Since there is no shared secret between the verifier $\mathcal{V}$ and the device $\mathcal{E}$, any impostor could generate the correct hash, since the hash algorithm, key and the image are all known to the impostor. This idea was also used by Umesh et al. [4] to attack *Genuinity* [2].

Thus the solution to the verification problem is to find an *irreversible* hash or checksum function which generates a unique hash $\mathcal{H}$ for every verification. This function should be such that within the given time $\mathcal{T}$ the only way to generate $\mathcal{H}$ is to execute the given verification function. Also this function should share a secret with the verifier. Thus if $\mathcal{E}$ returns the required $\mathcal{H}$ within the specified time $\mathcal{T}$ then it verifies the integrity of the device $\mathcal{E}$ as well as the image in $\mathcal{E}$. Thus heart of the solution is in defining the irreversible hash function $\mathcal{F}$ which generates $\mathcal{H}$. This $\mathcal{F}$ and $\mathcal{T}$ together constitute the signature of $\mathcal{E}$ which is verified against the precomputed values by $\mathcal{V}$. This is the core of our proposed approach to integrity verification.

The required and desirable properties of the irreversible hash generation function $\mathcal{F}$ are as follows.

1. It should be very fast and efficient. Hence any change in $\mathcal{F}$ or its simulated/emulated version should result in a perceptible and observable change in the response time $\mathcal{T}$.
2. It should depend on the image I as well as on the challenge from the verifier $\mathcal{V}$. Thus for two distinct challenges, it should generate distinct hash values.

Algorithm 1. Irreversible hash function (Pseudocode)

---

for $l = 0$ to $N - 1$ **do**
    $hash = hash + (MEM[l] \oplus \pi(l))$
end for

Algorithm-1 shows such an irreversible hash function. This hash function calculates the checksum of the image I exor-ed with permutation function π. $MEM[l]$ refers to memory contents of the image at location l. π refers to the permutation function which takes in a value from $0 \cdots N - 1$ and returns a value from $0 \cdots N - 1$. There are $N!$ possible distinct permutation functions. Verifier $\mathcal{V}$ chooses a particular permutation function through the challenge. Device $\mathcal{E}$ should use that specific permutation function while calculating the checksum.

The notable characteristic of the hash function shown in Algorithm-1 is that it uses the permutation function π to create the dependency between checksum calculation and verifier's challenge. In contrast, SWATT [1] used pseudo-random generator and Genuinity [1] used architectural side-effects to introduce such dependency. The main reason behind our choice of permutation function is the additional capability of IP protection offered by these permutation functions.

Reverse engineering is the first step in determining IP of the software. In order to reverse engineer the control flow graph (CFG) of the image has to be reconstituted. This is done by disassembling and decompilation of the binary image. Various static obfuscation techniques ([22], [23], [24], [5]) try to achieve IP protection by either obscuring the disassembling stage or decompilation stage. But these techniques are limited by the fact that the statically obfuscated image should retain the same CFG as its original.

The degree of obfuscation required in our problem is significantly weaker. The verifier $\mathcal{V}$ needs the image only for verification or to establish address by address correspondence of the contents of $\mathcal{V}$'s and $\mathcal{E}$'s images. The binary image held by $\mathcal{V}$ is not executed. This weakens the obfuscation constraints as follows. Any static obfuscation applied to the binary image I distributed to $\mathcal{V}$ need not retain the original CFG. Any permutation of the sequence of the bytes in the binary image I would obfuscate the CFG, in turn making the reverse engineering extremely difficult. Thus obfuscated image I_{obf}, which is a permuted version of the image I could be distributed to the verifier $\mathcal{V}$ without compromising its IP. Section 6.1 discusses in detail the strength of obfuscation function realized by permutation.

Our solution to the integrity verification problem which combines the permutation function to generate I_{obf} and the permutation function to generate hash to form a unified solution is as follows.

1. For every $(\mathcal{V}, \mathcal{E})$, $\mathcal{D}$ generates a permutation function π_d and gives $(\pi_d(I), \mathcal{T})$ to $\mathcal{V}$.
2. $\mathcal{D}$ secretly embeds π_d in $\mathcal{E}$.
3. For every verification, $\mathcal{V}$ generates π_v and finds $\mathcal{F}(\pi_v(\pi_d(I)))$. It then gives π_v as a challenge to $\mathcal{E}$.
4. $\mathcal{E}$ generates hash using π_v and π_d and reports it back to $\mathcal{V}$.
5. $\mathcal{V}$ measures the response time $\mathcal{T}$.
6. $\mathcal{V}$ can verify this *signature* with the precomputed one.

Figure 1 shows an example calculation of checksum by both $\mathcal{V}$ and $\mathcal{E}$. In this figure obfuscated image I_{obf} is generated as follows. Let M_{obf} be the memory content of I_{obf} and M be the memory content of image I. Then $M_{obf}[\pi_d(i)] = M[i]$ for every i from 1 to N, where N is the size of the image. Note that image I is not necessarily limited to only instructions. The presence of static data could also obscure the disassembly which makes reconstruction of CFG more difficult. In this figure, verifier $\mathcal{V}$ has the obfuscated image I_{obf} and device $\mathcal{E}$ has the actual image I. $\mathcal{V}$ generates π_v and calculates hash $\mathcal{H}$ using Algorithm-1. Device $\mathcal{E}$ uses the composite permutation function $\pi_v(\pi_d)$ and the actual image I to calculate the same hash $\mathcal{H}$.

A permutation function π with N values is $N!$ strong, which is slightly higher than 2^N by Sterling's approximation of a factorial. Hence by choosing sufficiently large N we can reduce the probability of success through a *brute − force* attack. By choosing a different permutation function for every verification we avoid the *replay* attack. Attack by impostor is avoided as $\mathcal{V}$ and $\mathcal{E}$ share the permutation function π_d as the secret. Hence

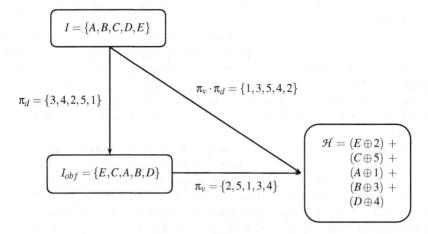

Fig. 1. An example *hash* or *checksum* function $\mathcal{F}$

the impostor needs to know π_d to generate $\mathcal{H}$. We have assumed that $\mathcal{E}$ is protected enough not to reveal its stored secrets.

The distribution of the software image now involves four operations, namely, distributing image I to the device $\mathcal{E}$, generating the permutation function π_d, generating the obfuscated image I_{obf} and distributing it to the verifier $\mathcal{V}$. Various existing solutions are applicable to this problem. In the case of embedded devices it is most likely that the device vendor distributes the image as well. Hence the device vendor can maintain the association of π_d with the device's unique ID. Whenever the device is purchased or obtained by the verifier the vendor can generate the obfuscated image using π_d and distribute it with the device. Whenever the device needs to be updated with newer version of the image I the device vendor has to generate the corresponding I_{obf} and distribute it to the verifier $\mathcal{V}$. In the following section, we describe the circuit to realize the reconfigurable permutation function. This logic needs to be embedded into $\mathcal{E}$.

4   Reconfigurable Permutation Function Unit (RPU)

This unit is responsible for realizing the permutation function π. There are $2^n!$ permutation functions possible for a n bit input. Reconfigurable logic is well-suited to generate a large dynamically variable subset of these functions. Figure 2 shows one such schema for permutation of 10 address bits, but note that this methodology is extensible to any number of bits. Before explaining the blocks of Figure 2, we observe that there are $\left(2^{2^n}\right)^n$ possible functions implemented in a $n \times n$ look up table (LUT) or n n-LUTs. But only a subset of them are bijective. We wish to implement only reversible (conservative) gates ([6], [8]) with LUTs.

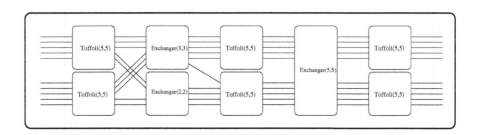

Fig. 2. Reconfigurable Permutation Unit (RPU)

A conservative gate does not lose any information in going from its inputs to outputs. We should be able to infer the input values uniquely by observing the output bits of such a gate. Thus a reversible gate needs to have as many outputs as inputs. Both Fredkin [6] and Toffoli [7] have defined classes of reversible gates.

Definition 1. *Toffoli gate, Toffoli(n,n)(C,T), is defined over a support set $\{x_1, x_2, \ldots, x_n\}$ as follows. Let the control set $C = \{x_{i1}, x_{i2}, \ldots, x_{ik}\}$ and the target set $T = \{x_j\}$ be such that $C \cap T = 0$. The mapping is given by*

$$Toffoli(n,n)(C,T)[x_1,x_2,\ldots,x_n] = [x_1,x_2,\ldots,x_{j-1},z,x_{j+1},\ldots,x_n]$$

where $z = x_j \oplus (x_{i1} \wedge x_{i2} \wedge \ldots \wedge x_{ik})$.

Definition 2. *Fredkin gate, Fredkin(n,n)(C,T), is defined over a support set $\{x_1,x_2,\ldots, x_n\}$ as follows. Let the control set $C = \{x_{i1},x_{i2},\ldots,x_{ik}\}$ and the target set $T = \{x_j,x_l\}$ be such that $C \cap T = \emptyset$. The mapping is given by*

$$Fredkin(n,n)(C,T)[x_1,x_2,\ldots,x_n] =$$

$$[x_1,x_2,\ldots,x_{j-1},p,x_{j+1},\ldots,q,\ldots,x_n]$$

where $k = x_{i1} \cdot x_{i2} \cdots \cdots x_{ik}$, $p = (x_j \cdot \bar{k}) + (x_l \cdot k)$, and $q = (x_j \cdot k) + (x_l \cdot \bar{k})$.

We use *Toffoli(5,5)* gates with 5-input bits and 5-output bits in our scheme as shown in Figure 2. However, we could easily replace them by *Fredkin(5,5)* gates. The domain of configurations mappable to each of these LUTs consists of selections of sets T and C such that $T \cap C = \emptyset$. For a support set of 5 variables, the number of unique reversible Toffoli functions is $4\binom{5}{1} + 3\binom{5}{2} + 2\binom{5}{3} + \binom{5}{4}$. Each of these terms captures control sets of size 1,2,3, and 4 respectively. Ignoring control sets of size 1, we get a total of 55 reversible functions. Thus total permutation space covered by all six of these gates is $(55)^6 \approx 2^{34}$. There are several redundant configurations in this space. We estimate this redundancy later in this section.

The exchanger blocks shown in Figure 2 perform *swap* operation. It has two sets of inputs and two sets of outputs. The mapping function is $S_{ok} = S_{ik}$ if $X = 0$, and

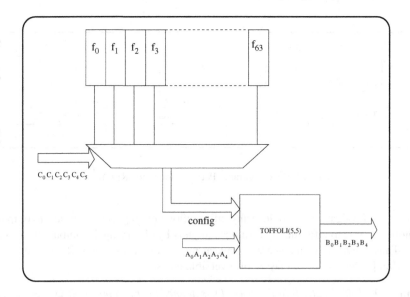

Fig. 3. Configuration Selection for each LUT

$S_{ok} = S_{i\bar{k}}$ if $X = 1$, where, S_{ik} is the input set, S_{ok} is the output set, X is configuration bit, and k is 0 or 1. Since *exchange* is also bijective, the composition of *Toffoli* gates and *exchangers* leads to a bijective function with large population diversity. Some other more interesting routing structures may also guarantee bijections. But a typical FPGA routing matrix configuration will require extensive analysis to determine if a given routing configuration is bijective. One point to note here is that we chose to implement a 10 *bit* permutation function with *Toffoli*(5,5) gates instead of a direct implementation of *Toffoli*(10,10). This is because an n-LUT requires 2^n configuration bits and hence 10-LUTs are impractical in the reconfigurable computing world.

Having fixed the reconfigurable logic to perform the permutation, we need to develop a schema for the LUT configuration. A simple mechanism would be to store all the 55 possible configurations at each of the LUTs (similar to DPGA of DeHon [9]). In addition to 4 *input bits*, each LUT will also have 6 *configuration bits* to choose one of the 55 configurations (assuming some configurations are repeated to fill the 64 locations), as shown in Figure 3. Each of the *exchanger* blocks also requires 1 configuration bit. Thus a total of 39 configuration bits are needed by the reversible logic of Figure 2.

4.1 Estimating Redundancy in Configurations

The most reasonable and efficient way to generate configurations is to generate each configuration bit independently and randomly. However this process may generate two configurations that represent the same mapping (from incoming address to the outgoing address). Such aliasing reduces the diversity of the address mapping functions making them more predictable to the adversary. We capture the degree of this aliasing with the concept of *redundancy level* of a reconfigurable permutation circuit. The redundancy level can be defined as the fraction of 2^{39} configurations that alias (generate a repeated, non-unique mapping function).

We assessed the redundancy level of the address permutation schema in Figure 2 through the following setup. We simulated this FPGA circuit with 2^{20} randomly generated configurations. For each of these configurations, we derived the corresponding bijective function by exercising all the 10-bit inputs sequences. Each unique bijective function was stored. When a bijective function f_i from a new random sequence from the 2^{20} runs is encountered, it is compared against all the stored bijective functions that have already been generated. At the end of 2^{20} runs, we end up with $k \leq 2^{20}$ unique functions f_i for $0 \leq i \leq k$ and their redundancy count r_i (function f_i occurs in r_i of the 2^{20} runs). The *redundancy level* is computed as $[\sum_{r_i > 1} 1]/2^{20}$. We repeated this experiment several times in order to get a statistical validation of our experiment. All the values are listed in Table 1.

This experiment can be modeled as a random experiment where we have $N(=2^{39})$ balls in a basket which are either *red*(=*redundant*) or *green*(=*non-redundant*). We need to estimate the number of red balls in the basket by picking $n(= 2^{20})$ balls where all the balls are equally likely. We define a random variable X such that $X = 1$ if the chosen ball is *red* and $X = 0$ otherwise. The mean of such a random variable is nothing but the redundancy level. We see from Table 1 that the mean is close to zero ($\approx 0.3\%$) and hence the variance is equal to the mean. Using the variance and mean we estimated the 99% confidence interval of the mean of X, *i.e.*, the average redundancy level of

Table 1. Redundancy Estimation: # of Rndm Configs = 2^{20}

Random Seed	# of Redundant Functions	Avg % Redundancy	99% CI
89ABCDEF	3359	0.320	0.3058 to 0.3342
11223344	3409	0.325	0.3107 to 0.3393
12345678	3441	0.328	0.3136 to 0.3424
34567890	3417	0.325	0.3107 to 0.3393
789012345	3469	0.330	0.3156 to 0.3444
8901234567	3460	0.330	0.3156 to 0.3444
56789012345	3460	0.330	0.3156 to 0.3444

reconfigurable permutation circuit. From the table, it is clear that with probability 0.99 the average percentage of redundant configurations will lie within 0.3058 to 0.3444, *i.e.*, only 3 out of 1000 randomly generated configurations will be redundant.

4.2   Area and Delay Estimation

Since we intend to use RPU in the embedded devices it should be both area and delay efficient. Figure 2 shows that RPU has 6 $5 \times 5 - LUT$s and 3 *shifters*. Each of these $5 \times 5 - LUT$s takes 6 *configuration selection* bits and 5 *input bits*. Each *LUT* can be visualized as having a direct mapped cache with 64 sets and 32 bit cache line. Each cache line stores the *configuration bits* and one of which is chosen by the 6 *configuration selection* bits. One of these 32 *configuration bits* is chosen by the 5 *input bits*. Thus an *LUT* has a 256B direct mapped cache and a 32-to-1 multiplexer. Since all the 5 *LUT* use the same configuration selection bits we can group all these direct mapped caches and make it a single direct mapped cache with 64 sets and 20 byte cache lines. Figure 4 shows such a schema.

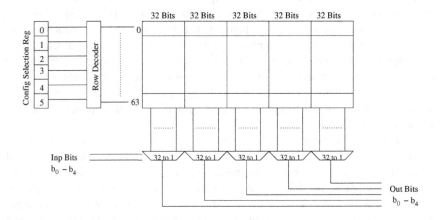

Fig. 4. A typical schema for 5x5-LUT

Table 2. Area estimate of RPU using CACTI [11]

Technology nm	Area mm^2
180	1.4526
130	0.7578
70	0.2196

Thus RPU has 6 1.25KB direct mapped caches. Since configuration selection bits will be preloaded, the delay incurred in accessing these caches would not have any impact on the access time of RPU. We used CACTI [11] to estimate the area requirement of RPU and Table 2 lists the area estimate for various process technologies. The other components of RPU are shifters and multiplexers. The shifters could be realized through 2-to-1 multiplexers. Since more than 99% of the transistors of RPU are contributed by the caches the area estimate of RPU could be equated to the area estimate of the caches.

To estimate the access time of RPU we should find the components which contribute to the access time. Since the configuration selection register will be preloaded the configuration bits will be available to the multiplexers. The access time can be given as,

$$T_{RPU} = 3 \times T_{32-to-1\ MUX} + 2 \times T_{2-to-1\ MUX}$$

We used HSPICE [10] to perform the delay estimation. We used pass transistor logic with appropriate drivers to design the multiplexers as they are area efficient. In order to optimize the delay of a 32-to-1 multiplexer we designed it as a 3-level multiplexer with first two levels being 4-to-1 multiplexers and the last one being 2-to-1 multiplexer. We used TSMC [14] and BPTM [15] models for the simulation. The results of the simulation are listed in Table 3. We will use these delay estimates while estimating the latency of this functional unit in the following section.

Table 3. Delay estimate of RPU using HSPICE [10]

Technology nm	Model	V_{cc} V	V_{th} V	$T_{32-to-1}$ ps	T_{2-to-1} ps	T_{RPU} ns
180	TSMC [14]	1.80	0.46	369	70	1.247
180	TSMC [14]	1.30	0.28	410	80	1.390
180	TSMC [14]	1.55	0.28	340	60	1.140
70	BPTM [15]	0.90	0.20	220	60	0.780

5 Integrity Verification Architecture

In Section 3 we outlined our basic solution for embedded device verification. In Section 4 we explained RPU which forms the basis of the proposed TIVA. In this section, we explain TIVA in more details. TIVA uses RPU, the hash function $\mathcal{F}$ and the response time $\mathcal{T}$ to provide the solution to the integrity verification problem.

5.1 XRPU

As explained in Section 3, the IP of image I is protected through π_d. In TIVA this is achieved by embedding this secret in the device $\mathcal{E}$. Hence $\mathcal{E}$ should have a protected

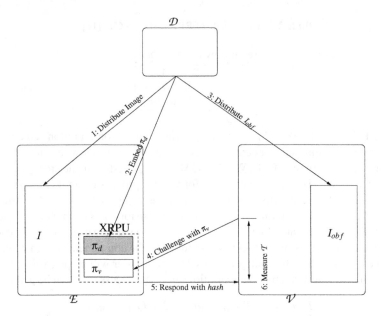

Fig. 5. Integrity Verification Architecture

hardware where this secret could be stored. From Section 4, we know that RPU has space to store all the 64 possible configurations for each LUT. Since π_d chooses only one of these configurations we do not need to store all of them. Thus $\mathcal{E}$ should have a special RPU$_{\pi_d}$ which stores only the chosen configuration bits which amounts to 120 bytes for the LUTs and 3 bits for the exchangers.

$\mathcal{E}$ should contain a second RPU$_{\pi_v}$ which is a generic one as explained in Section 4. This RPU is loaded with the configuration selection bits generated by $\mathcal{V}$. Since we want to protect the function π_d, we do not allow the input/output relation of RPU$_{\pi_d}$ to be visible. If π_d is allowed to be observed then I_{obf} could be de-obfuscated resulting in loss of its IP. Thus we create a single composite function unit XRPU, eX-tended RPU, which contains both RPU$_{\pi_d}$ and RPU$_{\pi_v}$. It takes start address and configuration selection as input and produces the *hash* as the output. This XRPU generates all 1024 addresses sequentially from the start address and computes $hash = hash + \{MEM[addr] \oplus \pi_d(\pi_v(addr))\}$. This could be implemented as microcode or implemented in hardware. Since π_v is public its permutation function is known. Hence given $addr$ and $MEM[addr] \oplus \pi_d(\pi_v(addr))$ it is easy to derive π_d. Thus XRPU only provides *hash* as the output from which π_d cannot be obtained as it is an irreversible function.

5.2 Verification

As is the case with any encryption function, the algorithm of RPU is public. The se-cret is the *configurations bits*. Thus $\mathcal{V}$ could be provided with a simulated version of RPU's algorithm or it could have a special application-specific hardware unit. To verify the authenticity of the image, $\mathcal{V}$ generates the configuration bits for π_v randomly and

```
      li    0,0    ; R0 counter
      li    5,0    ; R5 LS word of checksum
      li    6,0    ; R6 MS word of checksum
      lwz   1,st   ; R1 starting address
L1:   add   1,0,1  ; add counter to address
      xrpu  3,0    ; R3 = XRPU(R0)
      lwz   2,0(1) ; load the content in R2
      xor   3,2,3  ; R3 = R3 xor R2
      srawi 4,3,31 ; R4 = sign bit of R3
      addc  5,5,3  ; R5 = R5 + R3
      adde  6,6,4  ; R6 = R6 + R4 + Carry
      addi  0,0,1  ; R0 = R0 + 1
      cmpwi 0,0,1024; is R0 < 1024
      lt    L1     ; loop back
```

Fig. 6. An example PPC micro-code implementation of $\mathcal{F}$

computes the checksum as $sum = sum + (MEM[i] \oplus \pi_v(i))$. It then sends this π_v as a challenge to $\mathcal{E}$ and measures the time of verification (response time).

Since XRPU is a hardware unit, the verification function $\mathcal{F}$, which we assume to be a microcode, could be very fast. As an example, in PPC the execution of one iteration of loop body for this function takes only 10 cycles assuming XRPU takes 2 cycles per operation. Example pseudocode is shown in Figure 6. This is very fast and efficient. Any small modification in the verification code results in perceptible change in the time $\mathcal{T}$ of the verification process. Thus from the checksum and $\mathcal{T}$, $\mathcal{V}$ can establish the integrity of the binary image in $\mathcal{E}$. Figure 5 explains various steps involved in the verification architecture.

5.3 Overhead Estimation

Since RPU_{π_d} stores only one set of configuration bits area of XRPU $\approx$ area of RPU, whereas $T_{XRPU} = 2 \times T_{RPU}$ as RPU_{π_d} and RPU_{π_v} are in series. Using the estimates from Section 4.2 we estimated the area overhead and latency of XRPU for various commercial embedded processors and the results are tabulated in Table 4. In summary, the area overhead of this scheme is fairly insignificant. We see that for all the processors the area overhead is less than 1%. Even for low end embedded processor with 10 mm^2 of area the overhead comes out to be 2.2% for 70 nm technology to 14.5% in 180 nm

Table 4. Latency and Area overhead estimation of XRPU

Processor	Technology	Package mm^2	Max Freq MHz	% Area Inc	Delay ns	Latency cyc
PXA 255 [12]	0.18μ,1.80V	17x17	400	0.50	3.367	2
PXA 26x [12]	0.18μ,1.30V	13x13	400	0.86	3.367	2
PXA 27x [12]	0.18μ,1.55V	13x13	624	0.86	3.147	2
PXA 800F [12]	0.13μ,1.20V	12x12	312	0.53		
PPC 750FX [13]	0.13μ,1.45V	21x21	900	0.17		
PPC 750CXe [13]	0.18μ,1.80V	27x27	700	0.20	3.367	3

technology. The delay overhead is more easily hidden through pipelining. The overhead appears to be of the order of two cycles for most of these technology nodes, and hence fits nicely into any pipeline.

6 Discussion

6.1 Obfuscation Strength of Permutation Function (RPU)

In this section we quantify the *obfuscation strength* of the permutation function implemented using RPU. The aim of the permutation function is to obfuscate the instruction sequence. The first step in the process of reverse-engineering is disassembling the binary image. Once the instructions are disassembled their static sequence is used to reconstruct the control flow graph (CFG). Hence a measure of obfuscation could be derived from the dissimilarity between the original CFG and the CFG derived from the obfuscated static image.

The nodes in a CFG correspond to a basic block, a straight-line sequence of instructions. The permutation function rearranges the static instruction sequencing. This results in the modification of many basic blocks as constructed from the obfuscated/permuted image since there are no corresponding basic blocks in the original CFG. For instance, even if one instruction from an original CFG basic block is permuted away past a control instruction (a branch), a new basic block results in the obfuscated CFG. The edges in the permuted CFG similarly can either be completely new or may have a different source or target basic block. We will call a basic block or edge perturbed if there is no corresponding basic block (in the way of graph isomorphism accounting for new naming) or edge in the original CFG.

A permutation function that perturbs all the nodes (basic blocks) and edges from the original CFG achieves *complete* obfuscation. We define an analytical limited version of this notion that captures the similarities of the instruction sequences in the original image versus the permuted image. We will estimate what fraction of sequences of n instructions are preserved (or perturbed) from original to the permuted image for a large range of values for n. A typical basic block is 5 to 10 instructions long. Such a measure for $n = 5$ then estimates the fraction of perturbed basic blocks which constitutes a simplistic measure of obfuscation. We define such an obfuscation strength measure of size n, OS_n, for the permutation function as follows.

Definition 3

$$Let$$
$$I \rightarrow Unobfuscated\ binary\ image$$
$$I_{obf} \rightarrow Obfuscated\ binary\ image$$
$$N \rightarrow Number\ of\ instructions\ in\ I\ (|I| = |I_{obf}|)$$
$$S_n{}^j \rightarrow Sequence\ of\ instructions\ i_1, i_2, \ldots, i_n\ in\ I$$
$$from\ j^{th}\ position\ where\ 1 \leq j \leq (N - n + 1)$$
$$Then$$
$$OS_n = \%\ of\ S_n{}^j\ not\ in\ I_{obf}$$

Note that in our solution we permute the binary image in units of *words* (4 bytes). In some architectures (like x86) the instruction sizes are not fixed. Thus permutation could break some instructions giving rise to illegal or different instructions. Also the presence of static data in the image could cause the same effect. Hence this definition of *obfuscation strength* is very conservative and forms a lower bound.

To understand the definition of our *obfuscation strength* let us consider an example. Figure 7 shows an example permutation. In this example $|I| = |I_{obf}| = N = 5$ and $S_2{}^j$ exist for $j = 1, 2, 3, 4$. In I_{obf} only $S_2{}^1$ exists unobfuscated. Hence $OS_2 = 75\%$ and OS_n for $n > 2$ is 100%.

As explained in Section 4 RPU has 39 *configuration selection* bits. It is highly improbable to find the *obfuscation strength* of RPU by exercising all the 2^{39} configurations. We generated 2^{20} random configurations and found the average *obfuscation strength* for various sequence sizes. We repeated this experiment several times to get a statistical validation of our experiment. All the values are listed in Table 5.

Table 5. Average *Obfuscation Strength* for 2^{20} runs

Seed	OS_5	OS_6	OS_7	OS_8	OS_9	OS_{10}	OS_{11}
0x031245f8	94.74	95.96	96.80	97.35	97.83	98.29	98.63
0x7fc5a2d5	94.75	95.98	96.82	97.37	97.84	98.30	98.64
0x015e8f8c	94.73	95.97	96.80	97.36	97.84	98.29	98.63
0x00231eea	94.74	95.97	96.80	97.36	97.83	98.29	98.63
0x0153d22e	94.75	95.97	96.81	97.36	97.84	98.30	98.64

We have listed the *obfuscation strength* for sequences of size from 5 to 11 as this happens to be the most frequent length for basic blocks. We see from Table 5 that with at least 95% probability our permutation function will obfuscate basic blocks with 5 or more instructions. This makes reverse-engineering of CFG from I_{obf} as difficult as the permutation function itself, which is $\approx 2^{34}$ strong.

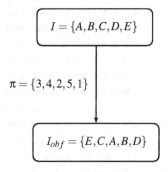

Fig. 7. An example Permutation

6.2   Attack Scenarios

A verification process using TIVA fails if one of following events occurs.

1. A malicious software executing on $\mathcal{E}$ is able to generate the expected checksum $\mathcal{H}$ in the expected response time $\mathcal{T}$.
2. An impostor system pretending to be $\mathcal{E}$, but with greater computational capabilities than $\mathcal{E}$, is able to generate the expected checksum $\mathcal{H}$ in the expected response time $\mathcal{T}$.

For both these attacks to be successful the malicious software running on the device $\mathcal{E}$ or the impostor system must know the composite permutation function $\pi_d \cdot \pi_v$. Since only microcode is able to exercise XRPU and it returns only the checksum value, it is not possible for the software running on the device to derive π_d. Thus the composite permutation function becomes as hard as the individual permutation functions which in our case is $\approx 2^{34}$ strong.

If an impostor system gets hold of I_{obf} then it is possible to generate the required hash without the knowledge of π_d. Only π_v and I_{obf} suffice. This attack could be avoided in two ways. The verifier $\mathcal{V}$ could make sure that I_{obf} is stored securely and trust the device vendor $\mathcal{D}$ to not release I_{obf} to anyone else. Another method is to extend the verification protocol in the application layer to add a unique ID to the device $\mathcal{E}$.

Secure storage of secrets in device $\mathcal{E}$ is essential for the functioning of TIVA. Any attack that could reveal π_d would de-obfuscate I_{obf} thus compromising its IP. However, storing secrets in hardware is a well researched topic and solutions like battery-backed RAM as used in IBM's 4758 [26] secure coprocessor could be used. Ishai et al. [25] proposed circuit techniques to protect circuits against probing attacks. This could be used to store the secret within the chip resistant to probing attacks.

6.3   Flexibility of TIVA

We explained TIVA for 10-*bit* permutation functions in a 32-*bit* architecture producing a 64-*bit* checksum, thus handling a memory size of 4*KB*. But TIVA is not restricted to this memory size. For bigger memory sizes the verification function could be easily extended to produce 64 *bits* for every chunk of 4*KB*. As we mentioned earlier the checksum or hash generation function proposed in our solution is not ideal. It could be replaced with any other checksum generation function of any size. TIVA is not restricted to 32-*bit* architectures. It could very well be applied to 8-*bit* or 16-*bit* architectures. The microcode for the verification function could be modified accordingly.

TIVA is not restricted to Von Neumann or Harvard architectures either. As explained in [1] to verify Von Neumann architectures, in which program and data share the same memory, the device should be brought into some known state and then verification could be performed. This known state should be the one which is distributed as binary image to the verifier. Software vendors could distribute multiple such images for various checkpoints. In the case of Harvard architectures the program and data memory are separate hence it is sufficient to find the checksum of program memory alone.

7   Related Work

Seshadri et al. proposed software only attestation mechanism in SWATT ([1]). A software only solution will incur lower cost than an attestation technique that requires additional hardware. It can also be used on legacy systems. These were the two major selling points for SWATT. But SWATT is probabilistic, i.e. it accesses the memory based on a pseudo-random sequence. The verification procedure performs $O(n \log n)$ memory accesses, for memory size n, in order to access all of the memory with high probability. They generate 16-bit addresses from an 8-bit RC4 pseudo-random number by adding to it the current value of checksum. This could very well affect the probability distribution of the PRG sequence. The effect of this change on the probability of accessing every memory location in the system is not studied in the paper. Additionally, embedded devices in most cases are limited by battery power. Deployment of such a probabilistic method will incur energy penalty.

Kennell et al. proposed software only solution *Genuinity* ([2]) to address the problem of autonomous integrity verification of remote systems. This solution is applicable only to general purpose systems which expose architectural parameters like TLB miss counters, etc. They used these architectural side effects to uniquely generate a checksum through the verification procedure. They argued that this checksum cannot be generated whenever the verification procedure is modified or through other emulated/simulated systems. But Shankar et al.([4]) proved that such a system based on architectural side effects is not sufficient to authenticate software.

Other solutions like IBM's IMA [16] use trusted hardware support [20] and require sophisticated OS support to verify the integrity. TPM provides root of trust for storage, for measurement, and for reporting. But TPM requires Public Key Infrastructure (PKI) and support of sophisticated message authentication algorithms like HMAC ([21]) to provide these trusts. The requirements of TPM and sophisticated OS support may be more than what an embedded device could offer. Moreover in IBM's IMA integrity verification is done only at the loading point. Hence any attack that occurs after the software is loaded will not be captured. Also the verifier is assumed to know the hash of the software or system configuration being verified. This again breaks our requirement of IP protection.

Thus earlier proposed solutions did not recognize IP protection as an important dimension in the problem of integrity verification. Our solution, TIVA, is different from these solutions in various aspects, such as

- TIVA uses a hardware component to aid the verification.
- TIVA is deterministic, i.e. it accesses each memory location at most once during verification.
- TIVA uses a shared secret between the embedded device and verifier to make simulating/emulating the device very difficult.
- TIVA uses permutation function to achieve both IP protection and randomness in hash generation function.

8   Conclusions

Embedded devices are omnipresent and pervade all facets of human life. This penetration is likely to only increase in the future. Their sheer numbers and wide presence make them amenable to tampering. A tampered sensor could misrepresent its environment (report no bio-hazard particles where there are some) or a tampered PDA could relay the private data of the user to a third party. Hence verification of these devices is a relevant problem. However, such verification needs to be extremely efficient and mostly automated given the sheer numbers of these devices. Moreover, the verification architecture will not be practical if it compromises the IP of the software running on these devices. This paper presents a novel hardware architecture TIVA and a schema for such a verification mechanism which satisfies all the requirements of a verification system without compromising the IP of the system being verified. We demonstrate that the silicon area overhead for TIVA is minimal, 1%, and its time overhead is completely absorbed in the pipeline.

Acknowledgments

Authors would like to acknowledge John Linwood Griffin and Ray Valdez of IBM TJ Watson Research Centre, Hawthorne for their valuable review comments.

References

1. Arvind Seshadri et. al. *SWATT: SoftWare-based ATTestation for Embedded Devices*, In Proceedings of ISSP 2004.
2. Rick Kennell and Leah H. Jamieson. *Establishing the Genuinity of Remote Computer Systems*, In Proceedings of 12th USENIX Security Symposium, 2003.
3. C. Collberg, and C. Thomborson. *Software watermarking: Models and dynamic embeddings.* POPL '99: The 26th ACM SIGPLAN-SIGACT Symposium on Principles of Programming Languages
4. Umesh Shankar, Monica Chew and J.D. Tygar. *Side effects are not sufficient to authenticate software*, In Proceedings of 13th USENIX Security Symposium, 2004.
5. Christian Collberg and Clack Thomborson. Watermarking, tamper-proofing, and obfuscation - tools for software protection, IEEE Transactions on Software Engineering, Vol. 28, Number 8, 2002.
6. E. Fredkin and T. Toffoli. *Conservative Logic*, In International Journal of Theoretical Physics, 21(3/4), April 1982.
7. T. Toffoli. *Reversible Computing*. Technical Report MIT/LCS/TM151/1980, MIT Laboratory for Computer Science, 1980.
8. R. Bennett and R. Landauer. *Fundamental Physical Limits of Computation*, Scientific American, pages 48-58, July 1985.
9. Andre DeHon. *DPGA-coupled microprocessor: Commodity ICs for the early 21st centry*, In Proc. of IEEE workshop on FPGAs for Custom Computing Machines, pages 31-39, April 1994.
10. Star-HSPICE 2001.4 Avant! Corporation.
11. Steven J. E. Wilton and Norman P. Jouppi. *An Enhanced Access and Cycle Time model for On-Chip Caches*, WRL Research Technical Report 93/5, July 1994.

12. Intel PCA Processors Data Sheets, *http://www.intel.com/design/pca/applicationsprocessors /index.htm.*
13. IBM Power PC Data Sheets, *http://www-306.ibm.com/chips/techlib/techlib.nsf/products/.*
14. Taiwan Semiconductor Manufacturing Company Ltd, *http://www.tsmc.com.*
15. Berkeley Predictive Technology Model, *http://www-device.eecs.berkeley.edu*
16. Reiner Sailer, Xiaolan Zhang, Trent Jaeger, and Leendert v. Doorn. *Design and Implementation of a TCG-based Integrity Measurement Architecture,* In Proc. of the 13th USENIX Security Symposium, 2004.
17. Reiner Sailer, Trent Jaeger, Xiaolan Zhang, and Leendert v. Doorn. *Attestation-based Policy Enforcement for Remote Access,* In Proc. of the 11th ACM Conference on Computer and Communications Security, pages 308-317, 2004.
18. AOL. The America Online Instant Messenger Application. *http://www.aol.com.*
19. PyxisSystemsTechnologies. AIM/oscar protocol specification: Section 3: Connection Management. *http://aimdoc.sourceforge.net/faim/protocol/section3.html,* 2002.
20. Trusted Computing Group, *Trusted Platform Module Specification,* Version 1.2, Revision 62, *http://www.trustedcomputinggroup.org*
21. HMAC. Internet RFC 2104, February 1997.
22. Cullen Linn and Saumya Debray. *Obfuscation of Executable Code to Improve Resistance to Static Disassembly,* In Proc. of 10th ACM Conference of Computer and Communications Security, pages 290-299, October 2003.
23. W. Cho, I. Lee, and S. Park. *Against Intelligent Tampering: Software tamper resistance by extended control flow obfuscation,* In Proc. of World Multiconference on Systems, Cybernetics, and Informatics, International Institute of Informatics and Systematics, 2001.
24. T. Ogsio, Y. Sakabe, M. Soshi, and A. Miyaji. *Software obfuscation on a theoretical basis and its implementation,* IEEE Transaction Fundamentals, E86(A)-1, January 2003.
25. Yuval Ishai, Amit Sahai, and David Wagner. *Private Circuits: Securing Hardware against Probing Attacks,* In Proc of CRYPTO 2003.
26. J. Dyer, M. Lindemann, R. Perez, R. Sailer, S.W. Smith, L. van Doorn, and S. Weingart. *Building the IBM 4758 Secure Coprocessor,* IEEE Computer. 34: pages 57-66. October 2001.

The Australian Sony PlayStation Case: How Far Will Anti-circumvention Law Reach in the Name of DRM?

Brian Fitzgerald

Head Law School,
Queensland University of Technology, Brisbane

Abstract. This chapter overviews the legal issues arising from the modification of the Sony PlayStation console under Australian Copyright Law – the so called anti-circumvention provisions. It will explain how these provisions have been interpreted by the courts and focus on the very recent decision of the Australian High Court. The article concludes by examining the extent to which the Australia-US Free Trade Agreement (AUSFTA) will impact upon this area of law.

Fearing the death of copyright in the digital networks of the Internet, states of the world agreed in Article 11, WIPO *Copyright Treaty* (WCT) 1996[1] to pass laws that would prohibit circumvention of (through hacking or interfering with) technological measures (DRM) used to protect copyright information e.g. passwords, and copy controls. These laws, known as anti-circumvention laws, are epitomized by the *Digital Millennium Copyright Act 1998* (DMCA) in the USA and a similar set of provisions in the amended Australian *Copyright Act 1968*. The US case that brought anti-circumvention laws to the fore was *Universal City Studios Inc v Reimerdes*[2]. In that case hackers posted software code (DeCSS) on websites that explained how to circumvent technological protection or encryption known as the Content Scrambling System (CSS). This encryption system is employed by the movie industry to regulate the usage of movies distributed on DVD. The Internet identities that distributed the decrypting code claimed that DeCSS allowed people to play DVDs on the free software platform GNU Linux and that this implemented digital choice or diversity.[3] However, the US court held that posting of the decrypting code on a website, including linking to a website, in certain circumstances was "providing or otherwise trafficking" in a circumvention device.

The first instalment in the Australian chapter of this story is the decision in *Kabushiki Kaisha Sony Computer Entertainment v Stevens*,[4] which is a part of world wide litigation concerning the Sony PlayStation2 console.

---

[1] See also art 18 *WIPO Performers and Phonograms Treaty 1996* (WPPT).
[2] 111 F. Supp. 2d 294 (S.D.N.Y. 2000) [affirmed on Appeal: *Universal City Studios Inc v Corley* 273 F.3d 429 (2nd Cir. 2001)].
[3] B. Fitzgerald, "Intellectual Property Rights in Digital Architecture (including Software): The Question of Digital Diversity?" [2001] *EIPR* 121.
[4] [2002] FCA 906; [2003] FCAFC 157.

R. Safavi-Naini and M. Yung (Eds.): DRMTICS 2005, LNCS 3919, pp. 32–51, 2006.

1 The Australian PlayStation Case

Eddie Stevens who was involved in the computer games industry in Sydney was sued by Sony pursuant to the anti-circumvention provisions of the Australian *Copyright Act* for modifying the Sony PlayStation (PS) computer games platform or console to allow it more functionality. In particular Sony argued that Stevens had breached s 116A of the *Copyright Act 1968* in that he had sold or distributed a circumvention device, namely mod chips, which he knew or ought reasonably have known would be used as a circumvention device. A circumvention device as defined by the *Copyright Act*, is something that has little other purpose than to circumvent a technological protection measure (TPM). A technological protection measure is something that is designed to prevent access to, or copying of, copyright subject matter. In this case the mod chips were alleged to have the purpose of circumventing Regional Access Coding – as activated by the Boot Rom – the technological protection measure[5].

1.1 The Technology

The Sony PlayStation is one of the most popular computer games consoles or platforms in the world. When a person wants to play a game they insert a disc into the PlayStation much like inserting a musical disc into a CD player. The PlayStation is coded (through what is called Regional Access Coding (RAC) contained within a track on each CD read by a chip known as a "Boot ROM" located on the circuit board of the PlayStation console (hereafter called "RAC/Boot Rom")) to play games available in the region in which the PlayStation was sold. This means that a game purchased in the USA or Japan cannot be played on a PlayStation purchased in Australia; the platform will not support it. As well a copied, burnt or unauthorised version of a game will not play on the PlayStation, as the copying process does not embed the necessary coding in the copy. As a consequence of consumers seeking greater choice of digital products or digital diversity, a device known as the "mod chip" or "converter" surfaced in the market place. It extended the functionality of the PlayStation allowing games from other regions as well as copied, unauthorised or burnt games to be played on the PlayStation.

1.2 The Digital Agenda Amendments: Anti-Circumvention Law

This was the first case to consider the anti-circumvention law introduced by the Copyright Amendment (Digital Agenda) Act 2000. Section 116A Copyright Act, effective 4th March 2001, introduced the anti-circumvention notion enshrined in Article 11 WIPO *Copyright Treaty* (1996) into Australian law. The section states:

> *Subject to subsections (2), (3) and (4), this section applies if:*
> (a)   *a work or other subject-matter is protected by a technological protection measure; and*
> (b)   *a person does any of the following acts without the permission of the owner or exclusive licensee of the copyright in the work or other subject-matter:*

---

[5] [2002] FCA 906 at [24].

> (i)   *makes a circumvention device capable of circumventing, or facilitating the circumvention of, the technological protection measure;*
>
> (ii)   *sells, lets for hire, or by way of trade offers or exposes for sale or hire or otherwise promotes, advertises or markets such a circumvention device;*
>
> (iii)   *distributes such a circumvention device for the purpose of trade, or for any other purpose that will affect prejudicially the owner of the copyright;*
>
> (iv)   *exhibits such a circumvention device in public by way of trade;*
>
> (v)   *imports such a circumvention device into Australia for the purpose of:*
>
> > *(A)   selling, letting for hire, or by way of trade offering or exposing for sale or hire or otherwise promoting, advertising or marketing, the device; or*
> > *(B)   distributing the device for the purpose of trade, or for any other purpose that will affect prejudicially the owner of the copyright; or*
> > *(C)   exhibiting the device in public by way of trade;*
>
> (vi)   *makes such a circumvention device available online to an extent that will affect prejudicially the owner of the copyright;*
>
> (vii)   *provides, or by way of trade promotes, advertises or markets, a circumvention service capable of circumventing, or facilitating the circumvention of, the technological protection measure; and*
>
> (iv)   *the person knew, or ought reasonably to have known, that the device or service would be used to circumvent, or facilitate the circumvention of, the technological protection measure.*

A technological protection measure (TPM) is defined under s 10 (1) *Copyright Act* as:

> *A device or product, or a component incorporated into a process, that is designed, in the ordinary course of its operation, to prevent or inhibit the infringement of copyright in a work or other subject-matter by either or both of the following means:*
>
> *(a) by ensuring that access to the work or other subject matter is available solely by use of an access code or process (including decryption, unscrambling or other transformation of the work or other subject-matter) with the authority of the owner or exclusive licensee of the copyright;*
> *(b) through a copy control mechanism.*

A circumvention device is also defined in s 10 (1) *Copyright Act* as:

A device (including a computer program) having only a limited commercially significant purpose or use, or no such purpose or use, other than the circumvention, or facilitating the circumvention, of an technological protection measure.

Section 116A (5) creates the civil cause of action against the infringer:

If this section applies, the owner or exclusive licensee of the copyright may bring an action against the person.

1.3 The First Instance Decision in the Federal Court on s 116A – RAC/Boot Rom Is Not a TPM and Therefore the Mod Chip Is Not a Circumvention Device

At first instance Sackville J held that Regional Access Coding (RAC)/Boot Rom was not a technological protection measure because it did not and was not designed to prevent access to the copyright content or to act as a copy control mechanism of the copyright content. The crucial finding being that RAC/Boot Rom did not prevent reproduction of a game, it only prevented use of a game that was not coded for the region in which the PlayStation was sold[6]. Therefore, the mod chip could not be a circumvention device because it was not designed for the purpose of circumventing a technological protection measure[7]. Sackville J rejected the argument that RAC/Boot Rom had the "practical effect" of inhibiting or preventing access or copying in that it created a disincentive for copying by making it difficult for copied games to be played. He explained:

There seems to be nothing in the legislative history to support the view that a technological measure is to receive legal protection from circumvention devices if the only way in which the measure prevents or inhibits the infringement of copyright is by discouraging infringements of copyright which predate the attempt to gain access to the work or to copy it[8].

However, the Judge did comment that if RAC/Boot Rom were a TPM then the mod chip would have satisfied the definition of a circumvention device[9]. Further, Justice Sackville rejected a submission from the ACCC that in order for a device to be a

---

[6] [2002] FCA 906 at [92, 118].

[7] cf. *Sony v Gamemasters* 87 F. Supp. 2d 976 (N.D. Cal. 1999); Sony Computer Entertainment v Owen [2002] EWHC 45; *Sony v Ball* [2004] EWHC 1738 (Ch); B Esler, "Judas or Messiah: The Implication of the Mod Chip Cases for Copyright in an Electronic Age" (2004) 1 *Hertfordshire L J* 1 http://perseus.herts.ac.uk/uhinfo/library/u20277_3.pdf See also an Italian decision (Court of Bolzano) on the legality of the mod chip at: http://www.alcei.it/english/actions/psmodchip.htm

[8] [2002] FCA 906 at [117].

[9] [2002] FCA 906 at [167].

"technological protection measure", its sole purpose must be to prevent or inhibit infringement of copyright, noting that a TPM may have a dual purpose[10].

The more complex argument made by Sony was that RAC/Boot Rom was a TPM because it prevented copies of the games being made in the RAM (Random Access Memory) or temporary memory of the PlayStation console.[11] The Judge rejected this argument predominantly on the basis that reproduction in RAM was of such a limited and temporary nature that it was not reproduction "in a material form" as required by s 31 (1) (a) (i) *Copyright Act*[12].

Sony continued this line of reasoning and alleged that playing PlayStation games created a copy of a cinematographic film in RAM. This argument was also rejected, explicitly on the ground that a substantial part of the film was not copied in RAM and implicitly because the film was not "embodied" in RAM[13].

The reasoning of Sackville J in *Stevens* along with that of Emmett J of the Federal Court in *Australian Video Retailers Association v Warner Home Video Pty Ltd*[14] establish a principle that reproduction of a computer program in RAM will not be regarded as an infringing reproduction for the purposes of the *Copyright Act* unless it is reproduced in a manner and on a technology that will allow that temporary reproduction to be captured and further reproduced[15]. The message being that "use/playing" of a computer game is not of itself an infringement under the *Copyright Act*.

1.4   The Full Federal Court – RAC/Boot Rom Is a TPM and the Mod Chip Is a Circumvention Device

On 30 July 2003, the Full Federal Court of Australia (French, Lindgren and Finkelstein JJ) overturned the decision of Sackville J at first instance, and held that the sale and distribution of PlayStation mod chips contravened s116A of the *Copyright Act*. The Court held that Regional Access Coding (RAC) embedded on PlayStation Games and activated by the Boot Rom chip on the circuit board of the PlayStation console was a technological protection measure for the purposes of s 116A *Copyright Act* even though it did not prevent copying as such but merely

---

[10] [2002] FCA 906 at [104].

[11] [2002] FCA 906 at [119 ff].

[12] [2002] FCA 906 at [137].

[13] [2002] FCA 906 at [158]-[160].

[14] (2001) 53 *IPR* 242 at 262-3.

[15] [2002] FCA 906 at [137, 147-8, 150] This position has now changed as a result of Article 17.4.1 of the Australia-US Free Trade Agreement which obliges Australia to enact laws giving copyright owners the right to prohibit all types of reproduction, in any manner or form, permanent or temporary. This change is implemented under the *US Free Trade Agreement Implementation Act* 2004 (Cth) which came into effect on 1 January 2005. The Act amends the definition of 'material form' and 'copy' in section 10 of the Act and creates an exception to infringement where the reproduction is made as part of the technical process of using a non-infringing copy of the copyright material (see ss 43B and 111B). The critical difference being that temporary reproduction of a whole or substantial part of a computer program (game) or film (game) in RAM generated from an infringing copy of the copyright material will be unlawful.

provided a disincentive for copying or burning games – the so called "practical effect argument"[16].

In the words of Lindgren J:

> If, as in the present case, the owner of copyright in a computer program devises a technological measure which has the purpose of inhibiting infringement of that copyright, the legislature intended that measure to be protected (subject to any express exception), even though the inhibition is indirect and operates prior to the hypothetical attempt at access and the hypothetical operation of the circumvention device. By ensuring that access to the program is not available except by use of the Boot ROM, or the access code embedded in the PlayStation games, or both in combination, Sony's measure does inhibit the infringement of copyright in the PlayStation games in that way[17].

Likewise French J explained:

> If a device such as an access code on a CD-ROM in conjunction with a Boot ROM in the PlayStation console renders the infringing copies of computer games useless, then it would prevent infringement by rendering the sale of the copy "impracticable or impossible by anticipatory action"[18].

However, in obiter the majority (French and Lindgren JJ, Finkelstein J dissenting) supported Sackville J's holding that playing a PlayStation game and reproducing it temporarily in the Random Access Memory (RAM) of the PlayStation console did not amount to a reproduction in a material form for the purposes of the *Copyright Act*[19]. Once again in obiter the majority (French and Lindgren JJ, Finkelstein J dissenting) supporting Sackville J's decision, apparently with slightly different reasoning, held that there is not a copy of cinematographic film made in RAM when a game is played, because there is no "embodiment in an article" as defined by ss 10 and 24 of the *Copyright Act*[20].

The case was appealed to the High Court of Australia[21].

1.5 The High Court – RAC/Boot Rom Is Not a TPM and Therefore the Mod Chip Is Not a Circumvention Device

The High Court rejected the holding of the Full Federal Court that RAC/Boot ROM was a TPM and confirmed the reasoning of Justice Sackville to find that Eddie

---

[16] *Kabushiki Kaisha Sony Computer Entertainment v Stevens* [2003] FCAFC 157 at   [20], [139], [189].

[17] Per Lindgren J at [139].

[18] At [20].

[19] At [168] [26]; cf [208-210].

[20] At [181-3], [26]; cf [222-4].

[21] See B Fitzgerald, "The Playstation Mod Chip: A Technological Guarantee of the Digital Consumer's Liberty or Copyright Menace/Circumvention Device?" http://www.law.qut.edu.au/about/staff/lsstaff/fitzgerald.jsp. An earlier and shorter version of this paper appears in (2005) 10 *Media and Arts Law Review* 89.

Stevens was not liable for infringement of s 116A of the Australian *Copyright Act*[22]. The Court also agreed with Sackville J and the majority in the Full Federal Court that Sony's arguments based on temporary reproduction in RAM could not be sustained[23].

The majority judgment of Gleeson CJ, Gummow, Hayne and Heydon JJ explained that Justice Sackville's interpretation was correct for the following reasons:

> It is important to understand that the reference to the undertaking of acts which, if carried out, would or might infringe, is consistent with the fundamental notion that copyright comprises the exclusive right to do any one or more of "acts" primarily identified in ss 31 and 85-88 of the Act. The definition of "technological protection measure" proceeds on the footing that, but for the operation of the device or product or component incorporated into a process, there would be no technological or mechanical barrier to "access" the copyright material or to make copies of the work after "access" has been gained. The term "access" as used in the definition is not further explained in the legislation. It may be taken to identify placement of the addressee in a position where, but for the "technological protection measure", the addressee would be in a position to infringe.

> This construction of the definition is assisted by a consideration of the "permitted purpose" qualifications to the prohibitions imposed by s 116A(1). First, s 116A(3) provides that, in certain circumstances, the section does not apply in relation to the supply of a circumvention device "to a person for use for a permitted purpose". The term "supply" means selling the circumvention device, letting it for hire, distributing it or making it available online (s 116A(8)). Secondly, s 116A(4) states that the section in certain circumstances does not apply in relation to the making or importing of a circumvention device "for use only for a permitted purpose".

> The expression "permitted purpose" in sub-ss (3) and (4) has the content given it by sub-s (7). This states that for the purposes of s 116A, a circumvention device is taken to be used for a permitted purpose only if two criteria are met. The first criterion is that the device be "used for the purpose of doing *an act comprised in the copyright in a work or other subject-matter*" (emphasis added). The second criterion is that the doing of that act otherwise comprised in the copyright is rendered not an infringement by reason of the operation of one or more of the exculpatory provisions then set out. (The listed provisions do not include the general fair-dealing exculpations in ss 40, 41 and 42 of the Act).

> The first criterion in s 116A(7) for reliance upon the permitted purpose provisions which are an answer to what would otherwise be a claim under s 116A thus in terms links the use of a circumvention device to the doing of one or more of the acts enumerated in s 31 of the Act (where these are done in relation to a

---

[22] *Stevens v Kabushiki Kaisha Sony Computer Entertainment* [2005] HCA 58.
[23] All judges made detailed comments regarding the method of statutory interpretation: [30]-[34] per Gleeson CJ, Gummow, Hayne and Heydon JJ; [124]– [127] per McHugh J; [168]-[169], [215]-[219] per Kirby J.

work) and in ss 85-88 (where these are done in relation to subject-matter other than a work).

If the construction of the definition for which Sony contends were accepted despite the linkage specified in s 116A(7) between the use of a circumvention device and the central provisions of ss 31 and 85-88 of the Act, the permitted purpose provisions would risk stultification. The facts of the present case are in point. The use of Mr Stevens' mod chip in order to circumvent the protections provided by (a) the access code on a CD-ROM in which a PlayStation game is stored and (b) the boot ROM device contained within the PlayStation console cannot be said to be for the "purpose" of reproducing a computer game within the sense of s 31 of the Act. Any such reproduction will already have been made through the ordinary process of "burning" the CD-ROM. The mod chip is utilised for a different purpose, namely to access the reproduced computer program and thereafter visually to apprehend the result of the exercise of the functions of the program[24].

Gleeson CJ, Gummow, Hayne and Heydon JJ explained that in 'choosing between a relatively broad and a relatively narrow construction of legislation, it is desirable to take into account its penal character.' While this was not a criminal proceeding the judges stated that the potential for criminal sanction called for caution in 'accepting any loose, albeit 'practical' construction of the section[25]. They added that:

...in construing a definition which focuses on a device designed to prevent or inhibit the infringement of copyright, it is important to avoid an overbroad construction which would extend the copyright monopoly rather than match it. A defect in the construction rejected by Sackville J is that its effect is to extend the copyright monopoly by including within the definition not only technological protection measures which stop the infringement of copyright, but also devices which prevent the carrying out of conduct which does not infringe copyright and is not otherwise unlawful. One example of that conduct is playing in Australia a program lawfully acquired in the United States. It was common ground in the courts below and in argument in this Court that this act would not of itself have been an infringement. [Footnotes omitted][26]

In finally disposing of the issue and settling the meaning of the word 'inhibit' Gleeson CJ, Gummow, Hayne and Heydon JJ explained:

...Sony contended that, unless the term "inhibit" had the meaning given by the Full Court, it was otiose, adding nothing to "prevent". One meaning of "inhibit" indeed is "prevent". However, it may be taken that "inhibit" is used in the definition of "technological protection measure" in one of its weaker senses, while still necessarily attached to an act of infringement. One such sense has been given above with respect to acts of secondary infringement by dealing in an

---

[24] Ibid at [39]-[43].
[25] Ibid at [45].
[26] Ibid at [47].

article created by an act of primary infringement. Further, the operation of a copy control mechanism to impair the quality or limit the quantity of a reproduction may be said to hinder the act of infringement. In that regard, there is a legislative antecedent in s 296 of the 1988 UK Act. This, it will be recalled, spoke of devices or means intended "to impair" the quality of copies made. In the present case, the Sony device does not interfere with the making of a perfect copy of Sony's copyright in its computer program or cinematograph film[27].

They also noted that the definition of TPM was a compromise between the respective interests and that 'there was a reluctance to give to copyright owners a form of broad "access control" and "this reluctance is manifest in the inclusion in the definition of "technological protection measure" of the concept of prevention or inhibition of infringement'.[28]

McHugh J explained that 'a device is a device that is "designed ...to... inhibit" copyright if the device functions, so as to make the doing of an act of copyright infringement – not impossible – but more difficult than it would be if the device did not operate'[29] He went on to further explain this notion by way of examples:

This interpretation does not render the term "inhibit" redundant because it applies to at least two categories of devices that do not have an absolute preventative effect on copyright infringement. Thus, there are protective devices that regulate a user's access, not to the work itself, but to the appliance through which works are accessed. For example, "device binding" is a measure through which the decryption key of a work is linked to the "unique identifier" of the computer of a person who is licensed to download and copy a work. The work may only be downloaded and saved (and thus, copied) onto a computer with this identifier. The fact that access to the work is available solely by use of a decryption key that is linked to the computer's identifier does not make it impossible for another user of the same computer – who has not been licensed to reproduce the material – to download and save the work. Nonetheless, in disenabling the access of all other computers to the work, "device binding" mechanisms function to make it more difficult for users – who are not licensed to download the work – to have access to an appliance that will enable the copying and infringement of copyright in the work. In this way, "device binding" inhibits, but does not prevent, copyright infringement.

Other devices are designed to make it impossible to do an act of copyright infringement by a particular method or methods, but are ineffective to prevent the doing of the same infringing act by other, more complex, methods. Online access controls are an example. They are measures that

---

[27] Ibid at [55] See also [51]-[52].
[28] Ibid at [49].
[29] Ibid at [139].

decrypt a work that is delivered to the computer through the Internet – "streamed" – when it is delivered to the computer. The work is then immediately re-encrypted, so as to enable only a small portion of the work to be decrypted at any given time. The result is that the work cannot be digitally copied onto the computer to which it is being delivered. However, the re-encryption of the work, after it has been delivered and played, does not restrain the user from reproducing the work on other recording devices while the work is being played. In making it impossible to do an act of copyright infringement (ie reproduction) using one method, but not making it impossible to do the same act of copyright infringement using a more tedious method, online access controls make it more difficult to reproduce the work. [Footnotes omitted][30]

McHugh J concluded by saying that 'if the definition of TPM were to be read expansively, so as to include devices designed to prevent access to material, with no inherent or necessary link to the prevention or inhibition of infringement of copyright, this would expand the ambit of the definition beyond that naturally indicated by the text' of the Act'[31].

Kirby J explained that as Parliament had chosen such an elaborate and a specific definition a court should be careful to respect this design. He added that the 'difficulty with Sony's interpretation is that it challenges the very assumption upon which the definition of TPM in terms of "devices" would operate to have the designated effect, namely the prevention or inhibition of the infringement of copyright'[32]. He explained:

The inclusion of the word "inhibit", in the context of a focus upon a self-operating device, does not alter this conclusion. A strict interpretation does not deprive the term "inhibit" in s 10(1) of meaningful content. That word still has work to do in a number of contexts that are not covered by the word "prevent". For example, it will apply to a protective device which regulates access to the mechanism that provides access to a work, rather than access to the work itself. Such a device will not prevent infringement in all cases. This is because a device limiting access to a work does not prevent infringing copies being made once access is legitimately achieved. However, by restricting access to the work in the first place, such a device makes infringement more difficult. Significantly, such an inhibition operates prospectively; the infringement against which the device is designed to protect occurs subsequent to the operation of the protection device in its ordinary course. ... Secondly, a device that prevents infringement by a particular method, but which is ineffective to protect against infringement by another more complex or involved method, is a device that will not be covered by the term "prevent" in s 10(1). This is because infringement will still be possible, through the more complex method, notwithstanding the

---

[30] Ibid at [139]-[143].
[31] Ibid at [143].
[32] Ibid at [204].

operation of the device. However, by making infringement more difficult (say by preventing a common or easily available method of infringement), such a device can be seen to inhibit infringement in the technical sense required by the definition. This further demonstrates the utility of the inclusion of the term "inhibit" in s 10(1), consistent with the strict interpretation that I favour.

Had it been the purpose of the Parliament, by the enactment of the Digital Agenda Act, to create a right to control access generally, it had the opportunity to say so. It even had overseas precedents upon which it could draw. The Australian Government was pressed to provide protection for all devices that "control access". This is evident in the definition of TPM suggested to the Australian Parliamentary Committee by the International Intellectual Property Alliance. Such a definition would effectively have mirrored the provision adopted by the Congress of the United States in the *Digital Millennium Copyright Act of 1998*. By the time the Australian definition of TPM was enacted, the United States Act had been in force for two years. Nevertheless, the propounded definition of wider ambit was not accepted. Instead, in Australia, the Parliament chose to focus its definition upon protection from infringement of copyright as such.

The preference inherent in the Australian Act has been viewed as one which "favours the use of protected works", by limiting the operation of TPMs in terms of control over infringement of copyright rather than a potentially broader control over access. When the competing legislation of other jurisdictions, giving effect to the relevant international treaties, is contrasted, it appears clear that the distinctive statutory formula adopted in Australia was a deliberate one. [Footnotes omitted][33]

Kirby J reinforced his interpretation by stating that:

Avoiding over-wide operation: There is an additional reason for preferring the more confined interpretation of the definition of TPM in the Copyright Act. This is because the wider view urged by Sony would have the result of affording Sony, and other rights holders in its position, a de facto control over access to copyrighted works or materials that would permit the achievement of economic ends additional to, but different from, those ordinarily protected by copyright law. If the present case is taken as an illustration, Sony's interpretation would permit the effective enforcement, through a technological measure, of the division of global markets designated by Sony. It would have the effect of imposing, at least potentially, differential price structures in those separate markets. In short, it would give Sony broader powers over pricing of its products in its self-designated markets than the Copyright Act in Australia would ordinarily allow.

---

[33] Ibid at [204]-[209].

The Australian Sony PlayStation Case 43

Upholding fundamental rights: A further reason, not wholly unconnected with the last, is relevant to the choice to be made in selecting between the competing interpretations of the definition of TPM. …The Full Court's broader view gives an undifferentiated operation to the provisions of s 116A that clearly impinges on what would otherwise be the legal rights of the owner of a Sony CD ROM and PlayStation console to copy the same for limited purposes and to use and modify the same for legitimate reasons, as in the pursuit of that person's ordinary rights as the owner of chattels …. Take, for example, the case earlier mentioned of a purchaser of a Sony CD ROM in Japan or the United States who found, on arrival in Australia, that he or she could not play the game on a Sony PlayStation console purchased in Australia. In the case postulated, there is no obvious copyright reason why the purchaser should not be entitled to copy the CD ROM and modify the console in such a way as to enjoy his or her lawfully acquired property without inhibition. Yet, on Sony's theory of the definition of TPM in s 10(1) of the Copyright Act, it is able to enforce its division of global markets by a device ostensibly limited to the protection of Sony against the infringement of its copyright.

The provisions of the Australian Constitution affording the power to make laws with respect to copyright operate in a constitutional and legal setting that normally upholds the rights of the individual to deal with his or her property as that individual thinks fit. In that setting, absent the provision of just terms, the individual is specifically entitled not to have such rights infringed by federal legislation in a way that amounts to an impermissible inhibition upon those rights constituting an acquisition. This is not the case in which to explore the limits that exist in the powers of the Australian Parliament, by legislation purporting to deal with the subject matter of copyright, to encumber the enjoyment of lawfully acquired chattel property in the supposed furtherance of the rights of copyright owners. However, limits there are. [Footnotes omitted][34]

The legislative option: An additional consideration for avoiding reversal of the *Sony* rule in the United States Supreme Court was mentioned by Breyer J in the recent opinion to which I have referred. This was, as the decision in *Sony* in that Court had earlier recognised, that "the legislative option remains available. Courts are less well suited than Congress to the task of 'accommodat[ing] fully the varied permutations of competing interests that are inevitably implicated by such new technology.'" In the Australian context, the inevitability of further legislation on the protection of technology with TPMs was made clear by reference to the provisions of, and some legislation already enacted for, the Australia-United States Free Trade Agreement. Provisions in that Agreement, and likely future legislation, impinge upon the subject matters of this appeal. Almost certainly they will require the attention of the Australian Parliament in the foreseeable future. [Footnotes omitted][35]

---

[34] Ibid at [213]–[216].
[35] Ibid. at [222]-[225].

2 The Effect of Australian – US Free Trade Agreement (AUSFTA) on the *Stevens v Sony* Decision

2.1 Background

The existing definition of TPM by including the words "prevents or inhibits infringement of copyright" is said to be narrower in effect than a provision that "controls access" without any reference to copyright infringement. At the time of enactment submissions were made by the International Intellectual Property Alliance (IIPA) to the House of Representatives Legal and Constitutional Affairs Committee that the definition of a TPM in the form of an "access control" should not be linked to copyright infringement[36]. It was argued that access controls should be reinforced by anti-circumvention law even if they do not prevent or inhibit infringement of copyright. The "real world" example provided by the IIPA to highlight the point was that of having a lock to prevent opening a door to a house (the access control) which contained a book which upon entry I could read without infringing copyright[37]. This view was said to have been endorsed in the *Digital Millennium Copyright Act* (DMCA) in the US. Critics of this approach had argued that such a broad ranging definition of TPM introduced a new form of economic exploitation over information called an "access right". At no point in time did the IIPA submission suggest that an access control should regulate "use" of copyright material that had already been copied. As well, the IIPA argued on the basis that the law reform being undertaken at that time related to the WCT and WPPT – both treaties dealing with copyright and convened by the World Intellectual Property Organisation. The IIPA's preferred definition of an effective TPM is the same as the one offered in Article 17.4.7 of AUSFTA and the DMCA.

2.1 The AUSFTA Obligations – Already Enacted

The AUSFTA has already been implemented in part through the *US Free Trade Agreement Implementation Act* 2004 (Cth) which came into effect on 1 January 2005. Article 17.4.1 of AUSFTA obliges Australia to enact laws allowing copyright owners the right to prohibit all types of reproduction, in any manner or form, permanent or temporary. The *US Free Trade Agreement Implementation Act* 2004 (Cth) amends the definition of 'material form' and 'copy' in section 10 of the Act and creates an exception to infringement where the reproduction is made as part of the technical process of using a non-infringing copy of the copyright material (see ss 43B and 111B). The critical difference being that temporary reproduction of a whole or substantial part of a computer program (game) or film (game) in RAM generated from an infringing copy of the copyright material will be unlawful. This will most likely mean that the arguments made by Sony concerning reproduction in RAM will be upheld in the case of

---

[36] S Metalitz , 7.10.1999, pages 3-5.
   http://www.aph.gov.au/house/committee/laca/digitalagenda/submiss.htm
[37] S Metalitz, Public Hearing 21.10.1999 pages 176-177
   http://www.aph.gov.au/house/committee/laca/digitalagenda/pubhear.htm

infringing material. The decision would remain intact in relation to non-infringing material namely games purchased overseas and possibly back up copies.

2.3   Will the Further Changes Required by AUSFTA Mean Regional Access Coding Is Now a TPM?

The clear intent of the AUSFTA evidenced in Article 17.4.7 is to bring Australian anti-circumvention law into line with that in the US through making actual anti-circumvention of an access control unlawful[38] and moving the definition of TPM from one that "prevents or inhibits infringement of copyright" to one that "controls access" to protected subject matter[39].

Article 17.4.7 of AUSFTA requires that:

> 7. (a) In order to provide adequate legal protection and effective legal remedies against the circumvention of effective technological measures that authors, performers, and producers of phonograms use in connection with the exercise of their rights and that restrict unauthorised acts in respect of their works, performances, and phonograms, each Party shall provide that any person who:
> (i) knowingly, or having reasonable grounds to know, circumvents without authority any effective technological measure that controls access to a protected work, performance, or phonogram, or other subject matter; or
> (ii) manufactures, imports, distributes, offers to the public, provides, or otherwise traffics in devices, products, or components, or offers to the public, or provides services that:
> (A) are promoted, advertised, or marketed for the purpose of circumvention of any effective technological measure;
> (B) have only a limited commercially significant purpose or use other than to circumvent any effective technological measure; or
> (C) are primarily designed, produced, or performed for the purpose of enabling or facilitating the circumvention of any effective technological measure, shall be liable and subject to the remedies specified in Article 17.11.13. Each Party shall provide for criminal procedures and penalties to be applied where

---

[38] On the possible exceptions see: AUSFTA art 17.4.7 (e) & (f).

[39] "There are two elements involved in implementing the TPM obligation. The first element is the development of amendments to the Copyright Act 1968 to ensure compliance with Article 17.4.7. The second element involves a determination of whether there are additional exceptions to TPM liability that would be appropriate for Australia to create. The Attorney-General's Department is currently undertaking the first element. At the request of the Attorney-General, the House of Representatives Standing Committee on Legal and Constitutional Affairs (the Committee) will undertake the second element. The Committee announced this reference on Wednesday 24 August 2005. Information about the reference can be accessed at http://www.aph.gov.au/house/committee/laca/previnq.htm. AG's Newsletter August 2005 and http://www.ag.gov.au/agd/WWW/enewsCopyrightHome.nsf/ Page/ eNews_Issue_37_-_August_2005

any person is found to have engaged willfully and for the purposes of commercial advantage or financial gain in any of the above activities. Each Party may provide that such criminal procedures and penalties do not apply to a non-profit library, archive, educational institution, or public non-commercial broadcasting entity.

(b) Effective technological measure means any technology, device, or component that, in the normal course of its operation, controls access to a protected work, performance, phonogram, or other protected subject matter, or protects any copyright[40].

The critical question concerning the continued relevance of the *Stevens v Sony* reasoning will be whether the amended Australian law will equate "access" with "use". If "controls access" means for example controlling access to copyright subject matter **before** any act of using, reproduction or communication occurs then the *Stevens v Sony* reasoning will remain important, as regional access coding does not "control access" before the relevant act. It does not stop someone being able to access the copyright subject matter for the purpose of using, copying or communicating it. This approach fits well with the argument proposed by the IIPA that access should be decoupled from the activity that goes on after access is achieved; access is merely the lock on the door. It does not concern itself with any activity (e.g. use)[41] that will occur after access has been achieved. However, if "controls access" means for example the right to control use or playing of a game on a PlayStation **after** access to copyright

---

[40] Consider: DMCA s 1201 (a) (1) (2) & (3)

(2) No person shall manufacture, import, offer to the public, provide, or otherwise traffic in any technology, product, service, device, component, or part thereof, that— (A) is primarily designed or produced for the purpose of circumventing a technological measure that effectively controls access to a work protected under this title;

(B) has only limited commercially significant purpose or use other than to circumvent a technological measure that effectively controls access to a work protected under this title; or

(C) is marketed by that person or another acting in concert with that person with that person's knowledge for use in circumventing a technological measure that effectively controls access to a work protected under this title.

(3) As used in this subsection— (A) to "circumvent a technological measure" means to descramble a scrambled work, to decrypt an encrypted work, or otherwise to avoid, bypass, remove, deactivate, or impair a technological measure, without the authority of the copyright owner; and

(B) A technological measure "effectively controls access to a work" if the measure, in the ordinary course of its operation, requires the application of information, or a process or a treatment, with the authority of the copyright owner, to gain access to the work.

[41] On one view it might be argued that you have not achieved access to a PlayStation game if you cannot play it on the console you have purchased. It is hard to justify such an approach as it ignores the fact that once access is established a consumer can use modified technology to play the game. If they could not achieve access to the game in the first place there would be nothing that could be done to enable use. By trying to draw the legality of the modified technology into the definition of access the proponents of this view are extending the notion of access control (having its origins in copyright law) to a broader right to control use (having significant impact on consumer law).

subject matter has been achieved then the *Stevens v Sony* reasoning will be of limited application[42].

The very great fear is that as software inhabits an enormous number of the consumer goods we purchase in this day and age there is tremendous scope for embedding TPMs in all kinds of products and thereby radically redefining the parameters of a sale of goods or services. If TPMs as protected by anti-circumvention law can be used to structure the scope/usability of the product through code or technology then what the consumer is buying may not be readily apparent and worse still, may not allow choice of, or interoperability with, other accessories[43].

If the definition of a TPM is to move from "prevent or inhibit copyright infringement" to "controls access" meaning "controls use" then we have not only legislated an access right in our copyright law but we have also legislated a far reaching right to control and define consumer use. This would be better placed in our consumer legislation and assessed in that light than articulated and justified as an aspect of copyright law. The AUSFTA in essence acknowledges such a point in Article 17.4.7 (d)[44].

As Australia has moved to open up the flow of goods and services across borders in line with free trade principles through the removal on the restrictions on parallel importation of copyright material in certain circumstances it seems odd that the AUSFTA should be interpreted as promoting the reintroduction of such barriers

---

[42] On this interpretation see, *Sony v Gamemasters* 87 F. Supp. 2d 976 (N.D. Cal. 1999):
'39. Defendant concedes in its opposition papers that "[t]he Game Enhancer makes temporary modifications to the [PlayStation] computer program ... [c]hanging these codes with the Game Enhancer does not alter the underlying software made by SONY." (Def. Opp. at 6). Based upon the declarations before this Court, the Game Enhancer's distinguishing feature appears to be its ability to allow consumers to play import or non-territorial SCEA video games. As discussed above, SCEA specifically designed the PlayStation **console to access only those games** with data codes that match the geographical location of the game console itself. The Game Enhancer circumvents the mechanism on the PlayStation console that ensures the console operates only when encrypted data is read from an authorized CD-ROM. (Pltf's Reply at 7). Thus, at this stage, the Game Enhancer appears to be a device whose primary function is to circumvent "a technological measure (or a protection afforded by a technological measure) that effectively controls access to a system protected by a registered copyright...." 17 U.S.C. § 1201(a)(2)(A). (Emphasis added.)' See also Gleeson CJ, Gummow, Hayne and Heydon JJ in *Stevens v Kabushiki Kaisha Sony Computer Entertainment* [2005] HCA 58 at [43 where they say 'The mod chip is utilised for a different purpose, **namely to access** the reproduced computer program and thereafter visually to apprehend the result of the exercise of the functions of the program.' (Emphasis added.)

[43] *The Chamberlain Group Inc v Skylink Technologies Inc* 381 F.3d 1178 at 1203, 1204 (Fed Cir. 2004); *Lexmark Int'l, Inc. v. Static Control Components, Inc.*, 387 F.3d 522; 2004 U.S. App. LEXIS 27422 (6th Cir 2004); B Fitzgerald, "The PlayStation Mod Chip: A Technological Guarantee of the Digital Consumer's Liberty or Copyright Menace/Circumvention Device?" http://www.law.qut.edu.au/about/staff/lsstaff/fitzgerald.jsp An earlier and shorter version of this paper appears in (2005) 10 *Media and Arts Law Review* 89.

[44] AUSFTA art 17.4.7 (d): Each Party shall provide that a violation of a measure implementing this paragraph is a separate civil or criminal offence and independent of any infringement that might occur under the Party's copyright law.

through technology. The barrier that law has taken away, AUSFTA is threatening to reintroduce through technological regulation.

Constitutional and statutory interpretation principle/s and international free trade principles suggest that "controls access" should not be given a broad interpretation so as to include use. In this way the fundamental reasoning and logic of *Stevens v Sony* would prevail and Australian consumers would be more secure in understanding what they are buying and allowed a broader choice and interoperability of accessories. Some will still argue that to be able to segment markets across the world through price differentiation is not bad in economics nor in anti-trust or competition law. However, once we have removed parallel importation restrictions and recognise that digital content can be distributed cheaply and efficiently across the globe in an instant, arguments taking us back to segmented markets reinforced through technology are not appealing. Arguments suggesting the cost of distribution in Australia are so high that a differential pricing structure is needed to make such distribution efficient are questionable in light of the increasing capacity to distribute online in a cost effective manner.

The lifting of parallel importation restrictions were meant to liberate us from the imperialism that British and US publishers have forced on us for many generations[45]. Why would we entertain the return to such imperialism in a digital environment that allows Australian consumers the possibility of immediate access to a global distribution market for the very first time? Today we can buy direct from New York and have it delivered via the Internet. Why should technology be allowed to stultify this and force us back to a situation where we buy the Australian edition at a marked up price?

Ultimately any TPM that is designed like regional coding to segment markets in digital entertainment products should not be reinforced by anti-circumvention law so as to make Australian consumers second class citizens in a global market. It is almost unthinkable that a copyright treaty and a copyright chapter in an FTA could end up being implemented in domestic law to the effect that the consumer's liberty is restricted by preventing them from using games lawfully acquired in New York on the games console purchased in Australia. That would be both frightening and outrageous.

Kirby J in *Stevens v Sony* questions whether such an enactment would be constitutional.[46] Parliament would act to legislate these amendments under the intellectual property power s 51 (18) and/or the external affairs power s 51 (29) (implementing the WCT,[47] WPPT and AUSFTA) with other powers such as the trade and commerce power or the corporations power having potential relevance. Any

---

[45] Consider the excellent overview of the history and context of Australian copyright law by Benedict Atkinson: "Copyright Law in Australia 1905-1968: Narrative, Counter-Narrative and the Challenge of the Historical Record" (Unpublished LLM Thesis, University of Sydney, 2002).

[46] At [216].

[47] E.g. Art 11 WCT: Contracting Parties shall provide adequate legal protection and effective legal remedies against the circumvention of effective technological measures that are used by authors in connection with the exercise of their rights under this Treaty or the Berne Convention and that restrict acts, in respect of their works, which are not authorized by the authors concerned or permitted by law.

inherent limits found in the intellectual property power (as yet undefined by the High Court)[48] or the guarantee of compensation ("just terms") for acquisition of property under s 51 (31) would be the obvious constitutional limits[49]. Section 51 (31) would have particular relevance where property rights to chattels have already vested and the AUSFTA amendments purport to reduce the value (through functionality) of such chattels to the benefit of the copyright owner[50].

3   Conclusion: The Limits of TPMS

The critical issue for Australia is to ensure that the implementation of the AUSFTA obligations does not result in the reinforcing of TPMs that deny Australian consumers their legitimate rights to participate in the global market for digital entertainment products. *Stevens v Sony* highlights for the very first time the need to bring into the balance and reconcile the fundamental rights of consumers with those of copyright owners. The next great battle in this digital copyright war will not necessarily be between pirates and copyright owners but between the digital liberties of the everyday Australian consumer and the increasing reach of copyright owners in the form of multi-national corporations.

My point is that if the definition of technological protection measure is amended to focus on "controls access" and this is equated to "controls use" then the liberties of Australian consumers will be radically altered by this legislation which serves to implement a part of the AUSFTA designated "Intellectual Property". The recent decision in *Stevens v Sony* has guaranteed Australian consumers a fair degree of liberty in the face of imperialistic regional coding restrictions. Will this significant decision reinforcing the liberties of Australian consumers be made redundant by the Australian Parliament's actions?

If TPM means "controls use" then we have entered a whole new dimension in which the interests of Australian consumers risk being subjugated to the needs of powerful multi-national corporations. In that situation the strongest consideration needs to be given to the exceptions that will apply to ameliorate this impact. My suggestion is that the Australian Parliament should clearly articulate the view that "controls access" do not reach so far as to "control use" of consumer products. We need to "unlock" the digital environment through interoperability and choice not suffocate it through an ill defined and unprincipled "grab" for control over the liberty of Australian consumers.

---

[48] See: *Grain Pool of WA v The Commonwealth* [2000] HCA 14 at f/n 218 per Kirby J.

[49] See further: B Fitzgerald, "The Playstation Mod Chip: A Technological Guarantee of the Digital Consumer's Liberty or Copyright Menace/Circumvention Device?" http://www.law.qut.edu.au/about/staff/lsstaff/fitzgerald.jsp An earlier and shorter version of this paper appears in (2005) 10 *Media and Arts Law Review* 89; B Fitzgerald, "Unjust Enrichment As A Principle of Australian Constitutionalism" (1995) available at http://www.law.qut.edu.au/about/staff/lsstaff/fitzgerald.jsp

[50] Consider: Kirby J in *Stevens v Sony* at [216].

At the end of the day the balanced definition of TPM will represent a part of what I term "digital constitutionalism"[51] and be fundamental in ensuring the emerging yet vitally important principle of "digital liberty".

PROFESSOR BRIAN FITZGERALD

BA (Griff) LLB (Hons) (QUT) BCL (Oxon.) LLM (Harv.) PhD (Griff)
Head of Law School, QUT Brisbane Australia
bf.fitzgerald@qut.edu.au
Website: http://www.law.qut.edu.au/about/staff/lsstaff/fitzgerald.jsp

Brian is a well-known intellectual property and information technology lawyer. He is co-editor of one of Australia's leading texts on E Commerce, Software and the Internet - *Going Digital 2000* - and has published articles on Law and the Internet in Australia, the United States, Europe, Nepal, India, Canada and Japan. His latest (co-authored) books are *Cyberlaw: Cases and Materials on the Internet, Digital Intellectual Property and E Commerce* (2002); *Jurisdiction and the Internet* (2004); *Intellectual Property in Principle* (2004).

Over the past four years Brian has delivered seminars on information technology and intellectual property law in Australia, Canada, New Zealand, USA, Nepal, India, Japan, Malaysia, Singapore, Norway and the Netherlands. In October 1999 Brian delivered the Seventh Annual Tenzer Lecture - Software as Discourse: The Power of Intellectual Property in Digital Architecture - at Cardozo Law School in New York. In October 2000 he was invited as a part of the Distinguished Speaker series hosted by the Ontario wide Centre for Innovation Law and Policy to deliver an address on "Digital Property" at the University of Western Ontario Law School in London, Canada.

Through the first half of 2001 Brian was a Visiting Professor at Santa Clara University Law School in Silicon Valley in the USA. In January 2003 Brian delivered lectures in India and Nepal and in February 2003 was invited as part of a distinguished panel of three to debate the Theoretical Underpinning of Intellectual Property Law at University of Western Ontario in London, Canada. During 2004 Brian has presented talks in Germany, India and China and was a Visiting Professor

---

[51] B. Fitzgerald (ed) *Cyberlaw* Volume 1 (2005) Ashgate London; B. Fitzgerald, "Software as Discourse: The Power of Intellectual Property in Digital Architecture" (2000) 18 *Cardozo Arts and Entertainment Law Journal* 382–5; Paul Schiff Berman "Cyberspace and the State Action Debate: The Cultural Values of Applying Constitutional Norms to 'Private' Regulation'" (2000) 71 *University of Colorado Law Review* 1263; Jack M. Balkin "Virtual Liberty: Freedom to Design and Freedom to Play in Virtual Worlds" (2004) 90 *Virginia Law Review* 2043; B Fitzgerald "Principles of Australian Constitutionalism" (1994) 1 (2) *Proceedings of the 49th ALTA Conference* 799; B Fitzgerald "Australian Constitutionalism" (20/6/97 Unpublished Manuscript on file with author); A Hutchinson, *Waiting for Coraf: A Critique of Law and Rights* (1995) University of Toronto Press, Toronto; *Associated Press v US* 326 US 1, 20. See further A Giddens, *The Constitution of Society* (1984) Polity Press, Cambridge; Alan Hunt *Foucault and law: towards a sociology of law as governance* (1994) Pluto Press, London; E Ehrlich *Fundamental Principles of Sociology of Law* (1936) trans. By WL Moll (NY: Arno Press edn 1975).

in the Oxford University Internet Institute's Summer Doctoral Program in Beijing in July 2004. He is also a Chief Investigator in the newly awarded ARC Centre of Excellence on Creative Industries and Innovation.

His current projects include work on digital copyright issues across the areas of Open Content Licensing and the Creative Commons, Free and Open Source Software, Fan Based Production of Computer Games, Licensing of Digital Entertainment and Anti-Circumvention Law.   Brian is a Project Leader for Creative Commons in Australia. From 1998-2002 Brian was Head of the School of Law and Justice at Southern Cross University in New South Wales, Australia and in January 2002 was appointed as Head of the School of Law at Queensland University of Technology in Brisbane, Australia.

Downloading vs Purchase: Music Industry vs Consumers

Supriya Singh[1], Margaret Jackson[1], Jenny Waycott[1], and Jenine Beekhuyzen[2]

[1] RMIT/SITCRC, Melbourne,
Victoria, 3000, Australia
{supriya.singh, margaret.jackson, jenny.waycott}@rmit.edu.au
[2] Griffith University/SITCRC, Brisbane,
Queensland, 4111, Australia
jenine@griffith.edu.au

Abstract. The music industry argues that unauthorised downloading of music is detrimentally affecting the industry; a breach of copyright that needs to be stopped. The industry has taken many actions to stamp out unauthorised music downloading, including prosecution of peer-to-peer software users for breach of copyright and against peer-to-peer software suppliers for contributory copyright infringement. Industry commentators have questioned this line of reasoning particularly as there is now significant revenue from legal music downloads in the United States and Europe. This paper draws on a qualitative study of music consumers in Australia to show there is not a clear dichotomy between downloading and purchase. It is more of a continuum. From the users' perspective, downloading is transformed to the activity of accessing and exploring music. The industry could more fruitfully focus on satisfying this basic aspect of the listening experience in DRM systems in order to work together with their customers.

1 Introduction

This paper examines the arguments around downloading vs purchase. Industry beliefs that downloading has led to a reduction in sales of music has led to prosecution of peer-to-peer software users. The essential argument here is that downloading is a breach of copyright. We have discussed the connections between copyright, fair use and personal use, and DRMs in another paper [10]. Suffice it to say that personal use and copyright is a grey area in the copyright jurisdictions of the United States, Europe and Australia. DRMs, by enforcing the letter of the law, in many cases are going against consumer experience of music in a digital age (see [4]). Their introduction has led to a rupture that has pitted the industry against young people, its most important consumer sector.

In this paper we consider industry arguments that unauthorised downloading is leading to less purchase and industry data that argues against such a simplistic relationship. We then move to our qualitative study of users to draw on the users' experience to show that the main music activity involved with downloading is the accessing, sharing and exploring of music. This qualitative study is carried out as part of a wider investigation by the Smart Internet Technology Cooperative Research

R. Safavi-Naini and M. Yung (Eds.): DRMTICS 2005, LNCS 3919, pp. 52–65, 2006.
© Springer-Verlag Berlin Heidelberg 2006

Centre into media use and digital technologies that aims to develop guidelines for the user-centred design of new digital rights management systems (DRMs). A DRM system is a technical system designed to protect and control access to, and use of, digital content such as music and video files, software, and e-books [11].

2 Downloads vs Purchase

The music industry has argued over the last five or six years that it is losing substantial earnings due to unauthorised downloading of copyrighted music. Peer-to-peer file sharing is seen to have a negative impact on CD sales, leading the record industry to file lawsuits against peer-to-peer file-sharing networks and users, starting with the Napster case in 2000. While illegal downloading and sharing of music online remains a problem that industry bodies are determined to quash, the industry has also begun to offer legal avenues for users to download, and pay for, music online. A prominent example of a legal downloading site is the iTunes online music store, established by Apple in the US, which enables users to buy songs on a track-by-track basis for 99 US cents a song. Although iTunes is not yet available in Australia, a number of other legal downloading services are available, such as Telstra's Bigpond (discussed later in this paper).

It has also been argued by industry commentators and others that music downloads are not adversely affecting revenues of music producers. At one level industry data has been questioned. At another level, it has been argued that the industry has not been able to use the potential of digitalization in an appropriate business model. Where that has happened, the Internet has led to sales that would not have been possible without the Internet.

2.1 Downloading: An Alternative Perspective

Industry statistics connecting downloading and falling CD sales have been questioned on two grounds. Firstly, decreasing CD sales are because of changes in industry practice. Secondly there are persuasive arguments that downloading leads to purchase. As Sirotic (2005) says, falling sales began in the pre-Napster era as a result of an economic downturn. Poor management and marketing decisions have also contributed.

> *In Australia, falls in CD prices may also play a role, although partly due to action taken by regulatory body, ACCC (Australia Consumer and Competition Commission)... Crunch the numbers further and music sales can appear healthier than ever. While dollar values appear down, volumes are up. In Australia, CD sales hit record highs of 63.9 million and 65.6 million from 2001 to 2003.... pre-Naptster days ...CD sales were at 40million (Sirotic 2005, pp 6-7).*

Oberholzer and Strumpf (2004) [15] observed the downloading behaviour of peer-to-peer file sharing users over a 17 week period and concluded that music downloads have a statistically indistinguishable effect on sales. The results of the study question industry claims that file sharing is the primary reason for the recent decline in music sales. The authors estimated that 5,000 downloads are required to replace one album sale.

They argued that the decline in music sales is not primarily due to file sharing and that other reasons such as a reduction in the number of albums released as well as growing competition from other forms of entertainment could be having a negative effect. Record sales in the 1990s may have also been abnormally high with individuals replacing older formats of music into compact discs.

Dufft et al (2005) reporting on an Internet survey of 4852 consumers across seven European countries conclude that downloading often leads to purchase. This is because the Internet is "an excellent tool to promote new music" (p. 50. They note:

> ...many Internet downloaders spend money on music after they have discovered new music: 64% of the digital music users who have discovered a new artist on the Internet have subsequently bought a CD by this artist, 31% have visited a concert, and 16% have bought more digital music by this artist [3] (p. 50).

They also say that a detailed analysis of frequent users of P2P networks shows that:

> P2P users that have discovered new music on the Internet, subsequently buy CDs or purchase music from online music stores almost as often as the average digital music user does (p. 51).

The fact that unauthorised music downloading and file sharing is illegal is also becoming more publicly known as a result of prosecutions initiated by the music industry. In 2005, for example, International Federation of the Phonographic Industry (IFPI) issued criminal and civil proceedings against 963 individuals who shared copyright material over the Internet without permission in ten European countries and in Japan [16].

Downloading of music has different effects on purchase depending on the record of the artist. Oberholzer and Strumpf [15] found that file sharing is likely to have a positive impact for major selling artists, whilst artists who sell few albums are likely to be negatively affected by file sharing.

Some artists, too, have begun embracing the Internet as a means of making their music available to the public. George Michael recently announced that he is to shun profits and make his music available to his fans for free [2]. Other less prominent artists have also been vocal in their support for free downloading and file-sharing on the Internet (e.g., Ian, 2002) [8].

A Pew survey (2004) on Artists, Musicians and the Internet found that the Internet was generally deemed to have a positive effect on musicians' ability to communicate with fans and promote their work:

> Two-thirds of those in the online musician sample say the internet has had a big effect on improving their ability to communicate with their audience and fans of their music ... When asked if the internet had allowed them to reach a wider audience with their music, the same portion, two-thirds say they have observed a big effect [13, p. 30].

It is not clear, though, whether these artists' views can be ascribed to the impact of digital technologies on music or whether they are reactions to the way the music industry has operated in the past.

2.2 An Alternative Business Model

In this section we consider legal download services, business models with unlimited rather than restricted supply and models where information is the unit.

Legal music downloads where introduced have begun to impact on revenue. The IFPI Digital Music Report 2005 has reported [9] that significant revenues from music downloads in the United States and Europe were made in 2004. Over 200 million tracks were downloaded in 2004 compared to 20 million in 2003. Illustrating the growth of this practice, in mid-2005 iTunes is celebrating the downloading of the 500 millionth song from their service.

More tracks are now available to download and more users are aware of the availability of legal download sites. The introduction of iPod and portable players has contributed to consumer awareness [9]. At the centre of the digital music model is the possibility of unlimited selection. As Anderson (2004) says

People are going deep into the catalog, down the long, long list of available titles, far past what's available at Blockbuster Video, Tower Records, and Barnes & Noble. And the more they find, the more they like. As they wander further from the beaten path, they discover their taste is not as mainstream as they thought (or as they had been led to believe by marketing, a lack of alternatives, and a hit-driven culture) [1. p. 2].

In a physical world, retailers will carry only hits, content "that can generate sufficient demand to earn its keep" (Anderson 2004, p. 2). But in a digital world with no expenses for space, hits and misses can be equally available. As Anderson says,

> ....the "misses" usually make money, too. And because there
> are so many more of them, that money can add up quickly to
> a huge new market....a miss sold is just another sale, with
> the same margins as a hit.... Suddenly, popularity no longer
> has a monopoly on profitability. (p. 2)

The other factor hindering the music industry is an imperfect understanding of the marketing value of information. As Horrigan (2002) says:

> The music industry is in the business of selling containers
> and using information as the bait. In contrast, music
> consumers seek information without commitment to any
> particular type of container. ...For the industry to persist
> in attempting to thwart this separation, and to continue to
> confuse the information with its package, indicates a basic
> failure of market understanding [7]{p. 155)

3 Music Experience

In this section we draw on literature focusing on the social and cultural context of the music experience – listening to music, sharing music, exploring new music, collecting music. These activities have been part of the music experience within different technological contexts. We will also draw on our qualitative study of 23 people in Melbourne and Brisbane, based on focus groups, group interviews and open ended individual interviews. At the centre of this section is the argument that there is continuum from downloading to purchase (See figure 1). The picture from the users' perspective is more complex than the dichotomy of downloading vs purchase that is painted by industry. The spectrum covers variations from free downloading and few purchases of CDs to no downloading and only purchase.

3.1 Social Studies of Music

The studies of music within the social and cultural context have seen music as a leisure activity. Music and talk of music has particularly been important to constitute and maintain friendship networks. Accessing, sharing and collecting of music has happened within different technological contexts.

Livingstone's 2002 study [12] of young people and new media reports on the United Kingdom portion of a substantive qualitative and quantitative study of 6-17 year olds in 12 European countries. The interviews were completed between 1997-1998 before DRM issues came to the fore. Her insights are particularly pertinent for they show how core facets of the music experience remain the same though the channels of access, sharing and exploring new music have changed. She says:

> ... new media rarely replace or even, displace, older media. Rather, new media add to the available options, to some extent prompting new, more specialised, uses for books, television ratio, etc. (p. 89).

She says,

> ...the great majority of children and young people (93%) say they talk abut media at least sometimes to their friends... While talk encompasses all media, it is newer media goods that are most commonly swapped, perhaps because they are the most expensive to buy. Music and screen entertainment items top the list: around one-third swap music tapes, CDs or records (37%) and videos (33%)... (pp. 195-196)

Other more recent research has also pointed to the importance of understanding the continuities as well as the discontinuities of users' music experience in the context of new technologies. Sirotic (2005) [18] studied a small sample of 11 teenagers 15-17 years old and found that:

> Typically, they search and download music while chatting with friends on msn, doing homework or while searching for school or personal information using their beloved google....The nature of P2P use is that it exists on the periphery of other activities and media use.... (p. 19).

Ebare (2004) [5] also found that talking and sharing music was at the centre of the music experience rather than the technology. He says the sharing of music takes place not only through downloading but through chat rooms and message boards. He points out that "the sharing of music between peers is nothing new to scholars of popular music audiences".

3.2 A Qualitative Study

We conducted a qualitative study between October 2004 and July 2005. We chose the qualitative approach for we needed to understand the music experience from the users' perspective, rather than generalize what was already known. Once the different facets of the music experience were understood, these insights could be translated to a design of DRM systems in the Smart Internet Technology Cooperative Research Centre.[1]

The study had at its centre the perspectives of user-centered design where the user's activities within their social and cultural context are at the centre of design (See [17, 19]). It was a 'grounded' study in that there was a fit between data and emerging theory, rather than a testing of hypotheses [6].

Our data is drawn from a qualitative study based on 23 people in Melbourne and Brisbane in Australia. They were between 18 and 44 years of age and thus a more diverse group than many studies (7 were between 18-24, 11 were between 25-34, 4 between 35-44, 1 unknown) There were 15 men and 8 women. All except two of the participants had university education or were currently university students. Except for four, the participants were Anglo Celtic.

The people were accessed through personal and professional networks and through advertising on the university group mail. All of them had experience downloading music or were knowledgeable about DRM and copyright issues.

We conducted two focus groups, three group interviews and six one to one open-ended interviews. The interviews and focus groups were transcribed. We used N6, a computer program for qualitative analysis. This meant we first broadly coded the data, then organized the data into matrices to check emerging themes in a transparent manner. We also used the N6 program to identify negative cases so that the study was rigorous. As Morse and Richards [14] say:

> *"The key to rigorous qualitative inquiry is the researcher's ability ... of being constantly aware and constantly asking analytic questions of data, which, in turn, constantly address the questions asked. Qualitative inquiry constantly challenges assumptions, constantly challenges the obvious, reveals the hidden and the overt, the implicit and the taken for granted, and shows these in a new light " (p. 170).*

Our study shows there is a continuum between downloads and purchase rather than the dichotomy that industry presents (See figure 1). The download side of the continuum is dominated by issues of affordability and access, where the purchase only side emphasises a professional concern for copyright issues accompanied by a lack of technological expertise.

3.2.1 Affordability and Access

In our study there were only two people who mainly downloaded and seldom purchased. Adrian, 25-34 is a bicycle courier. He says he has seldom bought a CD and always downloads. Carla also 25-34 is an academic from South America. She cannot find the music she likes in Australia. So her brother routinely copies and

---

[1]   The Smart Internet Technology Cooperative Research Centre website is at http://www. smartinternet.com.au

compresses music to CDs which he posts to her. It is these dozen CDs she listens to at work and home.

Issues of access crop up particularly when music tastes are wider than those supported by the majority culture in a city or country, or when the music is palpably new. For Ah Lin, 25-34, the local market does not support his taste in Korean and Japanese music. However his pleasure in the tangibility of the music means he purchases as well as downloads. Alice for instance downloads dance music for she finds it hard to get. For others described in section 3.2.3, downloading is a way of sampling new music.

3.2.2 Tangible Loyalty

There were two main reasons why active downloaders of music also purchased many CDs and DVDs. The first was loyalty to the artists, particularly if they were new, local artists. The second was the desire to hold a tangible piece of music, to display it in the collection, and to make visual one's taste in music.

Adam and Alice, both 25-34, downloaded as well as bought music. As did Ah Lin and Abe, who were in the same age group. Alice says:

> *I went through a stage for about the last few years of only buying normally small Australian music bands. Any kind of local bands that I like I'll always buy their CDs. Because they really do struggle ... Especially if they're selling them themselves at the concert I'll always buy the CD.*

Abe said he would always buy a Beastie Boys album, for example, because he was a fan and wanted to see them getting something for their music. Francis, 18-24 was rather concerned about the intangibility of purchased downloads:

> *It's just not worth it. If you are going to buy the CD then it (downloading) is worth it but if you buy it, it gets deleted, you have just lost your money. As soon as that file is deleted you have lost it or you have to pay for it again. And if the file becomes corrupt, just accidental things, how you just lose your money. What happens if you bought all these songs, spent hundreds of dollars and you lose it?*

Bert, 25-34, who not only downloaded music but had set up a peer-to–peer network to share music in his neighbourhood is also an enthusiastic buyer of CDs of local artists at their concerts. Craig, 35-44, a librarian, says

> *I've got a background in playing music ... My background is just independent music and I would have been rapt to know that people were downloading and sharing my music around. That would have been great. We sold records and made 12 cents a record and I think the record company made 15 dollars or something. So I don't see particularly the artists suffering from people downloading music.*

Some artists are proactive about sharing their new music through peer-to-peer networks. Francis (18-24) talked about his musician friends:

> *I access stuff that my friends have written. Some of my friends have bands and their stuff is on the Internet as well. They put their music on*

there so people can listen to it...through peer-to-peer and on the website ... Even one example of it is, the first one Napster, actually had a thing, you could download all the new artist music for free. You would put your music on Napster and ... you can download it. It's not as good quality so people are going to play the music loud, if it is good they are going to buy the CD anyway if they want to listen to it, you can notice the difference in the quality. And I think that's fine. What is the point of putting a licence on having to buy a song when it's limiting the musician?

Loyalty towards the artist was matched by an antagonism towards record companies. As the quote above suggests, record companies were seen as commercial bullies who did not allow enough of the profit from music sales to reach the artists. As such, participants did not, in general, support the idea that record companies should control access to music through DRM technologies.

3.2.3 Exploring Music

Sharing music with friends is one of the main ways that people find out about new music or revisit old music. It is often friends saying 'Have a listen to this'. The Internet has replaced the radio for many, though not all the participants, as the channel for listening to music. The Internet is particularly important when there is no time to socialise. As Christopher, 35-44 says,

When I was younger I had a lot more time to meet with all my acquaintances, then I tended to buy CDs and share them ... Whereas now I actually feel because my work is so busy, I feel socially isolated. So then I go to the Net to download what others have been listening to.

He doesn't see it as ripping anyone off. He says, if he likes the music, he buys it. "I've gone and seen bands (and bought their CDs) ... on account of listening to enough". Ben 25-34 has similar views:

I think the other side of it is all of the money that they make when you go and see a band live, that is another whole area that I actively spend money in, going to the concert and seeing them live. But when you look at it there is only a small percentage of bands that do that, that tour actively, especially visit Brisbane, Australia. So I think there are limitations there.

Exploring new music and regular exposure is often a precursor to purchase. Francis 18-24 says

It's not so much that I listen to it on the radio and I like it and then I go out and buy it. I listen to it on the radio. I like it. I hear it again. I like it. I hear it again and I like it. And then ... maybe I will buy the CD. But then if I hear another song of theirs ... I will go and buy the CD.

So is listening to old music, which is often difficult to find with music stores only stocking what is 'popular'. Adam, an academic, 25-34 says he used to be an avid downloader. But after he got caught at work downloading large amounts of music, he has only downloaded four songs. He says:

Usually what happens is I get a song in my head that's very old, that I haven't heard in a long time, and I get a hankering to listen to it then

and right away. That's part of the convenience of it...Usually, if it's a song I really like – I once downloaded a Stevie Wonder song and I really liked it, and my response was to go out and buy every single Stevie Wonder CD that was ever (made).

3.2.4 Paying for Downloads

Paid downloads are not a usual way of listening to new music in Australia because of the paucity of material and services available. The Australian version of iTunes is keenly awaited. This is mainly because of the large choice of tracks that can be bought, rather than albums. It is also because of the difficulty and time taken to download music and retain good quality.

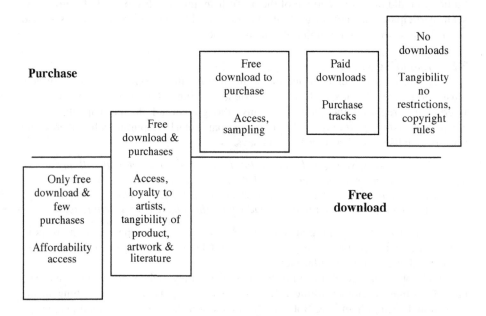

Fig. 1. A continuum from downloading to purchase

Alicia 18-24 says she will possibly buy when iTunes comes to Australia

> *"...because the American site is really cool. They have got lots and lots of different things. Even if you are just looking for what songs an artist has done it is really good to be able to go through and you can see a snippet of the songs which iTunes normally lets you do".*

Dominic, a DJ, downloads some of the more obscure jazz recordings that are hard to get. He subscribed to iTunes when he was in the US and also subscribes to an MP3 audio file store. Between these two, and buying CDs from the stores, he is usually able to get what he likes.

Alice buys CDs and would welcome paying for tracks because of her inadequate technology. Downloads are difficult on a 56k modem. She may download one song a month. She says:

> "... it can take up to an hour, sometimes more, to download a song. So I have to really, really want that song...if I hear a song on the radio that I really love, never heard of the artist before, I'll download it. But mainly I download dance music tracks that are not easy to get. ...Tomorrow...it might be very different. Tomorrow, we get ADSL".

It is information about your music that is also a plus when you use the iTunes application software. Ben 25-34 says:

> "ITunes... actually monitors how often you listen to each track. You can rank them and in the end you start seeing that maybe ten percent or something that you actually listen to out of the whole lot. So you start seeing those patterns which I think are interesting".

He however has difficulty with the notion of paying for music downloads.

> "...it sits on your system and essentially you don't end up with something in your hand at some point. In most cases if you buy a game online you end up with the box being mailed to you and if you don't, you normally buy it at a fraction of the cost".

Ben adds that downloading music that sits on his computer is different from his collection of 200 CDs.

> "You can sit there (and say) let's play music tonight. You can go through that person's collection... looking at things. ...You can open the covers up, find out about the person, the artist, the producers, even the lyrics for the songs. They are all there. (It is different from saying) 'This is my 18 gigs worth of music'".

However there were issues which clashed with consumers' wish to change format and share music.

3.2.5 No Downloads, Only Purchase

Douglas, 18-24 is one of the few participants in our study who does not download music. He only purchases. He says,

> "I basically buy it on CD, I have never really downloaded any music on the Internet. Normally what I do is go on a web site and I will listen to a few sample tracks and then go and buy the CD".

He sees two reasons for not downloading. Firstly he is still on dialup connections. And secondly he likes the visual aspects of music. He copies games however, and movies from videos.

For Craig, 35-44, a librarian, copyright issues have kept him away from downloading music. However wanting tracks rather than whole albums has made Craig thinking of legal download options he may use.

Christopher, 35-44 is quite similar. He buys CDs and puts them on the computer to preserve the original CD. So he listens to the CD almost exclusively on the computer. He says:

> *"...I download stuff, delete about three quarters of what I download straight away and then purchase the other stuff".*

4   Music Industry vs Consumers

Not a single participant in our qualitative study said anything good about the music industry. Ben, 25-34, encapsulated the general sentiment when he said, "The music industry is quite evil in some ways, quite greedy". The loyalty was for artists as seen in section 3.2.3. The Internet has opened up opportunities for artists to show their music and sell it direct to the consumer.

This schism between the music industry and consumers has also been documented by Sirotic [18]. She says:

> *Record companies have always seen new technology as threatening business. From pianolas through to blank cassettes, the recording industry has responded to technological changes by predicting its own demise and issuing the makers with million-dollar lawsuits. In keeping with past tradition, filesharing activity (incorporating providers and users alike) faces an aggressive publicity and litigation campaign aimed at protecting the industry's lucrative business model (p. 5)*

Sirotic adds that considering

> *...the changing nature of the media environment, it appears that record companies may be out of tune with their customers – music fans, enthusiasts, and especially, young people (p. 7).*

4.1   Reactions to DRMs

In our focus groups we elicited views about paid downloads and DRMs by showing participants two examples. The first related to Bigpond, an Australian site belonging to the telephone company Telstra which allows customers to purchase music. The second was from the US iTunes web site, a site for downloading music which can be easily transferred to play on the Apple iPod.

Participants were resistant to both examples. They felt that the DRM policies were driven by a lack of trust in the consumer to do the right thing. As discussed above, many participants saw themselves as honest consumers, and because of this they were affronted by the DRM restrictions: "I can see that they want to deter piracy but they're somehow treating everybody like criminals" (FGB1).

In general, participants saw themselves as honest consumers: their role was to purchase the music and use it in a way they considered to be fair. Charlotte, a publishing manager, was particularly adamant in her belief that downloading music was theft; therefore she was only interested in using the Internet to access music "if there was a business model attached to it and there was a digital rights component with it".

However, when confronted with two examples of DRM policies, this participant said that restrictions over the number of times one could copy an item made DRM solutions unattractive, as it complicated the activity of accessing and listening to music.

Thus, there was a primary contradiction in this participant's activity system: while she wanted to be able to download music legally and honestly (and therefore supported DRM in principle), she also felt that DRM systems complicated the activity of purchasing music.

There were similar contradictions in other participants' beliefs and actions.. Some participants like Adam went out of their way to purchase certain music by new artists legally at concerts. But he also preferred to download, rather than purchase music he considered to be "mass-produced bubblegum music where the people involved aren't really serious about doing anything but making a whole heap of cash."

In other words, there was a primary contradiction between this participant's belief that recording artists should be supported and his antagonism towards record companies and 'bubblegum music'.

In general, participants were less supportive of the Bigpond DRM statement, which is more restrictive than the iTunes policy. One of the main problems people had with it was the restriction that music purchased from the Bigpond site could only be downloaded in a certain file format This meant they could only play the music on the Windows Media Player through the computer and not, for example, on certain portable players such as the iPod. This was seen as an infringement upon what participants believed to be fair 'personal use'.

They felt that if they purchased the music, they should then be able to play and listen to it in any format that suited them, so as not to limit where and when they could listen to the music. In other words, the technical restrictions placed on digital music did not correspond with what participants expected to be able to do with the music they purchased.

This was also a problem with the iTunes policy. Although this policy allowed a greater number of copies to be made and recognised that people would want to access their music on a number of devices, it also limited downloads to a particular file format: the music could only be played using Apple application software. Although some participants (e.g., Adam and Alice) felt that this was okay because they approved of Apple software over Windows, there were others who felt that any such restriction was an infringement upon their personal rights.

There were also difficulties in comparing restrictions over the use of physical media (such as CDs) with restrictions over the use of electronic media. Participants felt they should be able to use music they had purchased over the Internet in much the same way they used a physical CD. With a physical CD they were able to copy it and play it on different devices. They wanted to be able to do the same with digital media: "[With DRM] I'm not really getting what I want, which is to have the music and be able to play it on all the devices that I own." (Carla). However, the use of CDs is, of course, restricted to devices that can be used to play CDs.

As one participant suggested, the advantage of having music in electronic form is that it could potentially be played on any number of devices, and the file format could be modified as people upgraded their equipment (rather than replacing records with cassette tapes, and then replacing tapes with CDs):

> *"...the whole idea about being able to do it through files is that then you can then pick the medium in which you play it on. It's much more transferable – you're not locked into buying all these individual devices. But they're essentially following that model by saying you've got to use this piece of software to listen to it". (Carla)*

The verdict is against DRMs that prevent this kind of exploring and sampling of new music. As Alicia 18-24 asks, Can they control the Internet across the world? Bert 25-34 also says that DRMs are trying to solve today's issues and generate revenue streams for the industry and creators. But the solution needs to be flexible. "You can stop peer-to–peer but now you can download from digital radio", he says. Seemingly another challenge.

5   Conclusion

Music consumers see their listening experience at the centre of their purchase behaviour. The industry sees the Internet working against copyright in terms of theft. A good DRM system that takes into account the interests of the consumers and the industry will need to devise a system that is flexible, that enables access for exploring and sharing music, for that is what leads to purchase. This has always been so, whether it is through borrowed tapes and CDs or through the radio. Online music also has to come to terms with the need for a tangible purchase, something you can see and hold and share with others.

The restrictions of current DRM systems also need to fit with the activities of users if they are to have any commercial success. Understanding the user experience is essential in developing a workable DRM business model.

Acknowledgements

We gratefully acknowledge our discussions with Rei Safavi-Naini and Nicholas Sheppard of the University of Wollongong. Our user study was done to contribute to their user-centered design for DRM systems. This multi-disciplinary and inter-university dialogue was made possible within the framework of the Smart Internet Technology Cooperative Research Centre.

References

1. Anderson, C. The long tail, Wired, (2004).
2. BBC_News. George Michael shuns music industry. London, BBC, (2005).
3. Dufft, N., Stiehler, A., Vogeley, D. and Wichmann, T. Digital Music Usage and DRM: Results from an European Consumer Survey, The Informed Dialogue about Consumer Acceptability of DRM Solutions in Europe, (2005).
4. Duncan, C., Barker, E., Douglas, P., Morrey, M. and Waelde, C. Digital Rights Management: Final Report. Study carried out by Intrallect Ltd on behalf of JISC., Joint Information Systems Committee, (2004).

5. Ebare, S. Digital music and subculture: Sharing files, sharing styles. *First Monday*, *9* (2) (2004).
6. Glaser, B.G. and Strauss, A.L. *The discovery of grounded theory: Strategies for qualitative research*. Aldine, Chicago (1967).
7. Horrigan, J.B. and Schement, J.R. Dancing with Napster: Predictable consumer behavior in the new digital economy. *IT& Society*, *1* (2). 142-160 (2002)
8. Ian, J. The Internet debacle: An alternative view *Performing Songwriter Magazine*, http://www.janisian.com/article-internet_debacle.html, (2002).
9. IFPI. IFPI:05 Digital Music Report, International Federation of the Phonographic Industry, London, (2005).
10. Jackson, M., Singh, S., Waycott, J. and Beekhuyzen, J. DRMs, Fair Use and Users' Experience of Sharing Music, *5th ACM Workshop on Digital Rights Management*, Alexandria, VA, US, (2005).
11. Liu, Q., Safavi-Naini, R. and Sheppard, N.P. Digital rights management for content distribution. in Weckert, J. ed. *2nd Australian Institute of Computer Ethics Conference (AICE2000)*, Conferences in Research and Practice in Information Technology, Canberra, (2001).
12. Livingstone, S. *Young People and New Media*. Sage Publications, London, (2002).
13. Madden, M. Artists, Musicians and the Internet, Pew Internet & American Life Project, Washington DC, (2004).
14. Morse, J.M. and Richards, L. *Readme First for a User's Guide to Qualitative Methods*. Sage Publications, Thousand Oaks, Calif., (2002).
15. Oberholzer, F. and Strumpf, K. *The Effect of File Sharing on Record Sales: An Empirical Analysis*. Harvard Business School, UNC, Chapel Hill, (2004).
16. Out-Law, N. 963 file sharers sued in Europe and Asia, out-law.com legal news, 12 April (2005)
17. Singh, S., Zic, J., Satchell, C., Bartolo, K.C., Snare, J. and Fabre, J. A reflection on translation issues in user-centred design. in Khalid, H.M., Helander, M.G. and Yeo, A.W. eds. *Work with Computing Systems 2004*, Damai Sciences, Kuala Lumpur, (2004).
18. Sirotic, D. Striking a 'digital' chord: How teenagers use online filesharing networks as part of music and internet consumption *School of Applied Communication*, RMIT UNIVERSITY, Melbourne, (2005).
19. Vredenburg, K. Increasing ease of use: Emphasizing organisational transformation, process integration, and method optimization. *Communications of the ACM*, *42* (5) (1999) 67-71.

Digital Rights Management: Merging Contract, Copyright and Criminal Law

Yee Fen Lim

Associate Professor of Law,
Dept of Law,
Macquarie University,
Sydney, Australia
YeeFen.Lim@mq.edu.au

Abstract. This paper examines the impact of digital rights management systems on the copyright regime. It argues that digital rights management systems in effect bestow copyright owners with more rights and control than what is stated in the copyright legislation. The end result is a regime that bears a remarkable resemblance to tangible property and which in some sense, is more powerful than tangible property.

1 Introduction

In the early nineties, John Perry Barlow predicted the demise of copyright law. He wrote:

> Intellectual property law cannot be patched, retrofitted, or expanded to contain the gases of digitized expression any more than real estate law might be revised to cover the allocation of broadcasting spectrum. We will need to develop an entirely new set of methods as befits this entirely new set of circumstances[1].

It is now nearly ten years since Barlow first penned those words and copyright law is still going strong. In some quarters though, what seems like the protection given by copyright law is slowly undergoing a transformation taking it beyond copyright law into some other genre of property law. Although Barlow may not have been correct in predicting the death of intellectual property law but he was not too far off the mark when he predicted the development of a new set of methods to deal with the new set of circumstances. Copyright law has been stretched to deal with digital technology but it is its strange coupling with contract law in the digital rights management system arena that has brought about a new set of methods.

2 Background

The WIPO Copyright Treaty 1996 requires states to prohibit circumvention of technological protection measures used to protect copyright,[2] as well as to prohibit the

---

[1] John Perry Barlow, 'The Economy of Ideas: Selling Wine Without Bottles on the Global Net' at <http://www.eff.org/~barlow/EconomyOfIdeas.html> 01/10/01.

[2] Article 11 WIPO Copyright Treaty 1996.

R. Safavi-Naini and M. Yung (Eds.): DRMTICS 2005, LNCS 3919, pp. 66–74, 2006.

removal or alteration of rights management information. In Australia, these have been implemented by the *Copyright Amendment (Digital Agenda) Act 2000*. Section 116A of the Australian *Copyright Act 1968* prohibits the making, dealing in, or distribution of circumvention devices for technological protection measures as well as their importation for commercial purposes through giving copyright holders civil remedies. The prohibition is not on the use of such devices. The section also contains a rebuttable presumption that the defendant knew, or ought reasonably to have known, that the device would be used to circumvent, or facilitate the circumvention of, technological protection measures.[3] There are exemptions from liability in instances where the device is supplied for 'permitted purposes',[4] such as to make interoperable products or to correct program errors. However, none of the fair dealing exemptions are included in the definition of 'permitted purposes'. What this means is that although legally a user is entitled to exercise her fair dealing rights over digital products and services by using anti-circumvention devices, the anti-circumvention provisions mean that no-one in Australia will be able to legally help her exercise her fair dealing rights[5] as she would not be able to legally obtain such a device in Australia. Such is the predicament of the average consumer of digital copyright protected material in Australia. The criminal equivalent of s116A is contained in subsections 132(5A) and (5B).

Section 116B prohibits the removal or alteration of electronic rights management information, and s 116C prohibits commercial dealings with works whose electronic rights management information have been removed or altered. In addition to the civil remedies available under these two sections, subsections 132(5C) and (5D) create criminal offences corresponding to the civil actions under sections 116B and 116C respectively.

On the face of it, these sections address the copyright problems posed by digital technology and in particular, the internet. They go some way in giving back to copyright owners some of the power they lost in controlling their works with the advent of digital technology. It is true that digital technology and the internet allow perfect copies of copyright protected materials to be made without permission and then enable these illegal copies to be widely transmitted. The use of copyright management systems prevents and curb illegal reproductions and illegal dealings with copyright protected materials. The validity of such systems is upheld by the copyright legislation. Further, the legislation effectively prevents any circumvention of these systems except in a few stated circumstances. This seems like a happy solution to the digital headache that copyright owners have faced since the early nineties. However, this theoretical model is slightly flawed in one respect: Digital rights managements systems may, and often do, ignore the user rights that exist under copyright law. As the anti-circumvention provisions of the *Copyright Act* give broad

---

[3] Section 116A(1)(c).

[4] Subsections 116A(3), 116A(4) and 116A(7).

[5] See sections 40, 41 and 42. The fair dealing rights are here referred to as rights for the sake of simplicity but the author acknowledges that there is continued debate on whether the fair dealing rights are in fact rights, or mere interests or mere exemptions. In many jurisdictions such as in the US and countries in Europe, there has been considerable debate on whether the copyright limitations actually grant certain rights to users or whether copyright limitations are mere defences against the rights of copyright holders.

protection for these digital rights management systems and thus, in effect, the *Copyright Act* is giving copyright owners implicit permission to ignore user rights. The current situation is one where theoretically, consumers have fair dealing rights enshrined in the *Copyright Act* but in practice, in the digital arena, these rights are not particularly useful or meaningful. Does this change in the digital realm transform the protection given by copyright law? Are we still dealing with intellectual property rights called copyright? This is the focal point of this paper[6].

3 Digital Rights Management Systems

The term "digital" refers to a representation that consists of electronic ones and zeroes, the binary code understood by computers. Before the advent of digital technology, analogue systems were the norm. Most real-world phenomena are fundamentally analogue, however, almost any analogue phenomena can be digitised, or transformed into digital format, for example, images, movies and sound. Digitisation is the technology that enables perfect reproductions of copyright protected materials that are easy and quick to perform. In order to stop the ease of copying and other forms of infringements created by digital technology, copyright owners have now resorted to employing secure content delivery standards and systems that implement digital rights management. These of course are only relevant for content delivered in digital form, so that content delivered in non-digital form can still be digitised and infringements can still occur.

A digital rights managements system, or a technological protection measure using the terminology of the *Copyright Act*, is essentially any system that digitally protects copyright owners against infringements of their works. They have usually been defined as fitting into two categories: Systems that control access to the works[7] and systems that control the use of the works. However, categorisation utilising the distinction between access and use may lead to difficulties, because increasingly, these two types of systems are merged into one single system. With this is mind, it can be said that access control systems are generally systems that prevent unauthorised persons from gaining access to a copyright protected work. They can be implemented in different ways, for example, in the online environment, access to the protected content is frequently controlled by an identification procedure using a login name and password. Or alternatively, for cable television services, the access control is implemented through the use of a set top box, which decrypts the encrypted signal received over the cable network.

Systems that control use of works are those that prevent uses of works that would infringe the exclusive rights of the copyright owner. They are often referred to as copy-controls[8] but they can in fact protect against not only the mere copying of the work, but also against acts infringing other exclusive rights of the copyright owners.

---

[6] There are also considerable issues relating to privacy but it's not the aim here to deal with them, see for example Sonia Katyal, "Privacy vs. Piracy" (2004/5) *9 Int'l J. Comm. L. & Pol'y 7.*

[7] See also the definition of technological protection measure as defined in s10(1) *Copyright Act* 1968.

[8] See Dean Marks & Bruce Turnbull, "Technical Protection Measures: The Intersection of Technology, Law and Commercial Licenses", 22 *E.I.P.R.* 198 at 199.

For example, some Cd-Rom products are protected against reproduction as well as its use on a network.[9] Audio content could also include a system to prevent its streaming on the internet to prevent infringement of the right of public performance and the right of distribution. As streaming does not involve reproduction,[10] such a system would not be preventing the infringement of the reproduction right.

Some digital rights management systems control both access and use of copyright protected material. For example, movies distributed on DVD (Digital Versatile Disk) are protected by an encryption scheme called the Content Scrambling System (CSS). CSS, in particular, the CSS licensing system, prevents most consumers from making perfect digital copies of all or any portion of a movie stored on DVD. CSS also requires the use of appropriately configured hardware (such as DVD players or computers) to decrypt, unscramble and play back motion pictures on DVDs[11].

Many of the technologies controlling access and use are based on encryption systems. Encryption is the process of using mathematical codes and algorithms to scramble data so that it appears random to all statistical tests and can, therefore, only be read by specified individuals using the appropriate key. Obviously no encryption system is perfectly secure and a sophisticated attacker can generally break any encryption scheme given adequate time and resources. There are many schemes for encrypting data ranging from the simple to the complex, from the easily broken to the highly secure. Encryption technology prevents all but the most sophisticated users from having unfettered access to the data on media they physically possess. However, the very existence of sophisticated users who are able to crack encryption schemes require legal regulation to prevent and discourage these practices. The legal regulation would have traditionally appeared in criminal law statutes but recently, they have begun to appear in copyright statutes, in the form of civil and criminal sanctions. For copyright material in digital form, there are now effectively three layers of protection. The first layer consists of the copyright regime that protects creative works. The second layer is the use of the digital rights management systems. And the third layer is the legal protection of the digital rights management systems through making it illegal and criminal to circumvent the digital mechanisms protecting copyright.

4   Copyright Law Stretched

Over the centuries, copyright law has developed into a very complex branch of property law. Generally, it still remains as a limited form of statutory monopoly that the public is willing to tolerate in order to encourage innovation and the creation of new works. To this end, the delicate balance of copyright has been maintained. Along with giving the copyright owner a bundle of rights, the public also has a bundle of rights. Fair dealing rights such as the right to reproduce certain portions for

---

[9] Kamiel Koelman & Natali Helberger (ed), *Protection of Technological Measures* (Institute of Information Law Amsterdam 1998) at 4.

[10] *A & M Record, Inc. v. Napster, Inc.* 114 F. Supp. 896 (N.D. Calif. Aug. 10, 2000) at 909.

[11] *Universal City Studio Inc. v. Reimerdes* 111 F. Supp. 2d 294 (S.D.N.Y. 2000) at 308.

research, private study, criticism or review are all rights that exist in Australia[12] and many copyright regimes around the world. Up till now, the rights of a copyright owner have been limited and have never been absolute like the rights of the owner of tangible property such as a table or a chair. If I own a table, I do not have to allow others to use my table, for free or for a fee. Copyright law has always required under the statutory regime that others be allowed to use portions of my work whether I like it or not. The "use" can come in various forms, such as reproduction for fair dealing purposes.

The two new extra layers of protection for copyright material in digital form seem to be on the face of it, extensions of the traditional copyright regime. However, on close examination, the owners of copyright material in digital form are in fact enjoying more rights and benefits even though in the law books, their rights do not appear to have increased. This is so because it is technology that has empowered the copyright owner. Digital rights management systems have effectively given copyright owners full control over access and use of the copyright protected material. When users want to access or use digital copyrighted material, they do so on the terms of the copyright owner. The transactions will be contract-based and the terms of the contract will generally be dictated by the copyright owner. Consumers are faced with 'take it or leave it' contracts that leave no room for negotiation.

Take the example of e-books available for sale on the World Wide Web.[13] You may choose to buy an e-book that you can only read on the screen but you cannot print the book or copy it or have the computer read it out aloud to you, and the book might expire in 3 months time. Quite surreptitiously, you seemed to have contracted out of the fair dealing rights that the *Copyright Act* gave you. If you are lucky, you might be able to pay more money and purchase a copy of the same e-book that allows you to read and print the book once. In this latter case, you would be able to exercise some of your fair dealing rights. It is true that consumers now have more choices as they can choose which contracts they want to enter into. And no doubt the competition lawyers will be pleased that there is now greater scope for price discrimination between the products. However, the fact still remains that it is the contract that governs the relationship between the consumer and the digital copyrighted material. Copyright owners are free to set whatever terms they wish, especially if they are in a dominant market position. And consumers are bound by these terms if they wish to access or use the copyrighted material. Whatever rights and obligations exist in the copyright law, these take a back seat to the contract between the copyright owner and the consumer.

The contract between the copyright owner and the consumer is not the only contract that is significant. There is also the contract between the technology developers and the copyright owners. Take the CSS encryption system for DVDs for example. The CSS system prevents routine copying. Even if a consumer wanted to pay more money so as to make a copy of a small portion for fair dealing purposes, and even if the copyright owner was agreeable to this, it would not be possible for such a contract to be drawn up. The reason for this is because CSS is not an open encryption system. It is a proprietary encryption technology developed jointly by

---

[12] See sections 40-42 *Copyright Act* 1968.
[13] See for example <http://www.ebook.com>.

Matsushita Electrical Industrial Co. and Toshiba Corporation. Matsushita and Toshiba licensed the technology to an industry trade group called the DVD Copy Control Association (the "DVDCCA") for the purposes of administering CSS and licensing the technology to vendors and content creators.[14] Anyone wanting a CSS decryption key must agree to the terms of the DVDCCA licence and pay certain fees to the DVDCCA. Not surprisingly, the DVDCCA is made up of all of the major motion picture studios and the terms of the DVDCCA licence strongly reflect their interests. Hence, the terms of the DVDCCA licence effectively impose certain restrictions on the copyright owner, including not permitting the consumer to perform any form of reproduction. The corollary of this is that the protections exerted by the copyright owner on the consumer, are determined not by the legislature but by members of the DVDCCA. Although the consumer's fair dealing rights are still contained in the *Copyright Act*, the means by which a consumer can exercise them are limited. As mentioned above, he or she would have to obtain an anti-circumvention device from overseas.

In addition to prohibiting reproduction, the CSS licence also contains provisions regarding region encoding.[15] Region Encoding is a system of marking DVDs so that compliant DVD players can check the countries in which the DVD can be played. For example, a United States DVD player will play only United States authorised DVDs and not those that have been imported or those foreign titles which have been resold. This means that if one purchased a DVD in the United States, and took that DVD to Japan where one's new place of residence is, the DVD will not play in a Japanese DVD player. This limitation is not in the copyright law and its source is the CSS licence that consumers have become victims to. Nothing in the current copyright law enables a copyright owner to prevent a legitimate purchaser of a work from using the work in another country.

The more alarming trend with digital rights management systems is the fact that the restrictions set out in the licence between technology developers and copyright owners are usually not expressed as terms of the contract the consumer enters into when the purchase of the copyrighted material is made. Rather, they simply appear as 'features' in the copyrighted items and the consumer only discovers their existence after the purchase is completed. This is a much greater concern as it is no longer the case that the consumer has any choice. Contracts are entered into without full information and there is very little choice available to the consumer. This kind of system, which relies on contracts and market dominance backed by strong anti-circumvention laws, allows copyright owners to exert very fine control over their intellectual property, certainly much finer control than otherwise possible under copyright law alone. Copyright owners of items that are in digital format very nearly have the exclusive right and power to control access to and use of their copyright protected material absolutely. Their power is limited only by what the parliament has exempted in the anti-circumvention provisions and the ability of consumers to obtain effective anti-circumvention devices from overseas. These rights go beyond the bundle of rights originally granted by the

---

[14] CSS License Agreement (V. 1.0) at Recital B (available, upon completion of forms, at <http://www.dvdcca.org/dvdcca/css/>, 03/02/01).

[15] CSS Procedural Specification (V. 1.1), p 6.2.1.4 (available, upon completion of forms, at <http://www.dvdcca.org/dvdcca/css/>, 08/02/01).

copyright regime. They seem reminiscent of the rights bestowed on owners of tangible property, such as chattels and real property.

5 The Tangible Property Paradigm

The next question of course is whether these rights that copyright owners have do in fact resemble those possessed by owners of tangible property. From a Lockean perspective, even if the rights do resemble those belonging to owners of tangible property, this would seem to be perfectly reasonable. Every person is entitled to the fruits of his or her own labour and the fruits are that person's property and that person is entitled to exclude others from the fruits. From a Lockean perspective, there may be nothing amiss about users not being able to exercise their fair dealing rights. However, the contention that the rights now belonging to copyright owners resemble those belonging to owners of tangible property needs further analysis. This will be examined utilising three elements: duration of rights, the number of persons against whom the rights may be enforced, and the availability of criminal sanctions for copyright infringements.

Firstly, the duration of the rights associated with ownership can often be substantially longer for copyrighted materials. For tangible property, one's rights over the property lasts as long as the property exists and as long as one owns the property. For many everyday items that are subjected to wear and tear, it is very unlikely that the tangible property will last for the lifetime of the maker plus 70 years, the current duration of copyright. It is true that items do vary in their lifespan in terms of their function and the care taken. A book for example may well be in existence for that period of time. A piece of furniture, clothing or household white goods on the other hand, would probably not last for more than 20 years. In this respect, comparison with tangible property may not be particularly instructive.

Secondly, the owner of tangible property will have a finite number of parties against whom she can take action against for violating some ownership rights. For example, if one's car is stolen, one would take action against the thief or thieves. When we consider copyrighted materials, the number of parties against whom a copyright owner can take action against can potentially be infinite. If there are a million copyright infringers, one could take action against a million infringers. It would appear that copyright owners have stronger or higher level of rights than owners of tangible property.

Lastly, the use of criminal sanctions for protecting digital rights management systems also raises issues. Tangible property has traditionally been protected by criminal law. Tangible property has required the protection of criminal law because the owner is entitled to the exclusive possession and control of the private property. For example, the ownership of a car comes with it the right to have exclusive possession of it. One may lend it to a friend to possess and to use, or one may deny lending it to a colleague to use or to possess. It would be difficult to describe copyrighted materials as strictly private property. Although the copyright owner owns the copyright, there are many facets of copyright regimes that would render copyrighted material ineligible for categorisation as private property. For example, the fair dealing rights given to users would render copyright ineligible for categorisation as private property. Similarly, the compulsory licensing schemes in operation in many countries would take copyrighted materials out of the realm of private property.

The argument then moves on to the rationalisation that criminal law can and does protect more than just private property. So for example, it may protect public property or private property for the public to use. A simple example is the protection of a park bench against vandalism or theft. Protection of such property however is grounded in the public good. Criminal law is required to protect the park bench against theft so as that as many people as possible can enjoy sitting on the park bench. Can the same public good argument be made about copyright? It is doubtful. In fact, the very fact that users can no longer exercise their fair dealing rights is in and of itself against the public good[16].

It is submitted that whilst copyright as a form of property right calls upon criminal sanctions for protection, the rationales for the criminal sanctions are not necessarily based on exactly the same rationales as tangible property. It is submitted that the use of criminal sanctions in the copyright regimes around the world is for the deterrence effect. Australia's legislation for example, is aimed at protecting commercial interests. Section 132 of the Australian *Copyright Act* contains some of the relevant offences. This section focuses on the concept of commercial advantage or profit, and it also takes into account whether the copyright owner is prejudiced in some way.

This then leads to the result that the criminal sanctions in the copyright regime are not present as a mere corollary of copyright being a form of property right. The connection between copyright law and criminal law is a direct one without any reference to copyright being a sub-category of property rights. This being the case, much theoretical analysis needs to be undertaken on the appropriateness of the use of criminal sanctions for copyright wrongs, and in particular, those relating to digital rights management systems.

6 Conclusion

Up till now, the relevance of contract law in copyright law has been limited to the dealings with copyright, such as assignments and licences. The dominance of contract law in the new layers of protection for creative output has catapulted the level of protection beyond that traditionally understood by copyright law. As a result of contract law's pivotal role in the extension of rights, copyright owners now have disproportionate rights in the digital realm. Whether the extension of rights is warranted or justified is yet another issue. The purpose here has been only to examine the role of contract law and the consequences of its role in the protection of creative

---

[16] The reference here to public good in copyright law is grounded upon the notion that authors are given property rights in their creative works with the ultimate goal of providing incentives for creation so that more works will exist for the public to consume and build upon. The scope of an individual's rights in his or her work is meant to be narrowly construed and should theoretically be limited only to protection that is necessary to maximize public welfare. See further the US cases of *Fogerty v. Fantasy, Inc.*, 510 U.S. 517, 526-27 (1994); *Sony Corp. v. Universal City Studios*, 464 U.S. 417, 429 (1986); *Twentieth Century Fox v. Aiken*, 422 U.S. 151, 156 (1975); *Tasini v. New York Times*, 533 U.S. 483, 523 n.20 (2001).

works. In particular, it has explored the nature of copyright with respect to the tangible property paradigm and the use of criminal sanctions.

Bibliography

1. Stefan Bechtold, "Digital Rights Management in the United States and Europe" (2004) 52 *American Journal of Comparative Law* 323
2. Joseph H. Sommer, "Against Cyberlaw" (2000) 15 *Berkeley Technology Law Journal* 1145
3. Declan McCullagh and Milana Homsi, "Leave DRM Alone: A Survey of Legislative Proposals Relating to Digital Rights Management Technology and their Problems" [2005] *Michigan State Law Review* 317
4. Raymond Shih Ray Ku, "Symposium: The Law and Technology of Digital Rights Management: Consumers and Creative Destruction: Fair Use Beyond Market Failure" (2003) 18 *Berkeley Technology Law Journal* 539
5. R. Anthony Reese, "Symposium: The Law and Technology of Digital Rights Management: Will Merging Access Controls and Rights Controls Undermine the Structure of Anticircumvention Law?" (2003) 18 *Berkeley Technology Law Journal* 619
6. Chris Jay Hoofnagle, "Digital Rights Management: Many Technical Controls on Digital Content Distribution can Create a Surveillance Society" (2004) 5 *Columbia Science & Technology Law Review* 6
7. Ryan Roemer, "Trusted Computing, Digital Rights Management, and the Fight for Copyright Control on Your Computer" (2003) *UCLA Journal Law and Technology* 8
8. Kristin Brown, "Comment: Digital Rights Management: Trafficking in Technology That Can Be Used to Circumvent the Intellectual Property Clause" (2003) 40 Houston Law Review 803
9. Michael A. Einhorn, "Copyright, Prevention, and Rational Governance: File-sharing and Napster" (2001) 24 *Columbia-VLA Journal of Law & the Arts* 449
10. Molly Torsen, "Lexmark, Watermarks, Skylink and Marketplaces: Misuse and Misperception of the Digital Millennium Copyright Act's Anticircumvention Provision" (2004) 4 *Chicago-Kent Journal of Intellectual Property Law* 117
11. Timothy Nielander, "Unchained Melody: Music Licensing in the Digital Age" (1998) 6 *Texas Intellectual Property Law Journal* 277
12. Terri Branstetter Cohen, "Anti-Circumvention: Has Technology's Child Turned Against Its Mother?" (2003) 36 *Vanderbilt Journal Transnational Law* 961
13. John Perry Barlow, 'The Economy of Ideas: Selling Wine Without Bottles on the Global Net' at <http://www.eff.org/~barlow/EconomyOfIdeas.html> 01/10/01
14. Sonia Katyal, "Privacy vs. Piracy" (2004/5) 9 *International Journal of Communication Law & Policy* 7
15. See Dean Marks & Bruce Turnbull, "Technical Protection Measures: The Intersection of Technology, Law and Commercial Licenses", 22 *European Intellectual Property Review* 198
16. WIPO Copyright Treaty 1996
17. *Copyright Act 1968*
18. Kamiel Koelman & Natali Helberger (ed), *Protection of Technological Measures* (Institute of Information Law Amsterdam 1998)

User-Attributed Rights in DRM

Milan Petković and R. Paul Koster

Philips Research, Information & System Security,
High Tech Campus 37 (WY 71), 5656 AE Eindhoven, The Netherlands
{milan.petkovic, r.p.koster}@philips.com

Abstract. Current Digital Rights Management (DRM) systems lack a functionality that allows a user to have more control over his content licenses to preserve his privacy or otherwise protect his interests. This paper presents an approach to increasing user's control of domain-based protected content without sacrificing content owner's control. The proposed method is based on a specific form of a delegation license and an activation mechanism. The paper also discusses a practical realization of the proposed concept as well as its cryptographic enforcement, architectural aspects and system complexity. The effectiveness and simplicity of the approach are illustrated by a practical realization of several motivating examples.

Keywords: Digital Rights Management (DRM), delegation, user-attributed rights.

1 Introduction

Current DRM systems protect the interests of the content industry and service providers by controlling the distribution of and access to commercial audio/video content. Users can use DRM protected content as they like within the rules of the DRM system and acquired license. However, it is very well possible that the DRM system allows content usage under circumstances undesired by the user because of privacy reasons, (parental) control or his other interests. For example, the user might want to have a fine-grained parental control, so that instead of just excluding children, he makes a content item available for them only in certain time slots or under supervision. In another example, he would like to prevent that somebody uses his one-time-play license. Support of domain concepts in DRM systems is another development that makes the current solutions ineffective, because content may be stored and rendered on a number of devices operated by many different users. In such environment, the needs for user privacy and value preservation are even more obvious. The user who just bought a piece of content for his domain might want to specify different restrictions for different domain members, e.g. prevent some domain members from deleting the content or burning it on a CD.

The above developments lead to the conclusion that users must have a mechanism to apply further restrictions on the original license, i.e. limit the distribution and use of content beyond the limits already set by the content provider. Since the threat model is equal to that of DRM, namely, that the receivers cannot be trusted, it is logical to

R. Safavi-Naini and M. Yung (Eds.): DRMTICS 2005, LNCS 3919, pp. 75–89, 2006.

search for a solution within the DRM space. Therefore, this paper presents a solution to extend the license aspects of a DRM system in such a way that users can add further restrictions to existing licenses on their terms and conditions, without interference of the service provider. From now on this functionality is referred to as **user-attributed rights**.

Related work to user-attributed rights can be found in the area of access control, more specifically delegation in access control. Our approach could be classified under constrained delegation which is a specific form of delegation, where the authority to create a permission and the permission itself are clearly differentiated. A formal definition of a constrained delegation model can be found in [1]. Delegation chains and delegation assertions form the basic elements of constrained delegation. In [2] it is shown how to extend the SAML 1.1 specification in such a way that it supports constrained delegation.

However, the aforementioned approaches either allow the end-user to control the final part of the delegation chain and override the original limitations or they are too restrictive requiring the final permission to be set immediately in the first license of the delegation chain. On one hand, unlimited control on the delegation process by the end-user may have severe implications on the trust content owners have in the system. Namely, the content owners clearly do not want the end-user to be able of delegating his rights to any other party than maybe his domain members. On the other hand, the user would like to have differentiations with respect to rights within his domain, while still preserving privacy towards the content provider. He does not want to go to the content provider every time he wants to change some rights, for example that his kid (which is part of his domain), who is now old enough, can watch the movie he bought for his domain five years ago. Sometimes, he does not want even to reveal the structure of his domain to the content provider. Therefore, we propose an approach in which the rights issued by the content provider are still respected, while the user is allowed to be in control by adding only extra restrictions on obtained licenses. The proposed solution is practically realized in a DRM context that is simple in structure and enforcement.

The rest of this paper is organized as follows. The next section provides some background for digital rights management and introduces domain concepts. Motivating use cases, requirements, and general concepts of our solution, as well as its practical realization are presented in Section 3. In Section 4, we revisit the motivating examples and show how they can be accomplished using the presented idea. Section 5 concludes the paper.

2 Digital Rights Management

Digital Rights Management (DRM) systems are employed to protect and enforce the copyrights of content owners. An important characteristic of DRM is that licenses determine the rights of a party to certain content items. Various options exist for the binding between a license and an entity, which furthermore is subject to change as technology and concepts develop. Initially entities were devices, i.e. content and licenses were bound to devices. More recent concepts bind licenses to groups of devices (domains), to persons (user accounts) and to hybrid groups of persons and devices.

Coming from the world of copy protection, DRM licenses were first bound to devices. As a consequence the content only rendered on a specific device. Consumers, however, want to enjoy content without hassle and with as few limitations as possible. They want to network their devices to enable all types of different applications and easily access any type of content anywhere. This also holds for sharing/transferring content in home environments. To address the requirements of content owners and consumers, companies [3] and standardization bodies such as DVB (Digital Video Broadcasting) [6] and OMA (Open Mobile Alliance) [7] are investigating and developing the concept of Authorized Domain (AD) [8][9]. Typical Authorized Domain DRM systems do not restrict content access to a specific device or medium, but rather define a group of devices (the domain) and allow content access on all of them as well as a free flow of content between them.

Noteworthy for device-based authorized domain concepts is that they are not all intended as delivery DRM systems, i.e. systems designed to deliver content from a content service provider's server to an end-user device. Instead, some are mainly designed to function in the home network and receive/import content from a delivery DRM system [3][4][9]. As part of this import process some form of license translation from a delivery DRM system into a license of the home network DRM system is performed. This process is typically under control of the device that performs the import.

Alternatively, licenses can be bound to a person or a group of persons. In a person-based AD configuration, content is bound to a person. A number of persons, e.g. all the members of one family, are grouped into an authorized domain, which allows them to share content. The idea underlying this configuration is that any content linked to any person in the domain can be accessed on any compliant device in close proximity to the user. A device can check user proximity by authenticating the user, e.g. via a token representing the user.

Finally, concepts are developed where domains of both user(s) and devices are entitled to access the content. One of such concepts is the Personal Entertainment Domain where content is bound to a person, and where a person can define a set of domain devices that can render his content [10].

Next to DRM for commercial audio/video entertainment content, DRM solutions also exist for use in enterprises to protect access to and usage of company documents. These systems typically have a license that grants certain rights to certain people, reusing as much as possible existing account management and authentication mechanisms [11]. A typical characteristic of enterprise DRM systems is that they offer fine-grained licenses with flexibility on who defines the policies and who gets access rights, instead of the rather static approach in DRM for entertainment content. An explanation for this difference can be found if one takes the different roles of the stakeholders into account: for entertainment content, a content provider wants to have a simple process and little complexity as long as there is payment for the content, while for enterprise data safeguarding the one who can access the content is of uttermost importance and may require more management complexity.

3 User-Attributed Rights

This section begins with a description of several use cases that motivate the work presented in the paper. Having the problem clarified, the section introduces the general concepts of our solution, as well as their practical realization via delegation and an activation mechanism. To further improve the security of the proposed solution, its cryptographic enforcement is presented. Finally, the section discusses architectural aspects and system complexity of the presented solution as well as user interaction with the system.

3.1 Motivating Examples and Requirements

As described in the previous section, the basic idea of domain based DRM systems is that if a user of a DRM system buys a piece of content, other users in his home (domain) may be allowed to access that content as well. However, while supporting the authorized domain idea, the system should preserve the user's privacy, e.g. by giving the user control over who else and under what conditions can access his content. Besides privacy, other reasons for user-attributed rights can be thought of such as parental control or value protection (in case of stateful/countable rights).

To further clarify the problems addressed by the paper we start with a few motivating use cases:

- Pete bought some content online, which can be used on all the devices in his domain. However, Pete would like to keep the content for himself instead of anybody who uses his devices, such as his family members. Therefore, Pete uses his content management application and indicates, for the content he just downloaded that it may only be accessed by 'Pete'. When Pete accesses his bought content item on his TV and tries to play it, he is asked to authenticate (by password/token/biometrics). The content plays after Pete has done so. Pete could also specify different rights for the different members of his domain for the content he bought. For example, he can keep for himself maximum rights while further restricting the rights for others (e.g. he can indicate that his kids do not have the right to delete the content or burn it on a CD). He can also split countable rights so that his kids cannot spend them all before he even watched it once.
- A grandma buys some content for her grandson Joy. During purchase the grandma asks the license issuer to bind this license immediately to Joy (which makes it cheaper because only one person can render it). However, grandma would prefer to have special rights with this license and be able to specify that content is only viewable after her grandson's birthday or after he passes an exam). Furthermore, she delegates the right to impose further restrictions to Joy's mum. At a later point in time, her daughter specifies that the content only plays between 10am and 18pm to prevent overuse (e.g. in case the content being a computer game).

From the abovementioned use cases, we can derive the main requirements for user-attributed rights, which are:

- The system shall allow authorized users to limit access to content to the intersection of both the rightsholder's (content owner's) and the rights licensee's (user's) wishes.
- The system shall allow rights differentiations (specified by the user) within domains: different users with different rights for the same piece of content
- The system shall keep security at the level which it was without user-attributed rights. This means that commercial rights must be as strongly enforced as before and also that user-attributed rights (the further) restriction, are enforced with the same level of security.
- The system shall provide mechanisms that prevent people from locking themselves out of their own content forever.
- The system shall provide user-friendly creation of additional licenses.

3.2 User-Attributed Rights Concept

To fulfill the aforementioned requirements one could think of different approaches. Advanced solutions could take into account concepts like DRM and delegation, e.g. people setting further restrictions while they themselves do not necessary have rights on the content. Note that basic properties of the further restrictions could also be accomplished by techniques such as access control on the content or license files. However, it is advantageous to integrate the further restrictions as user-attributed rights into the DRM system for a number of reasons:

- The restrictions are persistent regardless of where the licenses/content are stored and thereby prevent that the content/licenses end-up at unauthorized entities by alternative routes.
- DRM systems work by default with the threat model that the user of a device may be hostile.
- DRM systems have better potential of offering a single unified interface to the end-user.

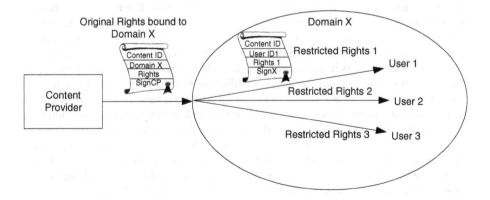

Fig. 1. Rights differentiations within a domain

There are several ways of allowing differentiation for rights within the domain. A straightforward solution would be to introduce differentiations during purchase of the rights when the user could immediately define different rights for different domain members and let the content provider encode this in the licenses. However, as already discussed in the introduction this is rather static, nonflexible, and privacy invasive approach. Furthermore, increasing the flexibility by having the content provider adapt licenses on user's request at a later moment would have the drawback that it increases the workload on the content provider. Another possibility is to introduce differentiations in the process of transcoding delivery DRM rights into domain DRM rights. Here, a person who bought the content (or domain administrator or a domain member who first accesses the license) will be allowed to add further restrictions/rights on top of the original rights (which are used to control the use of and access to content in a domain) specifically for domain members (see fig. 1). However, a very strong requirement by the commercial content providers is that they want complete control over the content distribution and usage. Very often, content providers do not trust and do not allow transcoding of original licenses. Therefore in this paper, an alternative solution is presented which supports user-attributed rights without transcoding of licenses. Another aspect of distribution control may be that the content providers would also like to have control on the further restrictions that the user defines for the content. The commercial interest of this approach however seems low, because it does not directly strengthen their business and as already mentioned, the content providers' goal is payment assurance in a simple process with low complexity. Furthermore, from technical perspective, interaction between the rights expression and the further restrictions would severely limit the cleanliness of the solution. This leads to the conclusion that from a content provider, user and technical point of view license management of the original bought license and the user-attributed right should be loosely coupled.

3.3 License Activation

To allow a user to have more control over his content, we introduce an activation mechanism and a special format of licenses that we call "**star-license**". In addition to the standard fields in a traditional license (such as content ID, protected content key, rights expressions, ID of the users or the domain to which the licenses is bound, etc.), a star-license specifies that it is not active, i.e. that it cannot be used by a user to access the content unless it is activated and used along with an additional license. The original license together with subsequent additional licenses will be called a license chain. Furthermore, the star-license specifies in a star-expression who is allowed to activate it and create a user-attributed license (and therefore an active chain of licenses). The differences between a star-license and a non-star-license are that the star-license contains a star-expression, is inactive and can therefore not complete an active chain of licenses. Next to the identity of the user to whom the rights to activate the license are delegated, the star-expression could comprise additional rights and constraints related to delegation. The format of a star-license is as follows:

L*: {ContentID, ProtectedContentKey, RightsExpr, BoundTo, ActivationInfo, Star-
        Expression}$_{signature}$

The main advantage of introducing star-licenses and the presented activation method is that there is no need for copy control of licenses. They can freely float around (assuming there are no other reasons such as associated state that prevent free floating of licenses). Another advantage of star-licenses is that users cannot be locked out of their own content as long as there is one license chain left that gives the user proper activation rights.

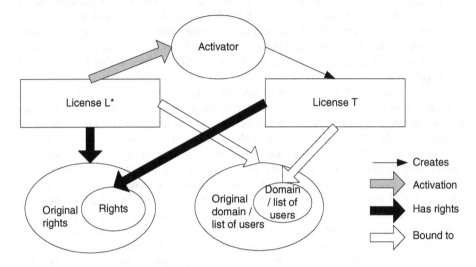

Fig. 2. General concept of star-license

While purchasing a content item for his domain a user can ask the content provider (license issuer) to issue him a signed star-license L* (instead of a standard one), which will give him more control on how the content will be used in his domain. The license issuer specifies in the star-license the identifier of the user who will be allowed to activate the license. Alternatively the license issuer could specify that the domain administrator is the default person who can activate the license.

It is depicted in fig. 2 that the user can activate the license by creating and adding an additional user-attributed license T, which could further restrict the rights given in the star-license and further limit (or change) to whom this license is bound. The further rights and binding restrictions are defined by the RightsExpr and BoundTo fields of the additional license T (see below). If the star-license is already bound to a domain and the star-expression does not allow changing the binding expression, the terminating license could only restrict specific persons from the domain to access the content. On the other hand, if there is no binding expression in the star-license or the star-expression allows changing the binding expression, the user who is allowed to activate the license can also specify to whom the license is bound. Note that the subsequent licenses are signed by the user who is authorized in the star-expression of the star-license (activator). This prevents other from activating the star-license.

The format of a user-attributed license that terminates the chain is as follows:

T: {L*, ContentID, RightsExpr, BoundTo, Active: Yes}$_{\text{signActivator}}$

License T restricts the rights specified in L* and activates license chain L*T. For this purpose, license T contains a reference to license L*. Only based on both licenses, which form now an active license chain, a specified user can access the content. However, the user who is allowed to activate license L* might be able to create another terminating license T' with different rights optionally binding that license to different domain members.

The described process can be used in a recurring way. The chain of licenses can be extended with a star or non-star-license. Each license in the chain (both star and non-star) may further restrict the rights and/or star-expression by specifying (narrower) rights expressions. So, after obtaining a star-license from the content provider a user might decide to create an additional star-license with restricted rights and restricted star-expression.

The functionality of a compliant device, i.e. a DRM client in a device, has to be extended to support license chains. The system allows access to content only based on license chains that end with a non-star-license. So, when a user wants to access a content item, the DRM client in the compliant device has to check if the user has an activated chain of licenses associated with him (chain which ends with a non-star-license and which intersection of binding expression contains the user identity). The DRM client must also enforce that the user can use the content according to the intersection of rights given in all rights expression in the license chain (containing both original and restricted rights). Note that license chains cannot be conflicting: either there is a valid license chain or not, but it is not possible that one prevents the other from being usable, i.e. no negative authorizations are supported. Therefore an issuer has to be careful with the rights it gives to others since these are hard to revoke or change in the future. This issue of license revocation/change is not limited to user-attributed rights and it is out of the scope of this paper. Furthermore, the DRM client allows a user to extend the chain (activate the license) only after a star-license in the chain that specifies his identifier in the star-expression. This would be in most cases at the end of the chain to prevent very complex situations for the end-user managing all of this.

A suitable representation for both rights- and star-expressions is required. For the rights expression the common rights expression technology can be reused, e.g. Rights Expression Languages (REL) as ODRL or XrML, since these typically contain the required facilities to express restrictions. The RELs can also support star-expressions if they are extended with a facility to specify that activation is required and an indication of the identities that can do that. In this paper, we will use an informal specification for both rights-expression and star-expression.

The user-attributed rights concept needs to deal with user identities. Typically, these identities are present in the context of the DRM system to enable person-based content access. These identities are typically issued and certified by a trusted authority. The user identities have cryptographic keys associated to them, e.g. to perform authentication and generic encryption and signing operations. A DRM system insisting on user presence could use token based authentication, e.g. by using a smartcard or biometrics. Signing a user-attributed right requires use of a private signing key, which a smartcard can provide, or a smartcard can perform the signing itself. This brings us to the conclusion that DRM identities can and should be reused where possible. Since the restrictions are determined by users and not by the content providers, theoretically non-DRM identities could be used for further restrictions too. However, in this paper, we assume that all identities and related cryptographic keys are trusted and certified by the DRM system.

3.4 Cryptographic Enforcement

The proposed solution using star-licenses, as presented in the previous sections, so far only referenced mechanisms that can be classified as being 'decision-based security'. This means that, regardless of further restrictions, a compliant trusted device/DRM client unrelated to the authorized set of recipients can theoretically access the content. However, it will not do so because it bases its decision on processing of all the licenses, i.e. the rights-expressions, the star-expressions and the signatures. Generally, security can be improved by switching from relying on trust to cryptographic enforcement. This implies that a key management solution must be used to provide a device with sufficient key material to decrypt the content only if content access is actually allowed by the license(s). This section describes a method to improve security of our solution. However, its application to user-attributed rights is not strictly necessary. The decision should be based on a trade-off between risk assessment and the complexity of the solution.

For star-licenses, cryptographic enforcement implies the following rule. Devices may only be able to decrypt the content if:

– the device itself is authorized to access the content; or
– a user is authorized to access the content and the user has interacted with the device transferring authorization to the device to render content on the users behalf (e.g. registering the device to a domain of the user or authenticating the user); or
– the abovementioned device or user have proper delegation rights expressed in the star-expression indicating that they could themselves complete a license chain into an activated license chain authorizing content access on that device.

Authorized content access in this case means that there is an active license chain that after evaluation of all individual licenses results in approval of a content access action given the context of a device, including authenticated users. A straightforward solution uses the following principles:

– For all entities that are authorized in the rights-expression (BoundTo) of a license key material is added to the key-chain that protects the content key. Key-chain here refers to the subsequent encryptions of the content key that make up the protected content key in the license. For example, if content is bound to a domain then it is encrypted with a domain key, if content is limited to a specific user then it encrypted with a key specific to that user.
– The key-chain protecting the content key is (also) protected by key material for entities authorized in the star-expression of an inactivated license. For example, if a specific user may activate a license then a key specific to that user is used to encrypt the abovementioned key-chain.

Note that although these principles provide cryptographically enforced security with respect to the entities (users, devices, domains) to which content access is limited,

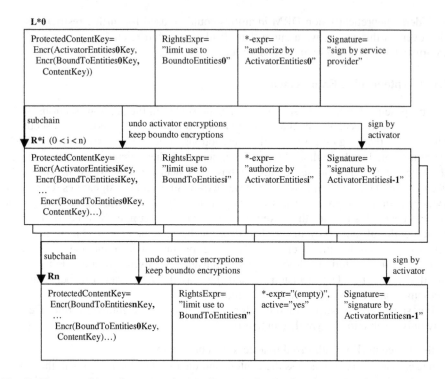

Fig. 3. Cryptographic enforcement for star-licenses given a license chain of arbitrary length. Encr($key, $data) means that $data is encrypted by $key.

other aspects of evaluation of licenses based on context are still decision-based, e.g. verification of authorized time interval specified in a license.

The general principle, illustrated in fig. 3, is that as part of issuing a new license in the chain, the new license encapsulates the ProtectedContentKey of the previous license using the following steps. First, the ProtectedContentKey is decrypted from the last star-license using a key of an entity authorized to active (ActivatorEntities) thereby enforcing that only authorized entities from the star-expression of the base license can do this. Second, the result is encrypted with keys associated to entities mentioned in the further restricting license expression (BoundToEntities), such as for example users, devices, domains, thereby enforcing that only those entities can access the content. Third, the result is encrypted with keys associated to entities that may further restrict or activate a license (ActivatorEntities).

Realizing cryptographic enforcement only requires limited technical complexity. Creation of further restricting licenses now involves a decryption and some encryptions. Recovering the content key for an active license chain involves the multi-level decryption of ProtectedContentKey in the last license. The method guarantees that if the combined rights expressions indicate that a content item may be accessed that a device can decrypt it.

With respect to the size of licenses an issue may appear when many entities are listed in a rights expression and/or in a star-expression because each have their own key. This means that the multi-level key hierarchy becomes a tree which requires more storage since for each authorized case a working key-chain must be embedded in the license.

3.5 Architectural Aspects and System Complexity

With respect to system complexity two roles can be considered: DRM clients and license issuers. For license issuers – operated by content service providers - hardly anything changes except the inclusion of a star-expression and an activation flag. DRM clients are more affected, though still manageable, as discussed below.

As indicated above, devices implementing DRM clients must be able to work with license chains. Fortunately, the impact on DRM clients to support processing of license chains can be very limited, because license evaluation can be realized in a straightforward way by processing all licenses of the chain serially and under the condition that each individual evaluation must be positive. Alternatively, consider the opposite approach where one would first try to determine the intersection of all rights expressions and evaluate that. This approach would be far more complex including the risk of introducing errors in the method for complex rights expressions. Simplicity in this case also contributes to security.

Adding new licenses to a license chain is rather straightforward. Most notably it includes interpretation of the star-expression and creation of the user-attributed license. An important point to pay attention to is management of the license chains. A good heuristic would consist in keeping a license chain together and treat a chain in the same way as a single license is managed in current systems. A related issue to complexity is the increased size of licenses, because a license now consists of a whole chain of licenses effectively increasing the average size by a factor of approximately two or three in most practical cases.

In most practical uses of star-licenses, the length of the license chain will be two or three. The reason for this is that a user probably creates user-attributed licenses (T) based on the original license (L*) or that he delegates that to somebody else which requires one additional license (T*). License chains longer than three are only foreseen if multiple group or domain definitions are present and used to limit access to the intersection of all these groups/domains, or if advanced delegation chains are used.

3.6 User Interaction and Experience

In a DRM system intended to give users more control, user interaction plays a very important role. From the user perspective, the processes of creating licenses must be easy and intuitive. The user must be able to specify what others are allowed to do with the content in the process of creation of user-attributed licenses. Furthermore, in this case, the user must understand what the original rights are and how he can restrict them. However, the rights expressions as used by a DRM system are usually not in a human readable form. If the system supports complex/advanced rights, it might be very difficult for the user to create a license or define restrictions. Therefore, we suggest using templates for the most common or useful right expressions, so that the user can choose the appropriate template when he creates a license for restricting the rights. Templates present the user-attributed rights to the user in a user-friendly way, providing him with the possibility to adjust them.

4 Examples

In this section we revisit the motivating scenarios given in Section 3.1 and explain how the activation mechanism and the concept of star-licenses could be used to fulfill the requirements specified in the scenarios. The RightsExpression and BoundTo license elements defined in L* in Section 3.3 have been combined in the RightsExpression in the examples below. Although the scenarios come from the entertainment domain, it should be noted that the general concept presented in this paper is applicable also to enterprise rights management systems to support, for example, personalized role-based access control.

4.1 Pete and His Family

Let us look how Pete could make sure that no one else in his domain will be able to access the content he bought. While purchasing the content for his domain Pete can ask the content provider (license issuer) to issue him a star-license (L*) to have more control on how the content will be used in his domain. The license issuer specifies in the star-license Pete's ID as the one who can activate the license. Then Pete creates an additional user-attributed license (T_1) which limits the license chain only to himself. Note that Pete can do this off-line without interacting with the content provider.

L*: { ContentID$_1$, RightsExpr: "ContentID$_1$ may be played and burnt once on a CD in Pete's domain", Active: No, StarExpr:"Pete may activate",
ProtectedContentKey: Encr(PubKey_Pete, Encr(DomainKey_Pete, ContentKey)) }$_{signContentProvider}$

T_1: { L*, ContentID$_1$, RightsExpr: "ContentID$_1$ may be played and burnt once on a CD by Pete", Active: Yes, ProtectedContentKey: Encr(PubKey_Pete, Encr(DomainKey_Pete, ContentKey)) }$_{signPete}$

Using the L* and T_1 chain of licenses, Pete can access the content ID$_1$. The DRM client evaluates the license chain L*T_1 and allows Pete to use the content according to the intersection of the rights expression specified in L* and the restricted rights expression in T_1. Note that Pete is able to specify any rights expressions in license T_1. However, the DRM client verifies that T_1 is used together with the original star-license L*. Furthermore, the DRM client always takes the intersection of rights from those two licenses. Therefore, the rights are actually limited to the ones defined in L* and might only be further restricted by ones defined in T_1.

On the other hand other family members cannot access the content, neither using L* nor the whole chain L*T_1. This demonstrates how domain members can be excluded, but still does not show how different family members could have different rights. Pete has paid a little more to obtain the right to burn the content on a CD once, in addition to the usual playing rights. However, as Pete can only burn a CD once, he would like to keep this CD in his archive as a back-up copy and does not want his children to use this right to burn a CD and give it to their friends. Therefore he wants to restrict that right only to him and his wife. To do so, Pete creates a license T_2.

T_2: {L*, ContentID$_1$, RightsExpr: "ContentID$_1$ may be played by Pete's children", Active: Yes, ProtectedContentKey: Encr(PubKey_Children, Encr(DomainKey_Pete, ContentKey)) }$_{signPete}$

License T_2 restricts the rights specified in L* and activates the licenses L*. Based on both licenses, i.e. the L* T_2 chain, Pete's children can play the content. However, Pete still has to create a license for his wife and for himself.

T_3: {L*, ContentID$_1$, RightsExpr: "ContentID$_1$ may be played and burnt on a CD by Pete and his wife", Active: Yes, ProtectedContentKey: Encr(PubKey_Pete+PubKey_Wife, Encr(DomainKey_Pete, ContentKey))}$_{signPete}$

License T_3 activates license L* and creates an additional chain which specifies that Pete and his wife can, burn the content on a CD in addition to playing it.

4.2 Grandma Makes a Gift to Her Grandson

To fulfill the requirements from the second scenario, a right issuer would create for Grandma star-license L_1*.

L_1*: {ContentID$_2$, RightsExpr: "ContentID$_2$ may be played by Joy", Active: No, StarExpr: "Grandma may activate", ProtectedContentKey: Encr(PubKey_Grandma, Encr(PubKey_Joy, ContentKey)) }$_{signCP}$

In order to allow her daughter to be able of further restricting the rights of Joy, Grandma creates an additional star-license L_2*.

L_2*: {L_1*, ContentID$_2$, RightsExpr: "ContentID$_2$ may be played after July 15, 2005", Active: No; StarExpr: "daughter may activate", ProtectedContentKey: Encr(PubKey_Daughter, Encr(PubKey_Joy, ContentKey)) }$_{signGrandma}$

Therefore, her daughter can further restrict the rights and activate the license by creating terminating license T_4.

T_4: {L_2*, ContentID$_2$, RightsExpr: "ContentID$_2$ may be played between 10.00 and 18.00", Active: Yes, ProtectedContentKey: Encr(PubKey_Joy, ContentKey)}$_{signDaughter}$

Using this chain of licenses (L_1*L_2*T_4), Joy can play his content but only after July 15, each day between 10.00 and 18.00 hours.

5 Conclusions

Current DRM systems protect the interest of the content provider while users' needs are typically not taken into account. The only possibility for a user to protect his interest and privacy is to apply some access control on licenses or content that he obtains from the content provider. Access control however only offers a limited functionality. Therefore a solution is proposed in this paper where a DRM system allows the user to set further restrictions on the licenses obtained from the content provider. The proposed method is based on a specific form of a delegation license, called star-license, and an activation mechanism. The star-licenses allow adding further restricting rights-expressions by indicating who may define further restrictions and activate the license.

The proposed approach has several advantages over existing methods. First of all, our solution keeps the security of a DRM system at the level it was before the introduction of user-attributed rights. While still respecting the rights issued by the content provider, the approach allows the user to be in control by adding extra restrictions on obtained licenses. In this way, the basis for the variety of enhanced functionality is provided (gifting, intra-domain control, etc.).

In addition to being a useful and practical concept for DRM systems, the user-attributed rights are also an excellent public relation feature for DRM which is very often accused of being operating only in the interests of the content providers without considering consumers' needs.

The paper also discusses a practical realization of the proposed concept as well as its cryptographic enforcement, architectural aspects and system complexity. It is demonstrated how a few example scenarios, namely rights differentiations within a domain and gifting, can be achieved. The practical realization also shows the effectiveness and simplicity of the approach.

The work presented in this paper suggests some interesting directions for future research. With the basic approach in place, it will be worthwhile to investigate how the user-attributed rights approach could be mapped on existing standards, for example OMA DRM. Furthermore, an interesting question is what the other possible applications of the activation mechanism of star-licenses are. For example, could we use the same approach for dealing with selling, and lending concepts? Finally, it is interesting to explore efficient ways to support multiple identities in rights expressions and star-expressions of user-attributed rights. Currently, the main option is to list the individual members which leads to inefficient results. Therefore, it would be very convenient for users to have some support for used-defined groups or sub-domains.

Acknowledgements

We would like to thank our project colleagues at Telematica Institute, Vodafone R&D and Philips Research for their valuable comments and suggestions. Furthermore, we would like to thank the reviewers for their constructive review comments.

References

[1] Olav Bandmann, Mads Dam, Babak Sadighi Firozabadi, Constrained Delegation, IEEE Symposium on Security and Privacy, 2002.
[2] Guillermo Navarro, Babak Sadighi Firozabadi, Erik Rissanen, Joan Borrell, Constrained delegation in XML-based Access Control and Digital Rights Management Standards, CNIS03, Special Session on Architectures and Languages for Digital Rights Management and Access Control, December 2003.
[3] Thomson Multimedia, SmartRight, www.smartright.org, 2003.
[4] IBM, IBM Response to DVB-CPT Call for Proposals for Content Protection & Copy Management: xCP Cluster Protocol, DVB-CPT-716, 19-10-2001.
[5] John Gildred, Ashot Andreasyan, Roy Osawa, and Tom Stahl, Protected Entertainment Rights Management (PERM): Specification Draft v0.54, Pioneer Research Center USA Inc, Thomson, 9-2-2003.
[6] Digital Video Broadcasting Project, www.dvb.org, for Authorized Domains see DVB-CPT Authorized Domain: Definition / Requirements, cpt-018r5, 2002.
[7] Open Mobile Alliance, DRM Architecture, version 2.0, 2005.
[8] R.Vevers and C.Hibbert, Copy Protection and Content Management in the DVB, IBC Conference Publication, p458-466, Amsterdam, IBC2002, 15-9-2002.
[9] S.A.F.A.van den Heuvel, W.Jonker, F.L.A.J.Kamperman, and P.J.Lenoir, Secure Content Management in Authorised Domains, IBC Conference Publication, p467-474, Amsterdam, IBC2002, 15-9-2002.
[10] Paul Koster, Frank Kamperman, Peter Lenoir and Koen Vrielink, Identity based DRM: Personal Entertainment Domain, Conference on Communications and Multimedia Security (CMS) 2005, LNCS 3677, pp. 42-54, Salzburg, Austria, September 19-21, 2005.
[11] Yang Yo, Tzi-cker Chiueh, Enterprise Digital Rights Management: Solutions against Information Theft by Insiders, RPE report, September 2004.

AVS-REL—A New Right Expression Language*

Ying Sha

AVS Workgroup, Software Division, Institute of Computing Technology,
Chinese Academy of Sciences, Beijing 100080
shaying@ict.ac.cn

Abstract. Advanced Audio Video Coding Standard (AVS) Workgroup
was established to provide the standards for compression, decompression,
manipulation and display in digital audio and video multimedia equipment and system. In order to provide a flexible and interoperable rights
expression mechanism for trade, distribution and usage on digital audio
and video resources, AVS DRM subgroup develops a new right expression language (AVS-REL) to describe rights on digital resources under
condition and permission. The new features of AVS-REL are illustrated
in details in this paper, including data model, data structure, the usage
of scenario and the management process of rights.

Keywords: AVS-REL, REL, AVS.

1 Introduction

Right expression language(REL) is one kind of formal language to express rights
on digital resources under conditions and permissions. The relationships among
subjects, rights and resources should be described in REL, to demonstrate the
conditions and authorities that users can execurte some operations on resources.
Hence, REL plays the key role in DRM systems through providing syntax and
semantic rules for them under the opened and trusted environment.

Users can embed REL into an open infrastructure to achieve DRM services
interoperability, or use REL as the independent rights expression mechanism on
existing DRM system.

Renato lamella[1] described that three parts should be included in rights expression languages, which were rights, also called "usage permissions", Constraints, such as times or territories, and payment.

Two XML-based RELs, XrML and ODRL, are widely used now.

XrML(eXtensible Rights Markup Language)[2] which includes two primary relationships: Grant and License, is an XML-based rights expression language developed by ContentGuard(httpd://www.contentguard.com), based on
the model comprised of rights, terms and conditions.

---

* Supported by The National High Technology Research and Development Program
  of China (863 Plan) (Project Number: 2004AA119010).

R. Safavi-Naini and M. Yung (Eds.): DRMTICS 2005, LNCS 3919, pp. 90–101, 2006.

ODRL (Open Digital Rights Language)[3], which includes two primary relationships: Offer and Agreement, is also an XML-based rights expression language developed by the international ODRL Initiative (http://www.odrl.net), based on a model comprised of assets, parties and rights.

There are some other RELs. For example, LicenseScript is a multiset rewriting/logic based right expression language[4].

AVS-REL: In order to establish the standard for compression, decompression, manipulation and display in digital audio and video multimedia equipment and systems, AVS Workgroup [5] was established by the Ministry of Information Industry on June 2002. To provide a flexible and interoperable rights expression mechanism for trade, distribution and usage on digital audio and video resources, AVS DRM subgroup presents AVS-REL in which relationship between resources, rights and principals can be protected.

AVS-REL is an important component of AVS-DRM; AVS-DRM provides mechanisms for protecting AVS audio and video resources. AVS-REL must meet the need of AVS-DRM. Because AVS are new standards for audio and video multimedia, AVS have special requirement for DRM and REL. So AVS DRM workgroup proposes special design principals for AVS-REL. According the design principals, AVS WG proposes a new type of REL: AVS-REL.

This paper is trying to provide some introduction and overview to those non-public AVS-REL documents. The rest of this paper provides an overview of AVS-REL data model, data structure, the usage of scenarios and the management process of rights. The differences between AVS-REL and other RELs are pointed out. Finally, the features of AVS-REL are also described.

2   AVS-REL

AVS DRM subgroup published "requirement for AVS-DRM" on Aug 2002, and "call for proposal for AVS-REL" on Mar 2003. Till 2004, "AVS DRM rights expression language specification" was completed, and "AVS REL&RDD" working draft has been passed. It was believed that the whole project would be finished by the end of 2005, including working draft, reference software and consistency versification tools. Data model, Relationship model and data structure of AVS-REL are all adapt to the requirement of AVS-DRM.

2.1   The Design Principles of AVS-REL

First, AVS-REL must meet the general design principles of rights expression language: 1.Comprehensiveness; 2.Generality; 3.Exactness; 4.Extensibility.

The following design principles are also focused in AVS-REL:

1. REL should express intellectual property rights information. REL not only can express right issuer's rights in technology, but also can express right holder's rights in law.

2. REL should support rights negotiation process, i.e., express contracts or permissions between principals. In the current version of REL, only one-way "flow", a flow from content owner to consumer, was considered. But there also exist rights flowing from consumers to content owner in a real world. For example, consumer may ask content owner to provide digital content in some quality. Thus AVS-REL should support two-way rights flow.
3. REL should consider the balance between rights and duties. Content owner has rights as well as duties, so do the consumers.
4. REL should express access or usage control.
5. With the progress of DRM, more and more attention are paid to to fair-use. AVS-REL should support solving fair-use problem to some extent by technology.

2.2   AVS-REL Data Model

AVS-REL data model consists of the following five entities: subjects, rights, resources, constraints and duties(Fig. 1). According to the design principles of AVS-REL, AVS-REL considers the balance of rights and duties. AVS-REL data model includes rights and duties; these can be content owner's rights and duties; these can also be consumer's rights and duties. Rights and duties have been talk by [6], and ODRL has rights and duties in Version 2.0 model. But there have differences between AVS-REL and ODRL regarding rights and duties. Section 2.2.2 and 2.2.4 will provide more discussions.

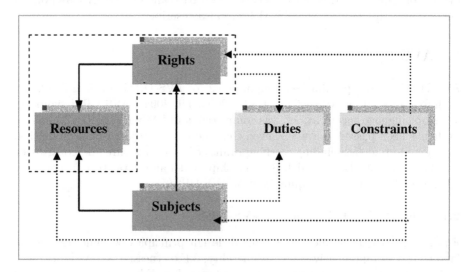

Fig. 1. AVS-REL data model

2.2.1   Subjects
A subject encapsulates the identification of a principal. According to the requirement of AVS standard, Subject can be a right issuer or a right requestor

on different steps of the whole digital content value chain. Human, groups, computer, applications and network device can all be called Subject. AVS-REL can also define a group of subjects as SubjectGroup. Subject includes distributor who is a right issuer and receiver who is a right requestor.

In AVS-REL, a Subject can be assigned with different roles. Subject can have a subset of rights as its fair-use rights by some roles. For example, a critic can cite a part of a writer's paper in his review paper without writer's permission. "Cite" is the critic's fair-use right.

2.2.2 Rights

Rights specify aections or activities that a subject can perform on some resources under some conditions. According to the requirement of AVS standard, Rights includes (1). Use rights: such as display, play; (2). Reuse rights: such as modify, split, package; (3) Resources management rights: such as move, copy, backup; (4). Rights management rights: such as revoke some special rights; (5). Fair-use rights.

Fair-use rights are an important component of rights. Subject can have some fair-use rights according its roles. Fair-use rights are rights that subject can hold without rights issuer's permission.

Rights are different from rights entity in ODRL 2.0. Rights in ODRL include statement, offer, request, ticket, etc. But Rights in AVS-REL are only operations on some objects. Rights in AVS-REL are similar Permissions in ODRL2.0; they only include operation, but don't include objects.

2.2.3 Resources

A Resource is the entity to which a subject can obtain a right. A resource could be digital content (such as e-book, an audio file, a video file or an image file), services (such as email services), or property information of a subject (such as someone's email address). AVS-REL can define a group of resources as ResourcesGroup. Resources usually includes some attribute of the resources such as resources quality, resources display format, resources storage format etc.

2.2.4 Duties

Duties are some requirements that a subject must satisfy when he want to obtain some rights. Duties can be divided into three types: (1). Payment: payment includes prePay, postPay, and perUse etc. (2) Interactive requirement; (3) Requirement for use.

Interactive requirement can further divide into: (1). Copyright Statement: Right issuer can use this part to state his copyright requirement. Before a consumer uses resources, he could browse the copyright statement. This feature can meet the design principle: REL not only can express right issuer's rights in technology, but also can express right holder's rights in law; (2). Pre-operation: When a subject wants to obtain some rights, he must complete some other operations, such as log on content provider web site and register personal information.

An example for Requirement for users is Record track: Record what a user has done on resources.

The interactive actions and fair-user can be implemented through Duties component. If a critic wants to extract several passages from a writer's work, he can use his fair-use right to implement it. Writer also can put some requirements for users on "duties" component. For example, the critic's review paper must have the writer's name, work's original link etc, when he publishes his review papers. Copyright statement or other descriptive information can also be put on "duties" component.

Duty in AVS-REL is different from Duty in ODRL2.0. Duty in ODRL2.0 defines a reward for certain permission. Duty in AVS-REL expresses some requirement. When someone gets some rights, he must fulfill some duties. Proposing duty in AVS-REL is mainly for the implement of negotiation between rights issuers and receivers. Rights receivers can put some requirement for rights issuers on duty component, and rights issuers can also put some requirement for rights receivers on duty component. Then they can get an agreement by some negotiation steps.

2.2.5   Constraints

Constraints are conditions that must be satisfied when user wants to obtain some rights. AVS-REL supports the following types of constraints, such as by space, by time, by hardware, by software, by network, by target, by use, by device, by transformation quality.

A set of the above five components is called LicenseUnit. LicenseUnit can be nested, that is to say, resources of one LicenseUnit can be another LicenseUnit.

2.3   Relationship Model

A licenseUnit must have Subject, Rights and Resources components. Constraints and Duties components are optional and can place on different other components, so several relationship models can be deduced by data model.

1. Subjects → Rights → Resources

   a) Subjects → Rights → Resources (ebooks, audio or video file, etc)
   b) Subjects → Rights → Resources (LicenseUnit).

In this model, a licenseUnit only has three components: Subject, Rights and Resources. a). Resources is a merely digital content, such as ebooks, a audio file or a video file. b). Resources is another LicenseUnit. In this situation, LicenseUnit is nested.

2. Subjects → Rights → Resources → Constraints

   a) Rights → Constraints
   b) Subject → Constraints
   c) Resources → Constraints

In this model, a licenseUnit has four components: Subject, Rights, resources and Constraints. This model includes model 1. According which component Constraints constrain, this model has three types: a) constraints restricts subjects, such as subject must belong to a special country. b) Constraints restrict rights, such as play a video three times. C) Constraints restricts Resources, such as software version requirement.

3. Subjects → Rights → Resources → Constraints → Duties

    a) Subjects → Duties
    b) Rights → Duties

In this model, a licenseUnit has five components: subject, rights, resources, constraints and Duties. This model includes model 2. This model has two types: a) Subjects must implement duties in advance, such as a consumer must pay 5\$ then he can play a video file. b) Duties refer to Rights. For example, John is a critic. He wants to write a report which has several passages extracted from a writer's works. He must request "edit" right of the writer's works. The writer can put some requirement of "edit" right on "duties" component. Such as, if someone wants to use "edit" right of works, he must put writer's name, works' original link in the report.

2.4 AVS-REL Data Structure

2.4.1 LicenseUnit
LicenseUnit is a base data structure of AVS-REL. It is composed of five entities: subject, rights, resources, constraints and duties. A LicenseUnit expresses who can obtain some rights on resources under constraints after he had implemented his duties.

2.4.2 License
License is a base unit for AVS-REL. License is a rights statement that was signed by a subject and was issued to another subject. License can express:

    a. Rights statement between copyrighter and distributors;
    b. Rights statement between distributors and consumers;
    c. Rights statement between consumers.

Fig. 2 gives the structure of a license. License includes issuer's information, LicenseUnits and signature of License. LicenseUnit is a base unit of License. A License can include more than one LicenseUnit. A license can also have more than one issuer and signature of license.

There are many types of License: (1). End-user license: when end user gets this type of license, he has rights to play a video file; (2). Attribute license: This type of license is used to state that someone possess some property; (3). Distribution license: Content provider uses this type of license to issue rights to content distributor; (4). Revocation license: Rights issuer can use this type of license to revoke some rights.

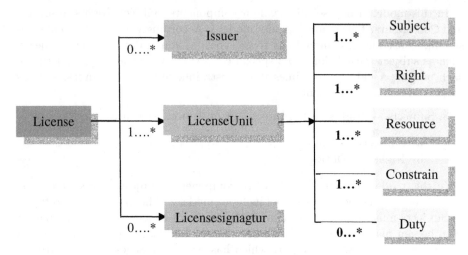

Fig. 2. License Structure

2.4.3   LicenseContainer

More than one License can form a LicenseContainer. A LicenseContainer can contain same type licenses, such as these licenses are all issued by the same one distributor. It is easy to manage and operate licenses using LicenseContainer.

2.5   AVS-REL Security Model

AVS-REL supports security methods, such as signature, encryption etc. AVS-REL is an XML-based language. AVS-REL use W3C XML Encryption to encrypt resources and use W3C XML Digital Signature to sign License.

2.6   AVS-REL Translate to Other RELs

There are two methods for translate AVS-REL to other REL standards.

1. AVS-REL can put forward some profiles for other REL standards.
2. AVS-REL can add some transformation model. These models can transform AVS-REL to other RELs and vice versa. For example, because AVS-REL, ODRL and XrML are all based on XML, they can translate to each other using XML XSLT technology.

3   Usage Scenario

This section illustrates how AVS-REL can be used. The Usage Scenario: A company can distribute a video file to individuals (John in this example case). Anyone can play this video file without any charge. But this file is only free before Feb 9 2005.

```
 1:  <?xml version="1.0" encoding="gb2312"?>
 2: <avs-rel:license xmlns:avs-rel="http://avs.net/v1.0/avs-rel"
 3: <xmlns:avs-rdd="http://avs.net/v1.0/avs-rdd"...... >
 4:    <avs-rel:licenseUnit>
 5:       <avs-rel:subject>
 6:          <avs-rdd:receiver>
 7:             <avs-rdd:entityDescription>
 8:                <avs-rdd:name¿John¡/avs-rdd:name>
 9:             </avs-rdd:entityDescription>
10:          </avs-rdd:receiver>
11:       </avs-rel:subject>
12:       <avs-rel:right>
13:          <avs-rdd:play/ >
14:       </avs-rel:right>
15:       <avs-rel:resource>
16:          <avs-rdd:entityDescription>
17:             <avs-rdd:id>doi:.../video/...</avs-rdd:id>
18:             <avs-rdd:name>XML:Movie¡/avs-rdd:name>
19:          </avs-rdd:entityDescription>
20:       </avs-rel:resource>
21:       <avs-rel:constraint>
22:        <avs-rdd:datetime>
23:         <avs-rdd:end>2005-2-9T23:59:59¡/avs-rdd:end>
24:        </avs-rdd:datetime>
25:       </avs-rel:constraint>
26:    </avs-rel:licenseUnit>
27:    <avs-rel:distributor>
28:       <ds:Signature>
29:          <ds:SignedInfo>
30:             <ds:CanonicalizationMethod Algorithm="......" />
31:             <ds:SignatureMethod Algorithm="......" />
32:             <ds:Reference>
33:                <ds:DigestMethod Algorithm="......" />
34:                <ds:DigestValue>......</ds:DigestValue>
35:             </ds:Reference>
36:          </ds:SignedInfo>
37:          <ds:SignatureValue>......</ds:SignatureValue>
38:          <ds:KeyInfo>
39:             <ds:KeyValue>
40:                <ds:RSAKeyValue> ...... </ds:RSAKeyValue>
41:             </ds:KeyValue>
42:          </ds:KeyInfo>
43:       </ds:Signature>
44:    </avs-rel:distributor>
45: </avs-rel:license>
```

Line 1-45 forms a complete XML-based AVS-REL License file. Line 1 is a XML declaration. Line 2-45 contains a AVS-REL License. Line 2-3 is some xml namespaces used by AVS-REL.

It is easy to see that this license has only one LicenseUnit. The LicenseUnit is from line 4 to line 26 and can be divided into four parts:

n Line 4-11 defines a person John who is this license's receiver.
n Line 12-14 describes that John has "play" right.
n Line 15-20 describes that resources is a movie.
n Line 21-25 describes a constraint which is a before-date.

Line 27-44 defines some information about license's distributor. This part can be divided into three components:

n Line 29-36 describes signature method and digest method;
n Line 37 is a SignatureValue;
n Line 38-42 defines a license's distributor by a rsa key.

4   Rights Management Process

Using an end-user license as an example, this section illustrates right management process: This process also illustrates how fair-use rights can be considered.

1. User downloads protected content;

2. When user wants to use this protected content, client program will send right request to Right Verification Engine (RVE), client program may also submit personal information, such as user's role, identity, public key, which rights wants to obtain, whether these rights are fair-use right etc.

3. First, RVE need to check whether rights the user want to obtain are fair-use right. Yes. Then it can be divided into three situations:

a. RVE supports local fair-use right check

According to user's role, RVE can check whether issue these fair-use right to use. If yes, then the user can use the content for free. If not, then go to step 4 .

b. RVE does not support local fair-use right check.

RVE need to use fair-use term in user's license to check user's fair-use right. When distributor issues license to users, it can put some fair-use terms into the license according user's roles.

If yes, then user can use content for free. If not, then go to step 4.

c. Neither of above two situations exists.

Then RVE can produce a fair-use right request for user, and negotiate with content owner.

4. RVE checks whether rights are conform to rights in user's license. It must also check constraints and duties term in user's license according environment context.

Similarly rights management process can be taken to other types licenses. In this usage scenario, the negotiation of rights or fair-use rights is very simple, but it can be seen that AVS-REL can meet these requirement in some extent. The details of negotiation and how to implement of fair-use rights will be another paper.

5   Comparison of RELs

5.1   Comparison of Components

There are some differences between XrML, ODRL and AVS-REL components. Table 1 shows a complete comparison of XrML, ODRL and AVS-DREL components.

Table 1. Compare of XrML, ODRL and AVS-DREL components(Y-YES, N-NO, M-MAYBE)

Components		XrML	ODRL	AVS-DREL
Right	Render	Y	Y	Y
	Reuse	Y	Y	Y
	Transport	Y	Y	Y
	Manage Object	Y	Y	Y
	Regulate Rights	M	M	Y
Obligation		Y	Y	Y
Object		Y	Y	Y
Subject		Y	Y	Y
Constraints	Temporal	Y	Y	Y
	Bound	Y	Y	Y
	Environment	Y	Y	Y
	Aspect	Y	Y	Y
	Purpose	M	Y	Y
	Status	M	M	Y

Table 2. Compare of XrML, ODRL and AVS-REL usage model(Y-YES, N-NO, M-MAYBE)

Model		XrML	ODRL	AVS-DREL
Revenue Model		Y	Y	Y
Provision Model	Conflicts	N	N	N
	Alternatives	Y	Y	Y
	Defaults	Y	Y	Y
Operational Model		Y	Y	Y
Contract Model		Y	Y	Y
Security Model		Y	Y	Y
Copyrights Model		N	N	Y

5.2   Comparison of Usage Models

REL usage models describe how REL can be used. There usually have six types of usage model. (1) **Revenue model:** Revenue model always have a relationship with payment method. (2)**Provision model:** When rights and obligation can not satisfy constraints, provision model will provide an optional choice. (3)**Operational model:** Operational model mainly pay attention to system technical problem, such as cache, watermark, network, bandwidth etc. (4) **Contract model:** Contract model mainly pay attention to term, contract and agreement between subjects. (5)**Copyrights model:** Copyrights model mainly pay attention to the enforcement of copyrights law and other laws, such as fair-use, first-sale (6)**Security model:** Security model define a series of security mechanisms, such as identify, authorization, access control, audit, etc.

Table 2 shows which usage model these RELs support.

6   The Features of AVS-REL

1. AVS-REL is an XML-based language:
    1   Interoperability;
    1   Can transform to other REL using XML XSLT technology;
    1   Define profiles for multiapplications.
2. AVS-REL can implement three layers right negotiation and control:
    (1) Copyright laws, Intellectual Property Law;
    (2) Contracts or licenses;
    (3) End-user access control.
3. AVS-REL can protect user's fair-use right in some extent.
4. AVS-REL recognizes the balance of right and duty.
5. AVS-REL is a dynamic rights expression language that can support the negotiation process. Right is no longer one-way flow.
6. AVS-REL supports right holder is a copyright holder. That is to say that the issuer of the license can also be a copyright holder by copyright law.
7. AVS-REL supports security methods to protect resources, right and licenses.
8. AVS-REL support super-distribution.

7   Conclusion

AVS-REL is an XML-based open, extensible rights expression language. It will be a REL standard of AVS DRM part. AVS-REL mainly focuses on fair-use, balance of right and duty, support negotiation process. The next work of AVS-REL is developing reference software, consistency versification tools and profiles for applications. Furthermore, AVS REL WG will try to implement transforming AVS-REL to other RELs and vice versa.

References

1. Renato Iannella, Digital Rights Management (DRM) Architectures, D-lib Magazine, v7, n.6, June, 2001, http://www.dlib.org/dlib/june01/iannella/06iannella.html
2. "eXtensible rights Markup Languae(XrML) 2.0 Specification", November 20, 2001. http://www.xrml.org.

3. Renato   lannella,   Open   Digital   Rights   Language   Specification   v1.1. http://www.odrl.net/1.1/ODRL-11.pdf
4. Cheun Ngen Chong, Ricardo Corin, Sandro Etalle, Pieter Hartel, Willem Jonker, and Yee Wei Law, "License Script: A novel digital rights language and its semantics. In K. Ng, C. Busch, and P. Nesi, editors, 3rd International Conference on Web Delivering of Music (WEDELMUSIC), pages 122-129, Los Alamitos, California, United States, September 2003a. IEEE Computer Society Press.
5. Audio Video Coding Standard Working Group of China (AVS Workgroup). http://www.avs.org.cn.
6. S. Guth, M. Strembeck: A Proposal for the Evolution of the ODRL Information Model. In Workshop-Proceedings of the International Workshop on the Open Digital Rights Language (ODRL), Vienna, Austria, April 2004.http://wi.wu-wien.ac.at/home/mark/publications/odrl2004.pdf

A Comparative Study of Specification Models for Autonomic Access Control of Digital Rights

K. Bhoopalam[1], K. Maly[1], R. Mukkamala[1], M. Zubair[1], D. Agrawal[2], and D. Kaminsky[3]

[1] Old Dominion University
[2] IBM, T. J. Watson Research Center
[3] IBM, Research Triangle Park

Abstract. One of the goals of Digital Rights Management Systems is the provision of a flexible access rights management system to specify and enforce digital rights. Policy-based access control is an important feature of flexible access management systems as it facilitates changes in access control with minimum or no changes to the system it protects. Two prominent policy based access specification models (and languages) are the Policy Core Information Model (PCIM) and the eXtensible Access Control Markup Language (XACML). In this paper we analyze and compare the two specification models for their suitability in building access rights for Digital Rights Management Systems.

1 Introduction

The protection of digital documents against improper use and distribution is one of the greatest concerns of digital libraries. Digital Rights Management (DRM) Technologies seek to address this concern in two ways, one is enforcement of rights after the user has legitimately accessed the resource and the second, the flexible management of access rights [10]. Our work provides an in depth discussion of two specification models for the flexible management of access rights, the Policy Core Information Model (PCIM) [4] by the Distributed Management Task Force (DMTF) [5] and the eXtensible Access Control Markup Language (XACML) [6, 7] by the Organization for Advancement of Structured Information Systems (OASIS) [11].

Both XACML and CIM are declarative, policy-based models suitable for the autonomic management of access rights. One of the goals of autonomic computing is Self-Protection. In the Digital Information domain, the important characteristic of "Self Protection" is to ease the management of access control for Digital Information and policy-based models enable the representation and enforcement of access rules in real time This paper provides a categorical comparison of the XACML and CIM along three axes, namely the information, computational and linkage models using Archon [9], a federated digital library as a case study.

This paper reports our experience in using these specification models and describes features of these models that are applicable for autonomic management of access for DRM. As a number of competing standards emerge to address similar goals, it is

R. Safavi-Naini and M. Yung (Eds.): DRMTICS 2005, LNCS 3919, pp. 102–112, 2006.
© Springer-Verlag Berlin Heidelberg 2006

essential to perform a structured analysis of the applicability of a standard for a particular application domain or requirement. This work provides such an analysis using a case-study. The evaluation criteria used in this work is applicable for evaluating a number of declarative languages for many domains, including, work flow management, IT infrastructure management, access control management etc.

The remainder of the paper is as follows: Section 2 presents some background on CIM and XACML, policy evaluation and the autonomic authorization framework. In Section 3 we describe the distributed access management system for Archon. In Section 4 we describe the differences between XACML and CIM as they relate to the specification and enforcement of access policies in our case study. In section 5 we conclude with a summary of our analysis.

2 Background

2.1 XACML and CIM

The CIM Policy Model and XACML are policy specifications models, in that, they do not specify details for implementation; however, many important aspects of a policy implementation such as its performance and scalability are directly influenced by the underlying policy specification. The styles of policy specification in the CIM Policy Model and XACML differ considerably. The normative specification of CIM Policy Model uses Meta-Object Facility and Unified Modeling Language. In contrast, XACML specification consists of XML schemas for access-control policies, requests, and decisions. This makes comparison of these models difficult.

In order to perform an impartial evaluation of specification models it is necessary to evaluate models expressed using similar specification styles or expressed at a similar granularity. We have evaluated XACML against Autonomic Computing Policy Language (ACPL), a CIM based language by IBM. As the grammar of ACPL, like XACML is also expressed using XML schemas, we are confident of the applicability of our comparative analysis of the two models for access control.

The XACML and CIM models, though not directly targeted for use in DRM, provide generic vocabulary to address DRM issues, such as user privacy, fair use and fee and non-fee based access. In both models, user privacy is facilitated by allowing role based or "characteristic (age, etc)" access specification for users; fair use is facilitated by the ability to specify complex conditions for usage; fee and non-fee based access is facilitated by providing flexibility in the way results can be configured to express access decisions.

2.2 Comparison Criteria for Policy Languages

The policy information, computation, and linkage models are three criteria that provide key insights into the capabilities of access specification models and their applicability to autonomic systems.

The *information model* explains how the abstract data model is specified as syntactical elements in the language and how it supports various access control requirements for self protection.

The *computational model* [12] explains the computational complexity of evaluating an access request against an access policy to guarantee an access decision and provides insight into the kinds of access control rules for which these models provide low latency access evaluation.

The *linkage mode* (or interaction model [14]) explains how these specifications interact with the environment, namely, the restrictions they place on the input (access request) and the output (access decision). The linkage model provides insight into the adaptability of these languages and models for various application domains. The features of the two models compared in this paper is similar in many aspects to those in [1], however this paper provides a clearer categorization of the compared features along the information, computational and linkage model axes.

2.3 Autonomic Authorization Framework

The autonomic cycle [13] in figure 1 consists of the monitoring, analysis, planning, and execution phases. Most access control applications are user driven and authorization is manifested by a request-reply paradigm, although answers may be impacted by asynchronous event, such as an intrusion attempt.

A request to access a resource is analogous to the "monitoring" phase receiving information through callbacks. The monitoring phase converts the information received from the environment (or attribute authority of the user) into a format suitable for access evaluation (or for consumption by the 'analysis' phase). The complexity of the conversion process is dependent upon the limitations of how the "analysis" phase receives input, which in turn is limited by the specification model. The "analysis" phase evaluates requests received from the "monitoring" against the policy specified in the knowledge base and provides its results to the "planning" phase. The "planning" phase understands the sequence in which the directives of the "analysis" phase needs to be executed.

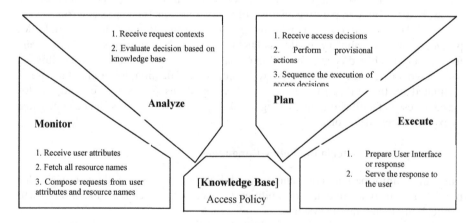

Fig. 1. Autonomic cycle for Access Control

It also determines the information that needs to be sent back to the requesting user and the actions that need to be performed prior to replying to the request (e.g., provisional actions [8]). Replying to the user is analogous to "execution" phase as authorization decisions are conveyed to the user in this phase.

3 Access Management Architecture

Our goals were to equip Archon [9], a federated digital library, with an autonomic authorization framework. Archon contains digital collections from different contributors and supports higher level services such as discovery, cross referencing, and classification services. Because of its varied contributors, Archon requires differential granularity of access both for its objects and services.

One of the most important aspects of our goal was to identity access specification models that assist us in specifying label based and content based access control and subsequently allow for the expression of cross organizational access rules for content sharing and access rules on hierarchically organized resources. As autonomic systems are typically policy-based, we chose first to evaluate XACML because it provided a generic and extensible access control model and specification, and subsequently a CIM based implementation as it was a dominant policy model for representing usage policies on IT infrastructure. This section briefly describes the digital library for which we have developed an authorization framework [2].

We want to provide selective access to the metadata of technical publications owned by various contributors (APS, CERN, etc.). Contributors have contractual agreements with subscribers enumerating the metadata that should be exposed to end-users who make assertions about their role in the subscribing institutions. When end users access the digital library, the Policy Enforcement Point (PEP) at the library receives the user's attributes through Shibboleth [3]. The PEP performs the necessary transformations (format conversion, mapping, etc) on the received credentials and supplies them to a Policy Decision Point (PDP) as access requests. The PDP evaluates these requests against a policy specification and responds with access decisions. Using the PDP's decisions, the PEP constructs a compendium of privileges for the requesting user and uses them to provide or restrict information and services to the user. A vendor supplied (Sun Microsystems XACML engine and IBM's CIM implementation) policy engine or PDP evaluates access requests against the corresponding specification models. The PEP implements the monitoring, planning and execution phases of the autonomic cycle and the PDP implements the analysis phase.

While this work is focused on digital libraries, the findings apply to other domain, such as medical and corporate records.

4 Access Control Using XACML and the CIM Policy Model

In this section we elaborate how XACML and the CIM Policy Model have influenced the implementation of access control policies for Archon.

4.1 Policy Information Model

As specified earlier, the *information model* explains how the abstract data model is specified as syntactical elements. The *information model* influences the decision engine of the analysis phase and also determines how the monitoring phase and planning phases interact with the analysis phase. Also, the planning and the execution phases need to be capable of understanding and implementing the directives encoded in the information model. In this section, we will first look into how simple <subject, object, action> rules are specified and how access requests and decisions are influenced by this representation, and then how provisional actions can be represented using the two models.

In XACML, a "Rule" forms the basic unit of a policy. Every rule has an "effect" clause which can take two values, namely "Permit" or "Deny". When the subject, resource and requested action in a request matches the "Target" of a "Rule," the access decision is based on the value of the "effect" clause for the "Rule". On the other hand, CIM does not have an equivalent for an "effect" clause. The basic unit of a CIM policy is a "PolicyRule", and each "PolicyRule" has a "PolicyCondition" and "PolicyAction". The "PolicyAction" encodes the directives that need to be enforced when a request matches the "PolicyCondition" of the "PolicyRule".

XACML's information model is used as follows in our system. The "Target" of a "Rule" encodes the subject attributes (e.g., faculty@odu.edu), the resources (identifier, author, description, etc.) and the action (read) permitted on the resources. A user choosing to use a digital library may have privileges to view (i.e., read) a number of resources. In order to evaluate the compendium of access rights using XACML,

```
<Rule ruleid="1" effect="Permit">
 <Target>
   <Subjects>
        <Subject>faculty@odu.edu</Subject>
   </Subjects>
   <Resources>
        <Resource>author</ Resource>
        <Resource>description</ Resource>
        <Resource>references</ Resource>
   </Resources>
   <Actions>
        <Action>read</Action>
   </Actions>
 </Target>
```

Fig. 2. XACML approximation

multiple requests, one for every resource (because of the limitation of XACML's request format) and permitted action is issued from the PEP (monitoring phase) to the PDP (analysis phase). The PDP uses simple decision logic to compare the subject, action and resource artifacts of the request, e.g., <faculty@odu.edu, author, read> against those of the "Target" of every "Rule" to evaluate the access decision. Figure 2 shows an approximation (as XACML is very verbose) of how we represented rules in XACML. Figure 2 specifies that a subject identified by the string "faculty@odu.edu" has read access to access the resources "author", "description" and "references" of technical articles.

CIM is used as follows. For each "PolicyRule," the "PolicyCondition" encodes the attributes of the requesting user (e.g., faculty@odu.edu), and the "PolicyAction" encodes a table of resources and the actions permitted on the resources) (e.g., <(author, read);(description, read)>). The CIM complaint decision engine needs only to compare the user attributes of request against those specified in the "PolicyCondition" elements of each "PolicyRule."

Although it is possible to represent a "PolicyCondition" as a Boolean matching function for <subject, resources, actions>, we used the ability of CIM to represent "PolicyAction" as a table of permitted actions on resources, as in doing so, only one request from the monitoring phase to the analysis phase is required to capture the compendium of access rights for a user. Also, if our system were enhanced to allow the users to perform multiple actions like "write" or "append" on resources, the number of access rules would remain unchanged in CIM, whereas, if XACML were used, additional rules would be required as its information model allows only one "action" to be specified in the "Target" of a "Rule". For the evaluation of simple access <subject, resource, action> rules, the policy information model of CIM imposes lesser burden than XACML in the monitoring, analysis phases of the autonomic cycle. Figure 3 shows an approximation of how we represented rules in a CIM compliant XML representation.

Now we examine how requirements such as specifying content-based access rights based and audits were represented in our system using the two models. Content-based access rights are of the form: 'do not provide access to a document containing the word "nudity" to accessing members younger than 18 years'. In XACML, we represented these access rights using an "Obligation" artifact, which can be associated with a set of access rules. XACML provides a clear distinction between an access decision for a rule and its obligation. In contrast, the CIM model does not; however, it is possible to reserve the usage of certain phrases in the "PolicyAction" clauses of CIM exclusively for the purpose of encoding such access rights. When XACML was used, the planning phase did not have to be enhanced to differentiate between access decisions and provisional actions, however, when CIM was used, the planning phase of the PEP had to be enhanced for this purpose.

The obligation artifact in XACML and the flexibility of expressing PolicyActions in CIM also accommodate the conditional specification of fee-based access to certain documents in a digital archive.

```
<PolicyRule priority="1">
      <PolicyCondition>
            <And>
                  <Role>faculty </Role>
                  <Affiliation>odu.edu</Affiliation>
            </And>
      </PolicyCondition>
      <PolicyAction>
            <author>read</author>
            <description>read</description>
            <references>read</references >
      </ PolicyAction >
</PolicyRule>
```

Fig. 3. CIM Approximation

4.2 Computational Model

The *computational model* is a key aspect in influencing the response time of the analysis phase. In this section we will examine two aspects of the computational model in XACML and CIM; (1) the computational complexity of Boolean expressions when requests are evaluated against access rules and (2) the conflict resolution schemes when a request matches the conditions of more than one access rule.

In XACML, the "Target" of a "Rule" element encodes a simple Boolean function in conjunctive and disjunctive normal form. In addition to the "Target" an optional "Condition" element can encode unrestrained Boolean expressions. This separation as shown in figure 4 allows for the optimization, and hence, a speedup in the comparison of the request with the "Target"; if this comparison evaluates to a 'false', the unconstrained condition encoded in the "Condition" is ignored. In contrast, the CIM model provides only for the specification of a unified unconditional Boolean expression and does not provide for the optimization of <subject, object, resource> evaluations, which are predominantly in conjunctive or disjunctive normal form.

In our system, unconditional Boolean expressions where not required and hence, we do not have empirical results to show the advantage of XACML over CIM, however, for access decisions involving complex Boolean expressions over the subject attributes, resources, permitted actions, access history and environment attributes (e.g., time, IP address of request, etc) the Boolean expression evaluation model of XACML is more optimized than that of CIM.

Now we examine the conflict resolution methods used in XACML and CIM. In XACML and the CIM Policy Model, policies are evaluated independent of each other and then the results are aggregated to compute the final outcome of policy evaluation.

The way results are aggregated differs in two models since XACML only needs to aggregate Permit/Deny actions, while the CIM policy actions can be much more varied. XACML provides conflict resolution schemes like "Deny Overrides", "Permit Overrides", etc.

```
<Rule ruleid="1" effect="Permit">
  <Target>
        <Subjects>…</Subjects>
        <Resources>…</ Resources >
        <Action>…</Actions>
  </Target>
  <Conditions>
        …
  </Conditions>
</Rule>
```

Fig. 4. XACML Boolean Expressions

```
<PolicySet PolicyCombiningAlgorithm="DenyOverrides">
<Policy policyId="p1" RuleCombiningAlgorithm="PermitOverides">
  <Rule ruleid="r1" effect="Permit">
    …
  </Rule>
  <Rule ruleid="r2" effect="Deny">
    …
  </Rule>
</Policy>
<Policy policyId="p2" RuleCombiningAlgorithm="DenyOverrides">
  <Rule ruleid="r3" effect="Permit">
    …
  </Rule>
  <Rule ruleid="r4" effect="Deny">
    …
  </Rule>
</Policy>
</PolicySet>
```

Fig. 5. Conflict resolution in XACML

The conflict resolution scheme for XACML shown in figure 5 is a domain decision that applies for all access rules specified in policy. In XACML, conflicts among access decisions may be resolved at multiple levels. The conflict resolution among decisions of various Rule elements is specified in the wrapping "Policy" element and those among policies are specified in the wrapping "PolicySet" element.

The conflict resolution method CIM is shown in figure 6. In CIM conflicts are resolved by assigning priority label each access policy. Unlike XACML, decisions in ACPL cannot be resolved at multiple levels (i.e, at the rule and policy level.) In CIM, considerable thought is required to specify the priority of one access rule over the other. We found both the schemes sufficient for our system.

```
<Policy id="policy1" priority="1" >
    <PolicyCondition>...</ PolicyCondition>
    <PolicyAction> ...</ PolicyAction>
</Policy>
<Policy id="policy2" priority="2" >
    <PolicyCondition>...</ PolicyCondition>
    <PolicyAction> ...</ PolicyAction>
</Policy>
```

Fig. 6. Conflict resolution in ACPL (CIM)

4.3 Linkage Model

The *linkage model* explains how the specification models interact with the environment, namely, the restrictions they place on the request and the access formats. It influences how the monitoring phase delivers requests to the analysis phase and how the planning phase receives decisions from the analysis phase of the autonomic cycle.

XACML, in addition to specifying syntax for policies, also specifies syntax for decision requests and decision responses. In contrast, the CIM model does not prescribe a format for requests and responses.

When using XACML for our system, the monitoring phase composes XACML compliant requests from user attributes that arrive as HTTP request parameters and delivers them to the analysis phase for evaluation. After evaluation, the PDP at the analysis phase responds to the planning phase with XACML compliant responses. The composition of XACML requests and subsequent processing of XACML responses is a significant overhead, however, such a requirement in the specification enforces standardization of the various implementations of the model.

In contrast, when the CIM model was used in our system, the monitoring phase converts the name value pairs of an HTTP request into a HashMap (a much simpler process than converting to XACML compliant format) and submits them to the PDP of analysis phase for evaluation. The output produced by the PDP is also a HashMap and required only a simple processing to be understood.

Here the *linkage model* of XACML forced us to enhance the monitoring and planning phases to convert and interpret XACML compliant requests and responses, whereas, these modules were not required when using the CIM implementation. The absence of a specification for input formats in the CIM Policy Model, and the provision for multiple input formats by the CIM implementation eased the task of request and response processing.

5 Conclusion

The choice of one specification model over the other is a very difficult to make as facets of both models offer advantages and pose hurdles. Certain information model aspects of XACML, namely the capability to represent provisional actions make XACML helpful for certain application whereas the ability to represent complex actions in CIM may make it attractive as fewer policies need to be managed. Also, the XML schema's of the XACML standard help ensure interoperability, in contrast the lack of standards-based XML schemas for CIM hinders interoperability.

The optimized Boolean expressions of XACML provides lower latency access evaluation when complex conditions need to be evaluated to obtain access to a single resource, whereas CIM provides an efficient mechanism when simple conditions need to be evaluated to obtain permissions on multiple resources.

In both XACML and CIM, access control features such as access to resource hierarchies and delegation for representing cross organizational access policies are rudimentary or non-existent. XACML allows for the specification of resources as XPath artifacts, but does not provide for features like privilege inheritance over resource subtrees. CIM does not support resource hierarchies either.

References

[1] Anderson, Key differences between XACML and EPAL, Workshop on New Challenges for Access Control, Ottawa, April 27, 2005

[2] Bhoopalam, K., Maly, K., Mukkamala, R., Zubair, M. Access Management in Federated Digital Libraries. Proceedings of IADIS, Madrid, October 6-9, 2004

[3] Cantor S., ed., Shibboleth Architecture – Protocols and Profiles, Working Draft 05, 23 November 2004, http://shibboleth.internet2.edu/docs/draft-mace-shibboleth-arch-protocols-05.pdf

[4] Common Information Model, Version 2.8. January 25,2004, http:// www.dmtf.org/standards/cim/cim_schema_v281/CIM_Policy28-Final.pdf

[5] Distributed Management Task Force, http://www.dmtf.org/home

[6] eXtensible Markup Language Working Group. www.oasis-open.org/committees/xacml

[7] Godik, S. and Moses, T. (eds.). OASIS eXtensible Access Control Management Language (XACML). Committee Specification 1.0, http://www.oasis-open.org/committees/xacml/repository/cs-xacml-core-01.pdf (21 April 2002

[8] Hada, S. and Kudo, M. XML Access Control Language: Provisional Authorization for XML Documents. (Tokyo Research Laboratory, IBM Research). October 16, 2000

[9] Maly, K., Anan, H., Tang, J., Nelson, M., Zubair, M. and Yang, Z. Challenges in Building Federation Services over Harvested Metadata. Proceedings of ICADL2003. pp.602-614, Kuala Lumpur, Malaysia, Dec 2003.

[10] M. Martin, G. Agnew, D.L. Kuhlman,J.H. McNair, W.A. Rhodes,R.Tipton, Federated Digital Rights Management: A Proposed DRM Solution for Research and Education, D-Lib Magazine, July/August 2002, Volume 8 Number 7/8, ISSN 1082-9873.

[11] Organization for Advancement of Structured Information Systems. http://www.oasis-open.org/home/index.php

[12] OWL Web Ontology Language: Overview, http://www.w3.org/TR/2004/REC-owl-features-20040210/#s5, Febuary 10, 2004.

[13] Understand the autonomic manager concept, March 2005, http://www-128.ibm.com/developerworks/library/ac-amconcept/

[14] S. Vinoski, Web Services Interaction Models - Part 1: Current Practice, IEEE Internet Computing, May – June 2002, pg 89 – 91

The Effect of Fidelity Measure Functions on the Capacity of Digital Watermarks

Yanjun Hu, Xiaoping Ma, Linming Dou, and Ying Chen

School of Information & Electronic Engineering,
China University of Mining and Technology,
221008, XuZhou, P.R. China
{yjhu, xpma, lmdou, ychen}@cumt.edu.cn

Abstract. Watermarking capacity determines how much information can be carried in an image. Shannon formula is usually used to calculate it. While in this paper, it is considered that the watermarking capacity relies directly on the fidelity measure function. After the watermarking embedding process model is discussed, watermarking capacity formula and maximum watermarking capacity formula are proposed. Then, the watermarking capacity using PSNR as fidelity measure function is discussed. The conclusion that PSNR is not suitable to evaluate watermarked image is obtained.

1 Introduction

Capacity is a very important property of digital watermarking. The purpose of watermarking capacity research is to analyze how much information can be hidden in an image by a watermarking algorithm.

Several works on watermarking capacity have been presented in recent years, such as [1, 2, 3, 4, 5]. Almost all previous works on image watermarking capacity are based on the model that an image is a communication channel and a watermark is the message to be transmitted. Therefore the Shannon channel capacity formula is naturally used to calculate the watermark capacity. Also, a conclusion is obtained that the capacity of image watermarking scheme is related directly to the image and noise signal.

The goal of a watermark algorithm is to embed watermark information into an image while satisfying invisibility and robustness. To achieve this goal, the algorithm must satisfy a condition and a rule, which are used in each algorithm but usually are not emphasized. The condition is: the original image must not be distorted in such a way that the watermarked image is useless. So, in each algorithm, there is a *fidelity measure function* used to measure the distortion between the original image and the watermarked image. The rule is: a watermark embedding process is considered successful if and only if the distortion, which measured by fidelity measure function, is acceptable. Therefore, two watermarking capacity conclusions are obtained: a) the watermarking capacity would be finite because the condition must be satisfied, b) no information could be embedded into an image if it is required that the original image and the watermarked image are the

R. Safavi-Naini and M. Yung (Eds.): DRMTICS 2005, LNCS 3919, pp. 113–122, 2006.

same. Thus, it is a reasonable conclusion that the digital image watermarking capacity relies directly to the fidelity measure function instead of others.

In this paper, the impact of the fidelity measure function on the capacity of digital watermarks is analyzed. The rest of this paper is organized as follows. After the definitions and symbols are introduced in Section 2, the watermarking capacity is analyzed and the watermarking capacity and maximum watermarking capacity formulas are given in Section 3. The maximum watermarking capacity of watermarking algorithm using PSNR is discussed in Section 4. Finally, conclusions are given in Section 5.

2   Definitions

Let $\mathbf{I}_o$ denote the original image which is a $M \times N$ matrix, $\mathbf{I}_w$ denote the watermarked image which is a $M \times N$ matrix too, d denote an acceptable threshold, and M denote the fidelity measure function.

Definition 1 (fidelity measure function). *The fidelity measure function is a mapping* $\mathbf{M} : (\mathbf{I}_o, \mathbf{I}_w) \rightarrow \mathbf{R}^+$*, where* $\mathbf{R}^+$ *denotes a nonnegative real number set.* $\mathbf{M}(\mathbf{I}_o, \mathbf{I}_w) = \infty$ *if and only if* $\mathbf{I}_o = \mathbf{I}_w$*.*

Definition 2 (watermark pattern). *A nonzero matrix* $\mathbf{T}_d$ *is called a watermark pattern over fidelity measure function* $\mathbf{M}$ *with fidelity measure above d, if*

$$\mathbf{M}(\mathbf{T}_d + \mathbf{I}_o, \mathbf{I}_o) > d \tag{1}$$

Fix $\mathbf{I}_o$, d and M, there may be many watermark patterns. Let $\mathbf{W}_d = \{\mathbf{T}_{d_i} |$ $M(\mathbf{I}_o, \mathbf{I}_o + \mathbf{T}_{d_i}) > d$, for each i$\}$ denote a set of all possible watermark patterns, $|\mathbf{W}_d|$ denote the number of elements of the set $\mathbf{W}_d$.

Suppose a discrete random variable X which represents choosing a watermark pattern from the set $\mathbf{W}_d$, and $p_i = P\{X = \mathbf{T}_{d_i}\}$ where $i = 1, 2, \cdots, |\mathbf{W}_d|$. Then, the entropy value of X is

$$H(X) = -\sum_{i=1}^{|\mathbf{W}_d|} p_i \log_2 p_i \quad \text{bit.} \tag{2}$$

3   Watermarking Capacity Analysis

3.1   Watermarking Embedding Process Model

T. Vogel and J. Dittmann proposed a generic model for digital watermarking in [6]. Based on the discussed notion, the watermark embedding process can be thought of being composed of the following two steps, shown as Fig.1:

Step 1. Generating the watermark pattern: Let $\mathbf{I}_h$ denote the information which is to be hidden in the original image $\mathbf{I}_o$. Therefor, this step can be considered an *hidden-information coding function*, which is a mapping $\boldsymbol{E} : \mathbf{I}_h \rightarrow \mathbf{T}_d$.

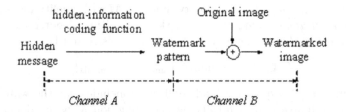

Fig. 1. Watermark Embedding Process

This function should be a surjection or bijection. If not, the hidden message can not be correctly decoded, and the watermarking scheme will fail.

Step 2. Embedding the watermark pattern: In this step, the chosen watermark pattern is embedded into the original image, and the watermarked image $\mathbf{I}_w$ is obtained. This step can be simply considered the calculation

$$\mathbf{I}_w = \mathbf{T}_d + \mathbf{I}_o \ . \tag{3}$$

3.2 Watermarking Capacity

The proposed communication model consists of two discrete channels:

- Channel A: The input is a random variable denoted as M_h; the channel output is denoted as X. Based on information theory, the capacity of this channel is

$$C_{\text{channelA}} = \max\{I(M_h; X)\} \tag{4}$$
$$= \max\{H(X) - H(X|M_h)\} \ . \tag{5}$$

As it was discussed that hidden-information coding function is a surjection or bijection, we have $H(X|M_h) = 0$. Therefore,

$$C_{\text{channelA}} = H(X) \ . \tag{6}$$

- Channel B: The input random variables is X; the channel output random variables is denoted as Y. The capacity of this channel is

$$C_{\text{channelB}} = \max\{I(X; Y)\} \tag{7}$$
$$= \max\{H(Y) - H(Y|X)\} \ . \tag{8}$$

From Eq.3, the conclusion is obtained that the channel B is a discrete memoryless noiseless channel. The transaction probabilities matrix of channel B is unit diagonal matrix. Therefore

$$C_{\text{channelB}} = \max\{H(Y) - H(Y|X)\} \tag{9}$$
$$= H(Y) \tag{10}$$
$$= H(X) \ . \tag{11}$$

Thus, given an image $\mathbf{I}_o$ over fidelity function M with fidelity measure above d, the *watermarking capacity* of watermarking algorithm, denoted as $C(\mathbf{I}_o, M_d)$, can be defined as the maximum capacity of channels A and B:

$$C(\mathbf{I}_o, M_d) = \max\{C_{\mathrm{channelA}}, C_{\mathrm{channelB}}\} . \tag{12}$$

Combining Eq.2, Eq.3, Eq.6 and Eq.9, we conclude that the watermarking capacity of an image $\mathbf{I}_o$ over fidelity measure function M with fidelity measure above d is

$$C(\mathbf{I}_o, M_d) = H(X) = -\sum_{i=1}^{|\mathbf{W}_d|} p_i \log_2 p_i \quad \mathrm{bit.} \tag{13}$$

It is clear that the watermarking capacity depends on the fidelity measure function and the choice of a watermark pattern. Although this conclusion is obtained without discussing the watermark detecting process and possible attacks, Eq.13 can be still used in any watermarking scheme because the random variable X contains other effect factors, such as the anti-attack ability and robustness of watermarking algorithm.

3.3 Maximum Watermarking Capacity

Based on the maximum entropy theorem in information theory, we have

$$-\sum_{i=1}^{|\mathbf{W}_d|} p_i \log_2 p_i \leq \log |\mathbf{W}_d| . \tag{14}$$

The *maximum watermarking capacity*, denoted as $C(\mathbf{I}_o, M_d)_{\max}$, is

$$C(\mathbf{I}_o, M_d)_{\max} = \log |\mathbf{W}_d| \quad \mathrm{bit.} \tag{15}$$

From the equation, it is obtained that enlarging the possible watermark patterns set $\mathbf{W}_d$, the maximum watermarking capacity will enhanced. On the contrary, the maximum watermarking capacity will be reduced while the $\mathbf{W}_d$ is made smaller.

This conclusion is reasonable. Considering an extreme situation that the original image and watermarked image are required to be the same. That means the fidelity measure is ∞. Therefore, $\mathbf{W}_d$ is an empty set, and $C(\mathbf{I}_o, M_0) = 0$ is obtained[1]. No information can be embedded into an image if the original image and watermarked image must be the same.

3.4 Example of Watermarking Capacity

Assume that $\mathbf{I}_o = \begin{bmatrix} 0 & 1 \\ 1 & 0 \end{bmatrix}$ is an binary-value image to be watermarked. Furthermore, set the acceptable threshold to $d = 0.9$, and let the fidelity measure function be $M(\mathbf{I}_o, \mathbf{I}_w) = 1/\sum_{i=1}^{2}\sum_{j=1}^{2} |\mathbf{I}_{o_{i,j}} - \mathbf{I}_{w_{i,j}}|$.

---

[1] In entropy definition, there is $0 \log 1/0 = 0$.

Based on the definition of a watermark pattern in Section 2, we obtain that $\mathbf{T}_{0.9_1} = \begin{bmatrix} 1 & 1 \\ 1 & 0 \end{bmatrix}$, $\mathbf{T}_{0.9_2} = \begin{bmatrix} 0 & 0 \\ 1 & 0 \end{bmatrix}$, $\mathbf{T}_{0.9_3} = \begin{bmatrix} 0 & 1 \\ 0 & 0 \end{bmatrix}$ and $\mathbf{T}_{0.9_4} = \begin{bmatrix} 0 & 1 \\ 1 & 1 \end{bmatrix}$ all are watermark patterns over fidelity measure function M with distortions measure above 0.9. Also, $\mathbf{W}_{0.9} = \{\mathbf{T}_{0.9_1}, \mathbf{T}_{0.9_2}, \mathbf{T}_{0.9_3}, \mathbf{T}_{0.9_4}\}$ and $|\mathbf{W}_{0.9}| = 4$.

According to Eq.15, we can calculate the maximum watermarking capacity as

$$C(\mathbf{I}_o, \mathbf{M}_{0.9})_{\max} = \log |\mathbf{W}_{0.9}| = 2 \quad \text{bit.}$$

If there is no robustness against attacks or noise required, every watermark pattern may be used. The probability of choosing a specific watermark pattern from the set $\mathbf{W}_{0.9}$ is set to $1/4$. In this case, the watermarking capacity is

$$C(\mathbf{I}_o, \mathbf{M}_{0.9}) = 2 \quad \text{bit.}$$

The calculation changes if watermarks should be resistant against attacks. The attack is assumed randomly change a pixel value of watermarked image. Thus, the $\mathbf{T}_{0.9_1} = \begin{bmatrix} 1 & 1 \\ 1 & 0 \end{bmatrix}$ and $\mathbf{T}_{0.9_4} = \begin{bmatrix} 0 & 1 \\ 1 & 1 \end{bmatrix}$ are apparently better than $\mathbf{T}_{0.9_2} = \begin{bmatrix} 0 & 0 \\ 1 & 0 \end{bmatrix}$ and $\mathbf{T}_{0.9_3} = \begin{bmatrix} 0 & 1 \\ 0 & 0 \end{bmatrix}$. The probability table of choosing a watermark pattern from the set $\mathbf{W}_{0.9}$ could be assumed as Table 1. In this case, the watermarking capacity is

$$C(\mathbf{I}_o, \mathbf{M}_{0.9}) = 1 \quad \text{bit.}$$

The example result is reasonable that the watermarking capacity will be reduced if the anti-attack ability increased.

Table 1. Hypothetic probability table of choosing a watermark pattern, which is possibly used in the case of considering the watermark pattern robust

X	$\mathbf{T}_{0.9_1}$	$\mathbf{T}_{0.9_2}$	$\mathbf{T}_{0.9_3}$	$\mathbf{T}_{0.9_4}$
p_i	$1/2$	0	0	$1/2$

This example also demonstrates that Eq.13 can be used in any watermarking scheme. The random variable X contains other possible effect factors, such as anti-attack ability and robustness of watermarking algorithm.

4   Watermarking Capacity over PSNR

The *Peak Signal to Noise Ratio (PSNR)* is usually used to evaluate the fidelity measures between the original image and the watermarked image. The PSNR is defined as [7]

$$PSNR = MN \, \mathbf{I}_{o_{\max}}{}^2 / \sum_{m,n} (I_{o_{m,n}} - I_{w_{m,n}})^2 , \tag{16}$$

where $\mathbf{I}_{o_{\max}}$ is the maximum value of $\mathbf{I}_o$. The watermarking capacity of watermarking algorithms which use PSNR as fidelity measure function is discussed in this Section.

4.1   Number of Watermark Patterns

Assume that d is the acceptable threshold. Therefore, after the watermarking embedding process is performed, we have

$$MN \, \mathbf{I}_{o_{\max}}{}^2 / \sum_{m,n} (I_{o_{m,n}} - I_{w_{m,n}})^2 > d \,. \tag{17}$$

Based on the definition of watermark patterns, Eq. 17 will be

$$MN \, \mathbf{I}_{o_{\max}}{}^2 / \sum_{m,n} \mathbf{T}_{d_{m,n}}{}^2 > d \,,$$

which can be re-written as

$$\sum_{m,n} \mathbf{T}_{d_{m,n}}{}^2 < MN\mathbf{I}_{o_{\max}}{}^2/d \,. \tag{18}$$

Thus, the set of all possible watermark patterns is $\mathbf{W}_d = \{\mathbf{T}_{d_i} | \sum_{m,n} \mathbf{T}_{d_{i_{m,n}}}{}^2 < MN \, \mathbf{I}_{o_{\max}}{}^2/d, i = 1, 2, \cdots, MN\}$.

Let $\mathbf{W}_d^k$ denote the set of watermark patterns which have k nonzero elements, and $s = \min\{MN, MN \, \mathbf{I}_{o_{\max}}{}^2/d\}$. It is obvious that

$$\mathbf{W}_d = \mathbf{W}_d^1 \cup \mathbf{W}_d^2 \cup \cdots \cup \mathbf{W}_d^k \cup \cdots \cup \mathbf{W}_d^s \,. \tag{19}$$

Thus,

$$|\mathbf{W}_d| = \sum_{i=1}^{s} |\mathbf{W}_d^i| \,. \tag{20}$$

Note that $|\mathbf{W}_d^i|$ can be computed algorithmically.

In theory, the watermarking capacity can be calculated by Eq.13. However, it is hard to calculate the capacity in practice because the hidden-information coding function is a complicated function, and the discrete random variable X, which represent the choice of a watermark pattern from the set $\mathbf{W}_d$, is hard to obtain.

4.2   Maximum Watermarking Capacity over PSNR

In contrast, the maximum watermarking capacity over PSNR can be calculated easily. Based on Eq.15, the maximum watermarking capacity of watermarking algorithm is

$$C(\mathbf{I}_o, \text{PSNR}_d)_{\max} = \log(\sum_{i=1}^{s} |\mathbf{W}_d^i|) \,. \tag{21}$$

This capacity again can be computed algorithmically. A C++ program segment shown in the Appendix demonstrates how to count $|\mathbf{W}_d^i|$.

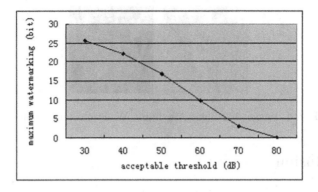

Fig. 2. Effect of the Acceptable Threshold on the Maximum Watermarking Capacity

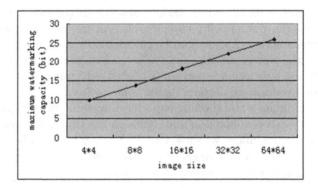

Fig. 3. Effect of the Image Size on the Maximum Watermarking Capacity

For example, consider the Lena image, which is a 256 gray-scale image. Fig.2 shows the effect of the acceptable threshold on the maximum watermarking capacity. The effects of the image size on the capacity are shown in Fig.3. The results are reasonable. The larger the image size or the smaller the acceptable threshold, the larger maximum watermarking capacity is.

From the C++ program segment, it is known that the maximum watermark capacity depends only on the image size, the maximum pixel value and threshold d. The conclusion is obtained: no matter which kind of watermarking scheme is used, the maximum watermarking capacity using PSNR as fidelity measure function is the same to a fixed threshold d and a fixed size image. Fig.4 shows two images. The right image is constructed by using the maximum pixel value of the left image as background and the letter's pixel value is 0. Hidding some information in the left image is easier than do it in the right image, which indicates the maximum watermark capacity should be different. But, the images have the same maximum watermark capacity when the PSNR is used as fidelity measure function. So, we consider that the PSNR is not a good fidelity measure function.

Fig. 4. Images has Same Maximum Watermarking Capacity

5   Conclusion

The important properties of digital watermarking, watermarking capacity and maximum watermarking capacity, are discussed. Based on the definitions of fidelity measure functions and watermark patterns, formulas for the watermarking capacity and the maximum watermarking capacity are proposed. Since the watermarking patterns over a fidelity measure function are countable and finite, the maximum watermarking capacity can be calculated by counting the watermark patterns. But, the watermarking capacity is hard to be calculated because the model of choosing a watermark pattern is needed, which it is still not built. So, how to choose a watermark pattern should come to front.

Since the maximum watermarking capacity of watermarking algorithm using PSNR as fidelity measure function only relies on the threshold d and the maximum value of original image, we show that PSNR is not a good fidelity measure function. A better fidelity measure function, which should tightly relate to image and watermarking scheme, is needed to be found.

References

1. S.D. Servetto, C.I. Podilchuk and K. Ramchandran: Capacity Issues in digital Image Watermarking. IEEE International Conference on Image Processing, Vol.1, Chicago, Illinoise, USA(1998) 445-449.
2. Fan Zhang and Hongbin Zhang: Digital watermarking capacity research. 2004 International Conference on Communications, Circuits and Systems, Vol.2, June 2004, 796 - 799.
3. M. Barni, F.Bartolini, A. De Rosa, A. Piva: Capcity of the watermarking-channel: how mang bits can be hidden within a digital iamge, Security and watermarking of Multimedia Contents, Springer Proceedings of SPIE, Vol.3657, San Jose, CA, USA(1999) 437-448 .
4. P. Moulin, M.K. Mihcak: A Framework for Evaluating the Data-Hiding Capacity of Image Sources, IEEE Transactions on Image Processing, Vol.11 2002, No.9, 1029-1042
5. C. Y. Lin, S. F. Chang: Zero-error Information Hiding Capacity of Digital Images. IEEE International Conference on Image Processing, Vol. 3. (2001) 1007-1010
6. T. Vogel, J. Dittmann: Illustration Watermarking: An Object Based Approach For Digital Images, Proceedings of SPIE-IS and T Electronic Imaging - Security,

Steganography, and Watermarking of Multimedia Contents VII, San Jose, CA, United States(2005) 578-589

7. M. Kutter and F. A. P. Petitcolas: Fair Benchmark for image watermarking systems. Security and Watermarking of Multimedia Contents. Electronic Imaging '99, vol. 3657, Sans Jose, CA, USA(1999) 1-14.

Appendix: C++ Program Segment

The following C++ program segment can be used to calculate the number of possible watermark patterns which have k nonzero elements($|\mathbf{W}_d^k|$). The main idea is that all potential watermark patterns are listed and tested. To show the idea clearly, the program is not optimized.

```
//
//Get the k value, image size and threshold
//
pValue=new int[kValue];
for(int i=0; i<kValue; i++) pValue[i]=1;
float s = imageX*imageY*maxPixel*maxPixel/threshold ;
sum=0;
while(imageLevel >= pValue[kValue-1])
{
    for(i=0;i<imageLevel;i++)
    {
        pValue[0]=i+1;
        int tempValue=0;
        for(int j=0; j< kValue; j++){
            tempValue=tempValue+pValue[j]*pValue[j];
            if(tempValue>=s){
                pValue[j]=imageLevel+1;
                goto LABEL1;
            }
        }
        if(tempValue<s) sum++;
    }
LABEL1:
    if(1==kValue) break;
    pValue[0]=1;
    pValue[1]=pValue[1]+1;
    for(i=1; i<kValue-1; i++)
    {
        if(imageLevel < pValue[i])
        {
            pValue[i+1]=pValue[i+1]+1;
            pValue[i]=1;
        }
```

```
        }
    }//end of while loop
    cout<<"total number is: "<<sum;

    delete[] pValue;
```

A MPEG-2 Video Watermarking Algorithm with Compensation in Bit Stream

Hongmei Liu[1,2], Fenglian Shao[1,2], and Jiwu Huang[1,2]

[1] Dept.of Electronics and Communication, Sun Yat-sen university,
Guangzhou, 510275, P.R. China
{isslhm, isshjw}@zsu.edu.cn
[2] Guangdong Province Key Laboratory of Information Security,
Guangzhou, 510275, P.R. China

Abstract. Some requirements for MPEG-2 video watermarking, such as invisibility, robustness, unchanged bitstream size and real time processing, are desirable. We firstly apply a DC-based embedding strategy to MPEG-2 compressed domain and embed the watermark by modifying the DC coefficients. The strategy has three advantages over the AC-based one. Then a MPEG-2 bitstream video watermarking scheme is proposed. The watermark is embedded in DC coefficients in I frames. Because these DC coefficients are differentially coded, error caused by watermark embedding will be propagated. In order to decrease the distortion to video quality caused by error propagation, we develop a compensation algorithm worked in bit-stream, which improves the quality of the watermarked video effectively. We also give a simple control scheme to ensure that the MPEG-2 bitstream keeps its original size after watermarking. The experimental results show that the watermark is robust while guaranteeing the invisibility and real-time processing.

1 Introduction

In the past decade, many video watermarking algorithms have been proposed[1]. Because video is usually stored in a compressed format before it is transmitted over networks, the watermarking techniques in compressed domain, such as MPEG-2/MPEG-4 bit stream, are considered more practical. A number of requirements, such as invisibility, robustness, unchanged bitstream size and real time processing, are desirable for video watermarking in compressed domain. This is also the objective of this paper.

The existing video watermarking methods in compressed domain can be classified into three classes according to where the watermark is embedded: 1) motion vectors[2-4], 2) VLCs[5-7], and 3) DCT (Discrete Cosine Transform) coefficients[8-9]. Our scheme belongs to class 2, which embeds watermark in DC VLC domain. In [5], Langelaar et al propose a real-time video watermarking scheme which embeds watermark by replacing AC VLCs. The quality degradation of a video after embedding can be almost negligible, but achieving robustness to MPEG-2 re-encoding becomes impossible. Langelaar et al also proposed a differential energy watermarking (DEW) algorithm [5]

R. Safavi-Naini and M. Yung (Eds.): DRMTICS 2005, LNCS 3919, pp. 123–134, 2006.
© Springer-Verlag Berlin Heidelberg 2006

which is based on partially discarding quantized DCT coefficients in the compressed MPEG video stream. DEW algorithm is considered as one of the representative video watermarking algorithms in compressed domain. Although DEW algorithm has relatively low complexity and is robust against the re-encoding of video bit streams, it still has several disadvantages [6]. The algorithms in [6, 7] improve the robustness and real-time performances of the DEW algorithm. We think there is still space for improving the robustness and real-time performances of VLC watermarking algorithms. According to the research of [10], the performance of embedding watermark in DC component of DCT is better than that of in AC components. So we try to propose a novel VLC watermarking algorithm.

We firstly apply the DC-based embedding strategy[11] to MPEG-2 compressed domain and embed the watermark by modifying the DC coefficients. The strategy has three advantages over the AC-based one. Then a MPEG-2 bitstream video watermarking scheme is proposed. The watermark is embedded in DC coefficients in I frames. Because these DC coefficients are differentially coded, error caused by watermark embedding will be propagated. In order to decrease the distortion to video quality caused by error propagation, we develop a compensation algorithm worked in bitstream, which improves the quality of the watermarked video effectively. We also give a simple control scheme to ensure that the MPEG-2 bitstream keeps its original size after watermarking. The experimental results show that the watermark is robust while guaranteeing the invisibility and real-time processing.

According to [12], the main drawbacks of bitstream watermarking methods are that embedding watermark may increase bitstream size and degrade the video quality. The scheme in this paper overcomes such drawbacks.

The watermarking method proposed in this paper heavily relies on MPEG-2 video compression standard [13]. In section 2, the relevant parts of MPEG-2 standard are discussed. In section 3, the embedding strategy in compressed DCT domain is presented. We describe the proposed watermarking algorithm with compensation in section 4. Section 5 shows the experimental results and analysis. At the end of this paper, we draw the conclusions for our work.

2   Relevant Parts of MPEG-2 Standard

2.1   Layers of MPEG-2 Coded Bitstream[13]

A real-time watermarking algorithm for compressed video should closely follow the compression standard to avoid computationally demanding operations, like DCT and IDCT or motion vector calculation[5]. Therefore, the algorithm should work on the lowest layer, called the block-layer, in which spatial 8x8 pixel blocks are represented by 64 quantized DCT-coefficients. Fig. 1 shows the different domains in which a quantized DC coefficient in DCT block can be represented. The first domain is the coefficient domain, each 8x8 block contains a quantized DC coefficient, denoted as DC_i, i is the block number. The second domain is the differential value domain, the differential value, denoted as dct_diff of current DC_i and the last DC_{i-1} is calculated. The lowest level domain is VLC domain, dct_diff is represented by VLC codeword.

Above the block layer is macroblock layer. In one marcoblock, there are four 8 by 8 blocks of luminance data. Above the macroblock layer is the slice layer. A slice is a series of an arbitrary number of consecutive macroblocks. The first and last macroblock of a slice shall be in the same horizontal row of macroblocks.

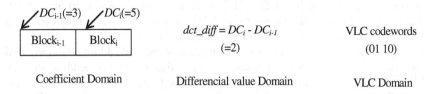

Coefficient Domain   Differencial value Domain   VLC Domain

Fig. 1. DC representation domains

2.2 DC Coefficients in I frame[13]

DC coefficients in blocks in I frame are encoded as a VLC denoting dct_dc_size as defined in Table B-12 (for Y) and B-13 (for Cb and Cr). If dct_dc_size is not equal to zero then this shall be followed by a fixed length code, $dc\_dct\_differential$, of dct_dc_size bits. A differential value (dct_diff) is first recovered from the coded data and then is added to a predictor to recover the final decoded coefficient (DC_i). The predictor, denoted dc_dct_pred, shall be reset to the pre-defined reset value at the start of a slice.

The Most Significant Bit (MSB) of $dc\_dct\_differential$ represents the sign of dct_diff. During decoding, DCi can be calculated from dct_dc_size and $dc\_dct\_differential$ by the following process: if dct_dc_size is 0, $dct\_diff=0$; otherwise if the MSB of $dct\_dc\_differential$ is 1, $dct\_diff=dct\_dc\_differential$; if the MSB of $dct\_dc\_differential$ is 0, $dct\_diff = dct\_dc\_differential+1 -2^{\wedge}(dct\_dc\_size)$, where $^{\wedge}$ denotes power; then $DC_i = dc\_dct\_pred + dct\_diff$ and $dc\_dct\_pred = DC_i$.

The watermarking method in this paper operates on the lowest level domain in Fig. 1, the VLC domain, and is based on modifying VLCs of quantized DC coefficients.

3   The Reason for Embedding Watermark in DC Domain

There are several embedding strategies in DCT domain. Cox et al [14] argued that the watermark should be embedded in those perceptually significant components. Hsu and Wu [15] proposed to embed watermark in middle frequency components of DCT. Huang et al [11] extended Cox's idea to insert the watermark in the DC components.

DCT is one of the key techniques adopted by MPEG-2 coding standard. Among the DCT coefficients in the MPEG-2 bit stream, which one is more suitable for embedding watermark? In this paper, we apply Huang's strategy[11] to choose the DC coefficients of DCT blocks in each intra frame (I frame) to embed watermark. This embedding strategy in MPEG-2 compress domain has the following advantages:

i) *Lower Complexity*. Embedding watermark in DC coefficients is simpler than that in AC coefficients. In VLC domain algorithm, partly decoding of the DCT coefficients is needed. Decoding one DC coefficient is relatively simpler than decoding (63-cc) AC coefficients such as that in DEW and DNW, where cc denoting the cut-off index in DEW[5] and DNW[6] algorithms.

ii) *Easy control of bitstream size.* DC coefficient in I frame is encoded as *dct_dc_size* followed by *dc_dct_differential* of *dct_dc_size* bits. The length in bits of a quantized DC coefficient in bitstream is decided by *dct_dc_size*. When embedding watermark bit in DC VLC domain, if *dct_dc_size* keep unchanged, that is, if the DC coefficient need not to be recoded, the size of bitstream keep unchanged. In Section 4.2 we will explain this point.

iii) *Higher Robustness.* Lou and Yin [10] compared some embedding strategies, and the results are shown in Fig.2, where "Huang" denotes DC embedding strategy [11], and "Cox" denotes that of embedding in low frequency components excepting DC component [14]. It is observed that the watermark embedded in DC component is more robust than that in AC coefficients under the same constraint of invisibility. As to MPEG-2 compressed domain, we think this conclusion will work all the same.

The algorithm described in following sections is based on this embedding strategy.

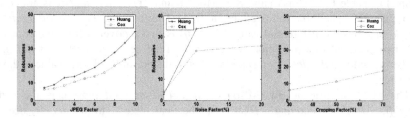

Fig. 2. Robustness comparison of embedding strategies

4   The Proposed Algorithm

4.1 The Embedding Scheme

The embedding process of the scheme is as follows:

1) Encode the watermark signal by using error correcting code (ECC) and get $X=\{x_j\}$, j = 0-K-1, where K is the number of ECC-coded watermark bits.
2) Partly decode the cover bitstream, and get *dct_dc_size* and *dc_dct_differential* for DCT blocks in I frame. Each block has its number according to its decoding order.
3) Randomly select a start block B_s with key K_1, where s is its number.
4) From Bs, embed one watermark bit every M (a parameter of the algorithm) blocks, the embedding block is denoted by Be, where $e = (s + M \times j)$ mod T_b, where T_b is the number of total blocks in Y component of I frame, j is the sequence number of the watermark bit to be embedded, j = 0-K-1. Bit x_j is embedded as follows:
   i)   When *dct_dc_size* of B_e is zero, go to the next embedding block
   ii) If *dct_dc_size* is not zero and the LSB of *dc_dct_differential* of B_e is equal to x_j, go to embed next watermark bit. Otherwise,

iii) If the LSB is not equal to x_j, replace it by x_j, and then search a suitable block between B_e and B_e', where $e' = (s + M \times (j+1))$ mod T_b to compensate this change. The compensation method is detailed in Section 4.3.

5) Repeat step 5 until all the watermark bits have been embedded and get the stego bitstream.

The detecting process is the reverse of the embedding process. But it is noted that compensation will not influence the detecting of watermark bit.

4.2 Control Scheme of Bitstream Size

Protect bitstream size from increasing is one of the main objects of video watermarking algorithm in bitstream. If the size increases, the buffers in hardware decoders can run out of space or the synchronization between audio and video can be disturbed. In our scheme, we embed watermark bits in DC VLC domain. The control scheme of bitstream size is simple, that is to ensure that, embedding process does not change the MSB (the sign bit of *dct_diff*) of the *dc_dct_differential*.

The following example explains what would happen during decoding if the MSB of *dc_dct_differential* has been changed, and show the idea of our control scheme.

Considering chrominance blocks, for example, here is the bitstream '110111...'. By looking up the Table B-13 in [13], we know that, the three bits on the left '110' denote that *dct_dc_size* is 3, the following 3 bits '111' denote *dc_dct_differential*, the leftmost bit is the MSB, the sign bit. The length in bits of this quantized DC coefficient is 6 before embedding.

We assume that we want to embed a watermark bit by adding 4 ('100') to *dc_dct_differential*, then *dc_dct_differential* becomes '111+100' and get '1011', the original MSB bit is changed from '1' to '0'. We need to recode this coefficient, that is, '1011' will be the new *dc_dct_differential*. According to Table B-13 in [13], '1011' will be recoded as '1110 1011'. The length in bits of new codeword, 8, is longer than that of old one, 6, so the bitstream size would be altered after embedding.

From this example, we can see that if we want to embed watermark by modifying only *dc_dct_differential*, we can not change it too much and have to keep the MSB of *dc_dct_differential* unchanged. In our scheme, we replace only the LSB of *dc_dct_differential*, it meet the requirements above. In the following compensation scheme, we also need to carefully choose the candidate DC coefficients to be modified in compensation to ensure that the MSB of *dc_dct_differential* keep unchanged.

4.3 Compensation Method in Bitstream

According to MPEG-2 [13], DC coefficients in blocks of I frame are decoded differentially. If one DC coefficient is modified in embedding process, the error will be propagated to other DC coefficients of the following blocks in the same slice. We show it by the following example.

The DCT blocks of Y component of I frame decoded from MPEG-2 stream are shown in Fig. 3, where the frame size is 704×576 and each block has its number according to its decoding order. Block B_n is the current embedding block and the next watermark bit will be embedded in block B_{n+10}. We suppose that the LSB of *dc_dct_differential* in B_n has been altered when watermark bit is embedded.

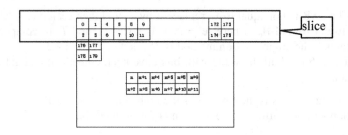

Fig. 3. Y blocks in I frame

Table 1 shows *dct_diff* and *DCi* of blocks from B_n to B_{n+9} before and after embedding a bit, where all the changed values are in parenthesis. We look at only the columns with headings "original *dct_diff*" "*dct_diff* after embed a bit *without* compensation" "original DC_i" and "DC_i after embed a bit *without* compensation". From these columns, we can see that although we change only the *dct_diff* of B_n for embedding a watermark bit, the *DCi* of the following blocks from B_{n+1} to B_{n+9} are also changed. This error propagation phenomenon will affect the video quality greatly, so we propose the following compensation method to decrease such influence.

For block B_n,

1) If LBS of *dc_dct_differential* of B_n is changed from '0' to '1', the process of compensation is to search a nearest suitable block between B_n and B_{n+10} and subtract 1 from this suitable block's *dc_dct_differential*. The suitable compensable block must meet this requirement: subtract 1 from its *dc_dct_differential* will not alter the MSB of its *dc_dct_differential*. For example, if *dc_dct_differential* is "111", the corresponding block is compensable block; but if *dc_dct_differential* is "100", the block is not compensable block. If such block exists, compensation is done by just subtracting 1 from its *dc_dct_differential*.

2) If LBS of *dc_dct_differential* of B_n is changed from '1' to '0', the process of compensation is to search a nearest suitable block between B_n and B_{n+10} and add 1 to this suitable block's *dc_dct_differential*. The suitable compensable block must meet this requirement: add 1 to its *dc_dct_differential* will not alter the MSB of its *dc_dct_differential*. If such block exists, compensation is done by just adding 1 to its *dc_dct_differential*.

3) According to MPEG-2 [13], the predictors shall be reset at the start of a slice, so there is no need to do compensation when the current embedding block is the rightmost block with the largest number in a slice, such as B_{175} in Fig. 3.

After compensation, error propagation is limited between current embedding block and the nearest compensable block.

We also show the effectiveness of our compensation method in Table 1. We look at columns with headings "*dct_diff* after embed a bit *without* compen-sation", "*dct_diff* after embed a bit *with* compen-sation", "*DCi* after embed a bit *without* com-pen-sation" , and "*DCi* after embed a bit *with* compen-sation". We can see that if compensation is done in B_{n+3}, error propagation is limited between B_n and B_{n+2}, DC coefficients of blocks beginning from B_{n+3} will keep their original values. We can say

Table 1. The demonstration of error propagation and function of compensation

blocks	Original dct_diff	dct_diff after embed a bit without compensation	dct_diff after Embed a bit with compensation	Original DC_i	DCi after embed a bit without compensation	DCi after embed a bit with compensation
Predictor	3	3	3	3	3	3
B_n	2	(3)	(3)	5	(6)	(6)
B_{n+1}	-1	-1	-1	4	(5)	(5)
B_{n+2}	2	2	2	6	(7)	(7)
B_{n+3}	3	3	(2)	9	(10)	9
B_{n+4}	-2	-2	-2	7	(8)	7
B_{n+5}	-1	-1	-1	6	(7)	6
B_{n+6}	2	2	2	8	(9)	8
B_{n+7}	4	4	4	12	(13)	12
B_{n+8}	3	3	3	15	(16)	15
B_{n+9}	-2	-2	-2	13	(14)	13

that compensation can decrease the degradation of video quality caused by error propagation effectively. We will further demonstrate the effectiveness of our compensation method in next section by Table 3, Fig. 5 and Fig. 6.

5 Experimental Results and Discussion

Three commonly used videos, "Flower Garden", "Table Tennis" and "Mobile Calendar" are adopted in our experiments. For each video, the number of frames is 80, with the frame size of 704x576. MPEG codec [16] is used to generate cover bitstream. The bit rate of cover bitstream is fixed at 8Mbits/sec, the length of a GOP(Group of Pictures) is 12. There are 7 I frames in each tested stream.

In our embedding scheme, the watermark is embedded in Y component. We embed one bit every M blocks. The larger value M takes, the fewer coefficients will be changed and thus the better invisibility will be obtained. In one I frame, T_b/M bits may be embedded in Y component. The larger value M takes, the fewer watermark bits may be embedded. In our experiments, M is set as $M=10$.

The watermark is bit string '1011' and coded using 127 repetition code. After ECC coding, 508 bits need to be embedded in each I frame. The performance in terms of invisibility, effectiveness of compensation, robustness to re-coding and Gaussian noise, real-time embedding and detection are examined in our experiments.

5.1 Invisibility

We compare the average PSNRs of the video sequences before and after watermarking, which are shown in Table 2. In Table 2, PSNR decreases at most 0.53dB is observed after watermarking. We also compare the cover frame with the stego frame by putting them together in Fig. 4, where Fig.4 (a), (c) and are the cover frames decoded from the cover bitstreams of "Flower garden" and "Mobile", respectively, while Fig. 4(b) and (d) are the corresponding stego frames decoded from the stego bitstreams. We can see that the stego frames are perceptually invisible when we compare them with the corresponding cover frames. In addition no visual degradations could be sensed when the stego video is played normally in our experiments.

(a)one cover frame of "Flower garden" (b) the corresponding stego frame of (a)

(c) one cover frame of "Calendar" (d) the corresponding stego frame of (c)

Fig. 4. Demonstration of invisibility

Table 2. Comparasion of PSNRs before and after watermarking

Sequence		Flower Garden	Mobile&Calendar	Table Tennis
PSNR (dB)	Cover	39.03	35.14	35.37
	Stego	38.50	34.88	35.22
ΔPSNR(dB)		-0.53	-0.26	-0.15

5.2 Effectiveness of Compensation

In order to verify the validity of compensation, we compare the PNSRs of the stego video sequences watermarked with and without compensation in embedding process. Average PSNRs of all the test sequences are shown in Table 3, where at least 0.51dB of PSNR increase can be observed when applying compensation in embedding process. We also compare the stego frames with and without compensation by putting them together in Fig. 5, where the left one is the stego frame with compensation, while the right one is the corresponding stego frame without compensation. The parts inside ellipses in Fig. 5 are zoomed in Fig. 6. From Fig.6, we can observed that there are some dark and bright slices in the stego frame without compensation, but these distortions are hardly found in stego frame with compensation. This indicates that the proposed compensation method can improve the quality of the stego video effectively.

Fig. 5. Stego frame with (left) and without (right) compensation

Fig. 6. Zoomed parts of frames in Fig. 6 with (left) and without (right) compensation

Table 3. Comparison of watermarking sequences with and without compensation

		Flower Garden	Mobile	Table Tennis
PSNR (dB)	with compensation	38.50	34.88	35.22
	Without compensation	37.26	34.19	34.71
ΔPSNR(dB)		1.24	0.69	0.51

5.3 Robustness to MPEG-2 Re-encoding

We test the robustness against MPEG re-encoding with lower bit rates by changing the original bit rate from 8M bps to 6M, 4M, and 2Mbps, respectively. The BERs (Bit Error Rate) of the extracted watermark bits are all zero, which are shown in Table 4.

Langelaar et.al [5] also test the robustness to MPEG re-encoding of DEW algorithm. Their results show that when the bit-rate deceases by 25% (from 8M to 6M), the BER of the watermark is 7%, and when the bit-rate deceases by 38% (from 8M to 5M), the BER of the watermark is 21%. The robustness of the DNW algorithm[6] is better than that of DEW algorithm[5]. If the video bit-rate is decreased to 5Mbps, about 38% label bit errors are introduced by DEW, while only 24% by DNW. From Table 4, we can see that ours robustness is much better. This result also supports our embedding strategy in DC.

Table 4. Robustness to MPEG re-encoing

Test sequence	Re-encoding bit-rate (bps)	The BER of the extracted watermark
Flower Garden	2M , 4M, 6M, 8M	0
Mobile&Calendar	2M , 4M, 6M, 8M	0
Table Tennis	2M , 4M, 6M, 8M	0

5.4 Robustness to Gaussian Noise

The existing video watermarking algorithms in compressed domain mainly focus on the test of robustness to MPEG-2 re-encoding, but we think robustness to noise also needs to be measured, so we also test the robustness to Gaussian noise. We first decode the stego bitstream into raw data, and then add Gaussian noise into the Y components, finally re-encode the noised raw data into MPEG-2 stream. Watermark is detected from these noisy videos. Table 5 shows the extracted watermark bits in 7 I frames, where s denotes the strength of noise, error bits are italic. From Table 5, we can see that the watermark of our algorithm can be robust to slight noise.

Table 5. Robustness to Gaussian noise

Sequence	S	PSNR (dB)	Extracted watermark bits						
			I-frame						
			1	2	3	4	5	6	7
Flower	3	35.54	1011	1011	1011	1011	1011	1011	1011
Garden	4	34.17	1011	*1001*	*1001*	1011	1011	1011	1011
Mobile	3	33.32	1011	1011	1011	1011	1011	1011	1011
&Calendar	4	32.42	1011	1011	1011	1011	*1010*	1011	1011
Table	3	33.56	1011	1011	1011	1011	1011	1011	1011
Tennis	4	32.61	1011	1011	1011	1011	*0011*	1011	*0011*

5.5 Real Time Processing

We test the speed of our algorithm on a PC, with CPU of 633 MHz and RAM of 128M. The average times took to embed watermark in I frames in three sequences, "Flower Garden" "Mobile Calendar" "Table Tennis", respectively, are 70ms, 52ms and 55ms. The average times took to extract watermark are 62ms, 44ms and 49ms, respectively. All the times above include the time taken by partly decoding I frame. It shows that our algorithm is a scheme of real-time watermark embedding and detecting.

6   Conclusions

In this paper, we propose a video watermarking algorithm in MPEG-2 bitstream. The contributions are as follows

i) To propose a watermark embedding strategy in compressed DCT domain by slightly modifying DC coefficients. This strategy has three merits over that AC coefficient embedding strategy.

ii) To propose an effective compensation method worked in bit-stream by using the feature of DC coding in MPEG-2 I frame. Experimental results show that the compensation can decrease the distortion to video quality caused by error propagation, thus improve the video quality greatly.

iii) To give a simple bitstream size control scheme based on the analysis of coding characteristic of DC coefficient in MPEG-2 I frame. The scheme is embedding watermark in DC VLC domain, and keeping the MSB of *dc_dct_differential* unaltered. It can guarantee that the bitstream will keep its original size after watermark is embedded.

The watermark with the proposed algorithm is robust to re-coding and slight noise. Embedding and detecting can be processed in real time.

In the experiments of this research, we use the repetition code for its simplicity. It is noted that other error correcting codes, either other linear block codes or nonlinear codes, can be exploited. In fact, convolutional codes may be an alternative noteworthy code [17]. Our future works includes using more efficient ECC in this algorithm to improve the robustness and capacity of the watermark, and combining the idea of compensation into other watermarking algorithm.

Acknowledgement

Supported by NSF of China (60325208, 60403045, 90604008), NSF of Guangdong (04205407, 021758), Key Project of Science and Technology of Guangzhou, China (2005Z3-D0391).

References

1. G. Do err, J.-L. Dugelay , "A guide tour of video watermarking", Signal Processing: Image Communication 18 (2003) 263–282
2. F.Jordan, M.Kutter, and T.Ebrahimi. "Proposal of a watermarking technique for hiding/retrieving data in compressed and decompressed Video". ISO/IEC JTCI/SC29/WG11, 1997
3. Y.Dai, L.Zhang, Y.Yang. "A new method of MPEG video watermarking technology". Proceedings of ICCT2003:1845-1847

4. Z.Zhu et.al , "New Algorithm for Video Watermarking," Proceedings of ICSP'02: 760-761
5. G.C. Langelaar, R.L. Lagendijk, J. Biemond. "Real-time labeling of MPEG-2 compressed video". Journal of Visual Comm. and Image Representation, 1998, 9(4):256-270
6. H.Ling, Z.Lu, and F. Zou, "New real-time watermarking algorithm for compressed video in VLC domain" in Proceedings of ICIP2004, pp.2171-2174
7. I.Setyawan, R.L.Lagendijk, "Extended differential energy watermarking (XDEW) algo-rithm for low bit-rate video watermarking," in the Proceedings of the Seventh Annnal Con-ference of the Advanced School in Computing and Imaging, Heijen, The Netherlands, pp.202-209.2001
8. F.Hartung, B.Girod. "Watermarking of uncompressed and compressed video". Signal Processing, 1998, 66(3): 283-301
9. D.Simitopoulos, S.A.Tsaftaris, N.V. Boulgouris, and M. G. Strintzis. "Compressed-domain video watermarking of MPEG streams," Proceedings of IEEE ICME'02, vol. 1, pp.569 – 572.
10. DC Lou, TL Yin, "Adaptive digital watermarking using fuzzy logic techniques," Optical Engineering, 41 (10): 2675-2687, 2002S.
11. J. Huang, Y.Q. Shi, and Y. Shi, "Embedding image watermarks in DC components," IEEE Trans. nn Circuits and System on Video Technology, 10(6): 974-979, 2000.
12. T.T.Lu, and P.C.Chang, "Key-based video watermarking system on MPEG-2," Proc. of SPIE: Security and Watermarking of Multimedia Contents V, vol.5020, pp516-525, 2003
13. ISO/IEC, Information Technology-Generic Coding of Moving Pictures and Associated Audio Informations: Video. ISO/IEC 13818-2,1995
14. I.J.Cox, J.Kilian, F.T. Leighton, and T. Shamoon, "Secure spread spectrum watermarking for multi media," IEEE Trans. on Image Processing, 6(12): 1673-1687, 1997.
15. C-T. Hsu and J-L. Wu, "Hidden signature in images," IEEE Trans. on Image Processing, 8(1): 58-68, 1999.
16. ftp://ftp.mpegtv.com/pub/mpeg/mssg/mpeg2v12.zip.
17. S. G. Wilson, Digital Modulation and Coding, Prentice-Hall, Inc., 1996.

Reversible Semi-fragile Image Authentication Using Zernike Moments and Integer Wavelet Transform

Xiaoyun Wu[1,2], Xiaoping Liang[1,2], Hongmei Liu[1,2], Jiwu Huang[1,2],
and Guoping Qiu[3]

[1] School of Information Science and Technology, Sun Yat-Sen University, Guangzhou,
Guangdong, 510275, China
isshjw@mail.sysu.edu.cn
[2] Guangdong Province Key Laboratory of Information Security, 510275, P.R. China
[3] School of Computer Science, University of Nottingham, NG8 1BB, UK

Abstract. Semi-fragile image authentication based on watermarking has drawn extensive attention. However, conventional watermarking techniques introduce irreversible distortions to the host signals and thus may not be allowable in some applications such as medical and military imaging. Though some reversible fragile authentication algorithms had been developed, reversible semi-fragile authentication presents a challenge. To the best of our knowledge, so far there are only two reversible semi-fragile authentication algorithms based on watermarking reported in the literature. The existing reversible semi-fragile authentication schemes have two shortcomings: i) Watermark security has not received attention; ii) They have weak capability to resist JPEG compression. In this paper, we propose a novel reversible semi-fragile image authentication scheme. The algorithm can distinguish malicious modification from incidental modification according to semi-fragile characteristics of Zernike moments magnitudes (ZMMs) of the low frequency subband in integer wavelet transform (IWT) domain of an image. Combining semi-fragile characteristics of ZMMs, the watermark can discern forgery attack, thus, improving watermark security. The algorithm can locate the tampered area of an image accurately while tolerating JPEG lossy compression at a low quality factor. Experimental results demonstrate the merits of the proposed algorithm.

1 Introduction

Using powerful image processing software, digital image may be arbitrarily modified. In many cases, a modified image may leave no visual clue of it being tampered with, therefore, in this digital age, "seeing is believing" is not always true anymore. As a consequence, in many real world applications, authentication for the integrity and authenticity of an image becomes an important issue.

A possible authentication technique to solve this problem is to embed a fragile watermark [1-3] or a semi-fragile watermark [4-7] into the image. The fragile watermark is sensitive to any modification imposed on the image which may be applied to exact authentication. However, in many real world applications, digital

R. Safavi-Naini and M. Yung (Eds.): DRMTICS 2005, LNCS 3919, pp. 135–145, 2006.
© Springer-Verlag Berlin Heidelberg 2006

image will inevitably be subjected to content-preserving operations such as JPEG lossy compression, noise, geometrical manipulations (scaling and rotation) etc. In this case, a practically useful authentication system should accept such manipulations even if the image has been modified. Furthermore, the authentication system should be able to detect content-altering manipulations such as cut and replacement. Semi-fragile watermark is able to fulfill this purpose and is applicable to semi-fragile authentication. Therefore, semi-fragile authentication is more practical than exact authentication. Because most proposed semi-fragile authentication schemes reject geometrical manipulations [8], we only focus the evaluation of semi-fragility on JPEG lossy compression in this paper.

The marking techniques mentioned above may introduce irreversible distortions due to quantization error, truncation error or bit replacement operations in watermarking embedding. In some applications, such as medical or military imaging, these distortions are not acceptable once the image is deemed to be authentic. In other words, once it is authenticated, the original image must be retrieved from the marked image in a lossless manner. The reversible watermarking technique can achieve such a goal.

The existing reversible data hiding algorithms can be classified into three categories [9]: (i) Those developed for high capacity data hiding [10-13]; (ii) Those developed for fragile authentication [14-16]; (iii) Those developed for semi-fragile authentication [17-18]. The main difference between category (i) and category (ii) as well as category (iii) is in their data hiding capacity which category (i) is much higher than that of categories (ii) and (iii) methods. Reversible semi-fragile authentication may have many applications, however, this is an area which has not been well studied. To the best of our knowledge, there are only two reversible semi-fragile authentication algorithms reported in the literature [17-18]. De Vleeschouwer et al. [17] proposed a reversible semi-fragile data hiding scheme based on patchwork theory. It can tolerate JPEG lossy compression at a high quality factor. However, the watermarked images may suffer from salt-and-pepper noise due to module 256 addition. Zou et al. [18] proposed a lossless semi-fragile authentication scheme based on integer wavelet transform (IWT). It adopted 5/3 IWT family recommended by JPEG2000 standard and is robust against compression by JPEG2000. Overflow/underflow and salt-and-pepper noise are avoided by adjusting LL_1 subband coefficients properly. Although the method in [17] is robust against JPEG lossy compression, it can only tolerate compression at a high quality factor. Both [17] and [18] have not tackled watermark security issues. By analyzing potential security vulnerabilities existing in the reversible watermarking schemes, Katzenbeisser et al. [19] generalizes three classes of attacks: the attacks against the key distribution, the attacks in the verification stage and the attacks in the reconstruction stage. Here, we concentrate security concern on the attacks in the verification stage, specifically forgery attack which is a deadly attack for image authentication using watermarking scheme. Such attack can modify image content without altering the mark data. As a result, an image that has been tampered with by forgery attack is able to pass authentication processes. As a good authentication algorithm for image using watermarking technique, it should resist forgery attack and tolerate JPEG compression to a certain extent.

In this paper, we propose a novel reversible semi-fragile image authentication scheme. Our new method is able to counter forgery attacks and is also robust against low quality factor JPEG lossy compression. If the marked image has not been modified, our method can retrieve the original image from the marked image. In our method, semi-fragile characteristics of the Zernike moments magnitudes (ZMMs) of the low frequency subband in the IWT domain of an image is used to distinguish malicious attack from incidental attack. By combining semi-fragile characteristics of ZMMs, the watermark can discern forgery attack, thus improving watermark security. The proposed method can locate the tampered region of an image accurately.

The paper is organized as follows. In Section 2, we give the integer wavelet transform of 9/7 biorthogonal wavelet and show the semi-fragile characteristics of the ZMMs of the low frequency subband in the IWT domain of an image. Section 3 describes the proposed algorithm, including outline of the scheme, reversible watermark embedding, tamper detection and recovery. Experimental results and conclusions are given in Section 4 and Section 5, respectively.

2 Integer Wavelet Transform and Zernike Moments

2.1 Integer Wavelet Transform

Because it can reconstruct the original image without distortion, we adopt IWT to implement reversible watermarking. Specifically, we use lifting scheme to realize IWT of CDF 9/7 biorthogonal wavelet. An example of the lifting of CDF 9/7 biorthogonal wavelet is given in [20]. To one dimensional signal $\{x_l\}_{l \in Z}$, the lifting steps are described as follows.

$$\begin{cases} s_l^{(0)} = x_{2l} \\ d_l^{(0)} = x_{2l+1} \end{cases} \quad \begin{cases} d_l^{(1)} = d_l^{(0)} + \alpha(s_l^{(0)} + s_{l+1}^{(0)}) \\ s_l^{(1)} = s_l^{(0)} + \beta(d_l^{(1)} + d_{l-1}^{(0)}) \end{cases} \quad \begin{cases} d_l^{(2)} = d_l^{(1)} + \gamma(s_l^{(1)} + s_{l+1}^{(1)}) \\ s_l^{(2)} = s_l^{(1)} + \delta(d_l^{(2)} + d_{l-1}^{(2)}) \end{cases} \quad (1)$$

$$\begin{cases} s_l = \zeta s_l^{(2)} \\ d_l = d_l^{(2)}/\zeta \end{cases} \quad (2)$$

$$\alpha = -1.586134342; \ \beta = -0.05298011854; \ \gamma = 0.8829110762;$$
$$\delta = 0.4435068522; \ \zeta = 1.149604398 \quad (3)$$

where s_l and d_l are generally referred to as lower frequency and detail coefficients, respectively. $s_l^{(i)}$, $d_l^{(i)}$ (i=0, 1, 2) are mid-outputs.

According to integer wavelet theory [21], we construct integer wavelet transform based on the framework mentioned above. That is:

$$\begin{cases} s_l^{(0)} = x_{2l} \\ d_l^{(0)} = x_{2l+1} \end{cases} \begin{cases} d_l^{(1)} = d_l^{(0)} + Int(\alpha(s_l^{(0)} + s_{l+1}^{(0)})) \\ s_l^{(1)} = s_l^{(0)} + Int(\beta(d_l^{(1)} + d_{l-1}^{(0)})) \end{cases} \begin{cases} d_l^{(2)} = d_l^{(1)} + Int(\gamma(s_l^{(1)} + s_{l+1}^{(1)})) \\ s_l^{(2)} = s_l^{(1)} + Int(\delta(d_l^{(2)} + d_{l-1}^{(2)})) \end{cases} \tag{4}$$

$$\begin{cases} d_l^{(3)} = d_l^{(2)} + Int((\zeta - \zeta^2)s_l^{(2)}) \\ s_l^{(3)} = s_l^{(2)} + Int((-1/\zeta)d_l^{(3)}) \end{cases} \begin{cases} d_l^{(4)} = d_l^{(3)} + Int((\zeta - 1)s_l^{(3)}) \\ s_l^{(4)} = s_l^{(3)} + d_l^{(4)} \end{cases} \begin{cases} s_l = s_l^{(4)} \\ d_l = d_l^{(4)} \end{cases} \tag{5}$$

where $Int(x)$ means integer part of x. The values of parameters α, β, γ, δ, ζ are given in formula (3). Equation (5) is an extra lifting step different from Equation (2). We adopt it here because it can achieve reversible transform according to [19] while Equation (2) cannot.

2.2 Zernike Moments

Zernike moments of a digital image are widely applied to pattern recognition, target classification, target identification and scene analysis. For a definition of the Zernike moments of order n with repetition m of a digital image, please, refer to [22].

The ZMMs of the LL_3 subband in the IWT domain of an image have semi-fragile characteristics. That is, they meet the following requirements:

    i)   High sensitivity to malicious modification.
    ii)   Robustness to incidental modification.

Such characteristics can be evaluated by computing the difference between the ZMMs of the original image and that of the image suffered from various attacks. Root-mean-square-error (RMSE) may be used to measure the difference of ZMMs. The RMSE of ZMMs is defined as below.

$$\Delta = \sqrt{\frac{1}{N}\sum_{i=1}^{N}\left(M_i - M_i^{'}\right)^2} \tag{6}$$

where Δ denotes RMSE of ZMMs, M_i and $M_i^{'}$ denote the ZMMs of LL_3 subband in the IWT domain of an image before and after attack, respectively. N is the numbers of the ZMMs of the LL_3 subband in the IWT domain of an image. Because the Zernike moments of order 12 have a moderate computational complexity and are enough to represent image features, therefore we compute Zernike moments of order 12, total of 49 moments here. We demonstrate such characteristics by making an experiment on two hundred images of 512×512×8 bits. Results on statistical quantities (mean and standard deviation) of RMSE of ZMMs for these images are shown in Table 1.

In Table 1, JPEG90 refers to JPEG compression with a quality factor of 90. Noise1, Noise2, Noise3 refer to zero-mean additive Gaussian noise with variance 0.0001, 0.0005, 0.0009, respectively. In our experiment, cut refers to replace a region with all white pixels. Replace refers to replace a region by another region from the same image or from another image. From Table 1, we can observe that mean and standard deviation of RMSE of ZMMs of JPEG40 and Noise3 are (128.59, 32.37) and (145.19, 55.08), respectively. The mean and standard deviation of RMSE of ZMMs of cut (16×16) and replace (16×16) are (5067.88, 3419.79) and (470.83, 248.12), respectively. The mean and standard deviation of RMSE of ZMMs of cut (32×32) and replace (32×32) are (5366.18, 3233.03) and (807.74, 437.63), respectively. That is if an image is suffered from incidental modifications, such as JPEG and noise, the differences of ZMMs are far smaller than those of malicious attack, such as cut and replace. It indicates that the semi-fragile characteristic of ZMMs of the LL_3 subband in the IWT domain of an image. Using this feature, we can distinguish incidental distortion from severe distortion according to a pre-selected threshold.

Table 1. Statistical quantities of RMSE of ZMMs of images before and after attack

Attack	Mean	Standard Deviation
JPEG90	54.05	35.35
JPEG70	74.78	45.22
JPEG50	100.01	28.92
JPEG40	128.59	32.37
Noise1	105.37	50.04
Noise2	120.33	47.44
Noise3	145.19	55.08
Cut(16×16)	5067.88	3419.79
Replace(16×16)	470.83	248.12
Cut(32×32)	5366.18	3233.03
Replace(32×32)	807.74	437.63

3   The Proposed Scheme

3.1   Outline of the Scheme

Fig. 1 and Fig. 2 are block diagrams of the watermark embedding, tamper detection and recovery procedure of the proposed scheme, respectively.

When embedding, we first pre-process the original image by histogram modification to prevent overflow/underflow. Then, we perform 3-level IWT on the pre-processed image. In the meantime, we compute Zernike moments of LL_3 subband of the pre-processed image. We embed watermark in HH_3 subband and the recovery information (bookkeeping date, original 1st bit plane of HH_3 subband etc.) in HH_1, LH_1 and HL_1 subband. Finally, inverse IWT is applied and the marked image is obtained.

In tamper detection and recovery stage, we first perform 3-level IWT on the suspected image. Then we compute Zernike moments of LL_3 subband of the

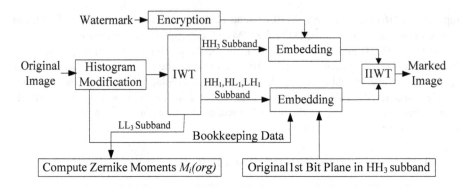

Fig. 1. Watermark embedding

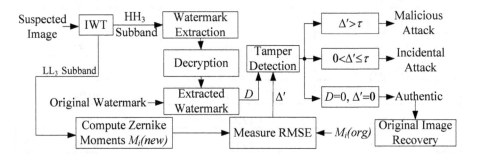

Fig. 2. Tamper detection and recovery

suspected image. Watermark is extracted from HH_3 subband. Finally, according to the difference image of watermark D and RMSE of Zernike moments Δ', we judge the image is authentic, incidental attacked or malicious attacked. If the image is authentic, we further recover the original image.

More details will be described in Section 3.2 and Section 3.3.

3.2 Reversible Watermark Embedding

The bit-plane of IWT coefficients in HH_1, LH_1 and HL_1 subbands has the following property: The higher the bit-plane, the larger the bias between 0's and 1's. By compressing bits in this bit-plane, it leaves room to hide data [10].

We use this property to implement reversible watermark embedding. Although the higher bit-plane may embed much more data, it will cause higher distortion. Considering lower embedding capacity, we choose the 4th bit-plane of the IWT coefficients in the HH_1, LH_1 and HL_1 subbands, which ensures sufficient space and better marked image quality, to hide data. We use a binary image, W, as the watermark for tamper detection. We encrypt it in consideration of security and denote the result as W^*. The embedding procedures are described as follows.

i)   Pre-process the original image by carrying out histogram modification to prevent overflow/underflow [10]. In order to restore the original image losslessly later, the bookkeeping information of histogram modification should be hidden as overhead. We denote it as B.

ii) Compute 49 ZMMs of LL_3 subband in IWT domain of the pre-processed image. Denote them $M_i(org)$, $1 \leq i \leq 49$. These 49 ZMMs needs to be transmitted to the receiver as the side information for distinguishing malicious attack from non-malicious attack.

iii) Denote the 1st bit-plane of the IWT coefficients in HH_3 subband as L. We replace L with $W*$ to embed mark data.

iv) Losslessly compress the original 4th bit-plane of the IWT coefficients in HH_1, LH_1 and HL_1 subbands using arithmetic coding. Let C denote the compressed data.

v)   Combine B, C and L into a bit stream S. Substitute S for the original 4th bit-plane of the IWT coefficients in HH_1, LH_1 and HL_1 subbands.

vi) Perform the inverse IWT to generate a watermarked image.

In this way, we implement reversible watermark embedding.

3.3 Tamper Detection and Recovery

To a suspected image, the authentication is performed via the following steps.

i)   Compute 49 ZMMs of LL_3 subband in IWT domain of a suspected image. Denote them $M_i(new)$, $1 \leq i \leq 49$.

ii) Extract the hidden watermark in the 1st bit-plane of the IWT coefficients in HH_3 subband. Via decryption, we denote the result as W'.

iii) Compute the difference image D and Δ' of ZMMs of LL_3 subband in IWT domain according to formula (7) and (8)

$$D = |W - W'| \tag{7}$$

$$\Delta' = \sqrt{\frac{1}{49} \sum_{i=1}^{49} (M_i(org) - M_i'(new))^2} \tag{8}$$

According to formula (7), if W is equal to W', all pixels in the difference image have value 0. Otherwise, some pixels in the difference image have value 1 which means mark extraction error. Thus white pixel in the difference image D represents the pixel is tampered. Hence, we can locate the tampered area according to D.

iv) If D and Δ' are all equal to zero, the image is supposed to be authentic. Extract B, C and L from the 4th bit-plane of HH_1, LH_1 and HL_1 subbands. Using these information, the original image can be recovered from the marked image losslessly.

v)   If Δ' is not equal to zero, let τ be a threshold which can be determined empirically to distinguish malicious tamper from incidental attack. If $\Delta' \leq \tau$, we decide that the image suffers from incidental modification. Otherwise, it is malicious attacked. In the latter case, if D is equal to zero, we conclude the image has suffered from forgery attack mentioned in introduction. So this forgery image can not pass authentication thus improving security. If D is not equal to zero, we can further locate the tampered region.

4 Experimental Results

We test the effectiveness of our proposed algorithm using the images shown in Fig. 3. The PSNRs of the watermarked images are shown in Table 2. Specifically, the marked images of Baboon and Peppers are shown in Fig. 4. We can observe no difference between the marked image and the corresponding original image. Fig. 5 shows the results of the fragility to malicious tamper such as cut and replacement. It is obvious that our algorithm can detect malicious modifications and locate the tampered areas accurately. Table 3 is the difference of ZMMs for Baboon and Peppers that suffered from malicious attack and JPEG compression. The cut and replace operations are shown in Fig. 5. It is seen that setting a threshold value (e.g. 200) will distinguish JPEG compression from cut and replace operation. Moreover, it also demonstrates that our scheme can tolerate JPEG lossy compression with a quality factor as low as 40. Since images compressed at a quality factor smaller than 40 may lead to obvious perceptual distortion, robustness to JPEG at a quality factor 40 is enough in most of applications.

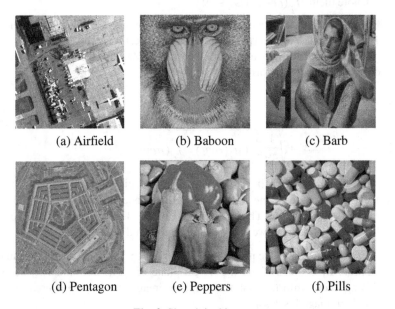

| (a) Airfield | (b) Baboon | (c) Barb |

| (d) Pentagon | (e) Peppers | (f) Pills |

Fig. 3. Six original images

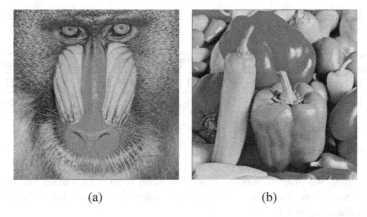

(a)   (b)

Fig. 4. Watermarked image (a) Baboon; (b) Peppers

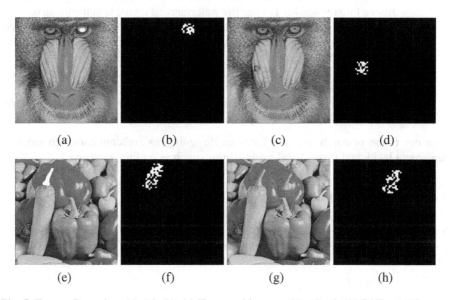

(a)   (b)   (c)   (d)

(e)   (f)   (g)   (h)

Fig. 5. Tamper Detection. (a), (c), (e), (g) Tampered images; (b), (d), (f), (h) Difference images of extracted watermarks.

Table 2. PSNR of six marked images

Test image	PSNR of marked image(dB)	Test image	PSNR of marked image(dB)
Airfield	35.54	Pentagon	36.91
Baboon	37.88	Peppers	39.04
Barb	36.72	Pills	37.44

Table 3. Diferrence of ZMMs of LL$_3$ subband in IWT domain of an image suffered from various attack

image \ attack	JPEG90	JPEG70	JPEG50	JPEG40	Cut	Replace
Baboon	47.99	73.36	145.04	158.56	5257.90	523.94
Peppers	60.66	74.65	82.50	86.95	3685.70	1352.20

5 Conclusions

In this paper, we propose a novel reversible semi-fragile authentication algorithm for images based on Zernike moments and integer wavelet transform. The main contributions are as follows:

i)   The proposed algorithm is able to recover an original image from the marked image losslessly after the watermarked image is authenticated.

ii) Using semi-fragile characteristics of Zernike moments, the proposed algorithm is able to distinguish malicious modifications from incidental modifications.

iii) Combining semi-fragile characteristics of ZMMs, the watermark can discern forgery attack and thus improve the watermark security.

iv) The proposed algorithm is capable of detecting tamper accurately while tolerat ing JPEG lossy compression at a low quality factor.

In our future research, we will focus on designing an authentication scheme that can accept incidental geometrical manipulations such as scaling, rotations.

Acknowledgement

Supported by NSF of China (60325208, 60403045, 90604008), NSF of Guangdong (04205407), Key Project of Science and Technology of Guangzhou, China (2005Z3-D0391).

References

1. M. M. Yeung, F. Mintzer, "An invisible watermarking technique for image verification," *Proc. of IEEE Int. Conf. on Image Processing*, vol. 2, pp. 680-683, 1997
2. P. W. Wong, N. Memon, "Secret and public key image watermarking schemes for image authentication and ownership verification," *IEEE Trans. on Image Processing*, 10(10):1593-1601, 2001
3. C. T. Li, F. M. Yang and C. S. Lee, "Oblivious fragile watermarking scheme for image authentication," *Proc. of IEEE Int. Conf. on Acoustics, Speech, and Signal Processing*, vol. 4, pp. 3445-3448, 2002
4. D. Kundur, D. Hatzinakos, "Towards a telltale watermark techniques for tamper-proofing," *Proc. of IEEE Int. Conf. on Image Processing*, vol. 2, pp. 409-413, 1998

5. C. Y. Lin, S. F. Chang, "Semi-fragile watermarking for authenticating JPEG visual content," *Proc. of SPIE Security and Watermarking of Multimedia Content II*, vol. 3971, pp. 140-151, 2000

6. J. Hu, J. Huang, D. Huang and Y. Shi, "Image fragile watermarking based on fusion of multi-resolution tamper detection," *IEE Electronics Letters*, 38(24):1512-1513, 2002

7. Z. Lu, C. Liu, D. Xu and S. Sun, "Semi-fragile image watermarking method based on index constrained vector quantization," *IEE Electronics Letters*, 39(1): 35-36, 2003

8. B. Zhu, M. D. Swanson, A. H. Tewfik, "When Seeing isn't Believeing," *IEEE Trans. on Signal Processing*, 21(2): 40-49, 2004

9. Y. Shi, Z. Ni, D. Zou, C. Liang and G. Xuan, "Lossless data hiding: fundamentals, algorithms and applications," *Proc of IEEE Int. Conf. on Circuits and Systems*, vol. 2 pp. 33-36, 2004

10. G. Xuan, J. Zhu, J. Chen, Y. Shi, Z. Ni and W. Su, "Distortionless data hiding based on integer wavelet transform," *IEE Electronics Letters*, 38(25): 1646-1648, 2002

11. M. Goljan, J. Fridrich and R. Du, "Distortion-free data embedding," *Proceedings of 4th Information Hiding Workshop*, pp. 27-41, 2001

12. J. Tian, "Reversible data embedding using a difference expansion," *IEEE Trans. on Circuits and Systems for Video Technology*, 13(8):890-896, 2003

13. M. U. Celik, G. Sharma, A. M. Tekalp, E. Saber, "Reversible data hiding," *Proc of IEEE Int. Conf. on Image Processing*, vol. 2 pp. 157-160, 2002

14. J. M. Barton, "Method and apparatus for embedding authentication information within digital data," U.S. Patent 5,646,997, 1997

15. C. W. Honsinger, P. Jones, M. Rabbani, and J. C. Stoffel, "Lossless recovery of an original image containing embedded data," US Patent: 6,278,791, 2001

16. J. Fridrich, M. Goljan and R. Du, "Invertible authentication," *Proc. of SPIE Security and Watermarking of Multimedia Contents III*, vol. 4314, pp. 197-208, 2001

17. C. De Vleeschouwer, J. F. Delaigle and B. Macq, "Circular interpretation of bijective transformations in lossless watermarking for media asset management," *IEEE Trans. on Multimedia*, 5(1):97-105, 2003

18. D. Zou, Y. Shi and Z. Ni, "A semi-fragile lossless digital watermarking scheme based on integer wavelet transform," *Proc of IEEE Int. Conf. on Multimedia Signal Processing*, pp. 195-198, 2004

19. S. Katzenbeisser, J. Dittmann, "Malicious attacks on media authentication schemes based on invertible watermarks," *Proc. of SPIE Security and Watermarking of Multimedia Content VI*, vol. 5306 pp. 838-847, 2004

20. I. Daubechies, W. Sweldens, "Factoring wavelet transform into lifting step," *Journal of Fourier Analysis*, vol. 4 pp. 245-267, 1998

21. R. Calderbank, I. Daubechies, W. Sweldens, B.L. Yeo, "Wavelet transforms that map integers to integers," *Journal of Applied and Computational Harmonic Analysis*, vol. 5 pp. 332-369, 1998

22. A. Khotanzad, Y. H. Hong, "Invariant image recognition by Zernike moments," *IEEE Trans. on Pattern Analysis and Machine Intelligence*, 12(5):489-497, 1990

Software Tamper Resistance Through Dynamic Program Monitoring

Brian Blietz and Akhilesh Tyagi

Dept. of Electrical & Computer Engineering,
Iowa State University,
Ames, Iowa 50011
tyagi@iastate.edu

Abstract. This paper describes a two instruction-stream (two-process) model for tamper resistance. One process (Monitor process, M-Process) is designed explicitly to monitor the control flow of the main program process (P-Process). The compilation phase compiles the software into two co-processes: P-process and M-process. The monitor process contains the control flow consistency conditions for the P-process. The P-process sends information on its instantiated control flow at a compiler specified fixed period to the M-process. If there is a violation of the control flow conditions captured within the M-process, the M-process takes an anti-tamper action such as termination of the P-process. By its very design, the monitor process is expected to be compact. Hence, we can afford to protect the M-process with a more expensive technique, a variant of Aucsmith's scheme. This scheme has been implemented with the Gnu C compiler *gcc*. There are several other monitoring, obfuscation, and dynamic decryption techniques that are embedded in this system. We quantify the performance overhead of the scheme for a variety of programs. The performance of such an anti-tamper schema can be significantly improved by leveraging a decoupled processor architecture to support the decoupled M- and P- processes. We describe one instance of such a two-stream decoupled architecture that can make the scheme more robust and efficient.

1 Introduction

The existing software intellectual protection (IP) protection schemes involve either some kind of authentication such as license keys or establish a proof of tampering after the damage is already done such as watermarking. A tamper resistance approach that detects and/or subverts/corrects the tampering actions in real time (concurrently with the program execution) is much more desirable. Ultimately, a technique that will protect the software transparently, without the user even knowing such actions are taking place, will succeed.

An observation of the historical trends suggest that the attack methods appear to be more mature than (lead in time) the security methods. Attacks use many readily available tools which allow them to monitor network connections, monitor a program's instructions with debuggers, modify an operating system's kernel[1], monitor address

---

[1] Operating systems such as Linux are open source, allowing modification of any part of a program's system interface.

R. Safavi-Naini and M. Yung (Eds.): DRMTICS 2005, LNCS 3919, pp. 146–163, 2006.

and memory buses, etc.. It seems somewhat ironic that the tools used to help design and implement complex software, are the same tools used to attack it.

Much has been done to thwart network originated attacks, but little has been done to thwart hardware and software based attacks on the intellectual property embedded within a program. These attacks include modifications to a program to skip crucial checks (such as license file/servers), or reverse engineering of a key piece of a program's functionality.

The anti-tamper techniques in general are designed to detect or sense any type of tampering of a program. Once such tampering is detected, one of many possible actions could be taken by the anti-tamper part of the software. These actions could include disabling the software, deleting the software, or making the software generate invalid results rendering it useless to the tampering adversary. This paper proposes one such anti-tamper methodology based on program monitoring. The monitoring process must have some knowledge of the monitored program's meta-structure, some notion of program semantics with respect to the tamper protected domain. This domain in our work is control flow integrity. We believe that all tampering methods, be they data tampering or memory tampering or network traffic tampering, eventually exhibit themselves in the control flow corruption. Hence, all types of tampering can be captured even if only control flow tampering is incorporated into an anti-tamper system design paradigm.

With this premise, we propose to use a two-process model for program integrity (one that is not tampered) checking. The original program runs as a program process (P-Process), whereas a monitoring co-process (M-process) runs concurrently with the sole objective of dynamically verifying the control flow of the P-process. The original program is compiled into the two process model by the modified Gnu C Compiler (*gcc*). The P-process performs periodic control flow integrity checks by communicating its instantiated control flow (since the last check) to the M-process. The M-process has the correct control flow of the P-process stored in it. The compiler can statically determine the piecemeal control flow information and compile it into a data structure resident in the M-process memory. The M-process performs the integrity check on the received control flow segment with respect to this data structure. If the check fails, it can take one of the few corrective actions such as killing the P-process and/or raising an interrupt. If the check passes, no information need be communicated back to the P-process. The frequency of the *check* primitives is user specifiable to control the overhead of the scheme. We have implemented the scheme with *gcc* on Linux. We present the performance overhead data on a variety of programs (interactive versus CPU intensive) in Section 6. The implementation details are given in Section 5.

The entire monitoring framework was first conceived by us as a decoupled architectural paradigm. The processor in such a case would have two decoupled computing engines: one for the P-process and one for the M-process. Such a two-instruction stream processor can perform these checks much more efficiently and stealthily. We describe such an architecture in Section 5.7.

Section 2 outlines some of the related work (both in use and proposed) to create a tamper resistant environment. Some of the background material is also covered in this section. Section 7 concludes the paper.

2 Background and Related Work

This section provides some of the related work and background material in tamper resistant software. The classical work in this field is Collberg & Thomborson [2].

2.1 Tamper Resistant Methods

There exists a wide range of tamper resistance methodologies. The following discusses some of the more widely know approaches. The main focus of this paper is on control flow monitoring, augmented with some new approaches, which are discussed in subsequent sections.

In order to increase the effectiveness of tamper resistance, multiple approaches must be combined. One should think carefully about how to combine different approaches, and strive to mask the weaknesses of one, with the strengths of another. For example, combining control flow monitoring with obfuscation can lead to a monitored program that requires significant effort to reverse engineer (NP-Complete).

Watermarking. Watermarking consists of statically, or dynamically inserting signatures into a program, which serve to identify the original owner. Static watermarks never change, and are therefore subject to some level of reverse engineering. Dynamic watermarks change with the program execution. Watermarks are either extracted from a programs image, or from the program execution itself. Because we are focusing on tamper resistance at the source, we will not be looking into watermarking as an effective technique. The watermarking only serves as a proof of tampering. While this performs a valuable function, the idea is to avoid the need for this all together by making the program impossible to tamper with in the first place. Good representatives of software watermarking methods are [2] and [11].

Obfuscation. Code obfuscation attempts to make the task of reverse engineering a program daunting and time consuming. This is done by transforming the original program into an equivalent program, which is much harder to understand, using static analysis.

More formally, code obfuscation involves transforming the original program P into a new program P' with the same black box functionality. P' should be built such that [2]:

i) It maximizes obscurity, i.e., it is far more time consuming to reverse engineer P' when compared to P.

ii) It maximizes resilience, i.e., P' is resilient to automated attacks. Either they will not work at all, or they will be so time consuming that they will not be practical.

iii) It maximizes stealth properties, i.e., P' should exhibit similar statistical properties, when compared to P.

iv) It minimizes cost, i.e., the performance degradation caused by adding obfuscation techniques to P' should be minimized.

Obfuscation techniques involve lexical, control and data transformations. Lexical transformations alter the actual source code, such as Java code. Control transformations alter the control flow of the program by changing branch targets to an ambiguous state.

Data transformations rearrange data structures such that they are not contiguous. Data can be transformed all the way down to the bit level. Bit interleaving is one example.

One particular obfuscation technique of interest is obscuring control flow of a program. By obscuring branch target addresses, static analysis of a control flow graph can be shown to be NP-hard [12]. Program address based obfuscation is presented in [7].

Hashing functions. Hashing is the act of scanning a section of the program's image, usually while running, and performing a hash function on the data. Each hash function performs a different algorithm, and each has different results. [5] has implemented such a system, using linear hash functions, which overlap each other. It is even possible for one hash function to hash another hash function, or even itself. This allows the hashing mechanism to not only protect the program, but to protect itself as well.

Control Flow Monitoring. Control flow monitoring involves tracing the execution of a program as it is running. A program is broken down into basic blocks using a Control Flow Graph (CFG) representation. Code is inserted into each of the basic blocks in order to keep a trace of the running application. At certain intervals, the trace is checked against a known good trace which is determined at compile time.

2.2 Types of Attacks

Attacks can be classified into three basic categories. Each of these depend on the relative location of the origination of the attack.

  i) **Outside attackers** attempting to gain entry over a networked connection. This is the most common type of attack today, and several preventive measures are already in place.
 ii) **Executable code** that is run on a target system, but not under the direct control of the attacker, such as viruses and Trojan horses. This is a fairly common attack which has several preventive measures already in place as well.
iii) **God Mode attacks.** The attacker owns a copy of the software, and has complete control over the system it is run on. This is one of most damaging attacks in that it allows the theft of Intellectual Property, and the execution of pirated software.

The God Mode attack model assumes that the attacker has full control over the system, *i.e.*, the attacker owns the system the program is running on, and has total access to the software and hardware in the system. The attacker may choose to run binary analysis tools, software and hardware debuggers, logic analyzers, etc.. The main hurdle for the attacker is rooted in the amount of technical know-how he/she possesses. These type of attacks are the focus of this paper.

2.3 Control Flow Graph Overview

During execution of a program, the path of execution will jump around inside the executable code for the program. This is typically done using instructions such as jump or branch. A control flow graph (CFG) can be viewed as a Directed Acyclic Graph

(DAG) of a program's control flow consisting of basic blocks as nodes, each of which are terminated by a control transfer instruction, such as a jump or branch.

Each basic block has at most two successors, and at least one predecessor (except for the entry block for a program which has no predecessor). At a high level, basic blocks are most commonly created from conditional statements such as *if then else* statements. The *if* block is the first successor ,and the *else* block is the second successor.

When the source code is compiled, the compiler translates the source into an intermediary representation called the Register Transfer Language (RTL). GCC maintains a representation of the CFG for a program based on its RTL. It would be of little use to have the CFG refer to C level source code, due to its higher level of abstraction. RTL code is very similar to assembly code. In fact, the RTL is used directly to generate the assembly code, which is then used by the assembler to generate object or executable files.

When the source code is in the RTL representation, the CFG is readily available to the compiler.[2] The CFG is used by several other optimization passes internal to GCC, and is updated accordingly after each pass. When GCC is ready to output the assembly code for the program, the CFG is in its final state. This is where the tamper resistant code is inserted.

At the beginning of each basic block, code is inserted to communicate with the M-Process. This code's function is to inform the M-Process of its unique ID. The M-Process will gather the trace information for basic blocks, and check them against the known CFG representation, that was determined at compile time. When it finds a control flow sequence that is invalid, it knows that the M-Process has been tampered with in some way. At this point, appropriate actions can be taken to secure the application from an attacker. Such actions can range from printing a warning message, to completely deleting the file from the disk. The action taken is application specific, which allows different *penalties* for tampering with a given program.

The CFG obtained from the compiler is a static representation of the flow of the program. Static analysis of the CFG is of much concern due to an attack's ability to automate a reverse engineering attack on the control flow. It is conceivable that someone could disassemble the program and recreate the CFG from the assembly code. This would allow an attack to succeed by communicating the fake set of unique identifiers associated with the original control flow graph instead of the new basic blocks inserted. This will allow the tampering to go undetected.

In order to prevent such an attack, the unique identifiers of each basic block must be dynamically determined at run-time uniquely for each run. Before the M-Process starts the P-Process, it will change the unique identifier associated with each basic block by replacing the value used by each basic block in its communication phase. The M-Process will also update its local CFG table with the new value.

To further protect the CFG table, the M-Process will remain in a mostly encrypted form during its execution. The M-Process will use Integrity Verification Kernels (IVK) variant [1] to allow only a small portion of the M-Process to be in plain text at any given time. This protects the CFG data structure from static analysis. As pointed out

---

[2] GCC has incorporated a CFG library into versions greater then gcc3.0. Other compilers have similar support such as SUIF2 from Stanford.

previously, static analysis will only give an abstract representation of the CFG. The actual unique identifiers that make up the CFG will be different with each run.

2.4   Monitor Process Overview

The Monitor Process (M-Process) is an application specific process that comes paired with the actual executable for the program (P-Process). When the M-Process starts up, it first performs some fix up tasks on the P-Process[3] It then *execs*[4] the P-Process.

Once the P-Process is running, for every basic block in the P-Process, a unique identifier will be sent to the M-Process. The M-Process will then verify the correct execution of the program by comparing it to the CFG that was determined at the compile time. The CFG data structure can be seen as a simple array containing 3-tuples of (Parent, Child1, Child2) entries for the entire CFG.

The M-Process will initially be in an encrypted form, using standard encryption methods. An IVK is decrypted, and allowed to execute, one at a time. When any portion of the executable code or the data section is needed, it is modified from its encrypted form to plain text, decrypted form which is then executed or read as data [1].

Having the M-Process stored as an encrypted file buys a significant advantage over a plain text M-process scheme. Not only will the CFG data structure be protected from static analysis, but several parts of the P-Process will reside as data structures in the M-Process as well.[5] We say more about this in Sections 5.5 and 5.6.

3   Application Transformation

The application, or P-Process, must be transformed such that a new P-Process, P' is created with the same black box functionality as the original process P. This means that any changes made to the P-Process must not be observable from the user's standpoint. The main goal is to create a tamper resistant version of P that is protected without any interaction from or inconvenience to the user.

3.1   Instruction Insertion

Instructions must be inserted into each basic block in order to communicate trace information to the M-Process. For example, consider a simple *if then else* statement as shown in Figure 1.

First decompose it into its basic blocks at the assembly level.[6] This is shown in Figure 2.

Notice the labels that have been inserted which start with the prefix ATP. These correspond to the beginning of a basic block. The number in each label corresponds to its unique identifier.

---

[3] The P-Process is not in a run-able state until the M-Process restores several parts of its executable code.

[4] exec refers to anything similar to the execv() call in Linux/Unix.

[5] Before the P-Process is paired to the M-Process, several parts of the P-Process are stripped out, and corresponding data structures are inserted into the M-Process. For example, the entire main() routine.

[6] All assembly given uses the x86 instruction set. All assembly is created using GCC3.2.3.

Next these labels are replaced with instructions to communicate the block's identifier to the M-Process as in Figure 3.

The inserted instructions correspond to the following steps:
1. Setup the stack pointer.
2. Push the unique identifier onto the call stack.
3. Call a function to write to the unique identifier to the pipe that the M-Process is listening on.[7]
4. Restore the stack pointer for the current function.

```
.ATP_270:
        movl    $0, −4(%ebp)
        movl    $0, −8(%ebp)
        cmpl    $1, −4(%ebp)
        jne     .L6
.ATP_271:
        leal    −8(%ebp), %eax
        incl    (%eax)
        jmp     .L7
.L6:
.ATP_272:
        leal    −8(%ebp), %eax
        decl    (%eax)
```

if(x == 1)
    y = y + 1;
else
    y = y − 1;

Fig. 1. Example C source code   **Fig. 2.** Assembly output with ATP labels

3.2 Communication

At this point, each basic block in the P-Process has the extra instructions to communicate its basic block identifier to the M-Process. In a perfect world, this would be all that is needed, but such an implementation is not feasible. In order to implement this functionality, the P-Process must also tell the M-Process when it should verify the current trace that it is keeping. This can be done by transmitting a *magic* number, i.e. the VERIFY code.

The key to making this work, is in determining where to insert the VERIFY code transmission. Inserting the VERIFY too often will yield very short traces, wherein one might be able to insert attack sequences. A short period between the verification also leads to large overhead. On the other hand, due to compiler limitations, function boundaries pose a problem for long trace lengths. The CFG library in GCC does not allow basic blocks to be broken based on a function call. This is understandable because, in the worst case, the function call could be in a library. If the function is in a library, then it is impossible to have a usable successor for the block. On top of this, because of the

---

[7] A separate source file was used to implement the P-Process communication. This file is compiled to an object file, and linked with the P-Process.

```
.ATP_270:
    subl    $12, %esp
    pushl   $270
    call    __AT__write_mp_pip
    addl    $16, %esp
    movl    $0, −4(%ebp)
    movl    $0, −8(%ebp)
    cmpl    $1, −4(%ebp)
    jne     .L6
.ATP_271:
    subl    $12, %esp
    pushl   $271
    call    __AT__write_mp_pip
    addl    $16, %esp
    leal    −8(%ebp), %eax
    incl    (%eax)
    jmp     .L7
.L6:
.ATP_272:
    subl    $12, %esp
    pushl   $272
    call    __AT__write_mp_pip
    addl    $16, %esp
    leal    −8(%ebp), %eax
    decl    (%eax)
```

Fig. 3. Modified assembly code with communication instructions inserted

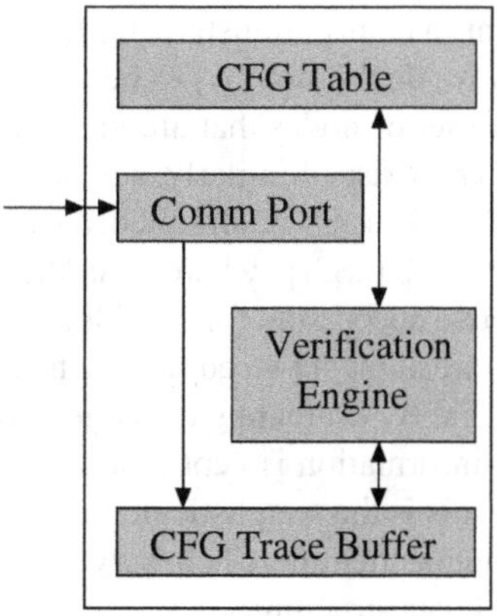

Fig. 4. M-Process

way GCC works, it is also very complicated to have a successor that is in another file or even in another function. GCC processes one function at a time, when it performs its passes. In other words, the CFG is only maintained per function, and not globally.

From an implementation standpoint, it is fairly easy to place the VERIFY code transmission at the end of every function. Through the use of temporary files, global CFG information could be maintained for each function's entry block identifier. This gets a little tricky at the RTL level, because one might find a function call to a function that the compiler has not seen yet. Because the compiler has not seen this function yet, there is consequently no identifier for it. One solution to this situation, is to process the function boundaries at the assembly level, instead of the RTL level. By this time all the files have been read, and every function has been seen. Any library calls are also easily detected at this point as well.

4   Monitor Process

The Monitor Process (M-Process) resides along side the P-Process. It's purpose is to monitor the control flow of the P-Process, and take appropriate actions when an inconsistency is found. The M-Process structure is shown in Figure 4.

4.1   Communication

The M-Process will sit and wait for any identifiers that are sent from the P-Process. As the identifiers are received, they are collected in a trace buffer for further use by the verification engine. Typically, the M-Process will wait for a VERIFY code from the P-Process before it invokes the verification engine. But, due to a fixed trace buffer size, it may also decide to verify on its own, when the buffer is full. A common situation that would fill up the buffer before a VERIFY code is seen is a *for* loop that iterates many times.

4.2   Control Flow Graph Representation

Let V be the set of nodes, and E be the set of edges in $V \times V$ that connect the nodes in V. Let C be the CFG of a program such that the set $C = \{V, E\}$, where $V = \{v_1, v_2, ... v_k\}$ and similarly $E = \{e_1, e_2, ... e_l\}$. Each v_i is a node of the CFG, and each e_i an edge that represents a control transfer, $ct_{i,j}$ from v_i to v_j.

Next we define $succ(v_i)$ to be the set of nodes that are successors to v_i, and $pred(v_i)$ to be the set of nodes that are predecessors of v_i. A node v_i belongs to $succ(v_j)$ if and only iff $ct_{i,j}$ exists. Similarly, a node v_j belongs to $pred(v_i)$ if and only if $ct_{j,i}$ exists [4].

As the P-Process is compiled, a CFG is created. This CFG consists of 3-tuples in the form of $\{P_i, S1_i, S2_i\}$, where P_i is the current basic block's identifier, and $S1_i$ and $S2_i$ are the two successors for this block. Each node (v_i) has a corresponding P_i. For every P_i there are at most two edges. Each e_i corresponds to an edge from node P_i to one if its successors. By evaluating the edges, $S1_i$ and $S2_i$ are calculated.

This information is kept in a linear array, which can be searched based on these 3-tuples. This is the simplistic description. Many enhancements such as sorting, caching, and dynamic identifiers help serve to increase performance further, and to better secure the CFG data structure.

4.3   Verification

Conceptually, during execution of the program, if any $ct_{i,j}$ exist that are not part of C, then an illegal control flow has been seen. Verification of a trace of identifiers involves sequentially scanning the trace buffer and comparing it to the CFG. To do this, let P_i equal the current identifier in the trace buffer, and let P_{i+1} be the next identifier in the trace. Scan the CFG table until a tuple containing P_i as $\{P_i, S1_i, S2_i\}$ is found. The following two entries $S1_i$ and $S2_i$ are the two successors of this basic block in a legitimate control flow. Each entry P_i is tested such that P_{i+1} must equal either S_i1 or S_i2. If this test fails, an incorrect path has been taken in the program, indicating that the program has been tampered with.

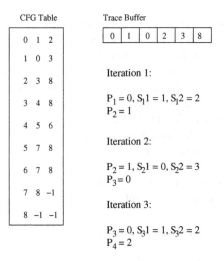

CFG Table

0	1	2
1	0	3
2	3	8
3	4	8
4	5	6
5	7	8
6	7	8
7	8	-1
8	-1	-1

Trace Buffer

| 0 | 1 | 0 | 2 | 3 | 8 |

Iteration 1:

$P_1 = 0, S_11 = 1, S_12 = 2$
$P_2 = 1$

Iteration 2:

$P_2 = 1, S_21 = 0, S_22 = 3$
$P_3 = 0$

Iteration 3:

$P_3 = 0, S_31 = 1, S_32 = 2$
$P_4 = 2$

Fig. 5. M-Process Verification Example

4.4   Protection Scheme (Aucsmith's IVKs)

[1] proposed a very interesting tamper resistant scheme. This scheme however has very high overhead. We present a simplified version of this scheme in the following. For a detailed treatment of an implementation of this scheme, the reader is referred to [3].

Each text section is broken down into several text subsections. The objective is that at any point in time, exactly one text subsection is in plaintext (the one that is currently executing). Whenever, there is a control flow edge between two such text subsections, the target text subsection is decrypted into plaintext along with encryption of the source text subsection simultaneously. Figure 6 illustrates a program (text section) broken into 8 text sub sections and the induced control flow graph at the text subsection granularity. Note that there can be multiple control flow edges between two subsections as in T_6 and T_7. There can be backward control flow edges as from T_5 to T_2.

Initially, all the text subsections T_1 through T_7 are in memory in some encrypted form (to be described later). Only the entry subsection T_0 is in plaintext. Let us say that the first inter-text-subsection control flow edge to be instantiated is from T_0 to T_3. The following actions are taken at that point.

Transfer control to a "decrypt & jump" module (similar to Aucsmith's) with a key as an argument. The key for the control flow edge from T_0 to T_3 is denoted by $K_{0,3}$. The decrypt & jump action XORs the key $K_{0,3}$ with each subsection. If the text subsections were assigned appropriate initial states, exactly one of the subsections would appear in plaintext. In this case, the text subsection T_3 must have been initialized to $T_3 \oplus K_{0,3}$, which would result in T_3 decrypting into plaintext from XOR with $K_{0,3}$. Each text subsection can either have a magic number or a special nop instruction (or some null instruction such as jump to next location) embedded at the beginning. The decrypt & jump function can check for that special instruction or magic number at the beginning of each text subsection. The text subsection with the special entry attribute is the one the control is transferred to. Note that a branch/jump instruction from T_0 only needed to specify the key $K_{0,3}$ to specify its target (and an offset from the beginning of the target text subsection T_3 to the actual branch target).

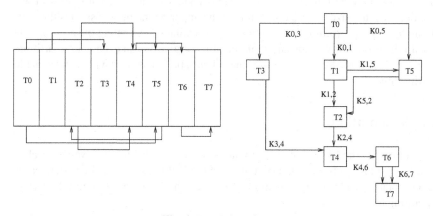

Fig. 6. Text Subsection Layout

The assumption is that each text subsection is designed to be the same size (it need not be as it depends on the key size). Maximum obfuscation is obtained if the key is as large as the text subsections (TS bytes). However, then the keys are large. The keys could be chosen in other granularities as well such as word size (4B) or cache block size (say 16B) or anything else up to TS. This is a tradeoff in memory overhead to maintain the keys versus obfuscation. If the key is chosen to be cache block size, then each cache block sized chunk in a text subsection is XORed with the key.

Key Consistency. Consider the text subsection T_4. It could either be reached from T_0 through T_3 (path $T_0 T_3 T_4$) or with path $T_0 T_1 T_2 T_4$. How should we initially encrypt the subsection T_4? If we make it consistent with the path $T_0 T_3 T_4$ then the initial state ought to be $T_4 \oplus K_{0,3} \oplus K_{3,4}$. Then the control flow edge from T_0 to T_3 would have XORed the initial $T_4 \oplus K_{0,3} \oplus K_{3,4}$ with $K_{0,3}$, and the control flow edge from T_3 to T_4 would have XORed the resulting $T_4 \oplus K_{3,4}$ with $K_{3,4}$ exposing T_4 as desired. But the path $T_0 T_1 T_2 T_4$ requires an initial encoding of $T_4 \oplus K_{0,1} \oplus K_{1,2} \oplus K_{2,4}$. Which one should it be? In general, many more paths could have led from the root node to this node placing many more constraints on the initial encoding. Can we always find consistent set of keys to satisfy all these constraints?

It turns out that the only constraint the keys need to satisfy is that if keys $K_{i_1}, K_{i_2}, \ldots,$ K_{i_k} label the control flow edges along a cycle (undirected induced) then $K_{i_1} \oplus K_{i_2} \oplus \ldots \oplus K_{i_k}$ must be 0! Note that $\oplus$ signifies bit-wise XOR of its arguments. By this token, in the example above, $K_{0,3} \oplus K_{3,4} \oplus K_{2,4} \oplus K_{1,2} \oplus K_{0,1} = 0$ since $T_0, T_3, T_4, T_2, T_1, T_0$ form a cycle. This would imply that $K_{0,3} \oplus K_{3,4} = K_{2,4} \oplus K_{1,2} \oplus K_{0,1}$ and hence these keys can be assigned consistently.

The general strategy would be to choose all the keys but one in a cycle randomly independently. The one key would have to be derived from all the other keys through the cycle constraint.

Text Subsection Partitioning. One of the objectives of the text section partitioning into text subsections could be to minimize the number of cross-subsection control flow edges. This is since each instantiated control flow edge costs a decrypt & jump operation. Hence, a k-mincut of the control flow graph of a text section into k text subsections of more or less equal size (with a constraint on the upper bound on this size) is the optimization objective. If profiling information is also available annotating the control flow edges with the probability of instantiation, the mincut gives us an even better partition. An approach based on Kernighan-Lin mincut heuristic [8] will provide a reasonable cell partitioning.

5   Implementation

Simply monitoring the CFG alone is fairly insecure. This is due to the adversary's ability to perform static analysis on the code itself in the P-Process. There are certain cases where an attacker could nullify functionality within the P-Process through the use of binary editing tools.

5.1 CFG Performance Enhancements

The CFG data structure is typically a large entity. Basics blocks are usually quite small, on average 10 instructions or so. This means that searching the CFG can become a costly task to perform. In the worst case, the identifier could be the last entry in the table, therefore requiring the search to look at every entry in the table. For large tables, a significant performance hit was observed.

One method to help speed up the CFG table search is to implement a caching mechanism. The cache would contain the last N 3-tuples which correspond to the last N identifiers seen, where N is the number of entries the cache can hold. The cache is implemented as a simple FIFO buffer, which holds a trace window for the most recent identifiers that the M-Process has seen. The M-Process will first check the cache to see if an entry is already there. Only if it is not found, will it perform a search on the full CFG. Due to locality of reference inherent in software programs, this improvement increases performance greatly. For ease of implementation, and more notably speed, duplicate entries in the cache are allowed.

Another method to speed up this operation is to sort the CFG table based on increasing P values, and perform a binary search. This method yields a search time of $O(\log N)$, where N is the number of basic blocks. Because this yields a vast improvement, the cache size can be reduced considerably. Earlier, when there were thousands of entries in the CFG table, a fairly large cache yielded good performance gains. However, with binary search, large cache sizes actually yielded poorer performance.

5.2 System Library Flaws

Another possible security hole is in the fact that the M-Process uses system libraries to perform several tasks. The most common of these is the pipe interface of `glibc`. Recall that the attacker has full control of the operating environment. Which means, in Linux, they have full access to the source code. To combat such attacks, it is recommended that proprietary interfaces be written for system library functionality. Pipes and random number generation are the most vulnerable to such attacks.

When an application makes a system call, there is significant overhead that the kernel must handle. First, the call is now in system space, invoking the kernel for assistance. This means that the application must wait for the kernel thread to execute, in order to perform the operation. In the case of reading or writing to a pipe, the kernel must also keep track of which pipes are open, which process is allowed to read/write to a pipe, and memory management.

Initially it was found that sending the unique identifiers at every basic block was significantly slow. To help reduce the performance loss due to system calls, an internal buffer is used. This buffer is used to hold a number of identifiers. Once it has queued up to its limit, it will send them all in one chunk to the M-Process. In much the same fashion, the M-Process will request as many identifiers as its buffer size. The `read()` system call under Linux, is implemented as a "blocking read", meaning that when a process calls the `read()` function, it will be put to sleep until the number of bytes that it requested have arrived.

5.3 Dynamic Identifiers and the CFG Template

At compile time, the CFG is a static representation of the application's control flow. In order to use dynamic identifiers, this particular CFG is only used as a template. At runtime, the M-Process will access each basic block in the P-Process and update the instruction sequence accordingly to insert the new identifier. Then the template is used to map the new unique identifiers creating a new CFG inside the M-Process, which holds the actual values in use. It is not recommended to use a static algorithm to create the unique identifiers at runtime. Using an algorithm to change the unique identifiers is also static in nature, and easily attackable. For our purposes, the use of the system library function rand() was employed.

5.4 M and P Process Coupling

Each P-Process has a corresponding M-Process that will only work with that particular version. Also, the P-Process is stripped down to a state that is not runnable on any architecture or tool. Several key pieces are missing, and it is the job of the M-Process to patch things.

After the executable is created, several pieces are taken out, and inserted as data structures in the M-Process. This allows these key pieces to be guarded by the encryption methods used to guard the M-Process itself.

First, the application's main function is stripped out. This puts the application in a state that is not runnable. The reason for this is that an adversary might be able to perform some analysis on the P-Process, if it is possible to get it to a runnable state which does not use the M-Process. This guarantees that if you try to run the P-Process by itself, it will cause a fatal error and be discarded by the operating system.

When the P-Process is compiled, it is linked against a common set of code that implements the communication functionality with the M-Process. It is feasible that an attack may *sterilize* the communication by modifying these functions. In order to combat such a scenario, these functions are also stripped out, and placed into the M-Process.

Another sanity check that the M-Process will do is to verify that the file size of the P-Process. After the P-Process is compiled, the size of the final executable is known. This value is placed into the M-Process for later use. When the M-Process opens up the P-Process file, the first thing it does is to verify that the sizes match. This means that an adversary cannot insert extra code into the file in the form of attacks. To further enhance this mechanism, a checksum could also be calculated on the P-Process. Some care must be taken, due to the fact that the P-Process goes through several transformations.

5.5 Data Hiding

When the P-Process is started by the M-Process, it needs to know how to communicate its unique identifiers. Namely, it needs the pipe identifier that the M-Process will be listening to. In order to facilitate this process, a placeholder is present in the P-Process' data section. Initially it contains some bogus value, which is of little concern. What is of concern is the flag variable in the P-Process data section that tells the P-Process that the pipe identifier has been fixed. There are several other flags of this nature that the M-Process will change before the P-Process starts.[8]

---

[8] The M-Process uses the Binary File Descriptor (BFD) library to edit the P-Process.

A possible attack scenario would involve editing the default values of some or all of these flags, consequently making the P-Process think the M-Process has correctly patched it, and thus not catching the fact that it has been modified. Such an attack alone would not do much, but it could be a significant building block, when combined with other attack methods.

Data Section Hiding is the process of stripping out the P-Process data section, and placing it inside the M-Process as a data structure. Also remember that the M-Process is protected using encryption techniques. This means that the real data section is only visible for a very short period of time, and depending on the size, may only be partially visible at any given time as well. When the M-Process is in the P-Process fix up phase, it will restore the data section and also modify any values or flags that the P-Process needs for communication.

5.6   Instruction Hiding

A common tamper mechanism is to modify key pieces of executable code to *fake out* the application. One such attack would be to nullify the communication with the M-Process. Because of performance reasons, the communication is one-way. The P-Process only sends data, and the M-Process only process the data it receives. To exploit this fact, one could simply place a return instruction as the first instruction in the function which performs the communication to the M-Process. The function would simply return, and the P-Process would continue running (as would the M-Process). To account for such an attack, the ability to strip out executable code, and place it as data in the M-Process has been added. When the M-Process starts up, it will restore the binary as needed, before it starts the P-Process.

5.7   Benefits of a Hardware Implementation

The key hurdle in an actual implementation is the overall performance of the tamper resistant code. A purely software solution has shown itself to be rather inefficient, thus slowing things down. While several enhancements have been made, such as caching,

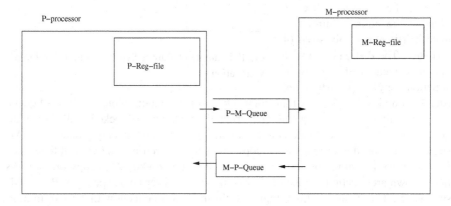

Fig. 7. Microarchitecture to support M-Process

and reduction of system calls, the overall performance can be vastly improved if a hardware based approach is used. We provide some details of such a two-stream decoupled architecture in the following. The verification engine's performance would increase significantly, and the communication could be performed with new instructions, also speeding things up.

There are several advantages from a security standpoint as well. The inner workings of the M-Process could be further hidden "inside the chip". This would protect against buss snooping, and other hardware monitoring types of attacks. Note that the two processes P and M are fairly tightly coupled. Hence if a two instruction stream processor microarchitecture to allow for the synchronization between the two streams is available, the overhead of the P and M process interaction will go down significantly. Large part of the overhead is in the operating system based signaling. All of that would be replaced by hardwired signaling, which would be significantly cheaper. Such a processor microarchitecture for a branch decoupled processor [10] has been proposed and evaluated. Figure 7 shows the elements of such a microarchitecture. The salient parts of this architecture are the synchronization queues P-to-M-Queue and M-to-P-Queue. These queues can be destinations of any instructions to deposit either a synchronization token into this queue, and/or to share the value of a register. The two logical processors, P and M, have their own register files. They can also have their own instruction caches.

Barriers & Synchronization.
Let us assume that the VERIFY step in the P-process is a barrier (The gcc based implementation does not use barrier semantics favoring asynchronous communication instead). The first step would be for the P-stream to deposit into P-to-M queue an identity of the program point to be verified. It could be the address in the memory where the control flow trace to be verified is stored. It could even be the entire control flow trace if it is reasonably sized (4-16 bytes). The P-stream can write into this queue with a copy instruction copyPMQ R3 where reg-

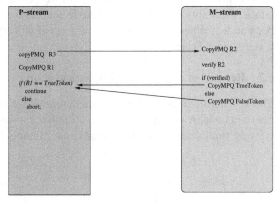

Fig. 8. Example of Barrier Synchronization for Tamper Verification

ister R3 contains the address of the control flow trace. contains Note that P-to-M queue is a first-in-first-out (FIFO) queue. The writer, the P-stream, is blocked /stalled on a full queue, and the consumer/reader, the M-stream, is blocked on an empty queue. The M-stream would need a corresponding copy instruction to retrieve the control flow trace address at the beginning of verification procedure, copy PMQ R2 to copy this address into its own architectural register R2. Note that the register name spaces of P- and M-streams are disjoint and distinct. Figure 8 illustrates this concept with a program fragment. In this example, we have created a barrier for the P-process as well for each verification point. It needs to wait for the result of verification from the M-process through the M-to-P queue. A token is enqueued by the M-process to indicate the status of verification. We have shown a scenario wherein the token is *true* for a successful verification and *false* otherwise. However, the presence of a token itself could be used to indicate a successful instance of verification. In that case, the P-stream blocks indefinitely waiting on a token when the verification fails, a reasonably effective anti-tamper action.

In order to maintain program semantics, the relative order of enqueuing actions in one stream ought to be the same as the relative order of the corresponding dequeuing actions in the other stream. Maintaining this invariant is relatively straightforward for the anti-tamper verification.

This architecture makes the cost of interprocess communication, which dominates when this communication is implemented as Unix pipes, fairly insignificant (order of a 1-4 processor) cycles. We are implementing such a decoupled architecture on top of our branch decoupled architecture [10] simulator to assess its performance benefits. Based on our experience with branch decoupling, we expect the overhead of anti-tamper to be below 5% with a decoupled processor implementation.

6 Performance Results

The following data shows performance results obtained with the Linux *time* function[9]. The time function takes a program as its argument, and measures the program's execution time. It is only an approximation due to the inaccurate modeling of the system mechanism (interrupts) to schedule the measurement events. However, even these imprecise measurements suffice from a comparative point of view. The results are parametrized by the pipe buffer size, and the cache size. The pipe buffer size effects the number of system calls that are needed for communication with the M-Process. The cache size is a trade off between search time overhead in the CFG table and in the cache. Once the cache gets too big, it itself constitutes a performance bottleneck.

Table 1 shows the execution time results for the well known compression utility, gzip. gzip-1.2.4 in particular was used. Table 2 shows the results for a network simulator, which simulates a prioritized version of the MPCP protocol. The simulation length was set at 0.10 seconds.

As is evident, the performance without the blocked control trace verification and CFG caching enhancements is significantly bad. The system time was significantly decreased by lowering the number of system calls (which were mostly needed for the pipe communication). A custom communication method, if correctly designed, could yield even better performance. The user execution time was decreased by implementing an identifier cache, and by binary search through a sorted CFG table.

These performance measures are based on applications which are computationally intensive programs such as gzip. For every OS allocated CPU timeslice, these programs use almost all of it. In applications that have inherent *sleep* times, such as waiting for user I/O, semaphores, or network I/O, performance degradation is minimal.

---

[9] Test system: 2.4Ghz Athlon, 512MB RAM, 266MHz system bus.

Table 1. Performance results using gzip on a 450kB file

orig. buff.	orig. cache	Real	User	Sys
		0.131s	0.030s	0.000s
1	0	49.000s	32.810s	5.930s
1	1	44.307s	28.980s	5.530s
1	2	44.331s	28.480s	5.850s
1	4	31.714s	16.170s	5.750s
1	8	28.564s	12.780s	7.580s
1	16	25.322s	9.260s	6.880s
1	32	19.874s	3.240s	6.380s
1	64	20.140s	3.530s	6.030s
1	128	21.216s	5.250s	6.670s
2	0	34.444s	31.620s	0.130s
4	0	32.941s	31.680s	0.070s
8	0	32.414s	31.650s	0.080s
16	0	32.941s	31.680s	0.070s
32	0	32.048s	31.620s	0.050s
32	32	1.204s	0.930s	0.040s

Table 2. Performance results using mpcp_sim for a .1 second simulation

orig. buff.	orig. cache	Real	User	Sys
		0.716s	0.120s	0.010s
1	0	19.914s	2.640s	6.470s
1	1	19.444s	2.660s	6.070s
1	2	19.831s	2.660s	6.220s
1	4	19.600s	2.370s	6.220s
1	8	19.630s	2.820s	6.480s
1	16	18.698s	2.650s	5.980s
1	32	18.859s	2.370s	6.520s
1	64	18.952s	2.570s	6.020s
1	128	19.415s	2.650s	7.180s
2	0	10.896s	1.670s	3.170s
4	0	6.459s	1.190s	1.750s
8	0	4.083s	1.030s	0.790s
16	0	2.973s	0.900s	0.430s
32	0	2.153s	0.840s	0.190s
64	0	1.788s	0.710s	0.170s
128	0	1.626s	0.730s	0.090s
256	0	1.570s	0.730s	0.080s
128	32	1.253s	0.350s	0.040s
256	32	1.179s	0.360s	0.000s

We use a clone of a well known game, *Breakout* to test performance on the general class of user interaction programs. This game is a good test of performance because of not only the user interaction, but also due to the fact that it needs CPU time consistently to display the constantly moving ball. Results showed no jitter in either the ball movement, or the paddle movement as a result of dynamic monitoring of the control flow. For such programs, the quality of the user interaction is the ultimate test of the acceptable performance overhead. It appears as if the proposed anti-tamper technique is more than acceptable for such programs.

Gcalc is a simple calculator written for the Linux Gnome desktop environment, also known as Galculator, which uses the GTK graphics libraries. This type of application involves relatively little user interaction. Most of the time, the application is sleeping, waiting for input from the user. There was no distinguishable difference in the anti-tamper version of Gcalculator from the original one.

7   Conclusions

We proposed a novel two-process based anti-tamper scheme, wherein a monitoring process monitors the control flow integrity of the monitored process constantly. We implemented such a scheme with gcc which compiles into two such co-processes: one for monitoring and one for the original monitored program. We verified empirically that the performance overhead for user interaction dominated programs is not even observable.

For the CPU dominated programs, the implementation can be performed at a variety of axes to trade anti-tamper degree with efficiency. We also propose a two-instruction stream processor microarchitecture to perform the same task with much higher efficiency and more stealth.

Note that such CFG verification can be viewed as one form of proof carrying code [9] wherein the proof is the control flow integrity table.

References

1. Aucsmith, David. "Tamper Resistant Software: An Implementation". *Proceedings of the First International Workshop on Information Hiding*, 1996
2. Christian Collberg and Clack Thomborson. Watermarking, tamper-proofing, and obfuscation - tools for software protection, 2000.
3. Ge Jun. "Software Obfuscation with Program Permutation". *M.S. Thesis*, Dept. of Computer Science, Iowa State University, Ames, IA, 2004.
4. O. Goloubeva, M. Rebaudengo, M. Sonza Reorda, M. Violante. "Soft-error Detection Using Control Flow Assertions". *Politecnico di Torino, Dipartimento di Automatica e Informatica*, Torino, Italy 2003
5. B. Horne, L. Matheson, C. Sheehan, and R. Tarjan, "Dynamic Self-Checking Techniques for Improved Tamper Resistance," *ACM Workshop on Security and Privacy in Digital Rights Management*, 2002
6. D. Lie, C. Thekkath, M. Mitchell, P. Lincoln, D. Boneh, J. Mitchell, and M. Horowitz. Architectural support for copy and tamper resistant software, 2000.
7. Cullen Linn, Saumya Debray, and John Kececioglu, Enhancing Software Tamper-Resistance via Stealthy Address Computations. In *Proceedings of 19th Annual Computer Security Applications Conference (ACSAC 2003)*, Decemeber 2003.
8. Brian W. Kernighan and S. Lin. An efficient heuristic procedure for partitioning graphs. *Bell System Technical Journal*, 49:291–307, 1970.
9. George C. Necula. Proof-carrying code. In *Conference Record of POPL '97: The 24th ACM SIGPLAN-SIGACT Symposium on Principles of Programming Languages*, pages 106–119, Paris, France, 1997.
10. Akhilesh Tyagi. Branch Decoupled Architectures. In *Proc. of Workshop on Interaction between Compilers and Computer Architectures at 3rd Int'l Symp. on High-Performance Computer Architecture*, Feb 1997.
11. Ramarathnam Venkatesan, Vijay V. Vazirani, and Saurabh Sinha. A graph theoretic approach to software watermarking. In *Information Hiding*, pages 157–168, 2001.
12. C. Wang, J. Hill, J. Knight, and J. Davidson. "Software Tamper Resistance: Obstructing Static analysis of Programs". *Technical Report CS2000-12*, Department of Computer Science, University of Virginia, 2000

Call Tree Transformation for Program Obfuscation and Copy Protection

Valery Pryamikov

Harper Security Consulting AS, Vestre Rosten 81, 7075, Tiller, Norway
valery@harper.no
http://www.harper.no/valery

Abstract. In this paper we propose a new scheme for software obfuscation and license protection that is based on an original transformation of the program's call tree. The idea is based on the observation of similarities between a program's call tree and Context Free Grammars. First, this paper proposes a practical technique for applying well studied LALR methodologies to transforming a program's call tree. Second, we suggest methods of effective binding of the transformed program to the program's installation site. Finally, we note that the given scheme provides us with a series of difficult to remove unique identifications integrally embedded into the transformed programs that could be used for software watermarking purposes.

Keywords: Software Obfuscation, Software Copy Protection, Software Watermarking.

1 Introduction

Intellectual Property Protection (IPP) related to software distribution and production is a longstanding problem. Early works in that area were mainly focused on copy protection. For examples of early work, see [9] where the author proposes some technical means of software copy protection. IPP problems related to reverse engineering and de-compilation were not considered to be as important at the time of Gosler's writing due to perceived complexity of reverse engineering of large binary-compiled programs. However, the problems of program protection against reverse engineering and de-compilation became increasingly more important and anticipated since the invention of Architecture Neutral Distribution Format (ANDF) and Virtual Execution Environment (VEE) such as Xerox-PARC's Smalltalk, Sun's Java and Microsoft's .Net. One of the major reasons for that change is that VEE/Virtual Machine (VM) Architecture Independency usually requires inclusion of rich metadata for the VEE/VM. Presence of rich metadata allows much easier de-compilation with higher than ever readability of reverse-engineered code.

In this paper we propose a new software obfuscation and copy protection scheme that is based on an original idea of program call tree transformation. We believe that the presented scheme opens a new venue for solving problems related to Software IPP.

A series of excellent theoretical and practical work in area of general Software IPP was published during the last decade. The most relevant preceding works are listed in

R. Safavi-Naini and M. Yung (Eds.): DRMTICS 2005, LNCS 3919, pp. 164–179, 2006.
© Springer-Verlag Berlin Heidelberg 2006

the references section. In the remaining part of our introduction we want to emphasize the most important publications. Among these are: [5] with the first systematic classification of known obfuscating transformations, [7], [6], [16] and [18] which describes techniques that either are used or could be effectively used for augmenting the software protection framework presented in this paper.

An elegant mathematical framework studying security aspects of obfuscating transformation was introduced by [1], where authors prove the existence of classes of unobfuscatable functions. Also note a couple of later mathematical works with positive results of obfuscation [14] and [19] using the mathematical framework introduced by [1].

Context Free Grammars, LR and LALR Parsers, Call Graphs

The concept of Context Free Grammars (CFG) was first introduced by Noam Chomsky in his study of natural languages and syntactic structures. The earliest publications concerning CFG are dated to 1957-1959 with the introduction of CFG and their application to computer programming languages and formal systems. The most significant contribution to the study of CFG and parsers was done by A.V. Aho, F.L. DeRemer, J.C. Earley, D.E. Knuth and J.D. Ullman. LALR parsers were introduced by F.L. DeRemer. For further references and treatments on GFG we would refer to the reference [8].

For an account of the study of Call Graph analysis applicable to software profiling refer to works of S.L. Graham, P.B. Kessler, D. Grove and J.R. Larus. Also note [13] which suggests the use of Context Free Grammars for purposes of program profiling and introduces the notion of Whole Program Path. Other related works in the area of Program Path profiling includes publications by Melski, Ammonds, Larus, Andler and others.

Scope of Writing and Remarks

In this paper we only present an application of the algorithm to the simplest form of a call tree. Even so, the presented algorithm works well with any other type of Call Graph.

We will not discuss any details of the generation of LR(k)/LALR(1) automaton, state tables, lookup/lookahead tables but refer to related work listed in the references section.

We refer to [5] for a definition of obfuscation transformation.

For software copy protection we limit our scheme to the following:

- illegal program execution shall result in undefined random behavior;
- correct program execution shall only be guaranteed when the protected program is running in a designated environment.

The methods of identification of the program installation site, protection of the delivery path of the identification data or methods of processing of identification data are out of scope for this paper.

In this paper we will not provide any details of the application of the algorithm to exception handling; virtual methods, events and delegates; multithreading; and other advanced elements of the program control flow graphs. However we strongly believe that all mentioned programming constructs could be properly handled by an enhanced version of the presented algorithm.

2 Idea

A Context Free Grammar (**CFG**) is a formal grammar in which every production rule is of the form $A \rightarrow w$ where A is a non-terminal symbol and w is a string consisting of terminals and/or non-terminals.

CFG parsers could be implemented in several different ways, but the most usual ways are:

- a recursive descent parser – which could be thought of as a traditional procedural parser with the shape of the call tree quite closely reflecting the shape of the CFG;
- an LALR parser driver routine relying on a set of state, transition and lookahead tables with shallow and flat-shaped call tree structure;

Both are implementation of the same algorithm - «Parser», but the former implementation tends to be easier to understanding and reverse engineering than the latter.

From the other side, it's quite intuitive that CFG could be effectively used for representing a call tree; there are known works in the area of program profiling that relies on a CFG representation of a program call tree – see for example [13].

This makes us believe that we should be able to apply techniques found in LALR parsers for automatic generation of alternative representations of a program's call tree, which should provide us with an alternative representation of a program's algorithm and strong obfuscation of the source program.

In this paper we propose an obfuscation algorithm that combines several earlier ideas from C. Collberg, C. Thomborson and C. Wang[1] with original transformations of the program call tree that uses the LALR interpretation of the control flow. The algorithm also relies on obfuscation-time scrambling and runtime descrambling of LALR tables for achieving resilience against automatic de-obfuscation tools and strong copy protection. As an extra benefit, it also allows us to apply difficult to remove one-way transformations of the input alphabet, which could be useful for software watermarking purposes. The overall algorithm is:

2.1) create CFG lexer by
    a)   merging all non-terminal methods of the original call tree together
        i)   by merging their argument arrays;
        ii) flattening the Control Flow Graph by techniques similar to [18]; and
        iii) merging their Control Flow Graphs together;
    b)   replacing the call-method instructions with return of the call-site index[2];
2.2) apply one-way transformation/(permutation) to the input alphabet from step 2.1.b) for watermarking purposes;

---

[1] Esp. see [5], [6], [7], [16], [17] and [18].
[2] Call-site indexes are used as an input alphabet for the CFG representation of the Call Tree.

2.3) generate an LALR driver routine that embeds terminal methods of the original call tree as CFG reduce actions;

2.4) scramble the LALR state, transition and lookahead tables by
- a) unstructuring and merging them together, and
- b) applying a set of transformations that
  - i) use identification of program installation site as key material/seed; and
  - ii) could be compensated/descrambled at runtime.

As a result of the application of the algorithm for transforming a source program, the original call tree becomes encoded and emulated by the LALR parse stack, which is controlled by the LALR state, transition and lookahead tables. Even minor problems during a runtime descrambling of these tables would lead to unpredictable results during a program execution. If a runtime descrambling affects a substantial part of LALR tables then it should provide a very strong copy protection because the emulated call-tree will be unusable without access to the designated installation site id[3].

Another major advantage of this algorithm is its strong obfuscation property that combines several well known obfuscation techniques due to C. Collberg, C. Thomborson and C. Wang with the original strong obfuscation of an inter-procedural control flow by flattening and reversing the actual call tree while relying on an LALR parsing for an interpretation of the logical call tree.

In cases when copy protection is considered to be a major goal, and because an LALR interpretation of the original call tree induces some performance hit to each interpreted method call; we suggest that often called, but trivial methods[4] should be excluded from a call tree CFG construction (as we will demonstrate in the following introductory example).

A strong software watermarking property comes as a convenient side-effect due to the fact that generation of an LALR parser is independent from numeric values assigned to an input alphabet as long as they stay in synch with a source CFG. We believe that the task of removing these watermarks[5] should be at least as difficult as the task of recovering the CFG (and recovering the original program call tree).

One of our design goals for the protection scheme presented in this paper was an attempt to ensure that recovering CFG/(the original call tree) from a generated LALR presentation of the call tree is indeed a difficult task; however, all questions concerning complexity of this problem is left for further study.

3 Introductory Example and Preprocessing Steps

Here we want to outline an idea of a practical implementation of the suggested scheme. For explanatory reasons we will present it on a minimal sample program. However, we believe this scheme is applicable to most real-life programs with just some adjustments/improvements. We will discuss security, performance and related considerations later in this paper.

---

[3] which we use as a keying material for scrambling/descrambling of LALR tables;

[4] such as property setters and getters;

[5] or switching from one permutation of an input alphabet to another permutation;

Sample Pseudo-code

During the first step we will prepare an input alphabet for our call tree CFG Parser by enumerating call sites and segments of a Control Flow Graph flattened with Wang's technique.

See Figure 1 for the pseudo-code of our sample program.

```
void Main() {
        A();
        B(message1);
}
int A()   {
        int i = C();
        while (i < D()) {
                A(); i++;
        }
        E(message2);
        return i;
}
void B(string message)   {
        F();//F will be excluded from Call-Tree CFG
        E(message);
}
int C() { //do some calculations here.
        return calculationResults;
}
int D() { //D will be excluded from Call-Tree CFG
        return --RemainingLoops;
}
void E(string message) {
        G();//G will be excluded from Call-Tree CFG
        print(message);
}
```

Fig. 1. Source Code

Preprocessing of Call Tree

Let's start with building the program call tree and preparing a set of indexes that will be used as an input alphabet for our call tree CFG parser.

3.1. Build a call tree by enumerating call sites and ignoring all methods external to the analyzed assembly (Figure 2);
3.2. Filter out trivial but often called methods[6]:
3.3. Mark all leafs (nodes without children):
3.4. Mark all joints (nodes that have at least one child):
3.5. Mark all recursive functions:
3.6. Enumerate call sites[7] (Figure 3).

---

[6] These methods will be treated the same way as methods external to the analyzed program.
[7] i.e. associate sequential numbers {1,2,3...} with points of calling functions on leafs (3.3) , joints (3.4) and recursive (3.5).

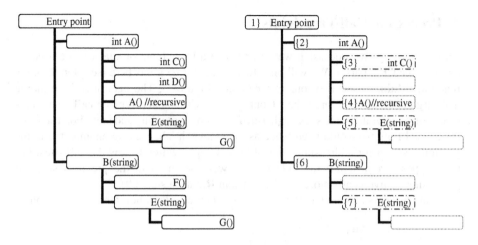

Fig. 2. Initial Call Tree   **Fig. 3.** Enumerated Call Sites

Application of our algorithm requires a separation of program segments surrounding the enumerated call sites. We will proceed by flattening the control flow graphs in a couple of following steps.

3.7. All loops containing at least one enumerated call site[8] should be dismantled with an algorithm such as [16]/[18] – see Figure 4.

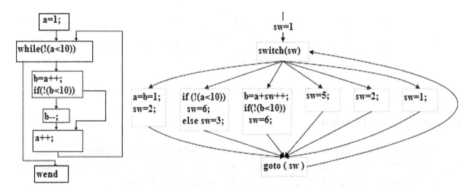

Fig. 4. Dismantling Cycles [18]

3.8. Enumerate fragments of dismantled cycles (switch labels from step 3.7);
3.9. Store the first index unused by an enumeration during steps 3.6 and 3.8 in a variable **R**. The stored value will be used for generating unique indexes required for the implementation of the CFG lexer function several steps later.

---

[8] Note that the source code from Figure 1 contains one cycle inside function A that requires dismantling.

4 Processing Call Tree Joints

During this stage of processing we will prepare a lexer function that will be used by our call tree CFG parser. We will only focus on call tree joints here (see step 3.4), i.e. functions **Main**, **A** and **B** of our sample code (Figure 1). The main idea is to merge their argument arrays; merge their Control Flow Graphs and replace **call** statements inside of enumerated call sites with **return** of corresponding indexes. For retaining the control flow we would need twice as many switch labels as we enumerated in the previous section for addressing Control Flow Graphs which follow the call sites. For that purpose we will use the indexes that were not used in the previous stage of processing (conveniently stored in the constant **R** during step 3.9).

Figure 5 shows an annotated version of the source code of non-terminal functions.

```
void Main() { //• entrypoint {1}
  A(); //• call site {2}
  B(message1); //• call site {6}; argB_1
}
int A() { //• return value A_ret
  int i = //• A_I_loc;
    C();//• call site {3}; C_ret;
  while (i < D()) //• loop criteria {8}
  { //• loop body {9}
    A(); //• call site {4}
    i++;
  } //• loop {10}
  E(message2); //• call site {5}; argE_1
  return i;
}
void B(string msg)//• argument argB_1
{ //• local storage argB_1_loc
  F(); //F will be excluded from Call-Tree CFG
  E(msg); //• call site {7}; argE_1
}
```

Fig. 5. Annotated Source Code

Preparing Lexer Function

4.1. Create a new function **int yylex** containing a single switch statement;
4.2. Arguments and return values of leafs and joints should be placed in a container (for example an array) which is accessible by callers of **yylex**;
4.3. Local variables that are used across any of enumerated points should be placed in the same container as in 4.2;
4.4. A reference to the container variable from the step 4.2 could be passed as a function parameter to **yylex**;
4.5. Split the source (Figure 5) on Control Flow Graph fragments (code between enumerated points);
4.6. Place all fragments from the step 4.5 into the switch statement inside **yylex**. Use the fragment indexes as case labels;

4.7. If a function inside an enumerated call-site is expecting any arguments – update correspondent arguments in the container from step 4.2 just above the call-site;

4.8. Replace the function-call inside the enumerated call-sites with return of the call site index;

4.9. Add **R** cases with the code that follows the call-sites that we replaced with return during step 4.8;

The resulting **yylex** function with the explanatory annotations is shown in Figure 6.

```
int yylex(object[] args) {
  switch (currentPosition) {
    case 1: return 2; //Main entry point; calls function A()
    case 2: return 3; //A entry point; calls function C()
    case R+2:args[argB_1]=message1; // argument to B();
      return 6; //call function B();
    case R+3:args[A_I_loc]=args[C_ret];
      // i ← return from C();
      goto case 8; //go to loop criteria;
    case 4: goto case 2; //A - recursive call; goto A's entry point
    case R+4:goto case R+9; //A returns; continue loop.
    case R+5:args[A_ret]=args[A_I_loc];
      //return from E(); update A's retval
      break; //exit A;
    case 6:args[argB_1_loc]=args[argB_1];
      //B's entry point; argument → local storage
      F(); args[argE_1]=args[argB_1_loc]; //arg. to E();
      return 7; //calls E();
    case R+6:break;//return from B(); exit Main
    case R+7:break;//return from E(); exit B();
    case 8: //loop condition
      if (args[A_I_loc] < D())
        goto case 9; //go to loop body;
      else
        goto case R+10;//exit loop
    case 9: return 4; //calls A() - recursive;
    case R+9:args[A_I_loc]++;//increment loop variable
      goto case 10; //go to loop;
    case 10: goto case 8; // go to loop criteria;
    case R+10:args[argE_1]=message2; //argument to E();
      return 5; //calls E()
  }
  return 0; ///(end-of-branch/reduce);
}
```

Fig. 6. The annotated pseudo-code of the yylex function

5 CFG and LALR Transformation of Call Tree

In this section we will construct a Context Free Grammar over a set of terminal symbols $V_T \subseteq T$, where T is a set of lexical tokens/values returned by the **yylex** function which we built in the previous section. Our CFG will be representing the original call tree. After that we will build an LALR parser function that will be emulating the original call tree by means of an internal parse stack. Finally, we will build first the version of the obfuscated program consisting of our LALR parser and the **yylex** from the previous section.

We will not elaborate on algorithms used by LALR parser generators or LALR parser driver routines, but instead we will refer to work of F. L. DeRemer, S. C. Johnson, R. Corbett and the related literature listed in the reference section (see [8]), as well as source codes of open source implementations of LALR parsers[9].

The LALR parser driver routine used in our scheme should ensure that updates of the internal parse stack position will be correctly reflected in the **currentPosition** variable that we used in the **yylex** function as a switch control variable (see Figure 6).

Additionally, the leaf functions **C** and **E** (Figure 1) will be inlined in the reduce actions of our CFG.

In Figure 7 is a raw sketch of a grammar definition of our call tree.

```
Main: BranchA BranchB ⊥;
A_1: A C        {inline C;};
A_2: A_1 A      {/*recursive A()*/;}
 | A_2 A        {/*recursive A()*/;}

 | A_2 ⊥;
A_3: A_2 E      {inline E;};

BranchA: A_3 ⊥;
B_1: B E        {inline E;};

BranchB: B_1 ⊥;
```

Fig. 7. Call Tree Grammar Definition

5.1. Use a grammar definition to generate an LALR parser driver routine that is also updating the **currentPosition** variable of the **yylex** function;

5.2. The leaf functions (**C** and **E**) should be inlined as reduce-actions of the LALR Parse function by using any standard inlining method. They also require the use of the container from the step 4.2 for retrieving parameters and storing return values.

Figure 8 shows the relevant fragments of the **yyparse** function that illustrates the call of **yylex** and the inlining of reduce-actions. The rest of logic of the LALR parser driver routine is omitted from Figure 8.

---

[9] Such as YACC/BYACC and BISON.

```
int yyparse() {
  object[] yyargs;
  //...intialize yyargs here
  . . .
  //...LALR logic here
  pcyytoken=yylex(yyargs);
  //...LALR logic here
  . . .
   switch (m)  { /*actions associated with grammar rules*/
      case 3: { //do some calculations here.
       yyargs[C_ret] = calculationResults;
       //return calculations result
       } break;
      case 5: //falls through
      case 7: {
       G(); //G is often called method which we excluded from CFG
       print(yyargs[argE_1]); //prints message sent in parameter
      } break;
       . . .    }
  goto enstack; }
```

Fig. 8. Fragments of LALR Parse pseudo-code

Now we are ready to create the first obfuscated version of our program that uses the LALR call tree obfuscation technique.

5.3. Our LALR obfuscated program will be created by putting together:

a. **yylex** (generated during steps 4.1—4.9);
b. **yyparse** (generated during steps 5.1—5.2), which calls **yylex** (see a. above);
c. the entry point function which sets the **currentPosition** to 1 and calls **yyparse** (see b. above).

If we take another look at our transformation, it essentially means that we have reversed and flattened the call tree, so that:

– all leaf functions from the lowest level of the call tree are now moved into a single **yyparse** function at the top of the modified call tree;
– all other functions, that were directly or indirectly calling the former leaf functions (see above), are now moved to a single leaf function **yylex** (regardless of their original call tree position).

The functionality of the original program is preserved by moving the original call tree into the parse stack of an LALR parser.

The LALR Parse stack is controlled by the interpretation of the state, lookup and lookahead tables. Figure 9 shows a sample of the LALR tables generated by YACC.

```
const int yyact[] = {
      5,         0,         0,         4,         8,         3,        17,         8,
      7,         9,         6,         0,         9,         8,         7,         1,
      6,         0,         9,        10,        11,        12,        13,        14,
     15,        16,         0,         0,         0,         0,         0,         0,
...
};
const int yypact[] = {
    -40,       -29,     -4096,       -40,       -40,       -40,       -40,       -40,
    -40,       -40,     -4096,     -4096,       -35,       -38,       -38,     -4096,
  -4096,     -4096,
};
const int yypgo[] = {
      0,        15,
};
const int yyr1[] = {
      0,         1,         1,         1,         1,         1,         1,         1,
      1,
};
const int yyr2[] = {
      0,         1,         2,         2,         3,         3,         3,         3,
      3,
};
const int yychk[] = {
  -4096,        -1,       257,        45,        43,        40,        45,        43,
     42,        47,        -1,        -1,        -1,        -1,        -1,        -1,
     -1,        41,
};
```

Fig. 9. The state, lookup and lookahead LALR tables generated by YACC

6   Protecting LALR Tables and Adding Copy Protection

The main problem with the LALR tables shown in Figure 9 is that their well defined structure could be used for recovering the source CFG with the help of the specially designed programs. Fortunately, we believe that there are ways of protecting LALR tables from such a threat. In fact, there are known techniques of arrays obfuscations that could be used for such purpose, as for example Array manipulations and String Encoding transformations by C. Collberg and C. Thomborson [7].

Additionally, if we derive a transformation key[10] from some unique installation site ID, then it will also provide us with a very efficient copy protection, because if the LALR tables only could be recovered in the presence of an unique installation site ID, then any attempt to run such a program on a different installation site would lead to distorted LALR tables, a corrupt call tree and completely unpredictable results. Unfortunately, a simple derivation of a symmetric encryption key from an installation side ID; encrypting LALR tables during obfuscation time and decrypting them during runtime could only provide a marginal protection (if any at all). The latter is due to the simple fact that when a complete LALR table structure is decrypted in a process memory it immediately becomes a subject to various attacks including simple dumping of decrypted LALR tables and running analysis of the memory dump.

Therefore, we would require a complex set of counter-measures that includes the obfuscation of the tables structure; use of various table access obfuscation techniques,

---

[10] We will use it for scrambling of the LALR tables.

such as added indirection layers, alias-tables and alias rotations; ensuring that only small, immediately required parts of LALR tables be descrambled at any given moment in time, while the rest of this structure should be kept protected. Another important factor to ensure is that it should be difficult to distinguish scrambled parts of the tables from the descrambled parts. Reasonable candidates of our protection framework could be based on the ideas from [14] where authors show how to obfuscate a complex access control functionality, and demonstrate strong access obfuscation properties of regular expressions and related functions. Another protection measure could be modeled on unstructured LALR tables and/or alias-tables like expander graphs and using bytes of a cryptographic hash of an installation site id for choosing walk edges. The expanding property of the graph implies (via a non-trivial proof) that the vertices along random walks on an expander have surprisingly strong random properties [2]. We can also XOR bytes along the walking path with another result of cryptographic hash as a part of a scrambling and descrambling processes.

In other words our goals are:

- to scramble LALR tables at obfuscation-time by using some function dependent on an installation site id;
- a periodic descramble of required parts of these tables at runtime;
- ensure that descrambling of these tables without having access to a corresponding installation site id is a difficult task, while the runtime descrambling of these tables only has an insignificant impact on performance.

Draft Description

6.1. We need to start with expanding and unstructuring tables, e.g. merging them into a single array and applying an initial permutation that could be matched by one or more layers of an added indirection with a help of alias tables (or similar) [7].

6.2. A similar set of transformations could be applied to both LALR tables and alias tables.

6.3. Addressing subsets of these tables should expose strong access obfuscation properties and pseudo-random properties. We can:

- model unstructured tables as an expander graph and use bits from PRF(id ‖ hour)[11] for choosing the walk edges;
- use a regular expression over random variables that are mappings of (possibly unadjusted) bytes of PRF(id ‖ hour), where id should be some unique identification of a program installation site and PRF could be a cryptographic hash function (let say SHA-1).

6.4. Addressed subsets could be used with different transformations that are efficiently computed at runtime, such as:

- removing/inserting addressed subsets;
- XOR-ing two (or more) addressed subsets together;

---

[11] Implementation of the algorithm will use a cryptographic hash function as a practical substitution of PRF.

- Using a modular arithmetic with bytes of addressed subsets at runtime and an inverse modular arithmetic at obfuscation-time;
- other suitable transformations.

6.5. Transformations listed in the previous step could be executed by a function running on a separate execution thread and also executed at the startup of a protected program.

Processing Results

- If descrambling of relevant parts of LALR tables was incorrect, it will severely affect the ability of the generated LALR parser to depict a correct shape of the original call tree. This will lead to unpredictable results of the program execution.
- Correct descrambling of the relevant parts of the LALR tables and the alias-rotation tables will only be guaranteed in the presence of the correct installation site id.
- We believe that LALR tables obfuscated and scrambled this way will provide an efficient protection against attempts of recovering the source CFG.

7 Adding Watermarks

If we look back at our choice of the input alphabet (steps 3.6—4.9) it's clear that we only require unique indexes and our choice of sequential numbers is arbitrary, supported only by convenience and explanatory reasons. A generation of the LALR parser is independent from the numeric indexes assigned to the input alphabet as long as indexes stay in synch with the source CFG. We can add an extra step with a permutation of the input alphabet before we generate the **yylex** and the **yyparse**.

Here is a draft description of the algorithm:

7.1. put all indexes (call sites, dismantled cycles fragments and all previous indexes incremented by **R**) into an array or a table;

7.2. the table from the previous step (7.1) could be augmented with aliases (e.g. 23 aliases for each index so that we can cycle indexes once per hour);

7.3. generate a random encryption key and use it to encrypt the table;

7.4. in cases when a permuted input alphabet is intended for watermarking purposes – store the encryption key generated in the previous step together with the original tables from step 7.1. Otherwise, if a post-identification of the watermark is not required, the encryption key generated in step 7.3 simply could be destroyed;

7.5. map each number in the original table to the corresponding position in the encrypted table and use the numbers from the encrypted table in the body of the protected program;

7.6. cases of the switch statement could be sorted in an ascending or descending order or randomized;

7.7. a return of indexes from the **yyparse** function could be replaced with a return of elements of an indexed (rotated) collection of input alphabet aliases (step 7.2);

7.8. excessive cases with a slightly modified/buggy code could be randomly placed in the switch body of the **yylex** and **yyparse** functions;

7.9. excessive cases could be combined with aliases to behave as a buggy code before they are selected by the alias scheduler;

7.10. the alias scheduler could be implemented by the same routine that descrambles parts of the LALR tables (step 6.5).

Processing Results

- The permuted input alphabet becomes an integral part of the **yylex** and **yyparse** functions as well as the state, lookup and lookahead tables generated by our obfuscating transformation.
- We believe that replacing a whole permuted input alphabet with another permutation is as a difficult task as a task of recovering a source CFG.
- Partial replacements of just a few symbols from an input alphabet could be easily matched by using "tree proximity" measurements for a detection of watermarks.

8 Performance Impact and Final Remarks

It is clear that the call tree emulated by the parse stack of the **yyparse** routine would not provide as a good performance as a direct function call. However, we believe that by adjusting how many often-called-but-trivial methods shall be excluded from the transformation, it is possible to achieve a strong-enough protection without affecting an overall performance of the protected program. The latter is especially true when concerning interactive applications, where a performance impact could be made completely unnoticeable. Very preliminary results of our tests show that occasional fluctuations of an execution environment (such as window scroll, thread context switch, processor speed steps, auxiliary inputs, such as mouse movement and others) could have a greater effect on the performance than the emulation of a call tree by the parse stack of the **yyparse** function. We have run our tests on three different computer configurations – Intel Centrino with Pentium M 1.6 MHz/1 GB; Dual Pentium 4 3.2 MHz / 2 GB and Intel Pentium 4 Celeron 2.2 MHz/512MB; all running Windows XP. All three computers used for tests didn't show a performance difference between the original and the transformed programs. Figure 10 shows results of several runs of the test program on the Pentium M computer. The test program source code could be found on the author's web page [20].

Source.exe /noninteractive	Transformed.exe /noninteractive
completed in 547.90 ms.	completed in 558.25 ms.
completed in 557.24 ms.	completed in 555.48 ms.
completed in 550.65 ms.	completed in 554.38 ms.
completed in 554.61 ms.	completed in 549.05 ms.

Fig. 10. Sample results of performance test on the Pentium M 1.6/1GB computer

Even so the results of our test may appear surprising, there is a simple explanation of the results. The percentage of a processing time that a normal program spends on transforming a control flow between different functions is usually very small when compared to the processing time used for actual calculations and/or calling external functions. For purposes of a closer emulation of a normal processing behavior of interactive programs, we avoided adding calls to an LALR emulated functions from tight loops. Therefore an LALR emulation of the call tree has only affected a very small (by percentage of execution time) part of the program and the absolute performance impact happened to be lesser than effects of occasional fluctuations of the execution environment. We want to note that the results of our performance test are very preliminary for drawing conclusions about a performance impact on real life programs. A bigger size of a call tree and a bigger size of LALR tables are the two most obvious factors that could affect a performance. We are very optimistic in our expectations, however an additional study is required for presenting more accurate estimates of a performance impact and providing recommendations for minimizing it for different classes of real life applications.

Finally, we want to note that even a simple examination of the source code of our sample test application appears to be quite reassuring about obfuscation properties of the suggested transformation. Additionally, other known methods of a program and data obfuscation could be effectively used in a combination with our scheme for augmenting resilience and potency of the obfuscation transformation proposed in this paper.

Acknowledgements. The author would like to thank Dr. Christian Collberg for his invaluable help on this paper.

References

1. Boaz Barak, Oded Goldreich, Russell Impagliazzo, Steven Rudich, Amit Sahai, Sali Vadhan, Ke Yang. On the (im)possibility of obfuscating programs. In Proceedings of CRYPTO 2001.
2. N. Biggs. Algebraic graph theory, 2nd ed., Cambridge University Press, 1994. ISBN 0-521-45897-8.
3. Christian Collberg, Clark Thomborson. Watermarking, tamper-proofing and obfuscation – tools for software protection. Technical Report TR00-03, The Department of Computer Science, University of Arizona, February 2000.
4. Christian Collberg, Clark Thomborson. Watermarking, tamper-proofing and obfuscation – tools for software protection. IEEE Transactions on software engineering, vol.28, No.8, August 2002.
5. Christian Collberg, Clark Thomborson, Douglas Low. A Taxonomy of Obfuscating Transformations. Technical Report 148, Department of Computer Science, University of Auckland. July 1997.
6. Christian Collberg, Clark Thomborson, Douglas Low. Manufacturing Cheap, Resilient, and Stealthy Opaque Constructs. Principles of Programming Languages 1998, POPL'98, January 1988.
7. Christian Collberg, Clark Thomborson, Douglas Low. Breaking Abstractions and Unstructuring Data Structures. IEEE International Conference on Computer Languages, May 1998.
8. A.V. Aho, R. Sethi and J.D. Ullman, Compilers: Principles, Techniques and Tools. Addison Wesley, 1986, ISBN 0201100886.

9. James R. Gosler. Software Protection: Myth or Reality? Sandia National Laboratory. Advances in Cryptology – CRYPTO'85. 1985.
10. D. Grove, G. DeFouw, J. Dean, C. Chambers. Call Graph Construction in Object-Oriented Languages. Proceedings of OOPSLA '97. pp. 108-124, 1997
11. Horwitz, S., Precise flow-insensitive may-alias analysis is NP-Hard, ACM Transactions on Programming Languages and Systems, Vol 19. No.1, pp 1-6. 1997.
12. W. Landi, Undecidability of static analysis. ACM Lett. Program. Lang. Syst. 1, 4, 323-337. 1992
13. James R. Larus, Whole Program Paths, Proceedings of the SIGPLAN '99 Conference on Programming Languages Design and Implementation (PLDI 99), May 1999, Atlanta Georgia.
14. Benjamin Lynn, Manoj Prabhakaran, Amit Sahai. Positive Results and Techniques for Obfuscation. In Proceedings of Eurocrypt 2004.
15. G. Ramalingam, The undecidability of aliasing, ACM Trans. Program. Lang. Syst. 16, 5,1467-1471, 1994
16. Chenxi Wang. A Security Architecture for Survivability Mechanisms. PhD Dissertation, Department of Computer Science, University of Virginia, October 2000.
17. Chenxi Wang, Jonathan Hill, John Knight, Jack Davidson. Software Tamper Resistance: Obstructing Static Analysis of Programs. Technical Report CS-2000-12, Department of Computer Science, University of Virginia. May 2000.
18. Chenxi Wang, Jonathan Hill, John Knight, Jack Davidson. Protection of Software-based Survivability Mechanisms. International Conference of Dependable Systems and Networks. July 2001.
19. Hoeteck Wee. On Obfuscating Point Functions. Computer Science Division University of California, Berkeley. Jan 2005
20. Valery Pryamikov. Call Tree Transformation. Test Program – Source Code http:// www.harper.no/valery/CallTreeTransformation

Algorithms to Watermark Software Through Register Allocation

William Zhu and Clark Thomborson*

Department of Computer Sciences,
University of Auckland, Auckland, New Zealand
fzhu009@ec.auckland.ac.nz, cthombor@cs.auckland.ac.nz

Abstract. Software security is a significant issue in the Internet age. In order to prevent software from piracy and unauthorized modification, many techniques have been developed. Software watermarking is such a technique that can be used to protect software by embedding some secret information into the software to identify its copyright owner. In this paper, we discuss algorithms of software watermarking through register allocation.

The QP Algorithm [1, 2] was proposed by Qu and Potkonjak to watermark a solution to a graph coloring(GC) problem to protect its intellectual property. In a recent paper by Myles and Collberg [3], the QP algorithm was corrected, and was, for the first time, implemented to watermark software through register allocation. It is called the QPS algorithm.

Our paper discusses some difficulties with the published descriptions of the QP and QPS algorithms, points out the problem in the extractability of the watermarks inserted by the QP algorithm through examples, proves the correctness of a clarified version of the QPS algorithm, and proposes an improvement for the QP algorithm. Finally, we give some potential topics for further research.

Keyword: Software Watermarking, Graph, Interference Graph, Graph Coloring.

1 Introduction

With the rapid development of the software industries, computer security [4, 5] and the protection of intellectual property of software from piracy becomes more and more important issues in computer business and academicia. Software watermarking is an approach to embed a message into software to claim the ownership of it [6, 7, 8, 9]. It is one of effective mechanisms to protect the intellectual property of the developers for a software.

Qu, Potkonjak, et al. developed some techniques to watermark the solutions to constraint problems such as the GC problem [1, 2, 10, 11, 12]. The GC problem is to color the vertices of a graph with the fewest number of colors such that

---

* Research supported in part by the New Economy Research Fund of New Zealand.

R. Safavi-Naini and M. Yung (Eds.): DRMTICS 2005, LNCS 3919, pp. 180–191, 2006.

no vertices connected by an edge receive the same color. In compiler, the GC problem is used to allocate the registers for variables of a program. Potkonjak and Qu proposed the QP algorithm [1, 2] in 1998, but they have not published any detailed implementation for QP algorithm; they even have not considered any attacks in their analysis, however resistance to attack is of vital importance in digital and software watermarking.

In 2004, Myles and Collberg [3], for the first time, implemented the QP algorithm to watermark software through register allocation, and conducted an excellent and thorough empirical evaluation of this algorithm. They tried various attacks on the QP algorithm to analyze its robustness. Furthermore, they propose the QPS algorithm to compensate for the flaws they discovered in the QP algorithm. However, for the reasons shown in this paper, there are still some confusing points in the QPS algorithm.

Le and Desmedt also pointed out some other flaws in the QP algorithm [13]. They claimed that watermarked solution resulted from the QP algorithm could be modified in such a way that any message could be verified, and thus the watermark inserted could not be used to show ownership of the solution.

This paper is organized as follows. Section 2 discusses some basic concepts in software watermarking systems. Section 3 introduces the QP algorithm and points out some flaws in the QP algorithm as a method of watermarking. Section 4 discusses the QPS software watermarking algorithm, a variant of the QP algorithm for software watermarking. It is pointed out that there are not clear points in the if statement in the QPS algorithm. A potential clarified version of the QPS algorithms is explored and we proved the soundness of this version of the QPS algorithm. Section 5 details our improved QP algorithm, which we call the QPI algorithm. Section 6 summarizes our conclusions about the QP algorithm, the QPS algorithm, and our QPI algorithm. Section 7 points out several topics for further research.

2   Software Watermarking Systems

A software watermarking system can be divided into two subsystems: embedding subsystem and extracting subsystem. Embedding subsystem tries to insert watermarks in programs, while extracting subsystem aims to take watermarks from watermarked programs. There are several software watermarking algorothms currently avaiable, among them is the graph-based algorithm, in which a watermark is encoded as a graph with some special properties. Venkatesan, Vazirani and Sinha [14] proposed the first graph-based Software watermarking algorithm called the VVS algorithm. It is a static software watermarking algorithm. Collberg and Thomborson [7] proposed the first dynamic graph algorithm, the CT algorithm which inserts a watermark encoded as a data structure graph and only running a watermarked program with a special input, called a key, does the watermark in the watermarked program appear.

A public cryptographic key could be used as a watermark value W [7, 8]. Only the owner of the public key should know the corresponding private key. If the key is sufficiently long, and if the watermark graph-extracting algorithm and the decoding algorithm are sufficiently well-publicised, then an attacker would be unable to mount a convincing counterclaim of ownership. The attacker might produce a fraudulent decoder $d'()$ and/or a fraudulent graph-extractor $g'()$, such that $d'(g'(P)) = W'$, where $g'(P)$ is a graph found in a watermarked program P by extractor $g'()$ and W' is a public key whose corresponding private key is known to the attacker. However one or both of $d'()$ or $g'()$ would bear little resemblance to the well-publicised $d()$ and $g()$. Furthermore it would seem extremely difficult (and may someday be proved to be computationally infeasible) for the attacker to produce a watermark embedding process $e' : X \times W \rightarrow X$ such that their watermarking system will operate ideally, or near-ideally, over a wide range of programs X and watermarks W. In an ideal watermarking system, the extractor always finds an embedded watermark

$$\forall x \in X, \forall w \in W : d'(g'(e'(x, w))) = w$$

and it never finds a spurious watermark

$$\forall y \in X, \forall w \in W, \exists x \in X : (d'(g'(y) = w) \implies (y = e'(x, w))$$

Note that it is trivial for an attacker to produce a spurious watermarking system (d', g', e') that will operate ideally over a very small range of programs and watermarks, for the extractor could do a table lookup on its inputs and then report a watermark that is arbitrarily chosen by the attacker.

3   The QP Watermarking Algorithm

Qu and Potkonjak proposed a watermarking algorithm for watermarking solutions to Graph Colouring (GC) problems [1, 2], which is called the QP algorithm in [3, 15]. It requires the vertices of the graph to be indexed, that is, each vertex must be labeled with a unique integer in the range 1 to $|V(G)|$. The QP algorithm relies heavily on the ordering of node indices. The followings are some concepts used in the QP algorithm.

Definition 1. *Cyclic mod n ordering [1, 2]: We use "$<_i$" to denote the cyclic mod n ordering relation for a fixed i, such that $i <_i (i + 1) <_i \ldots <_i n <_i 1 <_i \ldots <_i i - 1$. Where there is no confusion over the value of i, we omit the subscript in $<_i$.*

Definition 2. *Two nearest vertices that are not connected to a vertex v_i [1, 2]: For a vertex v_i of a graph G with $|V| = n$, we say $v_{i_1} \in V$ and $v_{i_2} \in V$ are the two nearest vertices that are not connected to a vertex v_i if $i <_i i_1 <_i i_2$; $(v_i, v_{i_1}) \notin E$; $(v_i, v_{i_2}) \notin E$; $\forall j : i <_i j <_i i_1, (v_i, v_j) \in E$; and $\forall j : i_1 <_i j <_i i_2, (v_i, v_j) \in E$.*

In this paper, if the above two vertices exist for a vertex v_i, we also say vertex v_i has two candidate vertices v_{i_1} and v_{i_2}.

The essence of the QP algorithm is to add an extra edge between every vertex v_i and one of its two candidate vertices. The choice between these two nearest unconnected vertices is determined by the watermark bits to be embedded. It is important to notice that this concept is a dynamic one, since the two candidate vertices of v_i may change whenever an edge is added to the neighborhood of v_i.

After a watermark is inserted in a cover message using an embedding algorithm, an important question we may ask is if this watermark can be extracted by some algorithm.

3.1   The QP Embedding Algorithm

The original QP algorithm in Fig. 1 was proposed by Qu and Potkonjak [1, 2]. It inserts a watermark into a solution to a GC problem.

```
Input: an unwatermarked graph G and
       a message bits: W = w₁w₂...wₘ
Output: a watermarked graph G'.
Algorithm:
n = |V|
G' = G
for each i from 1 to n
       if vᵢ has two candidate vertices vᵢ₁ and vᵢ₂
           if wᵢ = 0 connect vᵢ to vᵢ₁ in G'(V, E')
           else connect vᵢ to vᵢ₂ in G'(V, E')
return G'
```

Fig. 1. The original QP algorithm [1, 2]

We note a subtle problem in the algorithm of Fig. 1. We cannot expect to insert one bit for every vertex in an arbitrary graph G. In Fig. 2, we show an "obvious" adaptation of the QP embedding algorithm, to handle arbitrary G.

```
Input: an unwatermarked graph G(V, E) and
       a message bits: W = w₁w₂...wₘ
Output: a watermarked graph G'.
Algorithm:
n = |V|
G' = G
j = 0
for each i from 1 to n
       if vᵢ has two candidate vertices vᵢ₁ and vᵢ₂
           j++
           if wⱼ = 0 connect vᵢ to vᵢ₁ in G'(V, E')
           else connect vᵢ to vᵢ₂ in G'(V, E')
return G'
```

Fig. 2. A clarified version of the QP algorithm [1, 2]

3.2   The QP Extraction Algorithm

The QP extraction algorithm in [2] is as follows. Given the graph G', for each vertex v_i we consider all vertices v_j such that v_i and v_j have different colors and $(v_i, v_j) \notin E(G)$. One bit of information can be decoded for each such pair of vertices, by counting the number $n(i, j)$ of nodes k with indices $i <_i k <_i j$ which are not connected to v_i. The value of the message bit is defined by the following case analysis on $n(i, j)$:

1. If $n(i, j) = 0$, the watermark bit is 0;
2. If $n(i, j) = 1$, the watermark bit is 1;
3. If $n(i, j) > 1$, then the watermark bit is 0 if $n(j, i)$ is 0; the watermark bit is 1 if $n(j, i)$ is 1; and the watermark bit is undefined otherwise.

The unwatermarked graph G plus its coloring is not enough to recognize the watermark embedded in the watermarked graph. Even the unwatermarked graph plus its coloring and plus the coloring of the watermarked graph is still not enough to recognize the watermark embedded in the watermarked graph. This can be seen from the following example.

Example 1. Let $G(V, E)$ have 3 vertices v_1, v_2, v_3 and no edges. We can color its all 3 vertices with color RED. After inserting a message $W = 0$, $G(V, E)$ becomes a new graph $G_1'(V, E_1')$ with 3 vertices v_1, v_2, v_3, v_4 and 1 edge $\{v_1, v_2\}$. We can color it so that v_1 with color RED, v_2 and v_3 with color BLUE.

For the above graph $G(V, E)$, we can also color its all 3 vertices with color RED. After inserting a message $W = 1$, it becomes another new graph $G_2'(V, E_2')$ with 3 vertices v_1, v_2, v_3 and 1 edge $\{v_1, v_3\}$. We can also color it so that v_1 with color RED, v_2 and v_3 with color BLUE.

The same original graph $G(V, E)$ has the same coloring for the watermarked graphs but different messages inserted.

Myles and Collberg has also pointed out that the above QP extraction algorithm is incorrect, but their example [3] for the extraction failure of the QP algorithm is itself not clear.

3.3 The QP Algorithm Is Not Extractable

The QP algorithm is not extractable, since, as shown in the following example, inserting two different messages into an original graph respectively, we get the same watermarked graph.

Example 2 (Extraction failure of the QP algorithm). Let $G(V, E)$ have 4 vertices v_1, v_2, v_3, v_4 and two edges $(v_1, v_3), (v_2, v_4)$.

The first message to embed is $W_1 = 010$.

$E' = E$

For $i = 1$, v_i has the two nearest vertices that are not connected to v_i with $i_1 = 2$, $i_2 = 4$. For $w_j = 0$, we connect v_1 and v_2. Now $E' = E' \cup (v_1, v_2) = \{(v_1, v_3), (v_2, v_4), (v_1, v_2)\}$.

For $i = 2$, v_i has no the two nearest vertices that are not connected to v_i, so we cannot embed a bit for this vertex.

For $i = 3$, v_i has the two nearest vertices that are not connected to v_i with $i_1 = 4, i_2 = 2$. For $w_j = 1$, we connect v_3 and v_2. Now $E' = E' \cup (v_2, v_3) = \{(v_1, v_3), (v_2, v_4), (v_1, v_2), (v_2, v_3)\}$.

For $i = 4$, v_i has the two nearest vertices that are not connected to v_i with $i_1 = 1, i_2 = 3$. For $w_j = 0$, we connect v_1 and v_4. Now $E' = E' \cup (v_1, v_4) = \{(v_1, v_3), (v_2, v_4), (v_1, v_2), (v_2, v_3), (v_1, v_4)\}$. The following figure shows this embedding process.

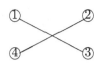

The original graph.

$i = 1$, $i_1 = 2$ and $i_2 = 4$, $w_j = 0$, so connect v_1 and v_2.

For $i = 2$, we cannot add any edge.

$i = 3$, $i_1 = 4$ and $i_2 = 2$, $w_j = 1$,,
so connect v_2 and v_3.

$i = 4$, $i_1 = 1$ and $i_2 = 3$, $w_j = 0$, so connect v_1 and v_4.

This is the watermarked graph.

The second message to embed is $W_2 = 111$.

$E' = E$

For $i = 1$, v_i has the two nearest vertices that are not connected to v_i with $i_1 = 2$, $i_2 = 4$. For $w_j = 1$, we connect v_1 and v_4. Now $E' = E' \cup (v_1, v_4) = \{(v_1, v_3), (v_2, v_4), (v_1, v_4)\}$.

For $i = 2$, v_i has the two nearest vertices that are not connected to v_i with $i_1 = 3, i_2 = 1$. For $w_j = 1$, we connect v_1 and v_2. Now $E' = E' \cup (v_1, v_2) = \{(v_1, v_3), (v_2, v_4), (v_1, v_4), (v_1, v_2)\}$.

For $i = 3$, v_i has the two nearest vertices that are not connected to v_i with $i_1 = 4, i_2 = 2$. For $w_j = 1$, we connect v_3 and v_2. Now $E' = E' \cup (v_2, v_3) = \{(v_1, v_3), (v_2, v_4), (v_1, v_2), (v_3, v_2), (v_3, v_2)\}$.

For $i = 4$, v_i has no the two nearest vertices that are not connected to v_i, so we cannot embed a bit for this vertex. Now we also have the same $E' = \{(v_1, v_3), (v_2, v_4), (v_1, v_2), (v_2, v_3), (v_1, v_4)\}$. The following figure shows this embedding process.

The original graph.

When $i = 1$, $i_1 = 2$ and $i_2 = 4$, $w_j = 1$,
so connect v_1 and v_4.

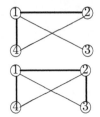

When $i = 2$, $i_1 = 3$ and $i_2 = 1$, $w_j = 1$,
so connect v_1 and v_2.

When $i = 3$, $i_1 = 4$ and $i_2 = 2$, $w_j = 1$, so connect v_2 and v_3.
For $i = 4$, we cannot add any edge.
This is the watermarked graph.

The problem is in that all bits of a message are embedded in an edge of E' which is not in E. For an edge (v_k, v_l), $k < l$, of E' but not in E, it may be connected in the following four possible cases:

1. when $i = k$ and $i_1 = l$
2. when $i = k$ and $i_2 = l$
3. when $i = l$ and $i_1 = k$
4. when $i = l$ and $i_2 = k$

In the first and third cases, the edge (v_k, v_l) means a bit 0 inserted, while in the second and fourth cases, it means a bit 1 inserted according to the QP embedding algorithm.

4   The QPS Software Watermarking Algorithm

After pointing out that a watermark inserted into a graph by the QP extraction algorithm cannot be extacted reliably, Myles and Collberg proposed the QPS software watermarking algorithm [3], a variant of the QP algorithm. In the QPS algorithm, two core concepts are used. They are "triple" and "colored triple" as follows.

Definition 3 (triple [3]). *For a graph $G = (V, E)$, if 3 vertices v, v', v'' of G satisfy the following two conditions:*

1. $v, v', v'' \in V$
2. (v, v'), (v, v'), $(v', v'') \notin E$

they are called a triple.

Definition 4 (colored triple [3]). *For a graph $G = (V, E)$, if a triple v, v', $v'' \in V$ are all colored the same color, then they are called a colored triple.*

Triples and colored triples change dynamically during the watermark embedding process, as did the cyclic mod-n ordering of our Definition 2. From the definition of GC, if three vertices are all colored the same, then condition 2 of Definition 3 is satisfied. If a triple is not a colored triple, then we call it a "multicolored triple".

4.1   The Original QPS Algorithm

Myles and Collberg applied the QP algorithm to software watermarking. The original QPS embedding algorithm [3] is in Fig. 3 and the QPS extraction algorithm [3] is in Fig. 4. In the QPS embedding algorithm, the input graph G of Fig. 3 would be the interference graph of a program P. The output graph G' would be the interference graph of a compiled program P', and the nodes of G and G' are the variables in P. Interference graph is a concept for register allocation in compilers [16]. If two variables interfere in P, then they cannot be assigned to the same register when P is compiled. This constraint on register allocation is modelled by introducing an edge between these two variables in P's interference graph G. A legal coloring of G is thus an acceptable register assignment for the compilation of P, if we consider each register to have a distinct color.

In the QPS embedding and extraction algorithm, the statement "v_{i_1} and v_{i_2} are not already in a triple G" is not clear.

4.2   A Clarified Version of the QPS Algorithm

From the example in [3], page 281, 4.2 Preliminary Example, a possible clarified version of the QPS embedding algorithm is given in Fig. 5. The corresponding extraction algorithm is as in Fig. 6.

This version of the QPS embedding algorithm works well in that a message embedded by itself can be recognized correctly by its corresponding extraction algorithm, however, the conditions in its "if" statement in it is so restricted that it can only embed much fewer bits of message into a graph than the QP algorithm can.

Proof of the correctness of the above QPS algorithm.

As said before, every bit of a message is embedded in an edge of E' which is not in E. For an edge (v_k, v_l), $k < l$, of E' but not in E, generally, there are two possible to connect it; when $i = k$ or when $i = l$. Now we prove that if we can get this edge when $i = k$, then we cannot get it when $i = l$ and vice verse. In fact, if

```
Input: an unwatermarked graph G(V, E)
       a message W = w₁w₂... to be embedded into the G(V, E)
Output: a watermarked graph G' with message W embedded in it
Algorithm:
n = |V|
G' = G
j=0
for each i from 1 to n
    if vᵢ is not in a triple G' AND possible find the nearest two vertices vᵢ₁ and vᵢ₂
       for vᵢ such that vᵢ₁ and vᵢ₂ are the same color as vᵢ in G'
       AND vᵢ₁ and vᵢ₂ are not already in a triple in G'.
    j++
    if wⱼ = 0
       connect vᵢ and vᵢ₁ in G'
    if wⱼ = 1
       connect vᵢ and vᵢ₂ in G'
return G'(V, E') and the inserted message W' = w₁w₂...wⱼ
```

Fig. 3. The QPS embedding elgorithm

```
Input: an unwatermarked graph G(V, E)
       a watermarked graph G'
Output: a message W embedded in G'
Algorithm:
n = |V|
j=0
for each i from 1 to n
    if v_i is not in a triple G' AND possible find the nearest two vertices v_{i_1} and v_{i_2}
        for v_i such that v_{i_1} and v_{i_2} are the same color as v_i in G
        AND v_{i_1} and v_{i_2} are not already in a triple in G.
    j++
    if v_i and v_{i_1} have the different colors in G'
        w_j = 0
        connect v_i and v_{i_1} in G
    else
        w_j = 1
        connect v_i and v_{i_2} in G
    return W = w_1 w_2 ... w_j
```

Fig. 4. The QPS extraction algorithm

we can get this edge in the case of $i = k$, then $i_1 = l$ or $i_2 = l$. First we consider the case of $i_1 = l$. According to the clarified QPS embedding algorithm, there is a number h, such that $k < l < h$ and v_l, v_h are the two candidate vertices of v_k. Since we can connect the edge (v_k, v_l) only when $i = k$ or $i = l$, if we does not connect it when $i = k$, we would connect the edge (v_k, v_h) when $i = k$. When $i = l$, the vertices v_k and v_l are still not connected, so are the vertices v_l and v_h. Therefore, $i_1 \leq h$ or $i_2 \leq k$. If $i_2 < k$, it is impossible to connect the edge (v_k, v_l). The only possibility to connect the edge (v_k, v_l) is the two candidate vertices of v_l are v_h and v_k, i.e., $i_1 = h$ and $i_2 = k$. In this case, v_i, v_{i_1} and v_{i_2} are not a triple, for the edge (v_{i_1}, v_{i_2}) has been connected, so we cannot connect the edge (v_k, v_l).

In case of $i_2 = l$, in the same way, we can prove that when $i = l$, we cannot connect the edge (v_k, v_l).

We can also prove that if we can get this edge when $i = l$, then we cannot get it when $i = k$ in the same way as above. Therefore, if an edge of E' which is not in E can be used to embed one bit of message 0, it cannot be used to embed a bit 1.

```
Input: an original graph G(V, E)
       a message W = w_1 w_2 ... to be embedded into the G(V, E)
Output: a watermarked graph G' with message W embedded in it
Algorithm:
n = |V|
G' = G
WV = V
j=0
for each i from 1 to n
    if possible find the nearest two vertices v_{i_1} and v_{i_2} in G'
        such that v_i, v_{i_1}, v_{i_2} have the same color and are a triple in G' and v_{i_1}, v_{i_2} ∈ WV
        WV = WV - {v_{i_1}, v_{i_2}}
    j++
    if w_j = 0
        connect v_i and v_{i_1} in G'
    if w_j = 1
        connect v_i and v_{i_2} in G'
    return G'(V, E') and the inserted message W' = w_1 w_2 ... w_j
```

Fig. 5. A clarified version of the QPS embedding algorithm

```
Input: an unwatermarked graph G(V, E)
       a watermarked graph G'(V, E')
Output: a message W embedded in G'(V, E')
Algorithm:
n = |V|
WV = V
j=0
for each i from 1 to n
    if possible find the nearest two vertices v_{i_1} and v_{i_2} from G
        for v_i such that v_i, v_{i_1}, v_{i_2} have the same color in G and are a triple in G'
        and v_{i_1}, v_{i_2} ∈ WV
        WV = WV - {v_{i_1}, v_{i_2}}
        j++
        if v_i and v_{i_1} have the different colors in G'
            w_j = 0
            connect v_i and v_{i_1} in G
        else
            w_j = 1
            connect v_i and v_{i_2} in G
return W = w_1 w_2 ... w_j
```

Fig. 6. A clarified version of the QPS extraction algorithm

5 The QPI Algorithm

We give an improved QP embedding algorithm, the QPI embedding algorithm, in Fig. 7. It is an informed software watermarking algorithm. We change the definition of the two candidate vertices $v_{i_1} \in V$ and $v_{i_2} \in V$ for a vertex $v_i \in V$. The original definition in [1, 2] used the cyclic mod n order for numbers $1, 2, \ldots, n$, while we use the order $1 < 2 < \ldots < n$ in our new definition.

```
Input: an original graph G(V, E)
       a message W = w_1 w_2 ... to be embedded into the G(V, E)
Output: a watermarked graph G' with message W embedded in it
Algorithm:
n = |V|
G' = G
j = 0
for each i from 1 to n
    if v_i has two candidate vertices v_{i_1} and v_{i_2}
        j++
        if w_j = 0
            connect v_i to v_{i_1} in G'
            change the color of v_{i_1} to different one from the current colors used in G'
        else
            connect v_i to v_{i_2} in G'
            change the color of v_{i_2} to different one from the current colors used in G'
return G'
```

Fig. 7. The QPI embedding algorithm

Definition 5. *Two candidate vertices: for a vertex v_i of a graph G with $|V| = n$ and a coloring of G, we say v_i has two candidate vertices $v_{i_1} \in V$ and $v_{i_2} \in V$ if $i < i_1 < i_2 \leq n$ and vertices v_i, v_{i_1}, and v_{i_2} have a same color and $(v_i, v_{i_2}) \notin E$; furthermore, $\forall j : i < j < i_1$ and $\forall j : i_1 < j < i_2 \leq n$, vertices v_i and v_j have different color.*

```
Input: an unwatermarked graph G(V, E) with n = |V|
       a watermarked graph G(V, E')
Output: the message W embedded in the watermarked graph G(V, E')
Algorithm:
j = 0
for each i from 1 to n
      if v_i has two candidate vertices v_{i_1} and v_{i_2}
          j++
          if v_i and v_{i_1} have different colors in G'
              w_j = 0
              connect v_i and v_{i_1} in G
              change the color of v_{i_1} to different one from the current colors used in G
          else
              w_j = 1
              connect v_i and v_{i_2} in G
              change the color of v_{i_2} to different one from the current colors used in G
      return W = w_1 w_2 ... w_j
```

Fig. 8. The QPI extraction algorithm

The QPI embedding algorithm is an extractable algorithm. The proof of it is similar to that of QPS algorithm in Subsection 4.2 of this paper; we also give an extraction algorithm corresponding to the QPI embedding algorithm in Fig. 8.

For our QPI embedding algorithm, every edge (v_k, v_l), $k < l$ in G' while not in G is only connected when $i = k$, so there is only one possibility for an edge in G' while not in G to embed a bit of message. Furthermore, this improved QP embedding algorithm works for all cases.

6   Conclusions

Now we reach our following conclusions about the QP algorithm through the above discussions.

1. The message embedded into a graph by the QP embedding algorithm is not extractable in general.
2. The QP extraction algorithm is not correct. It tries to recognize a message just by the unwatermarked graph; it does not use the watermarked graph.
3. The QPS algorithm proposed by Myles and Collberg is the first one that implemented the QP algorithm for software watermarking, though it includs some not clear descriptions.
4. The QPS algorithm is the first one algorithm that watermark software through register allocation.
5. The QPI algorithm proposed by us can correctly realize Qu and Potkonjak's idea and can be used to software watermarking through register allocation.

7   Potential Research Directions

From the paper [1, 2], we think it is important to distinquish an extraction algorithm and a recognition algorithm in software watermarking. An extraction algorithm tries to extract all bits of the message inserted in a software, while a recognition algorithm decides whether a watermark exists in a software. A good work to define these concepts is not as easy as it seems. We will explore this problem in our further works.

Another potential topic for future research is to design algorithms to embed a watermark into a graph such that it can still be recognized when the vertices of the graph have been reordered.

Acknowledgements. Thanks for Dr. F.-Y. Wang's stimulating suggestions on this paper. Thank Mr. Jun Ni, Mr. Han Zhang, and other colleages in the software security group at the University of Auckland for their helpful comments.

References

1. G. Qu, M. Potkonjak, Analysis of watermarking techniques for graph coloring problem, in: IEEE/ACM International Conference on Computer Aided Design, '98, 1998, pp. 190–193.
2. G. Qu, M. Potkonjak, Hiding signatures in graph coloring solutions, in: Information Hiding Workshop '99, 1999, pp. 348–367.
3. G. Myles, C. Collberg, Software watermarking through register allocation: Implementation, analysis, and attacks, in: LNCS 2971, 2004, pp. 274–293.
4. C. Collberg, G. Myles, A. Huntwork, Sandmark–a tool for software protection research, IEEE Security and Privacy 1 (4) (2003) 40–49.
5. W. Zhu, C. Thomborson, A provable scheme for homomorphic obfuscationin in software security, in: The IASTED International Conference on Communication, Network and Information Security, CNIS'05, Phoenix, USA, 2005, pp. 208–212.
6. C. Collberg, C. Thomborson, On the limits of software watermarking, in: Technical Report #164, Department of Computer Science, The University of Auckland, 1998.
7. C. Collberg, C. Thomborson, Software watermarking: Models and dynamic embeddings, in: Proceedings of Symposium on Principles of Programming Languages, POPL'99, 1999, pp. 311–324.
8. C. Collberg, C. Thomborson, Watermarking, tamper-proofing, and obfuscation - tools for software protection, IEEE Transactions on Software Engineering 28 (2002) 735–746.
9. W. Zhu, C. Thomborson, F.-Y. Wang, A survey of software watermarking, in: ISI 2005, Vol. 3495 of LNCS, 2005, pp. 454–458.
10. G. Qu, J. Wong, M. Potkonjak, Optimization-intensive watermarking techniques for decision problems, in: Design Automation Conference, '99, 1999, pp. 33–36.
11. G. Qu, M. Potkonjak, Fingerprinting intellectual property using constraint-addition, in: Design Automation Conference '00, 2000, pp. 587–592.
12. G. Qu, J. Wong, M. Potkonjak, Fair watermarking techniques, in: EEE/ACM Asia and South Pacific Design Automation Conference, '00, 2000, pp. 55–60.
13. T. Le, Y. Desmedt, Cryptanalysis of ucla watermarking schemes for intellectual property protections, in: LNCS 2578, Springer-Verlag, 2003, pp. 213–225.
14. R. Venkatesan, V. Vazirani, S. Sinha, A graph theoretic approach to software watermarking, in: 4th International Information Hiding Workshop, Pittsburgh, PA, 2001.
15. W. Zhu, C. Thomborson, On the QP algorithm in software watermarking, in: ISI 2005, Vol. 3495 of LNCS, 2005, pp. 646–647.
16. K. D. Cooper, T. J. Harvey, L. Torczon, How to build an interference graph, Software – Practice and Experience 28 (4) (1988) 425–444.

An Efficient Fingerprinting Scheme with Secret Sharing

Seunglim Yong and Sang-Ho Lee

Department of Computer Science and Engineering , Ewha Womans University,
11-1 Daehyun-dong, Seodaemun-gu, Seoul, Korea
dragon@ewhain.net, shlee@ewha.ac.kr

Abstract. The illegal copying and redistribution of digital data is a crucial problem to distributors who electronically sell digital data. Fingerprinting scheme is a technique which allows the copyright protection to track redistributors of digital data using cryptographic techniques. Anonymous fingerprinting scheme prevents the merchant from framing a buyer by making the fingerprinted version known to the buyer only. In addition, such a scheme makes it possible for the buyer to purchase goods without revealing his identity to the merchant.

In this paper, an efficient anonymous fingerprinting scheme based on secret sharing is introduced. A secret sharing scheme preserves the buyer's anonymity and traceability of traitor. When the buyer purchases a digital data, the buyer's identity is divided into two shares and two shares are embedded into the digital data. When the merchant finds a sold version that has been illegally distributed, he is able to retrieve the fingerprint and find the original buyer's identity by reconstructing it from two shares. When the merchant embeds the fingerprint in the digital data, the protocol uses the homomorphic encryption scheme for practicability. Plus, the digital signature prevents the buyer from denying allegations.

Keywords: Anonymous fingerprinting, secret sharing, copyright protection.

1 Introduction

Today's progress of computer networks along with the development of internet facilitates the illegal distribution of digital data. This has caused the protection of digital intellectual property to become a crucial problem to be solved. A lot of research has been invested in designing methods that technically support the copyright protection of digital data. One class of such methods consists of techniques called fingerprinting schemes.

The fingerprinting scheme is a cryptographic technique that supports the copyright protection of digital data[11]. Buyers who redistribute copies disregarding the copyright conditions are called traitors. The fingerprinting scheme enables copyright protection by allowing the merchant to identify the traitor who originally purchased the data item.

R. Safavi-Naini and M. Yung (Eds.): DRMTICS 2005, LNCS 3919, pp. 192–202, 2006.

Fingerprinting schemes can be classified into the following; Symmetric, asymmetric and anonymous asymmetric. In symmetric schemes, the merchant fingerprints the digital data, slightly differently from that of the original data and unique to that of each buyer's copy. Consequently, a malicious merchant could sell digital data with the same fingerprint to numerous buyers and accuse a buyer of being the traitor[1, 2, 17, 18].

In asymmetric schemes, the buyer and the merchant perform interactive protocol where the buyer embeds his own secret to fingerprint the copy. At the end of the protocol only the buyer knows the fingerprinted copy. The advantage of this solution is that the merchant can obtain proof against the buyer that can convince any honest third party. But the drawback is that the merchant knows the buyer's identity even when the buyer is innocent[12].

In anonymous asymmetric fingerprinting, the buyer can purchase a fingerprinted copy without revealing his identity to the merchant. The buyer no longer has to identify himself when purchasing the copy and remains anonymous as long as he keeps the purchased good secret, i.e., does not distribute it. More precisely, the merchant can learn the buyer's identity only if he obtains the purchased copy. Upon finding a fingerprinted copy, the merchant needs the help of a registration authority to identify a traitor. To insert the fingerprint anonymously, previous schemes used secure two-party computation or bit commitment[13, 8, 7, 11]. However, these schemes are inefficient and impractical because they are based on secure two-party computations[5] with high complexity or they use [2] schemes as the building block for collusion resistance. Recently, [10, 9, 6] proposed a buyer-seller watermarking protocol with homomorphic encryption scheme.

In this paper, we concentrate on practical anonymous fingerprinting protocols in the sense that buyers can buy goods anonymously, but can still be identified if they redistribute the goods illegally. A secret sharing scheme preserves the anonymity of the buyer as long as they do not redistribute the material. And Schnorr's digital signature prevents the buyer from denying the fact that he redistributed the product. When the merchant embeds the fingerprint into a digital data, the homomorphic encryption scheme is used for efficiency.

The remainder of the paper is organized as follows. Section 2 gives a brief cryptographic primitives adopted in this paper. In section 3 we describe the subprotocols in our scheme and statements for the security of the proposed scheme. In section 4 we present the proposed protocol in detail. We then discuss the security of the proposed method in section 5. Finally, conclusions are given in section 6.

2   Cryptographic Techniques

In this section, we introduce some cryptographic techniques used in our scheme briefly.

2.1   Secret Sharing

Secret sharing scheme is a kind of cryptographic protocol, which maintains secret information D securely by sharing a secret among lots of participants and secret information D is reconstructed by some valid shares. Shamir's polynomial based (t, n)-threshold secret sharing scheme operates in the following way.

A dealer generates a random polynomial of degree $t - 1$ polynomial $q(x) = a_0 + a_1 x + \ldots + a_{t-1} x^{t-1}$ subject to the constraint $a_0 = D$. The ith share, defined as $D_i (D_1 = q(x_1), \ldots, D_n = q(x_n))$ is generated. Each of the n shares (x_i, D_i) is distributed to n participants. If the secret D needs to be reconstructed, at least t participants must provide their shares. The secret $D = q(0)$ can be computed and reconstructed by reconstruction of coefficient of the polynomial using Lagrange interpolation. But none of $t - 1$ participants can obtain no information of the secret D[15]. We apply secret sharing to generate fingerprints which are two shares of buyer's secret information and trace traitor.

2.2   Schnorr's Digital Signature Scheme

The security of Schnorr's signature scheme depends on the difficulty of computing discrete logarithms. Users in the system can share a random number g and two prime numbers, p and q, such that q is a prime factor of $p - 1$, $q \neq 1$ and $g^q \equiv 1 \ mod \ p$. To generate a pair of private and public key, a user chooses a random number s $(0 < s < q)$ as her private key. And then computes her public key $v = g^{-s} \ mod \ p$. To sign a message m, user picks a random number r $(r \in_R Z_q)$ and does the following computations:

$$x = g^r \ mod \ p, \ e = h(m||x), \ y = (r + se) \ mod \ q$$

where h is collision-free one-way hash function. The signature on the message m is the pair (e, y). To verify the signature, sender computes $x' = g^y v^e$ and tests if e is equal to $h(m||x')$. If the test is OK, the signature is valid[15].

2.3   Homomorphic Encryption Scheme

A public key encryption function $E : G \rightarrow R$ defined on a group G is said to be homomorphic if E forms a homomorphism[3]. That is, for a certain defined operation, $\oplus$, then given ciphertext $E(x)$ and $E(y)$ for some unknown plaintext $x, y \in G$, anyone can compute $E(x \oplus y)$, or vice-versa, without any need for the secret key. For example, the RSA encryption[14] is homomorphic with respect to the multiplication operation. As in [10], we assume that the public key cryptosystem we are using is a privacy homomorphism with respect to the fingerprint insertion operation.

3   Proposed Anonymous Fingerprinting

In this section, we describe the overview of our anonymous fingerprinting scheme and its security.

3.1   The Model of Anonymous Fingerprinting

The involved parties in our protocol are a buyer $\mathcal{B}$, a merchant $\mathcal{M}$, a registration center $\mathcal{RC}$ and a judge $\mathcal{J}$. We assume that the registration center does not reveal the buyer's real ID if the buyer is honest. Also we assume that the judge $\mathcal{J}$ is a trusted third party. For the purpose of fingerprinting, it is required in this model that buyers register themselves to a registration center. There is no special restriction on the judge. The main subprotocols of the construction are registration, fingerprinting and identification, denoted by $P_{Reg}, P_{Fing}, P_{Iden}$, respectively.

- P_{Reg}: A probabilistic two-party protocol between $\mathcal{B}$ and $\mathcal{RC}$. $\mathcal{B}$ registers at $\mathcal{RC}$ and obtains certificates. $\mathcal{RC}$ stores a registration record of $\mathcal{B}$.
- P_{Fing}: A probabilistic two-party protocol between $\mathcal{B}$ and $\mathcal{M}$. $\mathcal{B}$ buys the digital data from $\mathcal{M}$ and jointly fingerprints it with him. The output to $\mathcal{M}$ is the purchase record and the main output to $\mathcal{B}$ is the fingerprinted data item.
- P_{Iden}: A probabilistic two-party protocol between $\mathcal{M}$ and $\mathcal{J}$. If $\mathcal{M}$ finds an illegally redistributed copy, he extracts some information from this copy and sends to $\mathcal{J}$ the user's information and traces traitor.

Now, we can state the main security properties of our protocol as followings.

- Security for the merchant: An honest merchant must be able to identify a traitor and win the corresponding trial for every illegally redistributed copy of the data item he finds, unless collusion do not exceed a certain size.
- Security for the buyer: No honest buyer should be guilty by an honest judge; at least no honest judge will believe it.
- Anonymity: Without obtaining an illegally redistributed copy, the merchant cannot identify the buyer.

3.2   Overview of the Scheme

The idea for using secret sharing scheme to design an anonymous fingerprinting scheme is as follows: The buyer generates a random polynomial of degree 1-polynomial $q(p) = k - px$ subject to the constraint x is a secret value. The secret value x is the buyer's anonymous private key. The first share $(a, D_1 = q(a))$ is generated by the response of registration center's challenge in registration protocol and the second share $(a', D_2 = q(a'))$ is generated by the response of merchant's challenge in fingerprinting protocol. Two shares are embedded into the digital data as fingerprints. When redistributed copy is found, the buyer can be traced by computing secret value x using the share (a, D_1) and (a', D_2) embedded into the digital data. In identification protocol, the merchant and the judge can find the buyer's anonymous private key by equation (1). But if the buyer does not distribute the purchased digital data, he remains anonymous because secret value x cannot be reconstructed.

$$D_1 = k - ax, \quad D_2 = k - a'x$$
$$x = \frac{(D_1 - D_2)}{(a' - a)} \tag{1}$$

The second idea of our scheme is to use homomorphic encryption in fingerprinting protocol for efficiency. When the buyer sends the buyer's first share $(a, D_1 = q(a))$ to merchant in fingerprinting protocol, which is embedded into the digital data as a fingerprint, the buyer encrypts the value in order to keep it secret from the merchant. Due to the property of homomorphic encryption, the merchant can embed the response into the digital data without decrypting the value. In spite of the value being encrypted, the merchant can verify the correctness of the value due to the certificate provided by the registration center.

4   The Protocol

In this section, we propose a fingerprinting scheme with secret sharing. We apply the secret sharing that the honest buyer remains anonymously. And we use the homomorphic encryption scheme for keeping the fingerprint secret from the merchant.

Algebraic structure. All arithmetic operations are performed in a group G_q of order q for which efficient algorithms are known to multiply, invert, determine equality of elements, test membership and randomly select elements. Any group G_q satisfying these requirements and in which the computation of discrete logarithms is infeasible and can be a candidate. For concrete constructions one can assume that G_q is the unique subgroup of prime order q of the multiplicative group Z_p^* where p is a prime such that $q = (p-1)/2$ is also prime and $q|(p-1)$. Let g be a generator of G such that computing discrete logarithms to the base g is difficult.

Notation. Let $item \in \{0, 1\}^*$ denote some digital data that is fingerprintable. The fingerprinted copy $item'$, some of its bits can be changed, remains "close" to $item$. But without knowing which particular bits were changed, altering of these bits is impossible without rendering the good useless. We refer to a formal definition of "marking assumption"[3]. We establish some notation as follows.

- $item$: Original digital data that is fingerprintable.
- $item'$: Fingerprinted digital data.
- $item \oplus W$: Embed W into $item$ with the fingerprint embedding operation.
- E_{H_k}/D_{H_k}: Encryption/decryption algorithm using key k with homomorphic property.
- H: Collision-free one-way hash function.
- σ: Random permutation function chosen (only known) by merchant.
- $||$: Concatenation

4.1   Registration Protocol

Assume that all buyers have the Schnorr's public and private key pairs. $\mathcal{B}$ has a secret random s $(0 < s < q)$ as a Schnorr's private key and $v = g^{-s} \bmod p$ as a public key. And all other participants have a pair of a private key and a public key (sk, pk) certified by certificate authority (CA).

When $\mathcal{B}$ wishes to register at $\mathcal{RC}$, $\mathcal{B}$ generates an anonymous key pair of a private key x and a public key $y = g^x$.

Protocol [registration] - P_{Reg}

1) $\mathcal{B}$ generates an anonymous key pair of a private and public key. $\mathcal{B}$ chooses $x \in_R Z_q^*$ randomly and secretly as a private key, and computes a public key $y = g^x \bmod p$.
   $\mathcal{B}$ chooses random numbers $r, k \in_R Z_q^*$, and computes $r' = g^r$ and $k' = g^k$. These values r' and k' show that $\mathcal{B}$ is responsible for this transaction. $\mathcal{B}$ generates Schnorr's signature (e, h) such that $e = H(H(y||k')||r')$ and $h = r + se$ using y, k' and r'. $\mathcal{B}$ sends y, k' and signature (e, h) to $\mathcal{RC}$, and convinces $\mathcal{RC}$ in zero-knowledge of possession of x. The proof given in [4] for showing possession of discrete logarithms may be used here.
2) $\mathcal{RC}$ computes that $z = g^h v^e \bmod p$ with $\mathcal{B}$'s public key v certified by CA. And then he verifies the Schnorr's signature by $e = H(H(y||k')||z)$ with the received value from $\mathcal{B}$. If it is verified, $\mathcal{RC}$ chooses a random $a \in_R Z_p^*$ and sends this number as a challenge to $\mathcal{B}$.
3) $\mathcal{B}$ computes $b = k - xa$ with his secret values x and k, and returns b to $\mathcal{RC}$.
4) $\mathcal{RC}$ checks that $k' = g^b y^a$. If it is verified, $\mathcal{RC}$ generates $W = a||b$, which is the first share of secret information x, and encrypts $EW = E_{H_y}(W)$ using y, and generates certificates $C_1 = Cert(H(y||k'))$ and $C_2 = Cert(EW)$. $\mathcal{RC}$ returns two certificates C_1 , and encrypted fingerprint EW to $\mathcal{B}$. Then $\mathcal{RC}$ stores y, W and $\mathcal{B}$'s signature (e, h) in its registration database.
5) $\mathcal{B}$ decrypts $W' = D_{H_x}(EW)$ using his private key x and checks that the value W' is equal to $(a||b)$. Then he verifies C_2 with $\mathcal{RC}$'s public key.

4.2   Fingerprinting Protocol

The fingerprinting protocol is executed between a buyer and a merchant. We use the homomorphic encryption to embed the fingerprint into the digital data.

Protocol [fingerprinting] - P_{Fing}

1) $\mathcal{B}$ sends y, EW, C_1, C_2 to $\mathcal{M}$.
2) $\mathcal{M}$ verifies the certificate C_2 in order to be assured that EW is indeed a valid fingerprint verified by the $\mathcal{RC}$. If it is verified, $\mathcal{M}$ chooses a random number $a' \in_R Z_q^*$ and sends the challenge a' to $\mathcal{B}$.
3) $\mathcal{B}$ returns $b' = k - xa'$ to $\mathcal{M}$.
4) $\mathcal{M}$ computes $k'' = g^{b'} y^{a'}$ and a hash value $H(y||k'')$. Then he verifies C_1 with $\mathcal{RC}$'s public key in order to be assured that y and k are registered to $\mathcal{RC}$.
5) If the verification holds, $\mathcal{M}$ finds a random permutation σ satisfying $\sigma(E_{H_y}(W)) = E_{H_y}(\sigma(W))$. The permutation σ is used to permute the elements of the buyer's fingerprints. $\mathcal{M}$ computes $\sigma(EW)$ and generates the value $emb = (a'||b')$. The value emb is the second share of $\mathcal{B}$'s secret information x. Then $\mathcal{M}$ computes $\sigma(emb)$ in order that $\mathcal{B}$ cannot know the value emb though he knows the values a' and b'.

6) $\mathcal{M}$ embeds the value $\sigma(emb)$ into the original digital data $item$ as a finger-print, and encrypts it with $\mathcal{B}$'s anonymous public key y. Then $\mathcal{M}$ embeds the received value $E_{H_y}(\sigma(W))$ into the digital data. As in [10], embedding finger-prints in the encrypted domain is possible that the public key cryptosystems being used is a homomorphism with respect to fingerprint embedding oper-ation $\oplus$. That is, $\mathcal{M}$ computes $E_{H_y}(item')$

$$E_{H_y}(item') = E_{H_y}(item \oplus \sigma(emb)) \oplus E_{H_y}(\sigma(W))$$
$$= E_{H_y}(item \oplus \sigma(emb) \oplus \sigma(W))$$

$\mathcal{M}$ transmits $E_{H_y}(item')$ to $\mathcal{B}$. $\mathcal{M}$ keeps records Rec_B of all transactions in his database, where each transaction is summarized as a six-order tuple $< y, \sigma(emb), EW, C_1, C_2, \sigma >$.

7) $\mathcal{B}$ decrypts $E_{H_y}(item')$ with his anonymous private key x and gets finger-printed digital data $item'$.

$$D_{H_x}(E_{H_y}(item')) = item'$$
$$= item \oplus \sigma(emb) \oplus \sigma(W)$$

4.3 Identification Protocol

When $\mathcal{M}$ detects illegal redistribution of $item'$, he performs the identification protocol. On finding an illegal copy redistributed, $\mathcal{M}$ extracts the fingerprint. Then $\mathcal{M}$ makes a proof, extracted information is combined with his record and send them to $\mathcal{J}$ with the proof $\mathcal{B}$ redistributed digital data.

Protocol [identification] - P_{Iden}

1) $\mathcal{M}$ extracts the fingerprints $\sigma(emb)$ and $\sigma(W)$ using the extraction algorithm and searches two certificates and permutation function σ corresponding to $\sigma(emb)$ from his database.

2) If $\mathcal{M}$ cannot find them, then this protocol returns failure. Otherwise he finds them, he sends to $\mathcal{J}$ the proof string

$$proof = (\sigma(emb), \sigma(W), EW, \sigma, C_1, C_2)$$

3) $\mathcal{J}$ finds the value (a, b) and (a', b') from $\sigma(W)$ and $\sigma(emb)$. Then he computes $x = (b - b')/(a' - a)$ using those values. After finding x, $\mathcal{J}$ decrypts EW using the value x and verifies the value $\sigma(W)$ with σ and checks that the certificates C_2 is valid. Then, he verifies $y = g^x$ and computes $k'' = g^{(b+xa)}$ and verifies C_1.

4) When the accused buyer denies the fact he redistributes the digital data $item'$, $\mathcal{J}$ asks $\mathcal{RC}$ for the signature (e, h) corresponding to anonymous public key y. Then $\mathcal{J}$ computes $z' = g^h v^e$ and verifies that $\mathcal{B}$'s Schnorr signature is a valid one on (e, h) with respect to $\mathcal{B}$'s public key v. If yes, it means that $\mathcal{B}$ has redistributed the digital data $item'$. Otherwise, $\mathcal{B}$ is innocent.

5   Analysis

In this section we present the proof sketch in detail for the security of our protocols. We assume that all the underlying primitives are secure. The merchant's security only relies on the security of the underlying embedding scheme and the buyer's on standard cryptographic assumptions.

5.1   Security for the Merchant

Due to the properties of the embedding scheme, we can assume that whenever the maximum tolerated size of a collusion is not exceeded, and the collusion redistributes a data item sufficiently similar to the original, then $\mathcal{M}$ can extract the fingerprints and relevant values that belongs to a traitor.

Traceability. In fingerprinting protocol, $\mathcal{B}$ must transmit the correct response b' of the challenge a. If this value is not correct, $\mathcal{M}$ needs not provide the digital data to $\mathcal{B}$ in the fourth step of fingerprinting. And the certificate C_1 guarantees that the anonymous key x, y and secret information k which is used to trace a traitor is registered at $\mathcal{RC}$. Thus $\mathcal{M}$ can be convinced that $\mathcal{B}$ knows the secret information k and x and that values are registered.

In fingerprinting protocol, $\mathcal{B}$ makes an attempt to provide a wrong value EW' not to accuse when he illegally redistributes the digital data later. But he cannot make a valid certificates C_2' on EW', $\mathcal{M}$ can notice that the value EW' is not correct value.

Besides, $\mathcal{B}$ cannot remove emb and W from $item'$ because he doesn't know the permutation function σ. And $\mathcal{M}$ should insert two fingerprints $\sigma(emb)$ and $\sigma(W)$ in the right manner for his own interest. If he does not correctly insert two fingerprints, he would not be able to identify the original buyer of an illegal copy. Thus the buyer who has distributed the digital data illegally can be traced in our scheme.

No repudiation. The buyer accused of reselling an unauthorized copy cannot claim that the copy was created by the merchant or a security breach of the merchant's system. In registration protocol, the buyer generates a signature on x and k. Since only the buyer knows his secret key x and can generate the Schnorr's signature, the others cannot re-create the buyer's copy.

5.2   Security for the Buyer

We assume that the registration center does not reveal the buyer's real ID if the buyer is honest. An honest buyer is secure if the attackers cannot convince the judge in the identification protocol, even if the other parties obtain other digital data that he bought.

Security from malicious merchant. $\mathcal{M}$ cannot frame $\mathcal{B}$ by generating two pieces of fingerprinted contents with the value emb or EW. Such cheating of $\mathcal{M}$, however, will be detected by $\mathcal{J}$ in our protocol. To cheat, $\mathcal{M}$ has the following two ways.

(1) Since $\mathcal{M}$ knows EW, $\mathcal{M}$ makes an attempt to embed it into other items and then frames $\mathcal{B}$. For doing this, he generates a random value $emb' = (a'', b'')$ and encrypts it with $\mathcal{B}$'s anonymous public key and embeds it into other item $item_*$ with $\mathcal{B}$'s EW.

$$item'_* = item_* \oplus \sigma(emb') \oplus \sigma(W) \tag{2}$$

Then $\mathcal{M}$ accuses $\mathcal{B}$ of redistributing the digital data. In such case, however, $\mathcal{M}$ cannot make a valid value (a'', b'') satisfying the function $b'' = k - xa''$. In our protocol, only the buyer knows his secret key x and secret information k if computing discrete logarithm is hard and used encryption algorithm is secure. Thus a malicious merchant cannot compute the valid fingerprint (a'', b'').

(2) Even though $\mathcal{M}$ knows the value emb and EW, he cannot spread the version sold to $\mathcal{B}$. $\mathcal{M}$ cannot reproduce the watermarked copy $item'$, because $\mathcal{M}$ only knows the encrypted value EW and cannot know the fingerprinted copy $item'$.

(3) Even though the merchant colludes with the judge, a malicious merchant cannot accuse an innocent buyer by a copyright violator like [9]. In [9], a merchant can obtain the anonymous public key of buyer's and encrypted form of secret key which is encrypted with the judge's public key, through insecure channel in the watermark generation protocol. If a merchant obtains those values, he researches the buyer's record corresponding with his anonymous key and send them to the judge. These are just plain text in the view of the judge. Thus the merchant can decrypt the buyer's content. But in our scheme, the judge can find the buyer's secret key by obtaining the fingerprint $\sigma(W)$ and that fingerprint is only obtained when the buyer redistributes the contents.

Security from adversary. An adversary takes part in the protocol as if he is $\mathcal{B}$. In this case, the adversary must generate a valid Schnorr's digital signature. But the adversary does not know the $\mathcal{B}$'s secret key for the signature, he cannot forge a valid signature. And the commitments in registration protocol are semantically secure, computing k and x from k' and y is as hard as computing discrete logarithm.

In our protocol, an honest buyer should not be wrongly identified as a copyright violator, because the others cannot re-create the buyer's copy or his signature and obtain the buyer's information even though participants collude with each other.

5.3   User's Anonymity

An honest buyer who follows fingerprinting protocol will not be identified. In fingerprinting protocol, the fact that $\mathcal{M}$ knows the value emb is no problem. $\mathcal{M}$ sees b', y, $E_{H_y}(W)$ and their certificates C_1, C_2. But $\mathcal{M}$ cannot see the value of W because $\mathcal{B}$ sends the value in the form of encryption. So, $\mathcal{M}$ cannot know $\mathcal{B}$'s one of fingerprints and fingerprinted copy $item'$. Finding W would require knowledge of x. However, if the encryption algorithm is secure, the only way for $\mathcal{M}$ to find x is to compute $\log_g y$. But polynomial algorithm proving discrete logarithm problem does not exist, so $\mathcal{M}$ cannot compute x.

When $\mathcal{B}$ registers to $\mathcal{RC}$, $\mathcal{B}$ generates an anonymous key pair and convinces $\mathcal{RC}$ by zero-knowledge proof. These method used in the registration protocol completely hides $\mathcal{B}$'s anonymous private key x. Furthermore using one-time random number r, k and anonymous key pair implies that $\mathcal{B}$'s different purchases are unlinkable.

5.4 Efficiency

Recently, for practical copyright protection, the fingerprinting scheme using homomorphic encryption has been proposed. The first-known scheme is proposed by Memon et.al[10]. Memon et.al proposed a fingerprinting protocol to protect the digital data using a homomorphic encryption algorithm. The drawback of this scheme is that it did not provide the buyer's anonymity. Other schemes providing the buyer's anonymity are attributed to Ju et. al[9] and Choi et. al[6]. Since the former scheme used verifiable encryption, can be expensive to computation, for providing anonymity, this scheme is not practical. The later scheme is not practical because fingerprint generation center generates n-different fingerprints for each buyer and the buyer should participate the identification protocol.

The proposed scheme is improved the efficiency compared to previous schemes [9, 6] by employing secret sharing to generate fingerprints and trace traitor. we do not need to apply the verification encryption for the buyer's anonymity since the secret sharing scheme guarantees that the buyer's identity is kept secret before he redistributes the digital data. We also do not need n-different fingerprints and the buyer's participation in identification protocol like [6].

6   Conclusions

In this paper, we have proposed an efficient protocol where all protocols are explicit and fairly efficient. The proposed scheme applied secret sharing scheme in order to allow both the tracing of the traitor and the preservation of the buyer's anonymity. Through a security analysis, we have shown that our protocol is secure from both the merchant and the buyer. And for inserting the fingerprint efficiently and anonymously, we applied the homomorphic encryption scheme. This scheme makes actual usage of anonymous fingerprinting attainable. Since non-repudiation is also provided by the digital signature scheme, the buyer and the merchant cannot deny their actions. The only drawback of our scheme is the requirement of an assumption that the registration center does not reveal the buyer's real ID if the buyer is honest.

References

1. G. Blakley, C. Meadow and G. B. Purdy, "Fingerprinting long forgiving messages," Advances in Cryptology - CRYPTO'85, LNCS 218, pp. 180-189, 1986.
2. D. Boneh and J. Shaw, "Collusion-secure fingerprinting for digital data," Advances in Cryptology - CRYPTO'95, LNCS 963, pp. 452-465, 1995.

3. E. F. Brickell, Y. Yacobi, "On privacy homomorphisms," EUROCRYPT'87, LNCS 304, pp. 117-125, 1987.
4. D. Chaum, "An impoved protocol for demonstrating possession of discrete logarithms and some generalizations," Advances in Cryptology - EUROCRYPT'87, LNCS 304, pp. 127-141, 1987.
5. D. Chaum, I. B. Damagaard and J. vad de Graaf, "Multiparty computations ensuring privacy of each party's input and correctness of the result," Advances in Cryptology - CRYPTO'87, LNCS 293, pp. 87-119, 1988.
6. J. G. Choi, K. Sakurai, J. H. Park, "Does it need trusted third party? Design of buyer-seller watermarking in digital contents," ACNS'03, LNCS 2846, pp. 265-279, 2003.
7. J. Domingo-Ferrer, "Anonymous fingerprinting based on committed oblivious transfer," PKC 1999, LNCS 1560, pp. 43-52, 1999.
8. J. Domingo-Ferrer, "Anonymous fingerprinting of electronic information with automatic identification redistributors," IEE Electronic Letters, 43(13), pp. 1303-1304, 1998.
9. H. Ju, H. Kim, D. Lee and J. Lim, "An anonymous buyer-seller watermarking protocol with anonymity control," ICISC2002, LNCS 2587, pp. 421-432, 2003.
10. N. Memon and P. W. Wong, "A buyer-seller watermarking protocol," IEEE Transactions on Image Processing, 10(4), pp. 643-649, 2001.
11. B. Pfitzmann and A. R. Sadeghi, "Coin-based anonymous fingerprinting," Advances in Cryptology - EUROCRYPT'99, LNCS 1592, pp. 150–164, 1999.
12. B.Pfitzmann and M. Schunter, "Asymmetric fingerprinting," Advances in Cryptology - EYROCRYPT'96, LNCS 1070, pp. 84-95, 1996.
13. B. Pfitzmann and M. Waidner, "Anonymous fingerprinting," Advances in Cryptology - EUROCRYPT'97, LNCS 1233, pp. 88-102, 1997.
14. R. L. Rivest, A. Shamir, L. Adleman, "A method for obtaining digital signatures and public-key cryptosystems," Communications of the ACM, vol. 21, no. 2, pp. 120-126, 1978.
15. C. Schnorr, "Efficient signature generation for smart cards," Journal of Cryptology, 4(3), pp. 161-174, 1991.
16. A. Shamir, "How to share a secret," CACM, 22(11), pp. 612-613, 1979.
17. W. Trappe, M. Wu and K. Liu, "Collusion-resistant fingerprinting for multimedia," IEEE International Conference on Acoustics, Speech, and Signal Processing, 4, pp. 3309-3312, 2002.
18. N. R. Wanger, "Fingerprinting," IEEE Symposium on Security and Privacy, 1983.

Worst-Case Optimal Fingerprinting Codes for Non-threshold Collusion

Takaaki Mizuki[1], Satoshi Nounin[2], Hideaki Sone[1], and Yousuke Toyota[3]

[1] Information Synergy Center, Tohoku University,
Aramaki-Aza-Aoba 6-3, Aoba-ku, Sendai 980-8578, Japan
tm-paper@rd.isc.tohoku.ac.jp
[2] Sone Lab., Graduate School of Information Sciences, Tohoku University,
Aramaki-Aza-Aoba 6-3, Aoba-ku, Sendai 980-8578, Japan
[3] KDDI R&D Laboratories Inc.,
Ohara 2-1-15, Fujimino-shi, Saitama 356-8502, Japan

Abstract. This paper investigates collusion-secure fingerprinting codes for digital data. Most previous works assume the threshold number of collusive users. Whereas, in order to treat a more general non-threshold collusion, we first introduce a notion of a potentially collusive family. Furthermore, we develop a novel way to measure collusion-secure codes according to combinatorial properties in a natural way. Our measurement immediately implies the definition of optimal codes. We then actually illustrate an optimal code. Finally, we give a necessary and sufficient condition for a code to be optimal by using a new notion of family-intersecting codes.

1 Introduction

Assume that there are k *users* who want to buy some digital content from a *distributor*. The distributor wishes to prevent the users from illegally copying the digital content. To this end, *fingerprinting* or *watermarking* techniques become being widely used; the distributor embeds a *watermark* into each copy of the digital content before she sells it to a user (e.g., refer to [10, 23] for a survey).

This paper considers the usual case where the embedded watermarks differ from each other so that the distributor can detect a user who made an illegal copy. More specifically, the copy of the digital content bought by each user $u \in U = \{1, 2, \ldots, k\}$ contains a unique watermark $w^{(u)} \in W$, where W is called a *watermarking space*. Throughout the paper, the set $U = \{1, 2, \ldots, k\}$ of all the users is fixed. If the distributor finds an illegal copy containing a watermark $w^{(u)}$, then she maybe judges that the user u is guilty. However, the distributor cannot always make such judgment because of the existence of *collusion attacks*. Roughly speaking, a collusion attack is that two or more users, in order to mask their identities, collude and alter the embedded watermarks by comparing their copies of the digital content. Since the seminal formalization given by Boneh and Shaw [4], so much research has been done extensively on modeling collusion attacks [13, 19, 20, 24], constructing collusion-secure fingerprinting schemes [8, 12, 14, 15, 21], analyzing bounds for collusion-secure fingerprinting

R. Safavi-Naini and M. Yung (Eds.): DRMTICS 2005, LNCS 3919, pp. 203–216, 2006.

[2, 17, 18, 25], and so on. Note that a more basic collusion problem was discussed first by Blakley, Meadows and Purdy [3].

1.1   Our Adopted Model

Although there are many models defining the problems of collusion attacks, this paper adopts the most well-known model, the so-called *Marking Assumption*, proposed by Boneh and Shaw [4].

We assume in this paper that a watermarking space W is binary, i.e. $W = \{0,1\}^n$ for some integer n. Therefore, a watermark $w \in W = \{0,1\}^n$ is a binary sequence (binary vector) of length n. As mentioned before, the watermark $w^{(u)}$ given to each user $u \in U$ is unique, that is, $w^{(u)} \neq w^{(v)}$ for every pair $u, v \in U$ with $u \neq v$. We call the set $\Gamma = \{w^{(1)}, w^{(2)}, \ldots, w^{(k)}\}$ of such watermarks an (n, k)-code or simply a *code*. We show a simple example.

Example 1. Let $\Gamma^{\mathrm{ex1}} = \{w^{(1)}, w^{(2)}, w^{(3)}, w^{(4)}\}$ be defined as follows.

$$w^{(1)} : 10111$$
$$w^{(2)} : 01100$$
$$w^{(3)} : 00010$$
$$w^{(4)} : 00001$$

Then, Γ^{ex1} is a $(5, 4)$-code.

Throughout the paper, the i-th bit of a watermark $w \in W$ is denoted by w_i. For instance, $w_1^{(1)} = 1$, $w_2^{(1)} = 0$, $w_3^{(1)} = 1$, and so on, where $w^{(1)}$ is the watermark in the code Γ^{ex1} (given in Example 1). Furthermore, given a code Γ, $w^{(u)}$ represents the watermark assigned to the user u in Γ if it is clear from the context.

We call a nonempty subset $C \subseteq U$ a *coalition*. Given a code Γ and a coalition C, consider the case where all the users in the coalition C collude. Then, since their watermarks in the code Γ are different from each other, by comparing their copies, they can realize some of the bit positions in which the watermark is really embedded. For instance, if $\Gamma = \Gamma^{\mathrm{ex1}}$ and $C = \{3, 4\}$, then users 3 and 4 can discover the watermarked bit positions (in their copies) corresponding to the 4th and 5th bits of their watermarks $w^{(3)}$ and $w^{(4)}$. We assume that these discovered bits cannot be deleted, but can be arbitrarily changed to either 0 or 1. For instance, the coalition $C = \{3, 4\}$ in the code Γ^{ex1} can illegally make two copies which do not contain the watermark $w^{(3)}$ or $w^{(4)}$; one is the copy containing the watermark 00011, and the other contains the watermark 00000. More formally, a coalition C in a code Γ can produce any illegal copy whose watermark is in the "feasible set" $F(C; \Gamma)$ defined as follows.

Definition 1. *The feasible set $F(C; \Gamma)$ for a coalition C and a code $\Gamma \subseteq \{0,1\}^n$ is defined as*

$$F(C; \Gamma) = \{w \in \{0,1\}^n \mid \forall i \in [1, n] \ \exists u \in C \ \ w_i = w_i^{(u)}\}.$$

For example,

$$F(\{3, 4\}; \Gamma^{\mathrm{ex1}}) = \{00010, 00001, 00011, 00000\}.$$

1.2   Previous Works

Let Γ be a code, and let each user possess her watermarked copy according to the code Γ. Once the distributor finds an illegal copy containing a watermark w, she tries to identify the guilty users from the code Γ and the illegal watermark w. That is, the distributor searches for the coalitions C such that the illegal watermark w is in the feasible sets $F(C; \Gamma)$. We call such a coalition a *suspected coalition*. In most previous works, the number of colluding users is assumed to be limited by a constant c, i.e. most previous works assume that at most c users collude. In other words, the distributor searches for only the suspected coalitions C such that $|C| \leq c$. This is captured by the following "suspected families."

Definition 2. *Let $\Gamma \subseteq \{0,1\}^n$ be a code, let $w \in \{0,1\}^n$ be a watermark, and let c be an integer with $1 \leq c \leq k$. Then, the* suspected family $\mathcal{S}(w, c; \Gamma)$ *is defined as*

$$\mathcal{S}(w, c; \Gamma) = \{C \subseteq U \mid w \in F(C; \Gamma),\ 1 \leq |C| \leq c\}.$$

For example,

$$\mathcal{S}(00011, 2; \Gamma^{\text{ex1}}) = \{\{1,3\}, \{1,4\}, \{3,4\}\}. \tag{1}$$

Notice that every coalition in the suspected family $\mathcal{S}(w, c; \Gamma)$ is possibly guilty, when the distributor used a code Γ and finds an illegal watermark w (assuming that at most c users collude).

Of course, depending on a code Γ, the "shapes" of suspected families

$$\mathcal{S}(w, c; \Gamma)$$

are determined. Therefore, one wishes to design a code Γ such that, from every suspected family $\mathcal{S}(w, c; \Gamma)$, the distributor can easily identify the guilty users. There have been various collusion-secure properties based on the "shapes" of suspected families, as below.

Boneh and Shaw gave the following definition.

Definition 3 ([4]). *Let c be an integer with $1 \leq c \leq k$. Then, a code Γ is* c-frameproof *if $\mathcal{S}(w^{(u)}, c; \Gamma) \subseteq \{C \subseteq U \mid u \in C\}$ for every user $u \in U$.*

A c-frameproof code implies that no coalition C with $|C| \leq c$ can frame a user not in C. One can easily observe that Γ^{ex1} is a 2-frameproof code. However, Γ^{ex1} is not a 3-frameproof code, because

$$\mathcal{S}(w^{(4)}, 3; \Gamma^{\text{ex1}}) \ni \{1, 2, 3\}.$$

Boneh and Shaw also gave the following definition.

Definition 4 ([4]). *Let c be an integer with $1 \leq c \leq k$. Then, a code $\Gamma \subseteq \{0,1\}^n$ is* totally c-secure *if*

$$\bigcap_{C \in \mathcal{S}(w,c;\Gamma)} C \neq \emptyset$$

for every watermark $w \in \{0,1\}^n$ such that $\mathcal{S}(w, c; \Gamma) \neq \emptyset$.

A totally c-secure code implies that, whenever an illegal watermark w is found, the distributor can necessarily identify at least one guilty user who surely made the illegal watermark w. However, it has been proved that there exists no totally c-secure code (provided that $c \geq 2$ and $k \geq 3$) [4], because there must exist a watermark w producing a "triangle" like Eq. (1) as a suspected family $\mathcal{S}(w, c; \Gamma)$ whatever code Γ is constructed.

As the alternatives to totally c-secureness, c-secure codes with ϵ-error [4] and error- and collusion-secure codes [13] were proposed. In these error probability approaches, which use randomization to generate a code, there has been much progress (e.g. [14, 15, 18, 21, 25]). In particular, Tardos [21] obtained beautiful results: he gave c-secure codes with ϵ-error of length $O(c^2 \log(k/\epsilon))$, which match lower bounds within a constant factor. (As seen later, this paper will take a "worst-case combinatorial approach," and hence considering such randomization makes no sense in our setting.)

Stinson, Trung and Wei gave the following definition.

Definition 5 ([20]). *Let c be an integer with $1 \leq c \leq k$. Then, a code $\Gamma \subseteq \{0,1\}^n$ is c-secure frameproof if*

$$C, C' \in \mathcal{S}(w, c; \Gamma) \quad \Longrightarrow \quad C \cap C' \neq \emptyset$$

for every watermark $w \in \{0,1\}^n$.

Yoshioka, Shikata and Matsumoto [24] have greatly investigated the relationships among c-frameproof, totally c-secure, ϵ-error c-secure, c-secure frameproof, and $(c, p/q)$-secure [2, 17] codes, and so on.

1.3   Our Results

As seen in Definition 2, most previous works have assumed that at most c users collude for some threshold c. That is, most previous works dealt with the "threshold model." In this paper, we will investigate a more general model, namely the "non-threshold model." To this end, we will introduce a notion of a "potentially collusive family," which generalizes the previous settings in the problems of collusion-secure fingerprinting.

Furthermore, we will develop a way to measure collusion-secure codes; our measurement can tell us which code is better or worse, given two codes. Using our measurement, one can define an "optimal" code. We will indeed construct such an "optimal" code. Furthermore, we will give a necessary and sufficient condition for a code to be "optimal," that is, we will completely characterize "optimal" codes. As will be seen, the idea behind our measurement of collusion-secure codes is based on combinatorial properties of suspected families in the worst case analysis. In addition, our measurement is quite natural and is in a reasonable way.

The remainder of the paper is organized as follows. In Section 2, we introduce a notion of a "potentially collusive family." In Section 3, we define an "optimal" code under our collusion model using our measurement. In Section 4, we actually construct an example of an "optimal" code. In Section 5, we give a necessary and sufficient condition for "optimal" codes. This paper concludes in Section 6 with some discussions and open problems.

2   Introducing a Potentially Collusive Family

In this section, we introduce a notion of a "potentially collusive family."

As mentioned before, most previous works have assumed that at most c users collude for some threshold c. However, this assumption may not be suitable for some actual situations. For example, consider the case where there are several users groups $U_1, U_2, U_3, \ldots$, and it has been known that any users in a certain group never collude with a user in other groups; then, one wishes to construct a collusion-secure code in a more general model other than in such a threshold model. For another example, there may exist a situation in which at most c users never collude, but at least $c + 1$ users may collude; in this situation, one cannot use the threshold model proposed previously. Indeed, in the real world, the social relations between users are not uniform; for instance, it has been known that such social networks possibly have a high clustering coefficient [22], a heavy-tailed degree distribution [16], a bipartite structure [11], and so on.

Thus, we wish to introduce a more general model, namely the "non-threshold model," which is trivial, as follows. We call a subset $\mathcal{R} \subseteq 2^U$ of the power set of U a *potentially collusive family*. A potentially collusive family $\mathcal{R}$ means that only coalitions C in the family $\mathcal{R}$ possibly collude. Of course, the "threshold model" can be obtained by setting

$$\mathcal{R} = \{C \subseteq U \mid 1 \leq |C| \leq c\}.$$

We now show an example.

Example 2. Let $U = \{1, 2, 3, 4\}$. Assume that any pairs of users possibly collude, and furthermore that coalitions $\{1, 2, 3\}$ and $\{2, 3, 4\}$ of three users possibly collude. Then, it suffices to set a potentially collusive family to

$$\mathcal{R}^{ex2} = \{\{1, 2\}, \{1, 3\}, \{1, 4\}, \{2, 3\}, \{2, 4\}, \{3, 4\}, \{1, 2, 3\}, \{2, 3, 4\}\}.$$

Similarly as in Definition 2, we can define a (generalized) "suspected family" $\mathcal{S}(w, \mathcal{R}; \Gamma)$ under a potentially collusive family $\mathcal{R}$, as follows.

Definition 6. *Let $\Gamma \subseteq \{0, 1\}^n$ be a code, let $w \in \{0, 1\}^n$ be a watermark, and let $\mathcal{R}$ be a potentially collusive family. Then, the suspected family $\mathcal{S}(w, \mathcal{R}; \Gamma)$ is defined as*

$$\mathcal{S}(w, \mathcal{R}; \Gamma) = \{C \in \mathcal{R} \mid w \in F(C; \Gamma)\}.$$

3   Measuring Codes and Defining Optimal Codes

In the previous section, we introduced the notion of a potentially collusive family $\mathcal{R}$; hereafter, we are always taking $\mathcal{R}$ into account, as will be seen. In this section, we design a novel way to measure collusion-secure codes; roughly speaking, given two codes Γ and Π, our measurement can tell us which code is better or worse. Using our measurement, one can easily define an "optimal" code under a potentially collusive family.

We first present our measurement of collusion-secure codes in Section 3.1. We then define an "optimal" code in Section 3.2.

3.1   Our Measurement of Codes

Let Γ be a code, and let $\mathcal{R}$ be a potentially collusive family. Then, remember that each watermark w determines the corresponding suspected family $\mathcal{S}(w, \mathcal{R}; \Gamma)$, whose "shape" is important for the distributor to trace the guilty users. Before selling copies of the digital content to the users, the distributor does not know which coalition in $\mathcal{R}$ will collude and which illegal watermark will be produced. Thus, we in advance "collect" all suspected families by considering all watermarks, as in the following Definition 7.

Definition 7. *Let $\Gamma \subseteq \{0,1\}^n$ be a code, and let $\mathcal{R}$ be a potentially collusive family. Then, the* suspected families collection $\Delta_{\mathcal{R}}(\Gamma)$ *is defined as*

$$\Delta_{\mathcal{R}}(\Gamma) = \{\mathcal{S}(w, \mathcal{R}; \Gamma) \mid w \in \{0,1\}^n, \ \mathcal{S}(w, \mathcal{R}; \Gamma) \neq \emptyset\}.$$

Note that the suspected families collection $\Delta_{\mathcal{R}}(\Gamma)$ depends only on a code Γ and a potentially collusive family $\mathcal{R}$.

Now, consider again the code Γ^{ex1} in Example 1 and the potentially collusive family $\mathcal{R}^{\mathrm{ex2}}$ in Example 2. Then, for the watermark 00011, we have

$$\mathcal{S}(00011, \mathcal{R}^{\mathrm{ex2}}; \Gamma^{\mathrm{ex1}}) = \{\{1,3\}, \{1,4\}, \{3,4\}, \{1,2,3\}, \{2,3,4\}\},$$

which is an element of the suspected families collection $\Delta_{\mathcal{R}^{\mathrm{ex2}}}(\Gamma^{\mathrm{ex1}})$. For another watermark 10011,

$$\mathcal{S}(10011, \mathcal{R}^{\mathrm{ex2}}; \Gamma^{\mathrm{ex1}}) = \{\{1,3\}, \{1,4\}, \{1,2,3\}\},$$

which is also in $\Delta_{\mathcal{R}^{\mathrm{ex2}}}(\Gamma^{\mathrm{ex1}})$, of course. Note that

$$\mathcal{S}(00011, \mathcal{R}^{\mathrm{ex2}}; \Gamma^{\mathrm{ex1}}) \supset \mathcal{S}(10011, \mathcal{R}^{\mathrm{ex2}}; \Gamma^{\mathrm{ex1}}),$$

and hence the suspected family of the latter is "smaller" than one of the former. Thus, for the distributor, the illegal watermark 10011 is preferable to the illegal watermark 00011; however, since the distributor has no power to choose such an illegal watermark made by the guilty coalition, we perform the worst case analysis. This is captured by the "maximal suspected families collection."

Definition 8. *Let $\Gamma \subseteq \{0,1\}^n$ be a code, and let $\mathcal{R}$ be a potentially collusive family. Then, the* maximal suspected families collection $\Delta_{\mathcal{R}}^{+}(\Gamma)$ *is defined as*

$$\Delta_{\mathcal{R}}^{+}(\Gamma) = \{\mathcal{H} \in \Delta_{\mathcal{R}}(\Gamma) \mid \forall \mathcal{F} \in \Delta_{\mathcal{R}}(\Gamma) - \{\mathcal{H}\} \ \ \mathcal{F} \not\supset \mathcal{H}\}.$$

Note that the maximal suspected families collection $\Delta_{\mathcal{R}}^{+}(\Gamma)$ also depends only on a code Γ and a potentially collusive family $\mathcal{R}$.

Given two codes Γ and Π, we determine whether Γ is better than Π or not, according to the inclusion of the suspected families in the maximal suspected families collections $\Delta_{\mathcal{R}}^{+}(\Gamma)$ and $\Delta_{\mathcal{R}}^{+}(\Pi)$, as in the following Definition 9. Remember that, intuitively, the "smaller" its suspected families in $\Delta_{\mathcal{R}}^{+}(\Gamma)$ are, the better a code Γ is.

Definition 9. *Let Γ and Π be two codes, and let $\mathcal{R}$ be a potentially collusive family. Then, we say that the code Γ is superior to the code Π under the potentially collusive family $\mathcal{R}$, and we write*

$$\Gamma \succeq_{\mathcal{R}} \Pi,$$

if the following holds:

$$\forall \mathcal{H} \in \Delta_{\mathcal{R}}^{+}(\Gamma) \ \exists \mathcal{F} \in \Delta_{\mathcal{R}}^{+}(\Pi) \ \ \mathcal{H} \subseteq \mathcal{F}.$$

Note that $\succeq_{\mathcal{R}}$ is a relation on the set of all codes; the relation $\succeq_{\mathcal{R}}$ satisfies reflexivity and transitivity (and hence is a quasi-order), but satisfies neither symmetry nor antisymmetry.

If two codes Γ and Π satisfy both $\Gamma \succeq_{\mathcal{R}} \Pi$ and $\Pi \succeq_{\mathcal{R}} \Gamma$ for a potentially collusive family $\mathcal{R}$, then we write

$$\Gamma \simeq_{\mathcal{R}} \Pi.$$

Definition 9 is our measurement of collusion-secure codes. Notice that our measurement, namely the quasi-order $\succeq_{\mathcal{R}}$, evaluates two codes Γ and Π depending only on the inclusion ($\subseteq$) of each pair of the suspected families $\mathcal{H} \in \Delta_{\mathcal{R}}^{+}(\Gamma)$ and $\mathcal{F} \in \Delta_{\mathcal{R}}^{+}(\Pi)$; no one disputes the fact that a suspected family $\mathcal{H}$ is preferable to a suspected family $\mathcal{F}$ when $\mathcal{H} \subseteq \mathcal{F}$. Note, therefore, that we need not bother to decide which suspected family is preferable for such as a pair of $\mathcal{H} = \{\{1,2\},\{2,3\},\{3,1\}\}$ and $\mathcal{F} = \{\{1,2\},\{1,3\},\{1,4\},\{1,5\},\dots\}$. (This is a reason why we take a worst-case combinatorial approach.) Thus, our measurement is in a natural way.

3.2   Optimal Codes

Using the definition of our measurement of collusion-secure codes, i.e. the relation $\succeq_{\mathcal{R}}$ given in Definition 9, one can easily define optimal codes in a natural way, as follows.

Definition 10. *We say that a code Γ is optimal under a potentially collusive family $\mathcal{R}$ if $\Gamma \succeq_{\mathcal{R}} \Pi$ for any code Π.*

Note that, in general, a quasi-order does not necessarily have such a "greatest" element as in Definition 10; however, the quasi-order $\succeq_{\mathcal{R}}$ has at least one optimal code, as will be seen in the next section.

Definition 11. *We say that a code Γ is optimal if it is optimal under any potentially collusive family.*

4   Illustrating an Optimal Code

In the previous section, we gave the definition of optimal codes as in Definition 11. In this section, we actually construct an example of an optimal code.

We first give the description of the code in Section 4.1. We then prove that the code is optimal in Section 4.2.

4.1   An Example of an Optimal Code

First, consider the $(2^k - 2, k)$-code $\Gamma^{\text{opt-long}}$ defined by the following $k \times (2^k - 2)$ binary matrix:

$$\Gamma^{\text{opt-long}} = \begin{bmatrix} 1\,0 \cdots 0\,0\,1\,1 \cdots 0\,1 \cdots 0\,0\,1\,1 \cdots 1\,0 \\ 0\,1 \cdots 0\,0\,1\,0 \cdots 0\,1 \cdots 1\,0\,1\,1 \cdots 0\,1 \\ 0\,0 \cdots 0\,0\,0\,1 \cdots 0\,1 \cdots 0\,1\,1\,1 \cdots 1\,1 \\ \vdots\;\vdots\;\ddots\;\vdots\;\vdots\;\vdots\;\vdots \cdots \vdots\;\vdots \cdots \vdots\;\vdots\;\vdots\;\vdots\;\ddots\;\vdots\;\vdots \\ 0\,0 \cdots 0\,0\,0\,0 \cdots 1\,0 \cdots 1\,1\,1\,1 \cdots 1\,1 \\ 0\,0 \cdots 1\,0\,0\,0 \cdots 1\,0 \cdots 1\,1\,1\,0 \cdots 1\,1 \\ 0\,0 \cdots 0\,1\,0\,0 \cdots 1\,0 \cdots 1\,1\,0\,1 \cdots 1\,1 \end{bmatrix}.$$

$$\underbrace{}_{\Gamma^{\text{opt}}}$$

The u-th row represents the watermark $w^{(u)}$ for each user $u \in U = \{1, 2, \ldots, k\}$. The columns list all bit patterns of length k other than "all-0" and "all-1" bit patterns. Especially, each column corresponds to a coalition $C \subseteq U$ such that $1 \le |C| \le k - 1$. The first $\binom{k}{1} = k$ columns list all bit patterns of length k, each having exactly one 1. The succeeding $\binom{k}{2}$ columns list all bit patterns, each having exactly two 1's, and so on.

We now construct a code Γ^{opt} by deleting half of the columns of the code $\Gamma^{\text{opt-long}}$ above. For every pair of two columns of $\Gamma^{\text{opt-long}}$ such that one is the bitwise complement of the other, we delete one of such two columns (because only one column of those suffices, as will be seen in Lemma 4): we set Γ^{opt} to the first half of the columns of $\Gamma^{\text{opt-long}}$. Thus, Γ^{opt} is a $(2^{k-1} - 1, k)$-code.

Concerning the code Γ^{opt} constructed above, the following Theorem 1 holds.

Theorem 1. *The code Γ^{opt} is optimal.*

We will prove Theorem 1 in the succeeding subsection.

Notice that the code Γ^{opt} is just an example of an optimal code, and that we have no intention of using the code Γ^{opt} in practical situations, of course; the length $2^{k-1} - 1$ of Γ^{opt} is too long. However, considering the optimal code Γ^{opt} helps us to derive a necessary and sufficient condition for optimal codes under a potentially collusive family $\mathcal{R}$, as will be seen in Section 5. In practice, it is more important to construct an optimal code under a certain appropriate potentially collusive family $\mathcal{R}$.

4.2   Proof of Theorem 1

In this subsection, we give a proof of Theorem 1.

We first give some notations. Given an (n, k)-code $\Gamma \subseteq \{0, 1\}^n$ and a binary sequence (column) $\gamma \in \{0, 1\}^k$, $\Gamma \| \gamma$ denotes the $(n + 1, k)$-code obtained by combining Γ with γ as the $(n + 1)$-th column. Similarly, given a watermark $w \in \{0, 1\}^n$ and a bit $v \in \{0, 1\}$, $w \| v$ denotes the watermark of length $n + 1$ obtained by concatenating w and v. Furthermore, Γ_i denotes the i-th column of a code Γ. Remember that w_i denotes the i-th bit of a watermark w.

In order to prove Theorem 1, we give five lemmas. First, Lemma 1 immediately follows from Definition 6.

Lemma 1. *Let $\Gamma \subseteq \{0, 1\}^n$ be a code, let $w \in \{0, 1\}^n$ be a watermark, and let $\mathcal{R}$ be a potentially collusive family. Then,*

$$\mathcal{S}(w, \mathcal{R}; \Gamma) = \mathcal{S}(w_1, \mathcal{R}; \Gamma_1) \cap \mathcal{S}(w_2, \mathcal{R}; \Gamma_2) \cap \cdots \cap \mathcal{S}(w_n, \mathcal{R}; \Gamma_n).$$

Next, we have the following Lemmas 2–5.

Lemma 2. *Let $\Gamma, \Pi \subseteq \{0, 1\}^n$ be two codes, and let $\mathcal{R}$ be a potentially collusive family. Assume that there exist two distinct indices i and j with $\Gamma_i = \Pi_j$ and $\Gamma_j = \Pi_i$, and that $\Gamma_\ell = \Pi_\ell$ for every $\ell \in [1, n] - \{i, j\}$. Then,*

$$\Gamma \simeq_{\mathcal{R}} \Pi.$$

Proof. Let $w \in \{0, 1\}^n$ be a watermark. Let w' be the (unique) watermark such that $w'_i = w_j$, $w'_j = w_i$, and $w'_\ell = w_\ell$ for all $\ell \in [1, n] - \{i, j\}$. By Lemma 1, we have

$$\mathcal{S}(w, \mathcal{R}; \Gamma) = \mathcal{S}(w_1, \mathcal{R}; \Gamma_1) \cap \mathcal{S}(w_2, \mathcal{R}; \Gamma_2) \cap \cdots \cap \mathcal{S}(w_n, \mathcal{R}; \Gamma_n)$$

and

$$\mathcal{S}(w', \mathcal{R}; \Pi) = \mathcal{S}(w'_1, \mathcal{R}; \Pi_1) \cap \mathcal{S}(w'_2, \mathcal{R}; \Pi_2) \cap \cdots \cap \mathcal{S}(w'_n, \mathcal{R}; \Pi_n).$$

Since $\Gamma_i = \Pi_j$ and $\Gamma_j = \Pi_i$, we have

$$\mathcal{S}(w_i, \mathcal{R}; \Gamma_i) = \mathcal{S}(w'_j, \mathcal{R}; \Pi_j)$$

and

$$\mathcal{S}(w_j, \mathcal{R}; \Gamma_j) = \mathcal{S}(w'_i, \mathcal{R}; \Pi_i).$$

Therefore, we have

$$\mathcal{S}(w, \mathcal{R}; \Gamma) = \mathcal{S}(w', \mathcal{R}; \Pi).$$

Hence, since w is arbitrary, $\Delta_{\mathcal{R}}(\Gamma) = \Delta_{\mathcal{R}}(\Pi)$. Thus, $\Gamma \simeq_{\mathcal{R}} \Pi$.   □

Lemma 3. *Let $\Gamma \subseteq \{0, 1\}^n$ be a code, let $\mathcal{R}$ be a potentially collusive family, and let $\gamma \in \{0, 1\}^k$ be a binary sequence (column). Then,*

$$\Gamma \| \gamma \succeq_{\mathcal{R}} \Gamma.$$

Proof. Let $w\|v \in \{0,1\}^{n+1}$ be a watermark, where $v \in \{0,1\}$. Then, by Lemma 1

$$\mathcal{S}(w\|v, \mathcal{R}; \Gamma\|\gamma) = \mathcal{S}(w_1, \mathcal{R}; \Gamma_1) \cap \mathcal{S}(w_2, \mathcal{R}; \Gamma_2) \cap \cdots \cap \mathcal{S}(w_n, \mathcal{R}; \Gamma_n) \cap \mathcal{S}(v, \mathcal{R}; \gamma)$$

and

$$\mathcal{S}(w, \mathcal{R}; \Gamma) = \mathcal{S}(w_1, \mathcal{R}; \Gamma_1) \cap \mathcal{S}(w_2, \mathcal{R}; \Gamma_2) \cap \cdots \cap \mathcal{S}(w_n, \mathcal{R}; \Gamma_n).$$

Therefore, we have $\mathcal{S}(w\|v, \mathcal{R}; \Gamma\|\gamma) \subseteq \mathcal{S}(w, \mathcal{R}; \Gamma)$. Hence, since $w\|v$ is arbitrary, for every $\mathcal{H} \in \Delta_{\mathcal{R}}(\Gamma\|\gamma)$, there exists $\mathcal{F} \in \Delta_{\mathcal{R}}^{+}(\Gamma)$ such that $\mathcal{H} \subseteq \mathcal{F}$. Thus, $\Gamma\|\gamma \succeq_{\mathcal{R}} \Gamma$. □

Lemma 4. *Let $\Gamma \subseteq \{0,1\}^n$ be a code, and let $\mathcal{R}$ be a potentially collusive family. Assume that either $\gamma = \Gamma_j$ or $\gamma = \overline{\Gamma}_j$ for some $j \in [1, n]$, where $\overline{\Gamma}_i$ denotes the column obtained by negating all bits of Γ_i. Then,*

$$\Gamma\|\gamma \simeq_{\mathcal{R}} \Gamma.$$

Proof. Let $w \in \{0,1\}^n$ be a watermark. We first consider the case of $\gamma = \Gamma_j$. By Lemma 1

$$\mathcal{S}(w, \mathcal{R}; \Gamma) = \mathcal{S}(w_1, \mathcal{R}; \Gamma_1) \cap \cdots \cap \mathcal{S}(w_j, \mathcal{R}; \Gamma_j) \cap \cdots \cap \mathcal{S}(w_n, \mathcal{R}; \Gamma_n),$$

$$\begin{aligned}
&\mathcal{S}(w\|w_j, \mathcal{R}; \Gamma\|\gamma) \\
&= \mathcal{S}(w_1, \mathcal{R}; \Gamma_1) \cap \cdots \cap \mathcal{S}(w_j, \mathcal{R}; \Gamma_j) \cap \cdots \cap \mathcal{S}(w_n, \mathcal{R}; \Gamma_n) \cap \mathcal{S}(w_j, \mathcal{R}; \Gamma_j) \\
&= \mathcal{S}(w_1, \mathcal{R}; \Gamma_1) \cap \cdots \cap \mathcal{S}(w_j, \mathcal{R}; \Gamma_j) \cap \cdots \cap \mathcal{S}(w_n, \mathcal{R}; \Gamma_n)
\end{aligned}$$

and

$$\begin{aligned}
&\mathcal{S}(w\|\overline{w}_j, \mathcal{R}; \Gamma\|\gamma) \\
&= \mathcal{S}(w_1, \mathcal{R}; \Gamma_1) \cap \cdots \cap \mathcal{S}(w_j, \mathcal{R}; \Gamma_j) \cap \cdots \cap \mathcal{S}(w_n, \mathcal{R}; \Gamma_n) \cap \mathcal{S}(\overline{w}_j, \mathcal{R}; \Gamma_j).
\end{aligned}$$

Therefore, $\mathcal{S}(w\|w_i, \mathcal{R}; \Gamma\|\gamma) = \mathcal{S}(w, \mathcal{R}; \Gamma)$ and $\mathcal{S}(w\|\overline{w}_i, \mathcal{R}; \Gamma\|\gamma) \subseteq \mathcal{S}(w, \mathcal{R}; \Gamma)$. Since $\Delta_{\mathcal{R}}^{+}(\Gamma\|\gamma)$ consists of maximal sets, $\mathcal{S}(w\|\overline{w}_i, \mathcal{R}; \Gamma\|\gamma) \notin \Delta_{\mathcal{R}}^{+}(\Gamma\|\gamma)$ whenever

$$\mathcal{S}(w\|\overline{w}_i, \mathcal{R}; \Gamma\|\gamma) \subset \mathcal{S}(w\|w_i, \mathcal{R}; \Gamma\|\gamma) = \mathcal{S}(w, \mathcal{R}; \Gamma).$$

Thus, one can observe that $\Delta_{\mathcal{R}}^{+}(\Gamma\|\gamma) = \Delta_{\mathcal{R}}^{+}(\Gamma)$, and hence $\Gamma\|\gamma \simeq_{\mathcal{R}} \Gamma$.

The case of $\gamma = \overline{\Gamma}_j$ is similar. □

Lemma 5. *Let $\Gamma \subseteq \{0,1\}^n$ be a code, let $\mathcal{R}$ be a potentially collusive family, and let either $\gamma = (0, 0, \ldots, 0) \in \{0,1\}^k$ or $\gamma = (1, 1, \ldots, 1) \in \{0,1\}^k$. Then,*

$$\Gamma\|\gamma \simeq_{\mathcal{R}} \Gamma.$$

Proof. Let $w \in \{0,1\}^n$ be a watermark. First, consider the case of

$$\gamma = (0, 0, \ldots, 0).$$

By Lemma 1, $\mathcal{S}(w\|0, \mathcal{R}; \Gamma\|\gamma) = \mathcal{S}(w, \mathcal{R}; \Gamma)$ and $\mathcal{S}(w\|1, \mathcal{R}; \Gamma\|\gamma) = \emptyset$. Therefore, we have $\Delta_{\mathcal{R}}^{+}(\Gamma\|\gamma) = \Delta_{\mathcal{R}}^{+}(\Gamma)$, and hence $\Gamma\|\gamma \simeq_{\mathcal{R}} \Gamma$.

The case of $\gamma = (1, 1, \ldots, 1)$ is similar. □

One can easily prove Theorem 1 by using Lemmas 2–5.

5   Characterizing Optimal Codes

In this section, we give a necessary and sufficient condition for a code to be optimal under a potentially collusive family $\mathcal{R}$. We first define an "$\mathcal{R}$-intersecting" code in Section 5.1, which will be used to describe our necessary and sufficient condition. We then give our characterization of optimal codes in Section 5.2.

5.1   Introducing $\mathcal{R}$-Intersecting Codes

We first review the definition of a "c-intersecting" code [5, 6, 7].

Definition 12. *A family $\mathcal{H}$ is* intersecting *if $C \cap C' \neq \emptyset$ for any two sets $C, C' \in \mathcal{H}$.*

Definition 13. *Let c be an integer with $1 \leq c \leq k$. Then, we say that a code $\Gamma \subseteq \{0,1\}^n$ is* c-intersecting *if $\mathcal{S}(w, c; \Gamma)$ is intersecting for every watermark $w \in \{0,1\}^n$.*

We now introduce a new notion of an "$\mathcal{R}$-intersecting" code, as follows.

Definition 14. *Let $\mathcal{R}$ be a potentially collusive family. Then, we say that a code $\Gamma \subseteq \{0,1\}^n$ is* $\mathcal{R}$-intersecting *if $\mathcal{S}(w, \mathcal{R}; \Gamma)$ is intersecting for every watermark $w \in \{0,1\}^n$.*

We can show that the code Γ^{opt} described in Section 4.1 is $\mathcal{R}$-intersecting, whatever $\mathcal{R}$ is chosen.

Lemma 6. *The code Γ^{opt} is $\mathcal{R}$-intersecting for every potentially collusive family $\mathcal{R}$.*

Proof. Let $C, C' \in \mathcal{R}$ be arbitrary coalitions such that $C \cap C' = \emptyset$. From the construction of the code Γ^{opt}, there is at least one column Γ_i such that

$$w_i^{(u)} = \begin{cases} v & \text{if} \quad u \in C; \\ \overline{v} & \text{if} \quad u \in C', \end{cases}$$

for some $v \in \{0,1\}$. Then, $F(C; \Gamma^{\mathrm{opt}}) \cap F(C'; \Gamma^{\mathrm{opt}}) = \emptyset$, and hence one can observe that $\mathcal{S}(w, \mathcal{R}; \Gamma)$ is intersecting for every w. Thus, Γ^{opt} is $\mathcal{R}$-intersecting. $\qquad\square$

Generalizing the discussion on the "triangle" mentioned in Section 1.2, one can have the following Lemma 7.

Lemma 7 ([2]). *Let Γ be a code, let $\mathcal{R}$ be a potentially collusive family, and let $\mathcal{H} \subseteq \mathcal{R}$ be an intersecting family. Then, there exists a watermark w such that $\mathcal{H} \subseteq \mathcal{S}(w, \mathcal{R}; \Gamma)$.*

5.2   A Characterization of Optimal Codes

In this subsection, we present our necessary and sufficient condition for optimal codes, as in the following Theorem 2.

Theorem 2. *Let Γ be a code, and let $\mathcal{R}$ be a potentially collusive family. Then, Γ is optimal under $\mathcal{R}$ if and only if it is $\mathcal{R}$-intersecting.*

Proof. We first show the necessity. Assume that Γ is optimal under $\mathcal{R}$. Suppose for a contradiction that Γ is not $\mathcal{R}$-intersecting. Then, there is a suspected family $\mathcal{H} \in \Delta_{\mathcal{R}}^+(\Gamma)$ such that $\mathcal{H}$ is not intersecting. On the other hand, since Γ is optimal under $\mathcal{R}$, $\Gamma \succeq_{\mathcal{R}} \Gamma^{\mathrm{opt}}$. Therefore, there is a suspected family $\mathcal{F} \in \Delta_{\mathcal{R}}^+(\Gamma^{\mathrm{opt}})$ such that $\mathcal{H} \subseteq \mathcal{F}$. Since $\mathcal{H}$ is not intersecting, $\mathcal{F}$ is not intersecting, and hence Γ^{opt} is not $\mathcal{R}$-intersecting, contrary to Lemma 6.

Next, we show the sufficiency. Assume that Γ is $\mathcal{R}$-intersecting, and let $\mathcal{H} \in \Delta_{\mathcal{R}}^+(\Gamma)$ be any suspected family. Then, $\mathcal{H}$ is intersecting. Hence, by Lemma 7, there exists a watermark w such that $\mathcal{H} \subseteq \mathcal{S}(w, \mathcal{R}; \Gamma^{\mathrm{opt}})$. Therefore, there exists $\mathcal{F} \in \Delta_{\mathcal{R}}^+(\Gamma^{\mathrm{opt}})$ such that $\mathcal{H} \subseteq \mathcal{F}$. Thus, we have $\Gamma \succeq_{\mathcal{R}} \Gamma^{\mathrm{opt}}$, and hence Γ is optimal under $\mathcal{R}$. □

Theorem 2 implies that all optimal codes under a potentially collusive family $\mathcal{R}$ can be characterized by the notion of $\mathcal{R}$-intersecting.

6   Conclusion

This paper dealt with collusion-secure fingerprinting codes. Whereas most previous works assumed that at most c users collude for some threshold c, we considered a more general model, namely a non-threshold model; we first introduced the notion of a potentially collusive family $\mathcal{R}$. A potentially collusive family $\mathcal{R}$ means that only a coalition C in the family $\mathcal{R}$ possibly colludes. In the real world, the social relations between users are not uniform such as "small-world" networks [22]; hence, our non-threshold collusion model may be effective.

We then gave a novel way to measure collusion-secure codes, based on combinatorial properties of suspected families in the worst case analysis. That is, we defined a relation $\succeq_{\mathcal{R}}$ on the set of all codes, which can tell us whether or not Γ is superior to Π under $\mathcal{R}$, given a potentially collusive family $\mathcal{R}$ and two codes Γ, Π. Our measurement is in a quite natural way, and it immediately implies the definition of optimal codes. Then, we illustrated an optimal code. Finally, we completely characterized optimal codes, that is, we proved that a code is optimal under a potentially collusive family $\mathcal{R}$ if and only if it is $\mathcal{R}$-intersecting.

This paper is the first attempt at dealing with a non-threshold collusion model; there is a lot to do in this direction. It is an interesting further task to construct an $\mathcal{R}$-intersecting code, whose length is practically short, for some realistic potentially collusive family $\mathcal{R}$. As there have been a lot of works on c-intersecting codes (or separating codes) for a threshold c (e.g. [1, 5, 6, 7, 9]), we hope that $\mathcal{R}$-intersecting codes for a family $\mathcal{R}$ would be widely investigated in the future. Besides, it is an important open problem to construct "$\mathcal{R}$-secure" codes with ϵ-error of reasonably short length, where one may regard $\mathcal{R}$ as a distribution over the potentially collusive families.

Acknowledgment

We thank the anonymous referees whose comments and suggestions helped us to improve the presentation of the paper.

References

1. N. Alon, V. Guruswami, T. Kaufman, and M. Sudan, "Guessing secrets efficiently via list decoding," Proc. the thirteenth annual ACM-SIAM Symposium on Discrete Algorithms (SODA 2002), pp. 254–262, 2002.
2. K. Banno, S. Orihara, T. Mizuki, and T. Nishizeki, "Best security index for digital fingerprinting," Proc. the Seventh International Workshop on Information Hiding (IH 2005), Lecture Notes in Computer Science, vol. 3727, pp. 398–412, Springer-Verlag, 2005.
3. G. R. Blakley, C. Meadows, and G. B. Purdy, "Fingerprinting long forgiving messages," Proc. CRYPTO '85, Lecture Notes in Computer Science, vol. 218, pp. 180–189, Springer-Verlag, 1986.
4. D. Boneh and J. Shaw, "Collusion-secure fingerprinting for digital data," IEEE Trans. Inf. Theory, vol. 44, no. 5, pp. 1897–1905, 1998.
5. G. Cohen, S. Encheva, S. Litsyn, and H. G. Schaathun, "Intersecting codes and separating codes," Discrete Applied Mathematics, vol. 128, pp. 75-83, 2003.
6. G. Cohen and A. Lempel, "Linear intersecting codes," Discrete Mathematics, vol. 56, pp. 35-43, 1985.
7. G. Cohen and G. Zemor, "Intersecting codes and independent families," IEEE Trans. Inf. Theory, vol. 40, no. 6, pp. 1872-1881, 1994.
8. J. Cotrina-Navau, M. Fernandez, and M. Soriano, "A family of collusion 2-secure codes," Proc. the Seventh International Workshop on Information Hiding (IH 2005), Lecture Notes in Computer Science, vol. 3727, pp. 387–397, Springer-Verlag, 2005.
9. M. Fernandez and M. Soriano, "Fingerprinting concatenated codes with efficient identification," Proc. the 5th Information Security Conference (ISC 2002), Lecture Notes in Computer Science, vol. 2433, pp. 459–470, Springer-Verlag, 2002.
10. T. Furon, "A survey of watermarking security," Proc. the 4th International Workshop on Digital Watermarking (IWDW 2005), Lecture Notes in Computer Science, vol. 3710, pp. 201–215, Springer-Verlag, 2005.
11. J.-L. Guillaume and M. Latapy, "Bipartite structure of all complex networks," Information Processing Letters, vol. 90, no. 5, pp. 215-221, 2004.
12. H. Guo and N. D. Georganas, "A novel approach to digital image watermarking based on a generalized secret sharing scheme," Multimedia Systems, vol. 9, no. 3, pp. 249–260, 2003.
13. H. Guth and B. Pfitzmann, "Error- and collusion-secure fingerprinting for digital data," Proc. the Third International Workshop on Information Hiding (IH '99), Lecture Notes in Computer Science, vol. 1768, pp. 134–145, Springer-Verlag, 1999.

14. T. V. Le, M. Burmester, and J. Hu, "Short c-secure fingerprinting codes," Proc. the 6th Information Security Conference (ISC 2003), Lecture Notes in Computer Science, vol. 2851, pp. 422–427, Springer-Verlag, 2003.

15. H. Muratani, "A collusion-secure fingerprinting code reduced by Chinese remaindering and its random-error resilience," Proc. the 4th International Workshop on Information Hiding (IH 2001), Lecture Notes in Computer Science, vol. 2137, pp. 303–315, Springer-Verlag, 2001.

16. M. E. J. Newman, "The structure and function of complex networks," SIAM Review, vol. 45, pp. 167–256, 2003.

17. S. Orihara, T. Mizuki, and T. Nishizeki, "New security index for digital fingerprinting and its bounds," IEICE Trans. Fundamentals, vol. E86-A, no. 5, pp. 1156–1163, 2003.

18. C. Peikert, A. Shelat, and A. Smith, "Lower bounds for collusion-secure fingerprinting," Proc. the fourteenth annual ACM-SIAM Symposium on Discrete Algorithms (SODA 2003), pp. 472–479, 2003.

19. J. N. Staddon and D. R. Stinson, "Combinatorial properties of frameproof and traceability codes," IEEE Trans. Inf. Theory, vol. 47, no. 3, pp. 1042–1049, 2001.

20. D. R. Stinson, T. van Trung, and R. Wei, "Secure frameproof codes, key distribution patterns, group testing algorithms and related structures," J. Stat. Plan. Inference, vol. 86, no. 2, pp. 595–617, 2000.

21. G. Tardos, "Optimal probabilistic fingerprint codes," Journal of the ACM, to appear.

22. D. J. Watts and S. H. Strogatz, "Collective dynamics of 'small-world' networks," Nature, vol. 393, pp .440–442, 1998.

23. M. Wu, W. Trappe, Z. J. Wang, and K. J. R. Liu, "Collusion-resistant fingerprinting for multimedia," IEEE Signal Processing Magazine, vol. 21, no. 2, pp. 15–27, 2004.

24. K. Yoshioka, J. Shikata, and T. Matsumoto, "Collusion secure codes: systematic security definitions and their relations," IEICE Trans. Fundamentals, vol. E87-A, no. 5, pp. 1162–1171, 2004.

25. K. Yoshioka, J. Shikata, and T. Matsumoto, "On collusion security of random codes," IEICE Trans. Fundamentals, vol. E88-A, no. 1, pp. 296–304, 2005.

Secure Remote Fingerprint Verification Using Dual Watermarks

Taehae Kim[1], Yongwha Chung[1], Seunghwan Jung[1], and Daesung Moon[2]

[1] Department of Computer and Information Science, Korea University, Korea
{taegar, ychungy, sksghksl}@korea.ac.kr
[2] Biometrics Technology Research Team, ETRI, Daejeon, Korea
daesung@etri.re.kr

Abstract. As user authentication by using biometric information such as fingerprint has been widely accepted, there has been a growing interest in protecting the biometric information itself against external attackers. In this paper, we propose a dual watermarking technique to protect fingerprint images in transmission/storage. As the proposed dual watermarking technique provides both robustness and fragileness with the embedded watermarks, it can guarantee the integrity of the fingerprint image transmitted and/or stored. In particular, when the embedding locations for fragile watermarks are selected, we consider the ridge information of the fingerprint images to avoid possible interference between the robust watermark detection and fingerprint verification systems. Based on experimental results, we confirm that our dual watermarking technique can detect the robust watermark accurately and avoid any significant degradation in the accuracy of fingerprint verification.

Keywords: Biometrics, User Authentication, Fingerprint Verification, Dual Watermarking.

1 Introduction

Traditionally, authorized users have gained access to secure information systems, buildings, or equipment via multiple PINs, passwords, smart cards, and so on. However, these security methods have important weakness that can be lost, stolen, or forgotten. Therefore, in recent years, there is an increasing trend of using biometrics, which refers the personal biological or behavioral characteristics used for user authentication[1].

In this paper, the fingerprint has been chosen as the biometrics for user authentication. It is more mature in terms of the algorithm availability and feasibility[1]. Current fingerprint verification systems are being developed for remote applications, such as Internet banking and e-government. In such remote applications, attackers can obtain a user's fingerprint image that is transmitted via a communication channel and/or stored in a database, and reuse the fingerprint image obtained to pretend to be the authorized user. Furthermore, once the fingerprint image is stolen, it cannot be changed easily (*i.e.,* the user has only ten fingers). To provide security and privacy of

R. Safavi-Naini and M. Yung (Eds.): DRMTICS 2005, LNCS 3919, pp. 217–227, 2006.
© Springer-Verlag Berlin Heidelberg 2006

the fingerprint image in remote applications, several techniques such as encryption and digital watermarking can be applied. Encryption can protect a fingerprint image in transmission and/or storage. Once decrypted, however the fingerprint image has no further protection. On the other hand, digital watermarking embeds some information into the fingerprint image itself. Therefore, it can provide additional security even after decryption. Note that, encryption can also be applied to the watermarked data, and we do not debate the pros and cons of using watermarks versus encryption as in [2-5]. Although, we focus on protecting fingerprint images transmitted in the following, the same technique can also be used to protect fingerprint images stored.

In this paper, we consider a digital watermarking technique that embeds information, called the **watermark**, within the content, called the **cover work**. Watermarking techniques used for protecting the copyright of multimedia data can be classified generally into *robust watermarking* and *fragile watermarking* according to the embedding strength of the watermark. Watermarks embedded by a robust watermarking technique are resistant to possible attacks, such as image compression or image processing. Watermarks embedded by a fragile watermarking technique, however, can be lost easily by embedding some other information. By using these characteristics, **dual** watermarking techniques can be used to guarantee the integrity of information transmitted with the fragile watermarking, and to hide some important information such as company logo with the robust watermarking.

In this paper, we use both the robust and the fragile watermarking techniques to protect fingerprint images. First, we embed watermarks by using the robust watermarking technique to embed some important information. For example, a fingerprint image stolen from one application by either an outsider or an insider may be used in another application. This issue is also important in terms of preserving privacy. Then, we apply the fragile watermarking technique to guarantee the integrity of the fingerprint image transmitted by embedding time stamp or challenge-response information.

We use Dugad's method [6] for the robust watermarking and modify Jain's method [3] for the fragile watermarking. When both watermarking techniques, however, are used without modification, the fragile watermark can be embedded into the result of the robust watermarking, and interference between the robust and the fragile watermarking can occur. Therefore, we consider the ridge information of the fingerprint image to avoid possible interference, noting that this does not affect the accuracy of fingerprint verification when the fragile watermark method is embedded. Based on experimental results, the proposed dual watermarking method can guarantee that the embedded robust watermarks are extracted accurately without interference, and the accuracy of the fingerprint verification is not affected by the embedded watermarks.

The organization of the paper is as follows. Section 2 explains the vulnerabilities in a typical fingerprint verification system and describes previous watermarking techniques used to protect biometrics information. A proposed dual watermarking method is described in Section 3, and we present experimental results in Section 4. Conclusions are provided in Section 5.

2 Backgrounds

2.1 Fingerprint Verification

A typical fingerprint verification system shown in Fig. 1 has two phases: *enrollment* and *verification*. In the off-line enrollment phase, an enrolled fingerprint image for each user is preprocessed, and the minutiae are extracted and stored in a server. In the on-line verification phase, the input minutiae are compared to the stored template, and the result of the comparison is returned.

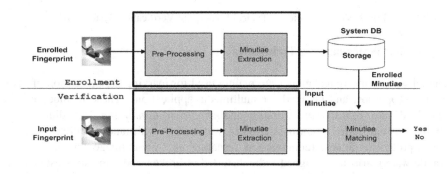

Fig. 1. Illustration of the Fingerprint Verification

In general, there are three steps involved in the verification phase[4]: Image Pre-Processing, Minutiae Extraction, and Minutiae Matching. Image Pre-Processing refers to the refinement of the fingerprint image against the image distortion obtained from a fingerprint sensor. Minutiae Extraction refers to the extraction of features in the fingerprint image. After this step, some of the minutiae are detected and stored into a pattern file, which includes the position, orientation, and type(ridge ending or bifurcation) of the minutiae. Based on the minutiae, the input fingerprint is compared with the enrolled database in the Minutiae Matching step[1].

2.2 Vulnerabilities in Fingerprint Verification

Typical fingerprint verification systems have many vulnerabilities as shown in Fig. 2 [1]: ① *attack at the sensor*, ② *attack on the channel between the sensor and the feature extractor*, ③ *attack on the feature extractor*, ④ *attack on the channel between the feature extractor and the matcher*, ⑤ *attack on the matcher*, ⑥ *attack on the system database*, ⑦ *attack on the channel between the system database and the matcher*, ⑧ *attack on the channel between the matcher and the application requesting verification*. Details of these attacks are explained in [1]. Attacks of type ②, ④, ⑦ have very similar characteristics, because they are applied to a communication channel. In this paper, we focus on this type of attack only.

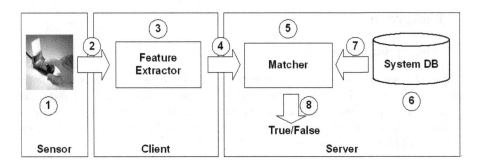

Fig. 2. Vulnerabilities of Typical Fingerprint Verification Systems[4]

2.3 Digital Watermarking Techniques

Digital watermarking techniques are mainly used for marking the possession of intellectual properties, and targeted for multimedia applications. These methods can be classified into *robust watermarking* and *fragile watermarking* according to the strength of embedded watermark. Robust watermarks withstand moderate to severe signal processing attacks (compression, rescaling, etc.) on an image. On the contrary, fragile watermarks are designed to be distorted or broken under the slightest changes to the image.

Such watermarking technique can be extended to protect biometric information such as fingerprint image. A fragile watermarking can be used for guaranteeing the integrity of the fingerprint image transmitted via non-secure communication channels. Also, the user generally uses the image of the same finger in various applications. In this case, a malicious attacker who steals the fingerprint image of a user in one application may try to impersonate the legitimate user in another application. Therefore, the robust watermarking by embedding some application-specific information is needed to prevent the unauthorized use of the compromised fingerprint image across multiple applications.

Also, watermarking techniques can be classified into *blind watermarking* that does not need an original image and *informed watermarking* that needs the original image to detect the embedded watermarks for fingerprint verification. Since the informed watermarking technique is unacceptable for fingerprint verifications, and we focus on the blind watermarking in the following.

2.4 Watermarking Techniques for Fingerprint Verification

Yeung and Pankanti [4] proposed a fragile watermarking for fingerprint images based on a verification key. The fingerprints captured by a scanner are watermarked by the scanner, and any tampering of the image data can be detected by the server using this method. Gunsel, Uludag and Tekalp [5] proposed a robust watermarking for fingerprint images where the watermark could be verified even if the fingerprint image was cropped.

In this paper, to preserve some application-specific information and check the integrity of fingerprint images simultaneously, we propose a dual watermarking method that applies a fragile watermarking to the fingerprint image resulted from a robust watermarking. Furthermore, we implement a blind watermarking technique which is practical for fingerprint verification systems.

3 A Proposed Dual Watermarking Method

In this section, a dual watermarking method for secure transmission of fingerprint images is described. Each watermark embedded by both watermarking techniques needs to satisfy the following conditions to verify the integrity and to embed some application-specific information simultaneously.

- Robust watermarks are embedded first, and then fragile watermarks are embedded
- Watermarks are free from interference between embedded information
- The effects on fingerprint verification accuracy is minimized

We chose the multi-resolution watermarking technique of Dugad *et al.* [6] for the robust watermarking, and the watermarking technique of Jain *et al.*[3] for the fragile watermarking. The former is executed in the frequency domain by Discrete Wavelet Transform (DWT), and the latter is executed in the spatial domain. Both watermarking techniques are suitable for fingerprint verification systems because of employing the blind watermarking technique.

For the purpose of completeness, we will briefly describe both techniques. The details of the techniques can be found in [3,6]. First, Dugad [6] uses a three-level DWT with a Daubechies 8-tap filter, leaves out the low pass sub-band, and picks all coefficients in the other sub-bands which are above a given threshold (T1). A watermark is embedded into these coefficients only. In watermark detection, Dugad chooses all the high pass coefficients above T2 and correlates them with the original copy of the watermark. Jain's technique [3] uses a spatial domain with a secret key which is shared by both sender and receiver. Every watermark bit is embedded into multiple locations. A random number generator initialized with the secret key generates locations of the pixels to be watermarked. Detection starts with finding the embedding locations, via the secret key used in the embedding stage. From the detected watermark bits, the watermark can be reconstructed.

If the both watermarking techniques are integrated without modification, however, the robust watermark may not be detected accurately because of the possible collisions in some embedding locations. Therefore, we first analyze the factors that can influence on detecting the embedded robust watermarks, and then propose a modified fragile watermarking technique that can avoid the possible interferences with the robust watermarking.

Fig. 3 shows the locations where collisions have occurred in the original fingerprint by both watermarking techniques. To show the interference caused by both watermarking techniques, the possible interference locations are overlaid in the ridge image after executing a Sobel operation(Fig. 3(b)). As shown in Fig. 3(b), most collisions take place near the ridges because the robust watermarking technique of

Dugad embeds the watermark near the ridges. It is easy to avoid such collusion areas with Jain's fragile watermarking technique because it is a spatial domain technique. However, it is hard to avoid collusion areas with Dugad's frequency domain, robust watermark technique. Therefore, to minimize the interference caused by embedding both watermarks, we embed the fragile watermark into the fingerprint image resulted from the robust watermarking. Especially, the fragile watermark needs to be embedded by considering the ridges where the robust watermark may be embedded into.

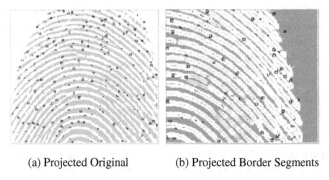

(a) Projected Original   (b) Projected Border Segments

Fig. 3. Possible Interference Locations between Two Watermarks

3.1 Processing at the Sending Side

First, we perform the robust watermarking. Then, we apply the fragile watermarking that modifies Jain's method to check the integrity of the fingerprint image resulted from the robust watermarking. The fragile watermarking embeds watermarks for guaranteeing the integrity and avoiding the collision using Eq. (1).

Note that β in Eq .(1) means the locations to be embedded and is determined based on a pseudo-random number generator initialized with a secret key. As mentioned in Section 3, the ridges should be excluded from β to avoid the collisions of the embedding locations between the robust and the fragile watermarking.

Though the embedding location β should be identical at both sending and receiving sides, the receiving side cannot generate the same embedding location β. This is because the original fingerprint image of the sending side and the watermarked fingerprint image of the receiving side generate different edge information by the Sobel operation. To solve this problem, we creates an approximated fingerprint image, $\hat{P}(i, j)$, using Eq. (2) before selecting the embedding location β at both sending and receiving sides. Therefore, the some location $\hat{\beta}(i, j)$ shown in Eq. (3) can be generated at both sides because the Sobel operation is applied to the approximated fingerprint image. Note that $\hat{P}_{GM}(i, j)$ shown in Eq. (3) can be generated by the Sobel operation.

$$P_{wm}(i, j) = P(i, j) + \{(2s - 1)P_{AV}(i, j)q(1 + \frac{P_{SD}(i, j)}{A})(1 + \frac{P_{GM}(i, j)}{B})\beta(i, j)\} \quad (1)$$

where,

$P_{wm}(i, j)$	: Watermarked Image	$P(i, j)$	: Cover Image
s	: Watermark Image Bit String	$P_{AV}(i, j)$	: 5×5 Square Average
$P_{SD}(i, j)$	: 5×5 Cross Standard Deviation	$P_{GM}(i, j)$	: Gradient Magnitude
$\beta(i, j)$	: Improved Embed Mask	q	: Strength of Watermarking
A	: Ratio of Standard Deviation	B	: Ratio of Gradient Magnitude

$$\hat{P}(i, j) = \frac{1}{8}\left(\sum_{k=-2}^{2} P(i+k, j) + \sum_{k=-2}^{2} P(i, j+k) - 2P(i, j)\right) \qquad (2)$$

$$\hat{\beta}(i, j) = \begin{cases} \beta(i, j) & \rightarrow if \ \hat{P}_{GM}(i, j) \leq t \\ exclusion & \rightarrow otherwise \end{cases} \qquad (3)$$

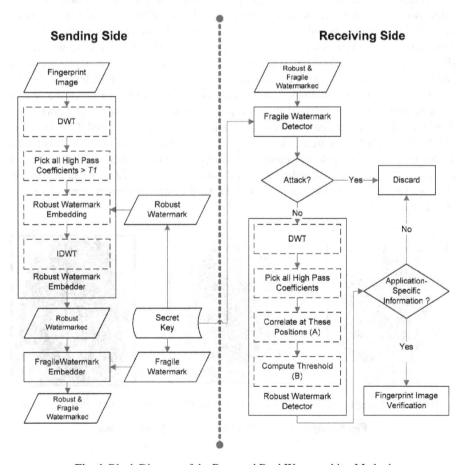

Fig. 4. Block Diagram of the Proposed Dual Watermarking Method

3.2 Processing at the Receiving Side

Watermark detection at the receiving side is performed in the reverse order of the watermark embedding at the sending side. After checking the integrity of the transmitted fingerprint image using the information detected from the fragile watermarking technique, we check the application-specific information detected from the robust watermarking technique. This application-specific information can be used to decide whether the fingerprint image transmitted is for the target application or not. If the application-specific information detected is different from the required one, we can recognize the fingerprint image as illegal and take necessary steps to prevent it from future usages. Fig. 4 illustrates the block diagram of the proposed dual watermarking method.

4 Implementation Details and Performance Evaluation

To evaluate the performance of the proposed dual watermarking method, we consider two experiment scenarios. We measured the robustness of the proposed method with various signal attacks (Experiment 1), and measured the effect of embedding the fragile watermark on the detection ratio of the robust watermark (Experiment 2). We left out the low pass sub-band coefficients and picked all coefficients in the other sub-bands which were above a given threshold ($T1$). The size of the watermark embedded in Experiment 1 was 200 bits. During the watermark detection, we selected all the high pass coefficients above $T2$ and correlated them with the original copy of the watermark. We used $T1 = 40$ and $T2 = 50$ ($T1$ is the threshold used for watermark casting). Also, we set $T2$ to be strictly larger than $T1$ for robustness because we should not compute the correlation over coefficients to which we have not embedded any watermark. Note that $T2 \geq T1$ is necessary, since some coefficients originally below $T1$ might become greater than $T1$ due to image manipulations.

  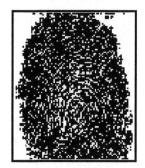

(a) Original Fingerprint Image   (b) Watermarked Fingerprint Image   (c) Embedding Locations

Fig. 5. Fingerprint Images with the Robust Watermarking

Fig. 5 shows fingerprint images that resulted from the robust watermarking. Fig. 5(b) represents the fingerprint image obtained from embedding the watermark into the original fingerprint image shown in Fig. 5 (a). The binary image of Fig. 5 (c) represents the difference between the original fingerprint image and the watermarked fingerprint image, *i.e.,* the locations of the embedded watermarks. We can see that the embedded locations are decided close to the fingerprint ridges.

To evaluate the robustness of the proposed watermarking technique, we considered four typical types of attacks. As shown in Table 1, the value of PSNR represents the image degradation due to the correlated attack. The detection ratio is acceptable even after attacks. The robust watermarking technique can provide the high robustness against the median filter attack compared to other attacks.

Table 1. Detection Ratio after Attacks

Attack	PSNR	Detection Ratio
Median Filter	60.161461 dB	1.000000
JPEG compression (30%)	25.241369 dB	0.777778
Blur Filter	27.950458 dB	1.000000
Cut	15.169233 dB	0.888889

Fig. 6 (a) shows the distribution of the detection ratio by using the proposed dual watermarking and the straightforward dual watermarking technique. The straightforward dual watermarking(represented as "wm2-st" in Fig. 6 (a)) that does not consider the ridge information has some influence on the detection ratio of the robust watermark(represented as "wm1" in Fig. 6). However, the proposed dual watermarking (represented as "wm2-pro" in Fig. 6) has no influence on the detection ratio of the robust watermark. This is because the ratios of wm1 and wm2-pro are similar, and 100% detections are possible for half of the cases as shown in Fig. 6 (a).

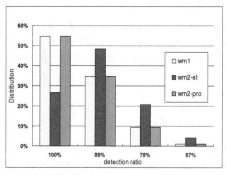

(a) Distribution of Detection Ratio

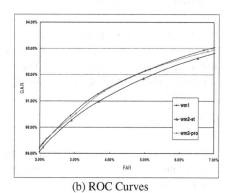

(b) ROC Curves

Fig. 6. Comparison of the Proposed Dual Watermarking(wm2-pro) with the Straightforward Dual Watermarking(wm2-st)

To evaluate the effects on the fingerprint verification accuracy with watermarked images, a data set of 4,272 fingerprint images composed of four fingerprint images per one finger was collected from 1,068 individuals by using the optical fingerprint sensor [7]. The resolution of the sensor was 500 dpi, and the size of captured fingerprint images was 248×292. A total of 12,000 genuine matchings was performed, and the impostor matching was performed 20,000 times. Fig. 6(b) shows three ROC(Receiver Operating Characteristic) curves of the fingerprint verification. In spite of embedding dual watermarks (represented as "wm2-pro" in Fig. 6 (b)), the effects on the fingerprint verification accuracy with watermarked images were negligible compared to the robust watermark only case (represented as "wm1" in Fig. 6 (b)).

5 Conclusions

In this paper, we proposed a method for the secure transmission of fingerprint images by using a dual watermarking technique. After embedding robust watermarks into the fingerprint images to hide the important information, we embedded fragile watermarks to guarantee the integrity of the fingerprint images transmitted. With the straightforward dual watermarking technique, the interference between the robust and the fragile watermarks can occur because the fragile watermark is embedded into the result of the robust watermarking. To reduce the interference, we considered the ridge information when the embedding locations for the fragile watermarking were chosen. Based on the experimental results, the proposed dual watermarking method can guarantee that the embedded watermarks are detected accurately without the interference. Also, it did not affect the accuracy of the fingerprint verification. Note that our dual watermarking method can also be applied to other biometrics such as faces, irises, and veins, although in this paper we considered fingerprints only.

Acknowledgements

This research was supported by the MIC (Ministry of Information and Communication), Korea, under the HNRC (Home Network Research Center) – ITRC (Information Technology Research Center) support program supervised by the IITA (Institute of Information Technology Assessment).

References

[1] D. Maltoni, et al., *Handbook of Fingerprint Recognition*, Springer, 2003.
[2] A. Jain and U. Uludag, "Hiding Fingerprint Minutiae in Images," *Proc. of AutoID*, pp. 97-102, 2002.
[3] A. Jain, U. Uludag, and R. Hsu, "Hiding a Face in a Fingerprint Image," *Proc. of ICPR*, pp. 756-759, 2002.
[4] M. Yeung and S. Pankanti, "Verification Watermarks on Fingerprint Recognition and Retrieval," *Journal of Electronic Imaging*, vol. 9, no. 4, pp. 468-476, 2000.

[5] B. Gunsel, U. Uludag and A. Tekalp, "Robust Watermarking of Fingerprint Images," *Pattern Recognition*, vol. 35, no. 12, pp. 2739-2747, 2002.

[6] R. Dugad, K. Ratakonda, and N. Ahuja, "A New Wavelet-based Scheme for Watermarking Images," *Proc. of the ICIP*, 1998.

[7] NiGen, http://www.nitgen.com.

Security Weaknesses of Certain Broadcast Encryption Schemes

Miodrag J. Mihaljević[1], Marc P.C. Fossorier[2], and Hideki Imai[3]

[1] Mathematical Institute, Serbian Academy of Sciences and Arts,
Kneza Mihaila 35, 11001 Belgrade, Serbia and Montenegro
miodragm@turing.mi.sanu.ac.yu
[2] Department of Electrical Engineering, University of Hawaii,
2540 Dole St., Holmes Hall 483, Honolulu, HI 96822, USA
marc@spectra.eng.hawaii.edu
[3] University of Tokyo, Institute of Industrial Science,
4-6-1, Komaba, Meguro-ku, Tokyo, 153-8505, Japan
imai@iis.u-tokyo.ac.jp

Abstract. This paper points out to a generic vulnerability of certain broadcast encryption schemes. This vulnerability can be effectively explored assuming chosen plaintext attacks, and in some cases even under ciphertext only attack. The developed methods for cryptanalysis are based on an attacking approach not taken into account in the security evaluations of the reported broadcast encryption schemes. The proposed attacks are based on employment of a dedicated time-data-memory trade-off approach for cryptanalysis. Two algorithms for cryptanalysis are proposed (both in the basic and the generalized versions) and their main characteristics regarding the complexity and required sample are pointed out. The algorithms are applied for cryptanalysis of particular recently reported broadcast encryption schemes implying that their security is far below the claimed ones.

Keywords: broadcast encryption, key management, cryptanalysis, time-memory-data trade-off.

1   Introduction

Broadcast encryption (BE), initially reported in [2] and [4], is a cryptographic method for providing the conditional data access distributed via the public channels. BE schemes employ the following approach for controlling the access privileges: the data are encrypted and only legitimate users are provided with the information on how to decrypt them (for some recent issues and particular applications see [11], [17] and [12] for example). The data encryption is performed based on a symmetric cipher and the secret session encrypting key (SEK). Ensuring that only the valid members of the group have the SEK at any given time instance is the key management problem. To make this updating possible, another set of keys called the key-encrypting keys (KEKs) is involved. The KEKs are used to encrypt and deliver the updated SEK to the valid members of

R. Safavi-Naini and M. Yung (Eds.): DRMTICS 2005, LNCS 3919, pp. 228–245, 2006.

the group only. Usually, in order to obtain the desired security, the KEKs must be kept in a protected storage. A number of advanced BE schemes has been reported in [15], [8] and [9].

The underlying paradigm of BE is to represent any privileged set of users as the union of s subsets of users of a particular form. A different key is associated with each one of these sets, and a user knows a key if and only if he belongs to the corresponding set. The broadcaster encrypts SEK s times employing the KEKs associated with the set in the cover. Consequently, each privileged user can easily access the data, but even a coalition of the non-privileged users cannot.

Security of the reported BE schemes was mainly considered via possible impacts of colluding the revoked users under assumption that the employed encryption techniques are secure ones.

Motivation for the Work. The main intention of this work was to consider some alternative attacking scenarios motivated by the following two issues: (i) KEKs have static nature - they are given to users at the very beginning and used later on during the entire "working life" of the system; (ii) a same SEK is encrypted a huge (usually) number of times by different KEKs and the corresponding ciphertexts are publicly available. As a result, knowledge of only one KEK can compromise the security of the entire BE system.

Particularly, a motivation was consideration of BE schemes resistance against dedicated time-data-memory trade-off attacks.

Contributions of the Paper. This paper points out to a generic vulnerability of certain BE schemes. This vulnerability can be effectively explored assuming chosen plaintext attacks, and in some cases even under ciphertext only attack. The developed methods for cryptanalysis are based on an attacking approach not taken into account in the security evaluations of the reported BE schemes. The proposed attacks are based on employment of a dedicated time-data-memory trade-off approach for cryptanalysis. Two techniques for cryptanalysis are developed, one related to the chosen plaintext attack scenario, and the other related to the ciphertext only scenario, and the corresponding algorithms are proposed in the basic and the generalized variants. The main characteristics of the proposed algorithms are given regarding the required sample, and time/space complexities. The algorithms are employed for cryptanalysis some of currently the most interesting BE schemes showing that their security levels are significantly below the claimed ones. One of the main consequences of the proposed methods for cryptanalysis is the impact regarding the design requirements of the BE schemes in order to avoid the identified vulnerabilities.

Organization of the Paper. Section 2 contains a summary, relevant for this paper, of the background on BE. The attacking model and scenarios are specified in Section 3. The basic forms of two developed algorithms for cryptanalysis are proposed in Section 4 including statements on theirs complexity and required sample. The generalized variants of these algorithms are proposed in Section 5. The security evaluations of the currently most interesting BE schemes employing the proposed algorithms for cryptanalysis are given in Section 6 and high vulnerability of these schemes is pointed out. A concluding discussion is given in Section 7.

2   Background: Broadcast Encryption

Let KEK_i denotes a KEK employed in the system, and let ID_i denotes its name, i.e. its identification (ID), noting that ID does not disclose any information on KEK_i itself. BE is based on the following approach. The system center generates all the employed KEKs. A user of the BE system is in advance provided with a subset of all KEKs employed in the system. Note that different users can have overlapping subsets of KEKs, but no one pair of users have the identical subset.

In a basic BE setting, the procedures at the center and each of the users are based on the following. When the current SEK should be updated, the center finds a subset I of KEKs $\{KEK_i\}_{i \in I}$ such that each of the legitimate users possesses at least one of these keys and none of the un-legitimate users possesses any of these keys. The center encrypts the data with SEK, generates encrypted forms of SEK employing all KEK_i, $i \in I$, and broadcasts the following

$$< [header]; E_{SEK}(data) > = < [\{ (ID_i, E_{KEK_i}(SEK)) \}_{i \in I}]; E_{SEK}(data) >, \tag{1}$$

where for simplicity we assume that the same encryption algorithm $E(\cdot)$ is employed for encryption of the data and KEKs.

Upon receiving (1), a legitimate receiver is able to find ID_i in its possession and based on the pair $(ID_i, E_{KEK_i}(SEK))$ it can recover SEK and the data based on the following:

$$SEK = E_{KEK_i}^{-1}(E_{KEK_i}(SEK)), \tag{2}$$

$$data = E_{SEK}^{-1}(E_{SEK}(data)), \tag{3}$$

where $E^{-1}(\cdot)$ denotes the decryption algorithm. As an illustration, note that a BE scheme called the complete sub-tree (CST) reported in [15] follows the above framework.

On the other hand in certain BE schemes the header should be modelled as following

$$[header] = < [\{ (info(i, q), E_{f_q(KEK_i)}(SEK)) \}_{i \in I}], \tag{4}$$

where $f_q(\cdot)$, $q = 1, 2, ...Q$, are certain publicly known one-way mappings, and $info(i, q)$ yields information on the employed $f_q(\cdot)$ and ID_i. Accordingly, upon receiving the header, a legitimate receiver is able to find the relevant $info(i, q)$ and learn about ID_i in its possession and the related $f_q(\cdot)$ so that it can recover SEK as follows:

$$SEK = E_{f_q(KEK_i)}^{-1}(E_{f_q(KEK_i)}(SEK)). \tag{5}$$

BE scheme called SD (Subset Difference) reported in [15] as well as the schemes reported in [8] and [9] follow the above paradigm based on (4)-(5).

3 Model and Scenarios for Cryptanalysis of Broadcast Encryption Schemes

3.1 Models Under Cryptanalysis

Basic Model. We assume that the key management in the considered BE schemes is based on (1)-(2) and accordingly in order to provide the legitimate users with the decryption key SEK_j at the time instance j, the following set of pairs H_j is publicly available

$$H_j = \{(ID_i, C_{i,j})\}_{i \in I(j)} , \tag{6}$$

where

$$C_{i,j} = E_{KEK_i}(SEK_j) , \tag{7}$$

and ID_i is the name of the key KEK_i employed for encryption of SEK_j using the symmetric encryption algorithm $E(\cdot)$, and $I(j)$ is a time dependent subset of integers $\{1, 2, ..., I\}$.

As an illustration, note that the above model directly fits to CST scheme [15].

Generalized Model. We assume that the key management in the considered BE schemes is based (6)-(7) and accordingly in order to provide the legitimate users with the decryption key SEK_j at the time instance j, the following set of pairs H_j is publicly available

$$H_j = \{(ID_i, f_q(\cdot), C_{i,q,j})\}_{i \in I(j)} , \ q \in Q(i,j), \ Q(i,j) \subseteq \{1, 2, ..., Q\} , \tag{8}$$

where

$$C_{i,q,j} = E_{f_q(KEK_i)}(SEK_j) , \tag{9}$$

$f_q(\cdot)$ is a known one-way mapping, ID_i is the name of the key KEK_i employed for encryption of SEK_j using the symmetric encryption algorithm $E(\cdot)$, and $I(j)$ is a time dependent subset of integers $\{1, 2, ..., I\}$.

Assumptions. Note that in the considered model $E(\cdot)$ could be a block-cipher or a stream-cipher.

Also, we assume that the following is valid:

- For each $i = 1, 2, ..., I$,
  - KEK_i is a randomly generated binary vector of dimension L and $2^L >> I$;
  - ID_i only indicates that the encrypted form $E_{KEK_i}(SEK_j)$ of SEK_j is obtained employing the key KEK_i and does not provide any information on the binary vector KEK_i;
- For each $j = 1, 2, ..., J$,
  - SEK_j is a binary vector of dimension L;
  - each $I(j)$ is a different subset of $\{1, 2, ..., I\}$;
  - a certain overlapping between different sets $I(j)$ could occur;
- The employed encryption algorithm $E(\cdot)$ is a secure one so that any $C_{i,q,j} = E_{f_q(KEK_i)}(SEK_j))$ does not yield any information on KEK_i and SEK_j;
- $f_q(\cdot)$ is a one-way mapping, $q = 1, 2, ..., Q$.

3.2 Scenarios Under Cryptanalysis

The attacker's knowledge is limited as follows:

– The attacker knows the entire structure of the BE scheme under cryptanalysis including the employed encryption algorithm $E(\cdot)$;

– For simplicity, we assume that the attacker does not know any of the keys KEK_i, $i = 1, 2, ..., I$, employed in the considered BE scheme. The scenario where we assume that a user knows his/her keys can be considered in the same manner but excluding certain keys from the set of the unknown ones.

The goal of the attacker is to recover at least **one of the secret keys** KEK_i, $i = 1, 2, ..., I$, employed in the BE scheme. We emphasize this last point as it constitutes the main difference in comparison with recovery of a single key employed in a block or stream cipher, and it is one of the main origins of the BE weaknesses pointed out in this paper.

Of course that usefulness of just one KEK recovered depend on its role, i.e. "position" in the underlying structure the key management, and the dynamics of users, but recovering even a single key has certain impact on the security of the entire system. The more detailed discussion of this issue is out of scope of this paper.

Scenario A. In this scenario, it is assumed that the attacker has the following data for cryptanalysis

$$(H_j, SEK_j = SEK) , \ j = 1, 2, ..., J .$$

This scenario corresponds to the chosen plaintext based cryptanalysis.

Note that the chosen SEK scenario is a legitimate attacking scenarios to consider and the obtained results show that the security claims from [15], [8] and [9] have overlooked this approach (e.g., because it is not required there that the SEKs should not be repeated). Indeed the chosen plaintext cryptanalysis usually corresponds to a misuse of a crypto system when an attacker enforces the system to work in a vulnerable mode. Accordingly, in the considered scenario it is assumed that (from time to time) the same SEK is employed which is unlikely in a regular use of the system but is a possible mode in a malicious use of the system. One can of course speculate about practical implications of this scenario in the context of BE systems, but clearly it pertains to the malicious entity which supplies the SEKs. For example, it can be the BE center who wishes to show that the system purchased from a vendor is insecure or a malicious content provider using the BE system (operated by the BE provider who controls KEKs) who wishes to recover any of the KEKs. In a general setting, the chosen SEK scenario can be considered as a consequence of a misuse of the system, and a more detailed discussion of this issue is out of scope of this paper.

Particularly note the following claims from [15] (Section 6.1, page 27): "The long term encryption method E_L should withstand a more severe attack, in the following sense: consider any feasible adversary B that for a random key L gets to **adaptively choose polynomially many inputs and examine** E_Ls

encryption and similarly **provide ciphertexts and examine** E_{LS} **decryption.**" According to the above claim not only a chosen SEK attack is a legitimate one, but also the chosen SEK-ciphertext attacks should be taken into account.

Scenario B. In this scenario, it is assumed that the attacker has the following data for cryptanalysis

$$(H_j, SEK_j) , \ j = const .$$

The requirement that the SEKs are known generally corresponds to the known plaintext attack, but in the considered scenario it also corresponds to the ciphertext only based cryptanalysis assuming that the attacker is a legitimate user of the system, which implies that SEKs are actually known to the attacker. Namely, it is a realistic scenario to consider the attacker joins the system as a legitimate (but malicious) user just to learn one SEK and collect the sample for cryptanalysis in order to recover one or more KEKs later on. Note that a SEK is valid only for a short time, but the KEKs are static and valid during the entire life span of the system.

4   Novel Methods for Cryptanalysis of Broadcast Encryption Schemes

4.1   Underlying Ideas

The main origins for developing the attacks are the following characteristics of the BE schemes:

(a) the entire secret key of a BE scheme, known only to the broadcasting center, consists of a huge number of the particular secret keys $\{KEK_i\}_{i=1}$;

(b) in a BE scheme, each session key is encrypted a number of times employing different KEKs;

(c) for simplicity of consideration, we assume that any user of a BE system does not know any of the assigned keys because they are in a tamper resistant storage, and accordingly the system should be considered as broken even if a user can recover only one of the KEKs employed in the system (this assumption does not change the generality of the attack but makes the notations and entire consideration easier for explanation).

Illustrative Example. The CST BE [15] is based on a secret key corresponding to a binary balanced tree in which each KEK is assigned to a node of this tree as illustrated in Fig. 1. The secret key consists of $2N - 1 = 63$ KEKs, and it is assumed that there are $N = 32$ receiving entities. Accordingly, the secret key consists of $2N - 1$ independent parts which could be considered as the randomly generated ones.

The above characteristics of BE open a door for developing cryptanalytic methods based on an attacking approach not taken into account in the reported security evaluations of the schemes.

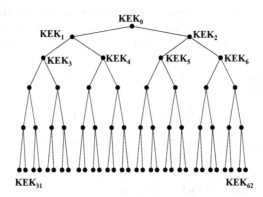

Fig. 1. An illustration of the secret key employed in certain BE schemes

The developed cryptanalysis could be called "list cryptanalysis" following the term "list decoding" and its related similarity. Recall that "list decoding" assumes that we have succeeded in decoding if the codeword is in the list of the candidate codewords. In our cryptanalysis we assume that the goal is achieved if it is possible to recover at least one key from the list of the all KEKs employed in the BE scheme.

This paper proposes dedicated time-memory-data trade-off based methods for cryptanalysis of the BE key management scheme. The proposed methods employ the following underlying ideas:

- develop a dedicated time-memory-data trade-off based cryptanalysis assuming the chosen plaintext attack corresponding to the attacking Scenario A;
- develop a dedicated time-data trade-off based cryptanalysis assuming the ciphertext only attack corresponding to the attacking Scenario B.

These approaches are different from reported ones related to the time-memory trade-off based cryptanalysis of block ciphers and time-memory-data trade-off based ones for stream ciphers. The differences are consequences of the attacking nature regarding BE schemes on one hand side and block or stream ciphers on the other hand. Regarding these issues, as an illustration note the following:

– the time-memory trade-off based cryptanalysis of block ciphers [7] (see [18], as well) assumes that the attacker's goal is to recover the employed secret key when at least one plaintext-ciphertext pair is known; in the BE setting with a block cipher, the cryptanalysis is based on a collection of the ciphertext of a same message generated employing different secret keys, and the attacker's goal is to recover at least one of these employed secret keys;

– the time-memory-data trade-off cryptanalysis of the stream ciphers [3] assumes that all the issues are related to recovering an internal state of the considered stream cipher; in the BE case even if the employed $E(\cdot)$ is a stream cipher, again the entire consideration is related to the secret key only, i.e. the internal state evolution appears as not relevant.

Particularly note the following differences:

– when a block cipher is employed as the algorithm $E(\cdot)$ in the BE scheme, the developed methods provide a gain proportional to the number of available plaintext-ciphertext pairs; on the other hand note that the a time-memory trade-off attack [7] does not provide any additional gain when more than only one ciphertext-plaintext pair is available;

– when a stream cipher is employed in the BE scheme, the developed time-memory-data trade-off based attack is related only to the stream cipher secret key and not to its internal state; on the other hand, the time-memory-data trade-off based attacks reported in [3] are related to the internal state of the cipher and they become infeasible when the internal state size is much larger than the employed key.

4.2   Attacking Scenario A

The algorithm for cryptanalysis of BE schemes under the attacking Scenario A (a particular chosen plaintext attack) consists of the following two main phases:

- pre-processing phase with the following main characteristics:
    - it should be done only once;
    - it depends on the employed encryption $E(\cdot)$ and the chosen SEK;
    - it is independent of the secret keys KEKs employed in the system;
- processing phase with the following main characteristics:
    - it should be performed for attacking a particular BE scheme where the employed set of keys $\{KEK_i\}_{i=1}^{i}$ is unknown assuming that a certain sample is available;
    - it employs the output of the pre-processing phase;
    - it yields, as the expected output, recovering at least one of the employed KEKs; and
    - for simplicity of consideration, we assume employment of just one table (memory) and multiple tables should be employed, as well, as it has been discussed in [7].

The developed algorithm for cryptanalysis under Scenario A follows the basic framework of the time-memory trade-off [7] (taking into account other related references as [3], [5], [18] and [14], for example) but with involving the multiple data into the consideration. In the pre-processing phase a table is prepared with certain pre-computed input-output pairs which enable that the processing phase could be performed with a significantly smaller time complexity.

When multiple data are available, the actual table preparation time will be less than exhaustive search. Since this is an offline activity independent of a particular attack, it might be reasonable to expect that the table preparation time should be more than the online time but less than exhaustive search time. Also note that the precomputation time will be in general more than the memory requirement. In the table preparation stage, the entire table will have to be computed and only a fraction of it stored. This shows that the offline time will be at least as large as the memory requirement. In [7] it is considered the condition where the online time is equal to the memory requirement. In the presence of multiple data, it appears as more practical to require that the data and memory requirement to be less than the online and offline time requirements.

Algorithm for Cryptanalysis

Basic Algorithm A

− Pre-Processing
  • Input Data: SEK, and the algorithm parameters M and T.
  • Pre-Processing Steps
    For $m = 1, 2, ..., M$, do the following:
    1. randomly select an L-dimensional binary vector $X_m(0)$
    2. For $t = 1, 2, ..., T$, perform the following recursive calculation

$$X_m(t) = E_{X_m(t-1)}(SEK) \qquad (10)$$

    3. Memorize the pair $X_m(0), X_m(T)$.
  • Output: The two-column matrix[1] of the pairs memorized in the pre-processing step 3.
− Processing
  • Input Data: sequence of D different values $C_{i,j} = E_{KEK_i}(SEK)$, $i \in I(j)$, $j = 1, 2, ..., J$.
  • Processing Steps
    For each $i, j, i \in I(j)$, $j = 1, 2, ..., J$, do the following:
    1. Set $t = 0$ and $X_t = C_{i,j}$.
    2. Check the identity of the considered X_t to any of the second column elements $X_m(T)$ of the matrix generated in the pre-processing phase; if for some index m the identity appears, go to the processing step 4; otherwise go to the processing step 3.
    3. If $t \le T$, calculate $X_{t+1} = E_{X_t}(SEK)$ and go to the processing step 2; if $t > T$, go to the processing step 5.
    4. (a) Select the corresponding $X_m(0)$ and set $X_0 = X_m(0)$;
       (b) perform the following iterative calculation: $X_{t+1} = E_{X_t}(SEK)$ until $X_{t+1} = C_{i,j}$;
       (c) memorize the pair $(X_t, C_{i,j})$.
    5. Select a previously not considered $C_{i,j}$ and go to the processing step 1.
  • Output: Set of the recovered KEKs obtained via the memorized pairs in the processing step 3.

Remark 1. For the simplicity of presentation, it is assumed that the sample for cryptanalysis $C_{i,j} = E_{KEK_i}(SEK))$, $i \in I(j)$, $j = 1, 2, ..., J$, is available before the processing phase starts, but this is not necessary, and the processing can work in the same manner when the data are available sequentially, i.e. the processing starts when $C_{i,1} = E_{KEK_i}(SEK))$, $i \in I(1)$, is available and continues when a new sample becomes available.

---

[1] For more flexibility regarding the eligible parameters, multiple matrices could be employed instead a single one.

Complexity of Cryptanalysis. This section yields the complexity analysis of the proposed Algorithm A assuming that the expected number of KEKs it recovers is equal to k, and that D is the expected cardinality of the union of the sets $I(j)$, $j = 1, 2, ..., J$.

According to the Algorithm A structure and the results reported in [7] and [3], the following statements can be proved.

Proposition 1. The pre-processing phase time complexity of Algorithm A is $O(k2^L D^{-1})$.

Proposition 2. The processing phase time complexity of Algorithm A is $O(k^2 2^{2L} M^{-2} D^{-2})$.

Proposition 3. Algorithm A provides different possible trade-offs between the required memory M, sample dimension D and time complexity of the processing T, assuming that the following trade-off condition holds:

$$TM^2 D^2 = k^2 2^{2L} . \tag{11}$$

Remark 2. Note that $k = D$ corresponds to [7] as our scheme can be viewed as [7] with kN/D instead of N.

4.3   Attacking Scenario B

For this attacking scenario, the developed algorithms for cryptanalysis do not require pre-processing phase. The main phases of the algorithm proposed in this section are: (i) sample collection; (b) processing over collected samples.

The proposed algorithm is a dedicated birthday paradox based method for attacking certain BE schemes under the assumed attacking scenario. This approach is a particular time-data trade-off attacking approach.

The birthday paradox based methods for cryptanalysis of stream ciphers have been proposed in [1] and [6] regarding recovering the cipher internal state. The approach proposed in this section follows the same framework as the employed one in [1] and [6] but it has a very different nature.

Algorithms for Cryptanalysis

Basic Algorithm B

- *Input Data:*
    - sequence of D different values $C_i = E_{KEK_i}(SEK)$, $i \in I(SEK)$, where SEK, is known;
    - the algorithm parameter T.
- *Processing Steps*
    For given SEK, do the following:
    1. Set $t = 1$ and randomly select an L-dimensional vector X_1.
    2. Calculate $C_t = E_{X_t}(SEK))$.
    3. Compare C_t with all C_i:

(a) If C_t is identical to C_i for some i, memorize the corresponding pair (X_t, C_i);

(b) If $t < T$, set $t \rightarrow t + 1$, randomly select previously not considered X_t and go to the processing step 2;

(c) If $t > T$ go to the processing step 1.

- *Output*: Set of the recovered KEKs obtained via the memorized pairs in the processing step 3(a).

Complexity of Cryptanalysis. According to Algorithm B processing steps the following statements can be directly proved.

Proposition 4. Assuming that Algorithm I should recover k KEKs the processing time complexity is $O(k2^L D^{-1})$ where D is the expected cardinality of the set $I(SEK)$.

Proposition 5. Algorithm I provides different possible trade-offs between the required sample dimension D and time complexity of the processing T, assuming that the following trade-off condition holds:

$$TD = 2^L k . \tag{12}$$

Remark 3. Note that $k = D$ corresponds to the preprocessing cost of [7].

5   Generalized Algorithms for Cryptanalysis

This section proposes algorithms for cryptanalysis of BE schemes which fit into the model specified in Section 3.1.2, i.e. when a SEK is encrypted employing not a KEK but $f_q(KEK)$ as the key, where $f_q(\cdot)$ is certain one-way mapping. The algorithms given in this section are developed as an extension of the Basic Algorithms A and B.

5.1   Attacking Scenario A

Generalized Algorithm A

- *Pre-Processing*
  - *Input Data*: SEK, and the algorithm parameters M, T and Q.
  - *Pre-Processing Steps*
    For $q = 1, 2, ..., Q$, do the following
    * For $m = 1, 2, ..., M/Q$, do the following:
      1. randomly select an L-dimensional binary vector $X_m(0)$
      2. For $t = 1, 2, ..., T$, perform the following recursive calculation

$$X_m(t) = E_{f_q(X_m(t-1))}(SEK) \tag{13}$$

      3. Memorize the pair $X_m(0), X_m(T)$ in the matrix M_q with two-columns and M/Q rows.

- *Output*: Matrices M_q of the pairs memorized in the pre-processing step 3.

- *Processing*
  - *Input Data*: sequence of D different values $C_{i,j} = E_{f_q(KEK_i)}(SEK)$, $i \in I(j)$, $j = 1, 2, ..., J$, $q \in \{1, 2, ..., Q\}$.
  - *Processing Steps*
    For each different q related to the sample, $q \in \{1, 2, ..., Q\}$, do the following:
    * For considered q and each related i, j, $i \in I(j)$, $j = 1, 2, ..., J$, do the following:
      1. Set $t = 0$ and $X_t = C_{i,j}$.
      2. Check the identity of the considered X_t to any of the second column elements $X_m(T)$ of the matrix M_q generated in the pre-processing phase; if for some index m the identity appears, go to the processing step 4; otherwise go to the processing step 3.
      3. If $t \leq T$, calculate $X_{t+1} = E_{f_q(X_t)}(SEK)$ and go to the processing step 2; if $t > T$, go to the processing step 5.
      4(a) Select the corresponding $X_m(0)$ and set $X_0 = X_m(0)$;
       (b) perform the following iterative calculation:
          $$X_{t+1} = E_{f_q(X_t)}(SEK) \text{ until } X_{t+1} = C_{i,j};$$
       (c) memorize the pair $(X_t, C_{i,j})$.
      5. Select a previously not considered $C_{i,j}$ and go to the processing step 1.
  - *Output*: Set of the recovered KEKs obtained via the memorized pairs in the processing step 3.

According to the structure of Basic and Generalized Algorithms A, it can be directly shown that the complexity of cryptanalysis when Generalized Algorithm A is employed has the same characteristics as those specified by Propositions 1-3.

5.2   Attacking Scenario B

Generalized Algorithm B

- *Input Data*:
  - sequence of D different values $C_{i,q} = E_{f_q(KEK_i)}(SEK)$, $i \in I(SEK)$, $q \in \{1, 2, ..., Q\}$, where SEK, is known;
  - the algorithm parameter T.
- *Processing Steps*
  For given SEK, do the following:
  1. Set $t = 1$ and randomly select an L-dimensional vector X_1.
  2. Calculate $C_t = E_{f_q(X_t)}(SEK))$.
  3. Compare C_t with all $C_{i,q}$:
     (a) If C_t is identical to $C_{i,q}$ for some i, memorize the corresponding pair $(X_t, C_{i,q})$;
     (b) If $t < T$, set $t \rightarrow t+1$, randomly select previously not considered X_t and go to the processing step 2;

(c) If $t > T$ go to the processing step 1.
- *Output*: Set of the recovered KEKs obtained via the memorized pairs in the processing step 3(a).

According to the structure of Basic and Generalized Algorithms B, it can be directly shown that the complexity of cryptanalysis when Generalized Algorithm B is employed has the same characteristics as those specified by Propositions 4-5.

6 Vulnerability of Particular Broadcast Encryption Schemes CST, SD, LSD and OWC

This section considers impacts of the methods for cryptanalysis proposed in the previous sections on the following recently reported BE schemes: (i) Complete Sub-Tree (CST) [15], (ii) Subset Difference (SD) [15], (iii) Layered Subset Difference (LSD) [8], and (iv) One-Way Chain (OWC) [9]. Also note that a number of applications of the schemas reported in [15] and [8] have been discussed in [11] and [12].

The schemes (i)-(iv) are cryptanalyzed as follows:

- BE scheme based on CST is cryptanalyzed employing Basic Algorithms A and B;
- BE schemes based on SD and LSD are cryptanalyzed employing Generalized Algorithms A and B where the one-way functions $f_q(\cdot)$, $q = 1, 2, ..., Q$, correspond to the pseudorandom number generator based mappings;
- BE scheme based on OWC are cryptanalyzed employing Generalized Algorithms A and B where the one-way functions $f_q(\cdot)$, $q = 1, 2, ..., Q$, correspond to the one-way permutations.

The results on the communications overhead of CST, SD LSD, and OWC-(p, c) reported in [15], [8] and [9], respectively, imply the following proposition.

Proposition 6. Assuming that there are J sessions of SEK updating, and that each of these sessions assumes R random revocations from a set of N users, the sample available for cryptanalysis of CST, SD and LSD, and OWC-(p, c) based BE schemes are upper-bounded by $JR\log_2(N/R)$, $2JR$, $4JR$ and $\frac{R}{p+1} + \frac{N-R}{c} + 1$, respectively.

According to Propositions 1, 2, 4 and 6, when $k = 1$, the complexities of cryptanalysis of CST, SD, LSD and OWC-(p, c) based key management schemes for BE are summarized in Table 1 and Table 2 regarding the attacking Scenarios A and B, respectively, assuming the following:

- the schemes include N users in total;
- each of the employed KEKs and SEKs consists of L bits;
- the sample for cryptanalysis is obtained from J sessions of SEK updating, and each of these sessions assumes R random revocations.

Table 1. Attacking Scenario A (chosen plaintext attack): Complexity of recovering one KEK (k=1) in CST, SD, LSD and OWC-(p,c) based key management schemes assuming that the schemes include N users in total, each of the employed KEKs and SEKs consists of L bits, the sample for cryptanalysis is obtained from J sessions of SEK updating and each of these sessions assumes R random revocations, and a memory of dimension M is available

	pre-processing time complexity	processing time complexity
CST [15]	$O\left(2^L(JR\log_2(N/R))^{-1}\right)$	$O\left(2^{2L}(MJR\log_2(N/R))^{-2}\right)$
SD [15]	$O\left(2^L(2JR)^{-1}\right)$	$O\left(2^{2L}(2MJR)^{-2}\right)$
LSD [8]	$O\left(2^L(4JR)^{-1}\right)$	$O\left(2^{2L}(4MJR)^{-2}\right)$
OWC-(p,c) [9]	$O\left(2^L J^{-1}\left(\frac{R}{p+1}+\frac{N-R}{c}+1\right)^{-1}\right)$	$O\left(2^{2L}J^{-2}M^{-2}\left(\frac{R}{p+1}+\frac{N-R}{c}+1\right)^{-2}\right)$

Table 2. Attacking Scenario B (ciphertext only attack): Complexity of recovering one KEK ($k=1$) in CST, SD, LSD and OWC-(p,c) based key management schemes assuming that the schemes include N users in total, each of the employed KEKs and SEKs consists of L bits, the sample for cryptanalysis is obtained from a session of SEK updating assuming R random revocations

	processing time complexity
CST [15]	$O\left(2^L\left(R\log_2(N/R)\right)^{-1}\right)$
SD [15]	$O\left(2^L(2R)^{-1}\right)$
LSD [8]	$O\left(2^L(4R)^{-1}\right)$
UWC-(p,c) [9]	$O\left(2^L\left(\frac{R}{p+1}+\frac{N-R}{c}+1\right)^{-1}\right)$

Table 3. Attacking Scenario A (chosen plaintext attack): Illustrative numerical examples on complexity of recovering one KEK ($k = 1$) in CST, SD, LSD and OWC-(p, c) based key management schemes assuming that the schemes include $N = 10^8$ users in total, each of the employed KEKs and SEKs consists of $L = 100$ bits, the sample for cryptanalysis is obtained from $J = 10, 100$, sessions of SEK updating and each of these sessions assumes $R = 10^6$ random revocations, and a memory of dimension $M = 2^{63}$ is available

	pre-processing time complexity		processing time complexity	
	$J = 10$	$J = 100$	$J = 10$	$J = 100$
CST [15]	$\sim 2^{70}$	$\sim 2^{67}$	$\sim 2^{43}$	$\sim 2^{36}$
SD [15]	$\sim 2^{76}$	$\sim 2^{73}$	$\sim 2^{54}$	$\sim 2^{47}$
LSD [8]	$\sim 2^{75}$	$\sim 2^{72}$	$\sim 2^{52}$	$\sim 2^{45}$
OWC-$(p = 1, c = 200)$ [9]	$\sim 2^{77}$	$\sim 2^{74}$	$\sim 2^{55}$	$\sim 2^{48}$

Table 4. Illustrative numerical examples on the complexity of recovering one KEK ($k = 1$) in CST, SD, LSD and OWC-(p, c) based key management schemes assuming that $L = 64, 100$ bits and the same scenario as in [9], i.e. $N = 10^8$, $R = 0.001N, 0.05N, 0.2N$ and the revocations imply the upperbound on the communications overhead

	processing time complexity					
	$L = 64$			$L = 100$		
$N = 10^8$	$R = 0.001N$	$R = 0.05N$	$R = 0.2N$	$R = 0.001N$	$R = 0.05N$	$R = 0.2N$
CST [15]	$\sim 2^{44}$	$\sim 2^{40}$	$\sim 2^{38}$	$\sim 2^{80}$	$\sim 2^{76}$	$\sim 2^{74}$
SD [15]	$\sim 2^{46}$	$\sim 2^{41}$	$\sim 2^{39}$	$\sim 2^{82}$	$\sim 2^{77}$	$\sim 2^{75}$
LSD [8]	$\sim 2^{45}$	$\sim 2^{40}$	$\sim 2^{38}$	$\sim 2^{81}$	$\sim 2^{76}$	$\sim 2^{74}$
OWC [9] $p = 1, c = 200$	$\sim 2^{48}$	$\sim 2^{43}$	$\sim 2^{41}$	$\sim 2^{84}$	$\sim 2^{79}$	$\sim 2^{77}$

Illustrative numerical examples related to Tables 1 and 2 are given in Tables 3 and 4, respectively.

Illustrative numerical examples related to Table 2 are given in Table 4 where the numerical scenario considered in [9] is employed which assumes that $N = 10^8$ and $R = 0.001N, 0.05N, 0.2N$, and the revocations imply the upperbound on communications overhead.

The above consideration points out that currently most interesting BE schemes, CST [15], SD [15], LSD [8] and OWC [9], are highly vulnerable by the developed methods for cryptanalysis proposed in Sections 4-5, implying that the security levels of these schemes are far below the claimed ones, and at least from the information-theoretic point of view they appear as the insecure ones.

7   Concluding Discussion

The vulnerabilities of BE schemes identified in this paper originate from the following generic characteristics of these schemes: (i) BE schemes employ "internal" secret key consisting of a huge number of independent static components (KEKs); (ii) BE schemes encrypt the session key (SEK) a huge number of times employing different KEKs and these ciphertexts are publicly available; (iii) the possibility for recovering even one active KEK, a part of the internal BE secret key implies weakness of the entire scheme.

This paper proposes methods for cryptanalysis of BE schemes via KEK by KEK recovering with complexity significantly lower than an exhaustive search over all KEK possibilities. The developed methods for cryptanalysis are based on the dedicated time-data-memory and time-data trade-off approaches employing chosen plaintext and ciphertext only attacks, respectively. Particularly note that the proposed cryptanalytical methods do not depend on the employed encryption primitive (it can be a block or a stream cipher, and for example, it can be AES or RC4, respectively).

The proposed algorithms for cryptanalysis are employed for security evaluation of the currently most interesting BE schemes, CST [15], SD [15], LSD [8] and OWC [9], and it is shown that these schemes are highly vulnerable, implying that the security levels of these schemes are far below the claimed ones, and at least from the information-theoretic point of view they appear as insecure ones.

The developed methods for cryptanalysis indicate requests for developing improved BE schemes which should be resistant against the proposed attacking approaches.

Regarding the attacking Algorithm B and the coincidence attack [10] note the following:

- the coincidence attack is a particular instance of the birthday paradox attacking scenario, and the coincidence attack is applied against the matrix based BE scheme (not against the tree based ones which had not been reported when [10] was published);
- Basic Algorithm B has been derived independently of the coincidence attack employing as the background the birthday attacking paradigm and particularly [1] and [6]; Algorithm B is employed against the tree based BE schemes CST, SD, LSD and OWC.
- The coincidence attack is related to the scenario where an attacker knows the ciphertexts of the employed KEKs. On the other hand, Algorithm B, in its generalized mode, works when not only the ciphertexts of KEKs are available but also the ciphertext of certain KEKs mappings is as well.

In addition to the considered models of BE specified in Section 3.1, according to statements from [10], [15] and [16], the following three models of BE can be identified, as well.

Model 1. According to [10] we identify the following BE paradigm.

$$< [header]; E_{SEK}(data) >=< [\{(ID_i, E_{KEK_i}(SEK \oplus ID_i))\}_{i \in I}]; E_{SEK}(data) >,$$
$$(14)$$

where for simplicity we assume that the same encryption algorithm $E(\cdot)$ is employed for encryption of the data and KEKs.

Model 2. According to [15]-[16] we identify the following BE paradigm. The center encrypts the data with SEK, generates encrypted forms of SEK employing a randomly selected parameter U and all KEK_i, $i \in I$, and broadcasts the following

$$< [header]; E_{SEK}(data) > =$$

$$< [\{ (U, ID_i, h(E_{KEK_i}(U)) \oplus SEK)) \}_{i \in I}]; E_{SEK}(data) > , \qquad (15)$$

where in the general case, $h(\cdot)$ denotes a truncating function, and in a special case it can be the identity function.

Model 3. According to [16] we identify the following BE paradigm.

$$< [header]; E_{SEK}(data) > =$$

$$< [\{ (U, ID_i, h(E_{KEK_i}(U \oplus ID_i)) \oplus SEK)) \}_{i \in I}]; E_{SEK}(data) > . \qquad (16)$$

The attacking approaches reported in this paper can not be directly employed for the attacking BE schemes which correspond to Models 1 - 3, but they can be employed as a background for developing methods for cryptanalysis of these schemes. As an illustration, we point out that the attacking scenario A in which different samples corresponding to the same SEK are collected appears as a model for certain attacking scenarios against the BE schemes proposed in [10], which correspond to the above Model 1 according to the following. When SEK_j is selected (assuming a chosen plaintext-SEK attack scenario) as

$$SEK_j = SEK \oplus ID_j \qquad (17)$$

then

$$E_{KEK_i}(SEK_j \oplus ID_i) = E_{KEK_i}(SEK \oplus ID_j \oplus ID_i) \qquad (18)$$

and for $i = j$ we obtain

$$E_{KEK_i}(SEK_j \oplus ID_i) = E_{KEK_i}(SEK) . \qquad (19)$$

As a result, for cryptanalysis we are able to collect samples which fit the attacking scenario A. The detailed analysis of the above cryptanalysis, as well as the cryptanalysis of Models 2 and 3 are out of the scope of this paper (just note that Models 2 and 3 can also be subject to certain malicious selections of the employed parameters).

References

1. S. H. Babbage, "Improved exhaustive search attacks on stream ciphers", European Convention on Security and Detection, *IEE Conference publication No. 408*, pp. 161-166, IEE, 1995.
2. S. Berkovits, "How to broadcast a secret", EUROCRYPT '91, *Lecture Notes in Computer Science*, vol. 547, pp. 536-541, 1991.
3. A. Biryukov and A. Shamir, "Cryptanalytic time/memory/data tradeoffs for stream ciphers", ASIACRYPT 2000, *Lecture Notes in Computer Science*, vol. 1976, pp. 1-13, 2000.

4. A. Fiat and M. Naor, "Broadcast encryption", Advances in Cryptology - CRYPTO93, *Lecture Notes in Computer Science*, vol. 773, pp. 480-491, 1994.

5. A. Fiat and M. Naor, "Rigorous time/space trade-offs for inverting functions", *SIAM J. Computing*, vol. 29, pp. 790-803, 1999.

6. J. Dj. Golić, "Cryptanalysis of alleged A5 stream cipher", EUROCRYPT'97, *Lecture Note in Computer Science*, vol. 1233, pp. 239-255, 1997.

7. M.E. Hellman, "A cryptanalytic time-memory trade-off", *IEEE Trans. Inform. Theory*, vol. IT-26, pp. 401-406, July 1980.

8. D. Halevy and A. Shamir, "The LCD broadcast encryption scheme", CRYPTO 2002, *Lecture Notes in Computer Science*, vol. 2442, pp. 47-60, 2002.

9. N. Jho, J. Y. Hwang, J. H. Cheon, M-H. Kim, D. H. Lee, E. S. Yoo, "One-way chain based broadcast encryption scheme", EUROCRYPT 2005, *Lecture Notes in Computer Science*, vol. 3494, pp. 559-574, 2005.

10. J. Lotspiech, V. Mirles, D. Naor and I. Nin, "Coincidence-free media key block for content protection for recordable media", *United States Patent 6,883,097*, filed May 2000.

11. J. Lotspiech, S. Nusser and F. Prestoni, "Broadcast encryption's bright future", *IEEE Computer*, vol. 35, pp. 57-63, Aug. 2002.

12. J. Lotspiech, S. Nusser and F. Prestoni, "Anonymous trust: Digital rights management using broadcast encryption", *Proc. IEEE*, vol. 92, pp. 898-909, June 2004.

13. A.J. Menezes, P.C. van Oorschot and S.A. Vanstone, *Handbook of Applied Cryptography*. Boca Roton: CRC Press, 1997.

14. J. Mitra and P. Sarkar, "Trade-Off attacks on multiplications and T-functions", ASIACRYPT 2004, *Lecture Notes in Computer Science*, vol. 3329, pp. 468-482, Dec. 2004.

15. D. Naor, M. Naor and J. Lotspiech, "Revocation and tracing schemes for stateless receivers", CRYPTO 2001, *Lecture Notes in Computer Science*, vol. 2139, pp. 41-62, 2001.

16. D. Naor, M. Naor and J. Lotspiech, "Revocation and tracing schemes for stateless receivers", IACR, Cryptology ePrint Archive, Report 2001/059, Dec. 2005, 34 pages, http://eprint.iacr.org/2001/059.pdf.

17. D. Naor and M. Naor, "Protecting cryptographic keys: The trace-and-revoke approach", *IEEE Computer*, vol. 36, pp. 47-53, July 2003.

18. P. Oechslin, "Making a faster cryptanalytic Time-Memory Trade-Off", CRYPTO 2003, *Lecture Notes in Computer Science*, vol. 2729, pp. 617-630, 2003.

A Broadcast Encryption Scheme
with Free-Riders but Unconditional Security

Andre Adelsbach and Ulrich Greveler

Horst Görtz Institute for IT Security,
Ruhr University Bochum, Germany
(andre.adelsbach, ulrich.greveler)@nds.rub.de

Abstract. We propose two schemes for efficient broadcast key establishment that enables a sender to communicate to any subset of the user-base by allowing a small ratio of *free-riders*. The schemes do not require stateful receivers and one scheme is unconditionally secure. The free-riders are unable to learn from the past whether they might become free-riders for a certain transmission again.

We present a new trade-off facet for broadcast encryption, namely the number (or ratio) of free-riders vs. the number of messages to be sent or the number of keys stored by each user.

1 Introduction

A number of applications need solutions to the problem of transmitting data to a group of receivers in a way that only the correct subset of all possible receivers can decrypt the data: Pay-TV, Digital Rights Management (DRM) controlled media, audio streaming, real-time business data, multicast communication are current examples. The subset of receivers can change for every transmission (e.g. pay-per-view) so an efficient scheme for a quick establishment of a secure channel to the new subset is desirable.

In the literature one can find very efficient revocation schemes which are suitable for a small set $\mathcal{R}$ with $|\mathcal{R}| \ll |\mathcal{N}|$ of revoked receivers (e.g. pirate receivers or traitors) compared to a huge number of total users $\mathcal{N}$ so that the broadcast communication can only be decrypted by the users $\mathcal{N} - \mathcal{R}$. The most efficient known schemes [1, 2, 3, 4] require a message header of length $O(|\mathcal{R}|)$ and user's individual private key size of $O(\log(|\mathcal{N}|))$. However, these revocation schemes are not intended nor suitable for a general subset case, e.g., cases where $|R| \approx \frac{1}{2}|\mathcal{N}|$.

The trivial scheme to address exactly all the users in the target set $\mathcal{N} - \mathcal{R}$ is to send the message encrypted individually for each user yielding a total number of $|\mathcal{N} - \mathcal{R}|$ messages to be sent via broadcast and only $O(1)$ keys to be stored by a user. This straightforward scheme is still the best known approach for the case where $|\mathcal{N} - \mathcal{R}| \ll |\mathcal{N}|$.

In this paper we will consider the case where *arbitrary* subsets are addressed by the sender. Assuming that any subset of $\mathcal{N}$ is chosen with equal probability

R. Safavi-Naini and M. Yung (Eds.): DRMTICS 2005, LNCS 3919, pp. 246–257, 2006.

for a transmission an average number of $\frac{1}{2}|\mathcal{N}|$ messages needs to be sent via the broadcast channel for every transmission if the trivial scheme is used. In order to reduce this number it is possible to assign keys to certain or all subsets of $\mathcal{N}$ and make these keys known only to the members of the subset. But even in the best (and not realistic) case where each user is provided with a key for all $2^{|\mathcal{N}|-1}$ subsets it belongs to, the numbers of bits needed to encode the subset key identifier is approximately $|\mathcal{N}|$ so any scheme which addresses the exact subsets would need to send $O(|\mathcal{N}|)$ message bits. Apart from that lower bound, a trade-off between the number of keys stored by each user and the number of messages to be sent to establish a transmission session key needs to be considered. The number of colluders (users outside the target group cooperating to break the scheme) the system can tolerate is another major parameter. Finally, we are interested in the level of security (existence of one-way functions, number-theoretic or information-theoretic security) we can establish.

1.1   Relaxed Requirements, New Trade-Offs

In order to set up schemes that are more efficient than sending $|\mathcal{N}| - |\mathcal{R}|$ messages we are relaxing the requirement that only the users in the target group $\mathcal{T} := \mathcal{N} - \mathcal{R}$ can decrypt the message by allowing a certain (small) number of users in $\mathcal{R}$ to decrypt the transmission as long as every user in $\mathcal{T}$ can receive the transmission. In this case new requirements on a relaxed scheme are to be considered: The number of users who can receive a transmission they have not subscribed to, i.e., the number of *free-riders*, shall be minimized and—following economic, game-theoretic requirements (see e.g. [5])—a user shall not gain any information whether she might be a free-rider for a future transmission by examining the past transmissions.

For example in a pay-TV scenario, we want to avoid a situation where two users $u_1, u_2 \in \mathcal{N}$ are put in one subscription set so that each time user u_1 subscribes to a transmission the user u_2 becomes a free-rider. The user u_2 might learn that he often becomes a free-rider for a certain kind of transmission preferred by u_1 (e.g., *Tarantino* movies) and will stop subscribing for these transmissions to avoid *unnecessary* payment.

The main area of trade-off parameters to be considered in this relaxed notion of broadcast encryption is the number (or ratio) of free-riders versus the message header length versus the user key size. Other major requirements on a scheme are collusion resiliency (i.e., the number of non-subscribers that may collude without being able to access the secured transmission) and underlying security assumptions (e.g., unconditional security versus computational security).

1.2   Related Work

The notion of broadcast encryption was introduced by Fiat and Naor in [6]. Their work described several methods making it possible to remove users from the target group by setting the requirement that only t users may collude where $t \leq k$ (*k-resiliency*). One method achieves a message header of size $O(k^3 \log |\mathcal{N}|)$ and a user key storage of $O(k|\mathcal{N}| \log |\mathcal{N}|)$ with unconditional security. The method is improved to user key storage of $O(k \log^2 |\mathcal{N}|)$ by assuming the existence of one-way-functions and to user key storage $O(k \log |\mathcal{N}|)$ by assuming hardness of root extraction modulo a composite.

Naor, Naor and Lotspiech [1] presented their *complete subtree* method that is secure under any number of colluders ($|\mathcal{R}|$-resiliency) and requires a header length of $|\mathcal{R}| \log(|\mathcal{N}|/|\mathcal{R}|)$ and $O(\log |\mathcal{N}|)$ keys per user. An improved version, the *subtree difference* method, requires header length $2|\mathcal{R}| - 1$ and $O(\log^2 |\mathcal{N}|)$ keys per user. Both methods are very efficient in the $|\mathcal{R}| \ll |\mathcal{N}|$ case and use PRNGs to assign keys in a tree structure.

Halevy and Shamir [2] presented a modified subset difference method with $O(\log^{1+\epsilon}(|\mathcal{N}|))$ key storage and $O(|\mathcal{R}|/\epsilon)$ message header size where ϵ can be chosen ($\epsilon = 1/2$ is a natural choice).

Dodis and Fazio [7] extended all three schemes, i.e., CS, SD and LSD, to the public key setting.

Boneh and Silverberg [8] showed that by using n-linear maps a collusion secure scheme with a fixed size public key and message header length can be achieved; Boneh and Waters [9] improved this by limiting a modified scheme to bilinear maps. Both schemes do not provide information-theoretic security.

Luby and Staddon [10] considered the information theoretic case and give general lower bounds for revocation schemes. Applying these bounds to the general case (i. e., not assuming $|\mathcal{R}| \ll |\mathcal{N}|$) shows that broadcast schemes with unconditional security are never efficient in the sense that either the message header length is large or the user key size is large.

1.3   Summary of Results and Outline

In the following section we will propose two new broadcast encryption schemes operating in a pseudo-probabilistic way. Both schemes realize their efficiency by accepting an adjustable ratio of free-riders. The first scheme is unconditionally secure, but puts certain undesirable constraints on the abilities of attackers; the improved scheme is information-theoretically secure and lacks these constraints. We will give a calculation of the parameter trade-offs of our schemes and discuss the collusion resiliency.

2   The Biased Sub-set Scheme[1]

2.1   Notations, Definitions and Basic Idea

Let $\mathcal{N}$ be the set of all users of a broadcast scheme and $\mathcal{T}$ be the set of users which shall receive a certain transmission[2].

---

[1] This work is subject of German patent DE 1020 0404 2094 B3 (issued 2005).

[2] We will not use the notion of a set $\mathcal{R}$ of revoked users in this paper further as we address the problem of broadcasting to arbitrary subsets, so the set $\mathcal{N} - \mathcal{T}$ does not refer to a small set of revoked users but to a set of users that have not subscribed to a certain transmission but might subscribe again to future transmissions.

Each user $u \in \mathcal{N}$ is provided with a fixed set of secret keys K_u which are assigned to him before receiving any transmission. Each user owns at least one individual key $k_u^{indv} \in K_u$ only known to him and the sender; the other keys might also be shared between several users, which is not known to the users sharing a key. During a transmission any user might receive further one-time usage keys (session keys, key encryption keys) which are not re-used and do not need to be stored after the transmission (thus we have a *stateless receiver*).

The basic idea of our scheme is to transmit the session key for a certain transmission bit-wise in a probabilistic way to all users in $\mathcal{N}$ so that the users in $\mathcal{T}$ receive on average more key bits than the users in $\mathcal{N} - \mathcal{T}$, thus only a small fraction of the users in $\mathcal{N} - \mathcal{T}$ is able to decrypt the transmission. Most users in $\mathcal{T}$ are provided with enough bits of the session key to derive the full key after exhaustive search. For the great majority of the users in $\mathcal{N} - \mathcal{T}$ it is infeasible to derive the session key in due time (e.g., before the transmission starts or before the transmitted data becomes outdated).

We choose a security parameter s and the generated session key k_S consists of $|k_S| = s$ bits. This key is valid for one transmission only. For the users in $\mathcal{T}$ a minimum of $d < s$ bits is needed to derive k_S (d is chosen according to the computation power of the users). We assume potential attackers could be more powerful than the ordinary users, so they only need $d' \le d < s$ bits to derive k_S in due time. The goal of the scheme is then that at a protocol step, the great majority of users in $\mathcal{T}$ has received more than d bits when at the same time only a small minority of users in $\mathcal{N} - \mathcal{T}$ has received d' or more bits (see Figure 1).

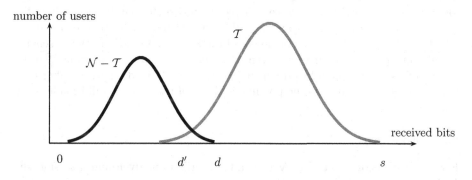

Fig. 1. Distribution of received key bits

Our scheme works in two phases: First a number of messages each carrying one key bit of k_S is broadcasted (each message can only be decrypted by a different subset of $\mathcal{N}$ provided with the right subset key) so that a certain number of the users $\mathcal{T}' \subset \mathcal{T}$ has received at least d bits (e.g., targeting $\frac{|\mathcal{T}'|}{|\mathcal{T}|} > 0.95$). In the second phase each user in $\mathcal{T} - \mathcal{T}'$ is provided individually with the full session key using the keys k_u^{indv} for all $u \in \mathcal{T} - \mathcal{T}'$.

Remark 1. Our approach broadcasts a secret by gradually broadcasting parts (bits or shares) of the overall secret to certain subsets so that any party having enough bits (or shares) can compute or recover the complete secret, e.g., the session key of a pay-TV broadcast transmission. The gradual transmission of secrets has been previously applied in the context of fair exchange [11]. In this context there is an additional "verifiability" requirement, as released parts of the secret have to be verifiable, such that a cheating party cannot gain valid parts of an honest party's secret, while sending random bits to this party. In the broadcast encryption setting the verifiability requirement can be neglected as the sender is trusted in this classical model and it is only a one-way release of secrets. This gradual probabilistic broadcast of secrets represents, to the best of our knowledge, a new probabilistic approach to broadcast encryption, which may foster further advance in broadcast encryption.

2.2   Setting Up the Scheme

The sender selects NK subsets $N_1' \ldots N_{NK}' \subset \mathcal{N}$, which are chosen uniformly from the set of all subsets of $\mathcal{N}$ with $\frac{1}{2}|\mathcal{N}|$ elements, so $|N_i'| = \frac{1}{2}|\mathcal{N}|$ for all $i = 1, \ldots, NK$. For each subset N_i' a *subset key* $k_{N_i'}$ is generated and let $k_{N_i'} \in K_u \Leftrightarrow u \in N_i'$. So each user knows the key assigned to each subset she belongs to, but she does not know any other subset keys, so she stores $\approx \frac{1}{2}NK$ subset keys in total (note that key storage could be reduced heavily if a PRNG-based algorithm is used to generate keys before usage, but then unconditional security is not achievable).

We simplify the notion here as for implementation we do intend to split the users $\mathcal{N}$ in equal-sized batches of users and choose the subsets and the keys for each batch individually so we can parameterize the batch size, reduce the number of necessary subsets and are able to add new users to the broadcast scheme batch-wise after the scheme is in broadcasting operation. As the scheme is then set up and run for each batch individually we can still assume $\mathcal{N}$ to be the set of users, although $|\mathcal{N}|$ might be a rather small fixed-length number (e.g. ten thousand) compared to the possible millions of users of the full broadcasting group.

2.3   Broadcasting

For a transmission a set $\mathcal{T} \subset \mathcal{N}$ of valid subscribers is given and a session key k_S is generated for this transmission.

In order to broadcast k_S to the set $\mathcal{T} \subset \mathcal{N}$ of users, the sender sorts the subsets N_i' so that we can assume for the sorted subsets $N_i := N_{\pi(i)}'$ that

$$N_i \geq_{\mathcal{T}} N_{i+1} \qquad \forall i : 1 \leq i < NK \tag{1}$$

where for arbitrary subsets N_a, N_b we define

$$N_a \geq_{\mathcal{T}} N_b :\Leftrightarrow |N_a \cap \mathcal{T}| \geq |N_b \cap \mathcal{T}| \tag{2}$$

using a suitable permutation π for sorting the subsets. Loosely speaking, we let N_1 be the subset containing the highest number of subscribed users, N_2 is next with the second greatest bias towards the number of subscribers, so for

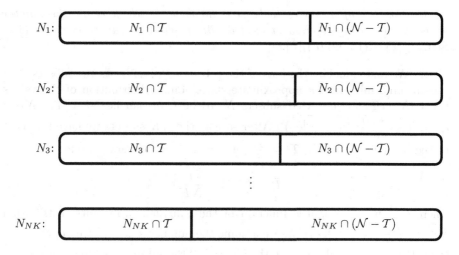

Fig. 2. Biased subsets

small indices i, the bias of the subsets N_i towards T is high, see Figure 2 for illustration.

The scheme consists of two phases.

Phase 1. The session key k_S will be transmitted bit-wise: Let $k_{S,1}$, $k_{S,2}$, ..., $k_{S,s}$ denote the session key bits. First bit $k_{S,1}$ is sent to subset N_1 using subset key k_{N_1}, then $k_{S,2}$ is sent to N_2 etc. until all bits are sent. Let $T'_j \subset T$ be the set of users in T which have received at least d session key bits after $k_{S,j}$ is broadcasted.

Phase 2. For each user in $u \in T - T'_s$ we provide the full session key by using her unique secret key k_u^{indv} to encrypt an individual message for her and send it via the broadcast channel.

We are now interested in the number of messages sent in the two phases and the number of free-riders who can decrypt the session key although being a user in $\mathcal{N} - T$ because they received d' key bits or more.

Theorem 1. *The number of free-riders given as a ratio of all users in $\mathcal{N}-T$ can be approximated by* $FR_{rat} = \Phi_{\mathcal{N}-T}(d')$ *where* $\Phi_{\mathcal{N}-T}$ *is the distribution function of the normal distribution* $N((1-\overline{t_s})s, \sqrt{s\overline{t_s}(1-\overline{t_s})^2})$ *and where* $\overline{t_s}$ *is the average key-bit information received by the subscribed users per key-bit transmission:* $\overline{t_s}$ *can be approximated by* $\overline{t_s} = \Phi^{-1}(1 - \frac{s}{NK})$ *where* Φ^{-1} *is the quantile function of the Gauss distribution* $N(\frac{|T|}{2}, \sqrt{\frac{|T|}{2}\frac{|T|}{|\mathcal{N}|}(1 - \frac{|T|}{|\mathcal{N}|})})$.

The ratio of users receiving at least d bits in phase 1 is $SUC_{rat} = \Phi_T(d)$ *where* Φ_T *is the distribution function of the the normal probability distribution* $N(t_s s, \sqrt{s\overline{t_s}^2(1-\overline{t_s})})$.

The number of messages to be sent in phase 2, which is the the number of users not having received at least d bits in phase 1, can be given by $(1 - SUC_{rat})|T| = (1 - \Phi_T(d))|T|$.

Proof. We first calculate the bias of the sub-sets $N_1 \ldots N_j$. As the subsets were chosen uniformly we can approximate the binomial distribution of the values $t'_i := |N'_i \cap T|$ for unsorted subsets N'_i to be Gaussian i.e. $\forall i = 1 \ldots NK$: $t'_i \sim N(\frac{|T|}{2}, \sqrt{\frac{|T|}{2}\frac{|T|}{|N|}(1 - \frac{|T|}{|N|})})$. After sorting the NK subsets we have the most biased s values $t_i := |N_i \cap T| > \frac{|T|}{2}$ for $i = 1 \ldots s$ with average values

$$\overline{t_i} = \Phi^{-1}(1 - \frac{i}{NK}) \tag{3}$$

where Φ^{-1} be the quantile function of the Gaussian probability distribution $N(\frac{|T|}{2}, \sqrt{\frac{|T|}{2}\frac{|T|}{|N|}(1 - \frac{|T|}{|N|})})$. As we assume the number $s \ll NK$ we approximate the value $t_i \approx \overline{t_s}$ for all $i < s$, so the bias' of all the subsets used for transmitting the key-bits are estimated to be equal to the bias of the last used sub-set in step s (note that, the scheme is more efficient than approximated here as the other biases are higher).

Using these approximations we can now calculate that each user in T has received every key-bit with probability $\overline{t_s} > \frac{1}{2}$, thus he has received $\overline{t_s}s$ key-bits on average and the number of key-bits received by each user is (by approximation) Gaussian distributed with parameters $N(\overline{t_s}s, \sqrt{s\overline{t_s}^2(1 - \overline{t_s})})$. For the users is $N - T$ we have the probability $1 - \overline{t_s} < \frac{1}{2}$, thus the distribution $N((1 - \overline{t_s})s, \sqrt{s\overline{t_s}(1 - \overline{t_s})^2})$.

Note, that on average a subscribed user has received $2s(\overline{t_s} - \frac{1}{2})$ more key-bits than non-subscribed users. □

Trade-off corollary result of the theorem. The scheme can be parameterized with the values s, d, d', NK (and with $|N|$ and $|T|$). From these values we can calculate (by approximation) the free-rider ratio FR_{rat} and success-ratio SUC_{rat}, hence the number of messages: $(1 - SUC_{rat})|T| + s$.

2.4 Batches of Users

As mentioned before we intend to divide the user set into batches of a certain size which we still denote $|N|$ to avoid unnecessary notations and run the scheme for each batch serially; let the number of batches that make up the real user-base be denoted by m so our total number of users is $|N|m$. We now face the problem of selecting the parameters during the set-up phase: batch size $|N|$, number of subsets NK – and for each transmission the parameters s, d and d'. There is obviously a tradeoff: For a smaller batch size, we have better biases and need less subsets (and less keys to be stored by the users), but we need to run the whole scheme more often and increase the transmission length.

Finally we have to identify the user's and attacker's computation power in order to select for a key size s the partial-key size values d and d'. In the next section we will improve our scheme so that this is not necessary anymore.

2.5   Improvements Based on Secret Sharing

The scheme introduced in the previous section uses a bit-wise distribution of the session key k_S. The scheme's security stems from the statistical certainty that unauthorized users receive on the average fewer bits (d' bits) of the session key than authorized users (d bits).

This basic scheme has some shortcomings, which are summarized below:

- The non-authorized users who are not free-riders do receive partial information as they receive a certain amount of key-bits.
- Authorized users have to perform an exhaustive search for up to $s - d$ bits of the session key. This could be costly.
- Each bit that an unauthorized user does not receive doubles his computational expense required for computing the full session key k_S. However, this still requires a rather large spread $d - d'$ between the number of bits received by authorized users in $\mathcal{T}$ and those received by unauthorized users in $\mathcal{N} \setminus \mathcal{T}$. Furthermore, estimating the computational power of adversaries is difficult, since exhaustive key-search can be easily parallelized and media content is sufficiently popular to attract many users in participating in a parallelized search for session keys.

Improved Biased Subset Scheme. Distributing the secret session key in a bit-wise manner can be seen as a naive way of sharing the secret and distributing its shares to certain sub-sets, which cover the set of authorized users. We will see in the sequel that we can overcome these disadvantages by applying a cryptographic secret-sharing scheme.

We will use the notion of a (k, n) *secret sharing scheme* consisting of two algorithms: Share and Reconstruct. Given a secret s the sharing algorithm Share(s) outputs n shares $s_1, \ldots, s_n$. Given shares $s_{i_1}, \ldots, s_{i_k}$, the reconstruction algorithm Reconstruct($s_{i_1}, \ldots, s_{i_k}$) outputs the original shared secret s so given any k of the n shares, the original secret s can be reconstructed, but knowledge of less than k shares does not reveal any information.

For our construction one of the first proposed schemes (Shamir's scheme: [12]) can be used. This scheme shares a secret $s \in F$ (e.g., $F = Z_p$ with $p > n$) by choosing a random polynomial *pol* of degree $k - 1$ and with constant term s (i.e., $pol(0) = s$) over F. The shares are defined as $s_i := (i, s(i))$, $i = 1, \ldots, n$, i.e., each share is a point of the polynomial. Given k different shares, the polynomial *pol* (and consequently the secret $s = pol(0)$) can be efficiently and uniquely reconstructed by performing a Lagrange interpolation.

The idea of applying secret sharing to overcome the limitations of the basic scheme is quite simple: The improvement is to replace the *bit-wise* broadcasting by broadcasting shares of the secret to the subsets instead.

In **Phase 1** of the improved scheme the sender applies a (d, s)-secret-sharing scheme to the key k_S, which results in the shares $s_1, \ldots, s_s$. Instead of encrypting and broadcasting single bits of the key k_S, the sender encrypts the share s_1 with sub-set key k_{N_1} and broadcasts the encrypted share (which can only be decrypted by members of N_1). Afterwards s_2 is sent to N_2, etc.

Given at least d shares a receiver can apply `Reconstruct` to efficiently reconstruct the secret k_S. Therefore, instead of performing an exhaustive search for the missing key bits, a receiver only performs a Lagrange interpolation to compute the complete session key. Moreover any unauthorized user in $N - T$ is unable to gain any information about the session key as long as he receives less than d shares. This is a significant improvement over the basic scheme, where an attacker could use extra time or extra computation power to derive more key-bits than ordinary users: the threshold value d in the improved scheme is a hard threshold and provides unconditional security.

2.6   Resiliency of the Schemes

The proposed schemes are highly vulnerable to colluders being able to combine their respective set of subset keys as these users would receive more key-bits or shares than any other user. In the case of two users sharing their subset key pool they would increase their portion of known subset keys from 0.5 to 0.75 each. This is higher than a reasonable bias being achieved by sorted subsets, thus the two users would become free-riders for all transmissions. Hence, the scheme does not offer any resiliency for colluders being a member of the same user batch. However, users from different batches can not gain anything from collusion as the scheme is run serially for each batch and different key encryption keys would be used. Therefore, the partial key information can not be combined at all.

The resiliency is therefore 1 from a worst-case point of view or dependent on the number of batches from an average-case point of view. It can easily be seen that the birthday paradox could be applied here if every user was assigned to a certain user batch uniformly chosen. So the resiliency of our proposed schemes can be approximated by the square root of the number of batches.

Fiat and Naor [6] describe a general applicable method to convert a scheme with low resiliency (1-resilient) to one with high resiliency by randomly grouping users in small *random* sets (batches) and applying 1-resilient broadcast encryption in parallel to broadcast shares of the broadcasted secret. This construction could also be used to achieve higher resiliency for our scheme.

3   Further Improvements in Practice

3.1   Getting Rid of Free-Riders

It is possible to avoid the existence of free-riders if the biased-subset scheme is connected with a revocation scheme (e.g., with Naor et al.'s subset-difference scheme [1]); the free-riders could be identified before the protocol starts and be removed from the set of all users by first establishing a broadcast key with revocation of the free-riders so that the biased-subset protocol only communicates to the target users and those users who will not become free-riders anyway. Note that this extension does not support information-theoretic security anymore, but it could still be useful for implementations, especially when the sender wants to avoid free-riders only for few transmissions.

3.2   Re-using Establishment Keys for Stateful Receivers

If the receivers are not stateless, the agreed key for a certain transmission can be learnt and re-used as a subset key for a future protocol run. In practice it is likely that the target set of one transmission is very *similar* to the target set of a related transmission, so if the key is used as a future subset key the bias towards the target set will often be much higher than that of a normal sorted subset. Hence, the scheme will become more efficient for future runs when the receivers have stored their transmission session keys for each time the receiver was in the privileged set of users.

4   Conclusion

We proposed schemes for efficient broadcast key establishment that offer a trade-off between the ratio of free-riders and other parameters (overall key size or message header size). The schemes do not require stateful receivers and the second one is unconditionally secure (disregarding the existence of free-riders). Free-riders can also be prevented if revocation schemes are used together with our proposed schemes.

5   Evaluation (Sample Data)

In this section we evaluate our probabilistic broadcast encryption scheme by comparing its performance with that of existing broadcast encryption schemes. Comparison will be mainly in terms of communication overhead (i.e., broadcast message length), storage (number of keys and public storage) per user, as well as computational complexity per user. The latter will be measured in terms of generic operations, i.e., we will count the number of XOR-, PRNG, multiplication-, addition- and exponentiation operations.

Furthermore, we focus our comparison on *1-resilient schemes* and rather *small numbers of users* n (in the order of 10000). These restrictions make comparisons between the different schemes possible: 1-resilient schemes are the basic building blocks for constructing k-resilient schemes by clever batching of users and serving each batch by an independent 1-resilient scheme. Note that this comparison is *unfair* to schemes being infinity-resilient; these are the trivial schemes and the revocation schemes (CS, SD).

Table 1 shows several sample data values for the proposed share-wise key distribution scheme. In all cases half of the user base is in the privileged set T

Table 1. Performance results: our 1-resilient scheme compared to the 1-resilient schemes of Fiat and Naor [6] and revocation schemes of Naor, Naor and Lotspiech [1]. $|\mathcal{N}| = 10000$, $|\mathcal{T}| = 5000$, size of keys and shares is 64 bits.

BE scheme	keys p. user	shares s	bits (header)	#ops p. user	FR_{rat}
Fiat&Naor [6]	10001	NA	10000	5001	0
Fiat&Naor [6] (OWF)	14	NA	10000	≈ 24974	0
Fiat&Naor [6] (Root)	10000 PKs	NA	10000	4999	0
Our scheme	1,000,000	1300	99200	650	0.05
Our scheme (Sect. 3.1)	1,000,014	1300	99200+138301	664	0
Trivial 1	2^{10000}	NA	64	1	0
Trivial 2	1	NA	320000	1	0
CS Revocation [1]	14	NA	320000	1	0
SD Revocation [1]	196	NA	639936	$14 + 1$	0

(i.e., $|\mathcal{T}| = |\mathcal{N}|/2$), while the other half is not (generic case), and resilience is fixed as $k = 1$.

We summarize the performance for different user batch sizes $|\mathcal{N}|$. The free-rider ratios FR_{rat} are a parameter so that different number of shares (the phase 1 messages of our scheme) s and total number of messages are calculated from that parameter. The values are approximated average numbers.

References

1. Naor, D., Naor, M., Lotspiech, J.B.: Revocation and tracing schemes for stateless receivers. In: CRYPTO '01: Proceedings of the 21st Annual International Cryptology Conference on Advances in Cryptology, Springer-Verlag (2001) 41–62
2. Halevy, D., Shamir, A.: The LSD broadcast encryption scheme. In Yung, M., ed.: CRYPTO '02. Volume 2442 of Lecture Notes in Computer Science., Springer (2002) 47–60
3. Goodrich, M.T., Sun, J.Z., Tamassia, R.: Efficient tree-based revocation in groups of low-state devices. In Franklin, M.K., ed.: CRYPTO '04. Volume 3152 of Lecture Notes in Computer Science., Springer (2004) 511–527
4. Jho, N.S., Hwang, J.Y., Cheon, J.H., Kim, M.H., Lee, D.H., Yoo, E.S.: One-way chain based broadcast encryption scheme. In: EUROCRYPT '05. (2005) to appear.
5. Shavitt, Y., Winkler, P., Wool, A.: On the economics of multicasting. Netnomics **6**(1) (2004) 1–20
6. Fiat, A., Naor, M.: Broadcast encryption. In: CRYPTO '93. (1993) 480–491
7. Dodis, Y., Fazio, N.: Public-key broadcast encryption for stateless receivers. In Feigenbaum, J., ed.: ACM Workshop in Digital Rights Management—DRM 2002. Volume 2696 of Lecture Notes in Computer Science., Springer-Verlag (2003) 61–80
8. Boneh, D., Silverberg, A.: Applications of multilinear forms to cryptography. Contemporary Mathematics **324** (2003) 71–90
9. Boneh, D., Waters, B.: Collusion resistant broadcast encryption with short ciphertexts and private keys. Cryptology ePrint Archive, Report 2005/018 (2005) http://eprint.iacr.org/.

10. Luby, M., Staddon, J.: Combinatorial bounds for broadcast encryption. In: EU-ROCRYPT '98. (1998) 512–526
11. Damgård, I.B.: Practical and provably secure release of a secret and exchange of signatures. Journal of Cryptology **8**(4) (1995) 201–222
12. Shamir, A.: How to share a secret. Commun. ACM **22**(11) (1979) 612–613

A Novel Broadcast Encryption Based on Time-Bound Cryptographic Keys

Miodrag J. Mihaljević[1], Marc P.C. Fossorier[2], and Hideki Imai[3]

[1] Mathematical Institute, Serbian Academy of Sciences and Arts,
Kneza Mihaila 35, 11001 Belgrade, Serbia and Montenegro
`miodragm@turing.mi.sanu.ac.yu`
[2] Department of Electrical Engineering, University of Hawaii,
2540 Dole St., Holmes Hall 483, Honolulu, HI 96822, USA
`marc@spectra.eng.hawaii.edu`
[3] University of Tokyo, Institute of Industrial Science,
4-6-1, Komaba, Meguro-ku, Tokyo, 153-8505, Japan
`imai@iis.u-tokyo.ac.jp`

Abstract. This paper proposes a novel broadcast encryption (BE) approach which combines the traditional one and time-bound cryptographic keys. The developed BE provides heavy reduced cumulative communication overhead and yields increased security. The reduction of the communication overhead is achieved via employment of time-bound session encrypting keys (TB-SEKs). The increased security against ciphertext only attack appears as a consequence of the reduced communication overhead and the increased security against the chosen-plaintext attack is obtained via employment of the time-bound key-encrypting keys (TB-KEKs). Appropriate methods for management of TB-SEKs and TB-KEKs are given. The proposed scheme is compared with traditional BE schemes and the advantages as well as the related trade-offs are pointed out.

Keywords: broadcast encryption, time-limited services, cryptographic keys management, time-bound keys, one-way mappings, pseudorandom number generators.

1 Introduction

Broadcast encryption (BE), initially reported in [1] and [3], is a cryptographic method for providing the conditional data (contents) access distributed via public channels. BE schemes employ the following approach for controlling the access privileges: the data are encrypted and only legitimate users are provided with the information on how to decrypt them (for some recent issues and particular applications see [7], [16] and [8] for example). The data encryption is performed based on a symmetric cipher and the secret session encrypting key (SEK). Ensuring that only the valid members of the group have the SEK at any given time instance is the key management problem. To make this updating possible, another set of keys called the key-encrypting keys (KEKs) is involved. The KEKs

R. Safavi-Naini and M. Yung (Eds.): DRMTICS 2005, LNCS 3919, pp. 258–276, 2006.

are used to encrypt and deliver the updated SEK to the valid members of the group only. Usually, in order to obtain the desired security, the KEKs must be kept in a protected storage. The underlying paradigm of BE is to represent any privileged set of users as the union of s subsets of users of a particular form. A different key is associated with each one of these sets, and a user knows a key if and only if he belongs to the corresponding set. The broadcaster encrypts the SEK s times employing the KEKs associated with the set in the cover. Consequently, each privileged user can easily access the data, but even a coalition of the non-privileged users cannot. A number of advanced BE schemes have been reported in [15], [4] and [5].

The time-bound cryptographic keys have been introduced in [17]. The most important feature of the time-bound cryptographic keys is that they have an exact activation and deactivation time. A particular technique has been proposed in [17] for establishing the time-bound keys and a particular application regarding time-limited contents access was discussed as well. It is reported in [18] that the method [17] for establishing the time-bound keys is not secure, but the idea of using time-bound cryptographic keys remains an interesting one. Another time-bound hierarchical key assignment scheme has been proposed in [2]. Very recently, certain time-bound key based schemes for controlling access privilege have been reported in [6] and [19].

In a traditional BE scheme the following properties hold: (i) The SEK should be updated according to the legitimate users dynamics; (ii) The KEKs are static, i.e. given at the very beginning and not updated later on. This paper proposes a different BE approach in which SEKs and KEKs are time-bound ones, i.e. they are valid only during time intervals specified in advance. The developed BE combines elements of traditional BE, time-bound cryptographic key approach and reconfigurable key management [10]-[11].

Motivation for the Work
The cumulative communication overhead of BE within certain time interval depends on the dynamics of legitimate users, and particularly can be heavily increased even when a frequent single-user change in the set of the legitimate users requires updating of the SEK. Furthermore, a generic vulnerability of BE has been reported in [14]. Accordingly, two main motivations for this work include:

- heavy reduction of the cumulative communication overhead of BE;
- developing a BE like scheme more resistant against the generic attack reported in [14].

Summary of the Results
A novel BE based on employment of time-bound SEKs and KEKs and the reconfigurability concept (regarding KEKs updating) is proposed. The main characteristics of the proposed scheme called BE with time-bound keys (BE-TBK) are analyzed and advantages over traditional BE are reported. The main advantages are reduced communication overhead in a number of scenarios and reduced vulnerability against generic chosen-plaintext and known-plaintext/ciphertext-only attacks (reported in [14]) on certain BE schemes. The employment of

time-bound SEKs provides reduction of the communication overhead. In addition, when combined with the employment of time-bound KEKs, it provides increased resistance against the security vulnerability. An efficient method for generation of time-bound SEKs based on a binary balanced tree and a keystream generator is employed. A particular one-way mapping technique suitable for updating TB-KEKs is pointed out.

Organization of the Paper
Background material is reviewed in Section 2. Section 3 introduces preliminaries, and the framework of the proposed BE with time-bound keys is presented in Section 4. The methods for management of time-bound SEKs and time-bound KEKs are proposed in Sections 5 and 6, respectively. The main characteristics of the developed BE are analyzed in Section 7. A comparison of the novel and traditional BE schemes is finally given in Section 8.

2   Background

2.1   Broadcast Encryption

Let KEK_i denotes a KEK employed in the system, and let ID_i denote its name, i.e. its identification (ID), noting that ID does not disclose any information on KEK_i itself. BE is based on the following approach. The system center generates all the employed KEKs. A user of the BE system is in advance provided with a subset of all KEKs employed in the system. Note that different users can have overlapping subsets of KEKs, but no one pair of users have the identical subset.

In a basic BE setting, the procedures at the center and each of the users are based on the following. When the current SEK should be updated, the center finds a subset I of KEKs $\{KEK_i\}_{i \in I}$ such that each of the legitimate users possesses at least one of these keys and none of the un-legitimate users possesses any of these keys. The center encrypts the data with SEK, generates encrypted forms of SEK employing all KEK_i, $i \in I$, and broadcasts the following

$$< [header]; E_{SEK}(data) > \; = \; < [\{ \, (ID_i, E_{KEK_i}(SEK)) \, \}_{i \in I}]; E_{SEK}(data) > ,$$
$$(1)$$

where for simplicity we assume that the same encryption algorithm $E(\cdot)$ is employed for encryption of the data and KEKs.

Upon receiving (1), a legitimate receiver is able to find ID_i in its possession and based on the pair $(ID_i, E_{KEK_i}(SEK))$ it can recover the SEK and the data based on the following:

$$SEK = E_{KEK_i}^{-1}(E_{KEK_i}(SEK)) , \qquad (2)$$

$$data = E_{SEK}^{-1}(E_{SEK}(data)) , \qquad (3)$$

where $E^{-1}(\cdot)$ denotes the decryption algorithm. As an illustration, note that a BE scheme called the complete sub-tree (CST) reported in [15] follows the above framework.

In other BE schemes the header should be modeled as follows

$$[header] = < [\{ \, (\, info(i,j), E_{f_j(KEK_i)}(SEK) \,) \, \}_{i \in I} \, , \tag{4}$$

where $f_j(\cdot)$, $j = 1, 2, ...J$, are certain publicly known one-way mappings, and $info(i,j)$ yields information on the employed $f_j(\cdot)$ and ID_i. Accordingly, upon receiving the header, a legitimate receiver is able to find the relevant $info(i,j)$ and learn about ID_i in its possession and the related $f_j(\cdot)$ so that it can recover SEK as follows:

$$SEK = E^{-1}_{f_j(KEK_i)}(E_{f_j(KEK_i)}(SEK)) \, . \tag{5}$$

The BE scheme called SD (subset difference) reported in [15] as well as the schemes reported in [4] and [5] follow the above paradigm based on (4)-(5).

Background on CST, SD and LSD Key Management Schemes. In [15], a generic framework is given by encapsulating several previously proposed revocation methods called subset-cover algorithms. These algorithms are based on the principle of covering all non-revoked users by disjoint subsets from a predefined collection, together with a method for assigning the "static" keys to subsets in the collection. An important consequence of this framework is the separation between long-lived keys (the KEKs) and short-term keys (the SEKs). Two types of revocation schemes in the subset-cover framework are proposed in [15] with a different performance tradeoff. Both schemes are tree-based, namely the subsets are derived from a virtual tree structure imposed on all receivers in the system. The first proposed scheme, complete sub-tree (CST) scheme, requires a message length of $R \log(N/R)$ and storage of $\log N$ keys at the receiver. The second technique for the covering is the subset difference (SD) [15]. The improved performance of the SD algorithm is primarily due to its more sophisticated choice of the covering sets in the following way.

Let i be any vertex in the tree and let j be any descendent of i. Then $S_{i,j}$ is the subset of leaves which are descendents of i but are not descendents of j. We observe: (i) $S_{i,j}$ is empty when $i = j$; (ii) otherwise, $S_{i,j}$ looks like a tree with a smaller subtree cut out; (iii) an alternative view of this set is a collection of subtrees which are hanging off the tree path from i to j.

The SD scheme covers any privileged set P defined as the complement of R revoked users by the union of $O(R)$ of these $S_{i,j}$ sets, provided that a receiver stores $O((\log N)^2)$ keys.

What is shown in [4] is that the SD collection of sets can be reduced: The basic idea of the layered subset difference (LSD) scheme [4] is to retain only a small collection of the $S_{i,j}$ sets used by the SD scheme, which suffices to represent any privileged set P as the union of $O(R)$ of the remaining sets, with a slightly larger constant.

The subcollection of the sets $S_{i,j}$ in the LSD scheme is defined by restricting the levels in which the vertices i and j can occur in the tree. This approach is based on specifying some of the $\log(N)$ levels as "special". The root is considered to be at a special level, and in addition we label every level of depth $k \cdot \sqrt{\log(N)}$

for $k = 1, ..., \sqrt{\log(N)}$, as special (we assume that these numbers are integers). Thus, there are $\sqrt{\log(N)}$ special levels which are equally spaced at a distance of $\sqrt{\log(N)}$ from each other. The collection of levels between (and including) adjacent special levels is defined as a "layer".

Since there are fewer possible sets, it is possible to reduce the number of initial keys given to each user. In [4], it is shown that if we allow the number of sets in the cover to grow by a factor of two, we can reduce the number of keys from $O(\log^2(N))$ to $O(\log^{3/2}(N))$. This technique was then extended and it has been shown how to reduce the number of keys to $O(\log^{1+\epsilon}(N))$ for $\epsilon > 1$.

Suppose that nodes i, k, j, occur in this order on a path from the root to a leaf, that i is not located on a special level, that i and j do not belong to the same layer, and that k is located on the first special layer from i to j. In this case the subset $S_{i,j}$ is not included in the basic LSD but it can be described using other subsets included in the LSD collection as follows:

$$S_{i,j} = S_{i,k} \bigcup S_{k,j} \ .$$

Accordingly, instead of a ciphertext encrypted under the subset key $S_{i,j}$ as in SD, two ciphertexts obtained from $S_{i,k}$ and $S_{k,j}$ should be broadcasted in the LSD scenario. Therefore, the communication overhead increases by at most a factor of two in comparison with SD, but on the other hand LSD yields a storage reduction at a receiver.

2.2   A Generic Vulnerability of Certain BE Schemes

In [14] a generic vulnerability of certain BE schemes has been pointed out. This vulnerability can be effectively explored assuming chosen plaintext attacks, and in some cases even under ciphertext only attack. The developed methods for cryptanalysis are based on an attacking approach not taken into account in the security evaluations of the reported BE schemes. The proposed attacks are based on employment of a dedicated time-data-memory trade-off approach for cryptanalysis. The main characteristics of the proposed algorithms are given regarding the required sample, and time/space complexities. The algorithms are employed for cryptanalysis of some of the currently most interesting BE schemes showing that their security levels are significantly below the claimed ones.

The vulnerabilities of the BE schemes identified in [14] originate from the following generic characteristics of these schemes: (i) the BE schemes employ "internal" secret key consisting of a huge number of independent static components (the KEKs); (ii) the BE schemes encrypt the same key (the SEK) a huge number of times employing different KEKs and these ciphertexts are publicly available; (iii) the possibility of recovering only one active KEK, a part of the internal BE secret key implies weakness of the entire scheme.

In [14], methods for cryptanalysis of BE schemes via KEK recovery with complexity significantly lower than an exhaustive search over all KEK possibilities have been proposed. The developed methods for cryptanalysis are based on the dedicated time-data-memory and time-data trade-off approaches employing chosen plaintext and ciphertext only attacks, respectively. Particularly the proposed cryptanalytical methods do not depend on the employed encryption primitive (it can be a block or a stream cipher, and for example, it can be AES or RC4, respectively).

The proposed algorithms for cryptanalysis are employed for security evaluation of the currently most interesting BE schemes, CST [15], SD [15], LSD [4] and OWC [5], and it is shown that these schemes are highly vulnerable, implying that their security levels are far below the claimed ones, and at least from an information-theoretic point of view they appear as insecure ones.

The developed methods for cryptanalysis indicate needs to develop improved BE schemes which should be more resistant against the proposed attacking approaches.

3   Preliminaries: Time-Bound Cryptographic Keys

The time-bound key scenario assumes that a number of keys $\{K_{i,t}\}_t$ is assigned to a privileged group G_i where $K_{i,t}$ is the group key of G_i during the time segment t, and time is in advance divided into the time segments. In the time-bound key approach, a legitimate member of group G_i during the time interval from t_1 to t_2 is provided with the information $I(i, t_1, t_2)$ from which the keys $K_{i,t}$, $t_1 \leq t \leq t_2$ can be recovered.

The above framework can be employed for establishing the time-bound SEKs (TB-SEKs) and the time-bound KEKs (TB-KEKs). The following discussion is related to TB-SEKs and a similar one holds regarding TB-KEKs.

TB-SEKs are organized as a time-varying sequence and a privileged user is provided with a segment of this sequence corresponding to the assigned privileges. TB-SEKs have the following characteristics:

- Each TB-SEK is valid only during a certain time interval; it is not valid both before its *activation* time and after its *deactivation* time;
- A collection of TB-SEKs which grant the access privileges during a certain time period can be delivered in advance at any arbitrary time instance before the activation time.

Let $TB - SEK_i$ denotes a TB-SEK valid during a time slot $[t + (i-1)\delta, t+i\delta)$, where t is the initial time instance and δ is the time slot duration. Accordingly, a privileged user obtains a segment of TB-SEKs, $[TB - SEK_j]_{j=1}^J$, where J depends on the duration of the privileged status. For simplicity, we assume that the time slots are of the same duration, i.e. δ is a constant, and in the same manner we could consider scenarios where δ is a certain function of the pair (t, i), i.e. $\delta = f(t, i)$.

In order to reduce the communication overhead, the center establishes an appropriate method to generate the TB-SEKs corresponding to certain time slots. This approach requires the design of an appropriate algorithm which generates all involved TB-SEKs, based on certain seeds. Each seed generates a segment of the entire sequence of TB-SEKs, $TB - SEK_i$, $i = 1, 2, ..., I$. When the appropriate algorithm is available, the center can transmit to the privileged users the seed values instead of the entire required TB-SEKs segment. The above model requires to solve the following two problems: (a) The development of an appropriate method to generate the segments of the TB-SEK sequence employing certain seeds, and (b) The development of an appropriate technique for secure delivery of the seeds to the privileged users via a public channel.

Regarding issue (a) note the following: (i) an approach is reported in [17] employing RSA but it has appeared as not secure as shown in [18]; (ii) the approaches reported in [6] and [19] provide certain frameworks only but actually do not cover the entire scheme.

4   Underlying Ideas and Framework of Broadcast Encryption Based on Time-Bound Keys

BE-TBK assumes the same underlying architecture as traditional BE: There are two main entities in the system, the center and the users. The system enables conditional access of the users to the services (contents) provided by the center based on employment of certain SEKs and KEKs.

The differences between BE and BE-TBK are related to the nature and management of the employed SEKs and KEKs. The following statements summarize the main differences.

- *Differences regarding SEKs*
    - BE SEKs are (usually) delivered "on line" at the activation time of a SEK, and the time delivery depends on the users' dynamic; it is unpredictable.
    - In BE-TBK, a legitimate user privileges are granted via delivering information about the related TB-SEKs (usually) in advance.
- *Differences regarding KEKs*
    - BE employs static KEKs delivered only once in advance and valid during the entire "life span" of the system.
    - BE-TBK employs TB-KEKs with activation and deactivation times specified in advance.

In order to reduce the communication overheads TB-SEKs are not delivered directly but indirectly employing certain seeds and an algorithm that generates the TB-SEKs based on these seeds. So, BE-TBK assumes that delivering a length-J sequence of TB-SEKs, $TB - SEK_1, TB - SEK_2, ..., TB - SEK_J$, is performed via transmitting a set of seeds $\{S_i^{(TB-SEKs)}\}_{i=1}^{I}$ where $I << J$, and the employment of a certain algorithm to generate the required TB-SEKs based on the received seeds.

The generation of TB-KEKs is based on the master secret key, appropriate public data and a suitable one-way mapping approach proposed in [12], as well as the updating of the public data at certain time instances specified in advance.

Accordingly, the framework for developing BE-TBK is based on the following:

- employment of a binary balanced tree at the center to specify the seeds $\{S_i^{(TB-SEKs)}\}_{i=1}^I$ required to generate a sequence of TB-SEKs (this tree is formally similar to the tree for delivering SEKs in a traditional BE, but it has a very different nature corresponding to the different natures of the seeds and TB-SEKs on one hand, and of the KEKs and users on the other hand);
- employment of a binary balanced tree at each user to determine the TB-SEKs based on the delivered seeds;
- employment of a generator of pseudorandom sequences (GPRS) over the above trees for a secure generation of the TB-SEKs based on the related seeds (following the underlying ideas reported in [3] and [15])
- employment of an appropriate scheme to deliver the seeds from the center to the privileged users;
- employment of a dedicated one-way mapping of the user's master key and certain updatable public information for generating the TB-KEKs.

5   Management of Time-Bound SEKs

5.1   Framework and Underlying Ideas

The developed key management for TB-SEKs is based on the following:

- TB-SEKs are changed periodically at predetermined time instances;
- Time evolution of TB-SEKs makes these keys (at any user) active and obsolete at certain time instances yielding time limited access privileges via their activation and termination;
- A method is employed to generate the TB-SEKs such that any subsequence of J consecutive TB-SEKs, $TB-SEK_j$, $j = J_0, J_0+1, ..., J_0+J-1$, can be derived from a set of I seeds $S_i^{(TB-SEKs)} = S_i$, $i = 1, 2, ..., I$, where $I << J$; Accordingly, delivering the seeds provides users with the access privileges;
- A method is employed for transmitting the required seeds $\{S_i\}$ from the center to the users in a secure and efficient manner which provides the users with the access privileges.

Accordingly, the underlying ideas for developing the key management scheme for TB-SEKs include:

(a) a method to specify the seeds and time-bound keys employing a binary balanced tree and a cryptographically secure GPRS (a keystream generator, [9]);
(b) employment of an appropriate scheme to deliver the seeds.

Fig. 1 illustrates a tree structure which relates the seeds and TB-SEKs. For example, Seed$_3$ specifies $TB-SEK_0$ to $TB-SEK_7$.

With respect to issue (a), to derive time bound keys based on certain seeds, we propose a method formally similar to the methods employed in [3] and to develop the SD based BE scheme [15]. As in the SD method [15], our proposal is also based on the employment of a binary balanced tree as an underlying structure

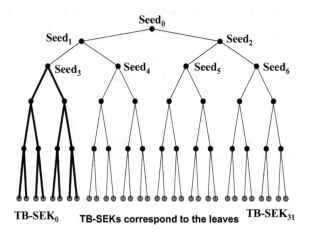

Fig. 1. An illustration of the TB-SEKs management

and a GPRS to specify the values at the nodes, but with different goals. A binary tree approach to specify of the time-bound keys but without employment of a keystream generator has been reported in [19], but this approach provides only a framework rather than a secure and practical scheme.

Similar approaches are employed at both sides, i.e. at the center and at the privileged users: Given the seeds, the same algorithm is employed to generate the time-bound keys noting that all the seeds are generated by the center and the legitimate users obtain only the seeds necessary to recover theirs TB-SEKs.

With respect to issue (b), BE-TBK assumes that the seeds $\{S_i\}_{i=1}^{I}$ are delivered to the users employing a scheme with low communications overhead.

5.2   Generation of TB-SEKs

Center. The specification of the sequence of time-bound SEK_t, $t = 1, 2, ...$, at the center is based on the following procedure.

- The Center adopts: (i) a suitable binary balanced tree of height h as an underlying structure to generate the time-bound keys, and (ii) a secure GPRS to assign the data to the tree nodes.
- The Center assumes that the time-bound keys are assigned to the tree leaves and that the internal nodes correspond to the seeds which can generate, employing the GPRS, certain segments of time-bound keys.
- The Center employs a GPRS with an ℓ bit initial state, and the master key MK of length ℓ to assign data to the internal nodes and leaves of the tree as follows:
  - Let A_0 be the tree root, and let B_0 and C_0 be its left and right-child nodes, respectively. The Center initializes the GPRS based on MK and the GPRS generates a pseudorandom binary sequence of length 2ℓ. The Center assigns MK to A_0, the first half of the generated sequence to B_0 and the second half to C_0.

- Let A be an internal tree node to which length-ℓ data have been already assigned, and let B and C be the left and right child-nodes of A, respectively. The data assigned to A are employed to initialize the GPRS and generate its length-2ℓ output sequence. The first half of the generated output sequence is then assigned to B and the second half to C.
- The procedure continues until the data have been assigned to all the leaves.
- The data assigned to the tree nodes are labeled as follows:
  - The data assigned to an internal node of the tree are labeled as the seed S_i and there are $2^t - 1$ different seeds;
  - The data assigned to the tree leaf t are labeled as $TB - SEK_t$ and $t = 1, 2, ..., 2^h$.

Users. A privileged user is provided by the center with a sequence of the triplets (S_i, h_i, t_i), $i = 1, 2, ..., I$, where S_i is a seed corresponding to a subtree of height h_i and t_i is the activation time of the SEKs at the leaves of the assigned subtree. These data enable the privileged user to recover the time-bound keys corresponding to the subscribed access privileges. Note that the seeds $\{S_i\}_{i=1}^{I}$, in form of length-ℓ binary strings, are delivered in a secure manner. Also, each user knows the algorithm of the GPRS because only the initialization data are secret.

Given (S_i, h_i, t_i), $i = 1, 2, ..., I$, a legitimate user derives the time-bound SEKs corresponding to the subscription period employing the following procedure.

- For each $i = 1, 2, ..., I$, the user performs the following:

  - Construct a binary balanced tree of the height h_i with $2^{h_i} - 1$ internal nodes and 2^{h_i} leaves;
  - Assign S_i as the root data and evaluate the data corresponding to all the tree nodes employing the following procedure:
    - Initialize the GPRS with S_i and generate 2ℓ output bits; assign the first half of the generated sequence to the root's left child-node and the second half to the root's right-child node;
    - Let A be an internal tree node to which the length-ℓ data have already been assigned, and let B and C be the left and right child-nodes of A; The data assigned to A are employed to initialize the GPRS and to generate its length-2ℓ output sequence; The first half of the generated output sequence is assigned to B and the second half to C;
    - The procedure continues until the data have been assigned to all the leaves.
    - The data assigned to the tree leaf j are labeled as $SEK_{i,j}$ and $j = 1, 2, ..., 2^{h_i}$;

- A privileged user constructs the sequence of TB-SEKs, $TB - SEK_t$, $t = t_i, t_{i+1}, ..., t_{i+\sum_{i=1}^{I} 2^{h_i}}$, which corresponds to the subscribed privileges, as the concatenation of the recovered $TB - SEK_{i,j}$, $j = 1, 2, ..., 2^{h_i}$, $i = 1, 2, ..., I$.

6   Management of Time-Bound KEKs

An important feature of BE-TBK is the employment of TB-KEKs in order to make the scheme more resistant against certain reported vulnerabilities of BE based on chosen plaintext attack [14], and to provide an extended flexibility of the scheme. This section proposes a method to manage TB-KEKs based on the approaches reported in [12] .

6.1   Underlying Ideas and Framework for TB-KEKs

The main underlying ideas to generate TB-KEKs include the employment of the following: (i) a master secret key (MK) uniquely related to each user; (ii) certain non-secret data which can be updated; (iii) an appropriate technique to map the MK and the public data into the required TB-KEKs.

Accordingly, the basic framework to manage the TB-KEKs includes the following.

- The center assigns a unique MK to each of the users. All the users are provided with these MKs once in advance.
- The center adopts an appropriate one-way mapping technique which maps the MK and certain data into the desired mapping output; All the users are provided with this mapping algorithm once in advance.
- The center generates TB-KEKs only valid during a pre-specified time interval and assigns certain subsets of these TB-KEKs to each of the users.
- For selected TB-KEKs, for each involved MK, the center generates certain data D such that each of TB-KEKs assigned to a user can be obtained employing the adopted mapping using the MK and D.
- Each user is provided with D to generate the required TB-KEKs.
- In general the data D can be subject to suitable time-varying one-way mappings.

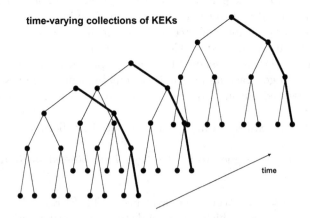

Fig. 2. An illustration of the basic TB-KEK management

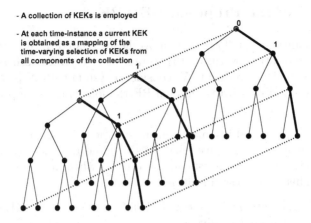

Fig. 3. An illustration of the TB-KEK management employing a combining approach

Implementation Note. There are a number of alternative approaches to deliver D. One approach is to deliver D to a user just once in advance. Another approach, applicable in certain scenarios, is to deliver D part-by-part at certain time instances specified in advance using an appropriate channel for transmission which provides a low communication overhead.

An illustrative basic structure of TB-KEKs is depicted in Fig. 2, and a more sophisticated approach in which TB-KEKs are obtained as a time-varying mapping from a collection of static KEKs is illustrated in Fig. 3.

6.2   Generation of TB-KEKs

Following the framework proposed in the previous section, this section proposes a method to generate TB-KEKs.

Let MK be a binary k-dimensional vector, and let I TB-KEKs, $TB-KEK_i^{(t)}$, be different binary ℓ-dimensional vectors, $k \geq \ell$, valid only during a certain time interval beginning at the time instance t, $i = 1, 2, ..., I$. The goal is to map the vector MK employing the data D into any of the vectors $TB - KEK_i^{(t)}$, $i = 1, 2, ..., I$, under the following conditions:

- it is computationally infeasible to recover MK knowing all $TB - KEK_i^{(t)}$, $i = 1, 2, ..., I$, and all the related public data D;
- the mapping of MK into any $TB - KEK_i^{(t)}$ should be a low complexity one and should include only mod2 additions and simple logic operations.

Particular mappings which can be employed to recover the TB-KEKs or to transform the master key MK into the required TB-KEKs have been recently proposed in [12] and [13]. An important feature of these mappings is that they provide provable security for the considered dedicated mapping scenario.

7   Analysis of the Proposed BE-TBK

This section analyzes the following main overheads related to the proposed BE-TBK: (i) communication overhead, (ii) storage at a receiver overhead; and (iii) processing at a receiver overhead. We consider a system with N possible users.

For a fair comparison with traditional BE the following assumptions are introduced.

Assumption 1. A SD based key management scheme [15] with minimized secure storage [12] is employed to deliver the seeds required to generate the TB-SEK segments (which reduces to unicast communications when the seeds are delivered to a small number of addressed legitimate users).

Assumption 2. The data D to generate M different sets of TB-KEKs required by a receiver are delivered in advance.

Assumption 2 is a particular communication-storage overhead trade-off in which the communication overhead is minimized at the expense of storage.

7.1   Communication Overheads

In general, the communication overheads of the proposed BE-TBK are related to the required delivery of TB-SEKs and TB-KEKs. The proposed algorithms for management of TB-SEKs and TB-KEKs (see Sections 4 and 5) imply the following:

- Providing a legitimate user with the sequence of TB-SEKs (corresponding to the user's privileges) requires the transmission in a secure way of the corresponding set of the seeds $\{S_i^{(TB-SEKs)}\}_i$;
- Updating the TB-KEKs requires the transmission of the non-secret data D once in advance or part-by-part at certain time instances which appear with low frequency. (Accordingly, this communication overhead does not appear as a dominant one.)

There is a significant difference between the proposed BE-TBK and a traditional BE: BE-TBK does not require any kind of revocation of the session keys because they are time-bound with pre-specified activation and expiration times. Accordingly, we focus on the communication overhead within a specified time interval instead of the communication overhead due to a change in the group of privileged users as in BE.

For simplicity we assume the following model for the dynamics of the users.

Assumption 3. Let N be the total number of users, and $N - R$ be the number of privileged users at the time instance t_1. We assume that within the time interval $[t_1, t_2]$ L changes in the number of privileged users occur, and that each change assumes that ΔR privileged users loose their privileges and that at the same time ΔR users obtains their privileges.

Assumption 4. J TB-SEKs correspond to the access privileges of a legitimate user.

Statement 1. The proposed BE-TBK does not require any communication for revocation of the access privileges because they are time-bound and expire at time instance specified in advance.

Based on Section 5.2 we readily obtain:

Proposition 4. The cardinality of the set $\{S_i^{(TB-SEKs)}\}_i^I$ which defines J TB-SEKs is upperbounded by $\log_2 J$.

According to the communication overhead related to SD (see [15]) and its variant with minimized secure storage [12], Statement 1 and Proposition 4 we obtain the following result regarding the communication overhead of the proposed BE-TBK under the given assumptions.

Proposition 5. Under Assumptions 1 - 4 and Proposition 4, the cumulative communication overhead of the proposed BE-TBK within a time interval $[t_1, t_2]$ is given by $O(L(\log_2 J)\Delta R)$.

7.2   Storage Overheads at Receiver

According to the proposed BE-TBK, the storage overheads at a receiver are related to the following requirements:

- a secure storage to keep the receiver's master secret key MK;
- a public storage to keep non-secret data D (due to Assumption 2) required to generate the currently valid TB-KEKs based on MK;
- a protected storage to keep "active segments" of the sequence of TB-SEKs: $TB - SEK_1, TB - SEK_2, ..., TB - SEK_J$ (note that these keys could be generated "on-line" one-by-one when required).

In general, a trade-off between the required storage overhead related to the public data D for TB-KEKs specifications and the communication overhead is possible, but according to Assumption 2 this analysis of storage overhead assumes that the data D are stored at each receiver in advance.

The results on the storage overhead reported in [15] and [12] regarding the SD scheme with minimized secure storage, and the given assumptions for the proposed BE-TBK imply the following proposition.

Proposition 6. Under Assumptions 1 - 4, the storage overheads of the proposed BE-TBK are:

- the required secure storage for the MK is $O(1)$ (independent of N) ;
- assuming "on-line" one-by-one generation of the involved TB-SEKs, the required secure storage is $O(1)$;
- the required public storage of the public data D is $O(M(\log_2 N)^2))$ where M is the number of TB-KEK updatings.

7.3   Processing Overheads at Receiver

According to the proposed BE-TBK, the processing overheads at each receiver are related to the following requirements:

- the processing overhead to recover the required $TB - KEK_i^{(t)}$ employed for secure transmission of the seeds;
- the processing to recover the seeds $\{S_i^{(TB-SEKs)}\}_i$ assuming, according to Assumption 1, employment of SD (with GPRS) for their secure transmission;
- the processing to generate J TB-SEKs based on $\{S_i^{(TB-SEKs)}\}_{i=1}^I$, $I << J$.

Assumption 1, the result on the SD processing overhead from [15] and Proposition 3 and 4 imply the following proposition.

Proposition 7. The processing overheads of the proposed BE-TBK are:

- the processing overhead to recover the required $TB - KEK_i^{(t)}$ is $O(1)$;
- the processing overhead to recover the seeds $\{S_i^{(TB-SEKs)}\}_{i=1}^I$ is $O(I \log_2 N)$ with $I \leq \log_2 J$;
- the processing overhead to generate J TB-SEKs is $O(J)$.

8   Comparison of BE and BE-TBK

This section points out a number of differences between BE and BE-TBK and the related advantages of BE-TBK as well as its main drawback.

8.1   Comparison of the Underlying Approaches

The following discussion points out certain characteristics of BE and BE-TBK and differences between the underlying characteristics of BE and BE-TBK.

BE is based on the following underlying characteristics:

- the KEKs are static data; they are set-up at the very beginning and do not change later on;
- the SEKs are updated irregularly and not-predictably;
- the updating of SEKs is driven by the dynamics of the legitimate users; whenever a user joins or leaves the group, the current SEK must be updated.

BE-TBK is based on the following underlying characteristics:

- the TB-KEKs are time varying data which are refreshed at certain time instances; these changes are based on updating certain public data and the employment of a dedicated one-way mapping controlled by a master secret key;
- the TB-SEKs are updated regularly at time instances specified in advance;
- the updating of TB-SEKs is not driven by the dynamic of the legitimate users but according to the rule established by the center.

Moreover we point out the following properties of BE-TBK access control:

- The basic paradigm can be described as "the users follow the system", i.e. the users adjust their actions according to the system rules;
- The updating of the session keys is independent of the user's actions;
- The activation and deactivation times of all the keys can be specified in advance and accordingly, the keys can be delivered "off-line".

On the other hand, the access control employed in a traditional BE scheme has the following characteristics:

- The basic paradigm can be described as "the system follows the users", i.e. key management depends on the behavior of the users;
- The updating of the session keys depends on the dynamics of the users;
- The users' actions are usually not-predictable and accordingly "on-line" delivery of the keys is needed.

8.2   Comparison of the Overheads

In any BE based scenario, the most critical overheads involved by the access control mechanism are the following ones: (i) the communications overhead; (ii) the storage overhead at a receiver, and (iii) the processing overhead at a receiver.

For a fair comparison we assume employment of the same key management scheme in the both BE and BE-TBK, and as an illustration we consider BE and BE-TBK with SD based key management. Also, for a fair comparison of BE and BE-TBK we consider the cumulative communication overhead which is the sum of the communication overheads corresponding to a change of the legitimate users.

Table 1. Comparison of BE schemes based on SD [15], its variant with minimized secure storage [12], and the proposed BE-TBK when Assumption 1 - 4 hold; N is the total number of users, R is the average number of the revoked users, ΔR is the fluctuation of revoked users (ΔR users terminate their privileges and at the same time ΔR users obtain their privileges), L is the number of changes of legitimate users during the considered time interval, J is the number of TB-SEKs at a legitimate user, and the public data D at a receiver should provide the possibility to generate M different TB-KEK collections

	SD based BE [15]	modified SD based BE [12]	proposed BE-TBK
secure storage overhead at receiver	$O((\log_2 N)^2)$	$O(1)$	$O(1)$
public storage overhead at receiver	/	$O((\log_2 N)^2)$	$MO((\log_2 N)^2)$
processing overhead at receiver	$O(\log_2 N)$	$O(\log_2 N)$	$(\log_2 J)O(\log_2 N) + O(J)$
cumulative communications overhead (under Assumption 3)	$L(O(R))$	$L(O(R))$	$L(\log_2 J)(O(\Delta R))$ $\Delta R << R$

Table 2. Illustrative numerical implications of Table I under Assumption 1 - 3 when the total number of users is $N = 2^{25}$, average number of revoked users is $R = 2^{20}$, the fluctuations of the revoked users $\Delta R = 2^7$ (ΔR users terminate the privileges and ΔR users obtain the privileges), there are $L = 2^{10}$ changes of the legitimate users during the considered time interval, each legitimate user should be provided with $J = 2^3$ TB-SEKs, and the public data D at a receiver should provide possibility for generating $M = 2^3$ different TB-KEKs collections

	SD based BE [15]	modified SD based BE [12]	proposed BE-TBK
secure storage overhead at receiver	~ 400	~ 1	~ 1
public storage overhead at receiver	/	~ 400	~ 3200
processing overhead at receiver	~ 20	~ 20	~ 78
cumulative communications overhead (under Assumption 3)	$\sim 2^{30}$	$\sim 2^{30}$	$\sim 2^{18}$

Regarding the storage overhead two different overheads are considered: the required dimension of a secure storage and the required dimension of a public storage.

Table 1 summarizes the main overheads of BE schemes based on SD [15], its variant with minimized secure storage [12] and the proposed BE-TBK. The comparison assumes the scenario specified by Assumptions 1 – 3. The overheads related to BE schemes based on SD [15] and its variant with minimized secure storage [12] are evaluated based on the results reported in [15] and [12]. The overheads of the considered particular BE-TBK are evaluated according to Propositions 5 – 7. Table 2 provides a numerical illustration of the overheads given in Table 1.

8.3   Vulnerability Discussion

A generic vulnerability of certain BE schemes has been reported in [14]. This vulnerability is a consequence of the following: (i) the same SEK is encrypted by a huge number of different KEKs; (ii) the static nature of the KEKs employed in BE which can not be updated. In [14] it is shown that (i) yields an opportunity to mount a ciphertext only attack, and that (ii) yields an opportunity to mount a more powerful attack assuming chosen-plaintext based cryptanalysis.

In BE-TBK, instead of a single SEK, a number of different seeds to generate TB-SEKs are employed. The same seed for TB-SEKs is encrypted with a significantly smaller number of different TB-KEKs, and the TB-KEKs which are updatable via changing certain public data involved in the generation of TB-KEKs are used. The increased security against ciphertext only attack appears as a consequence of the reduced sample for cryptanalysis whose dimension corresponds to the number of different TB-KEKs employed for encryption of a same seed for TB-SEKs. The increased security against the chosen-plaintext attack is obtained via employment of the TB-KEK.

Accordingly, when the life span of the TB-KEKs has been appropriately selected, BE-TBK appears much more resistant against attacks to which BE is vulnerable. Furthermore the resistance is obtained without changing the dimension of the cryptographic keys which is important in certain scenarios. The increased resistance of BE-TBK on the chosen plaintext attacks to which BE is vulnerable is obtained via a security-storage trade-off, noting that the required storage is a public one, which renders its increase appropriate.

8.4 Summary of the Comparison

The employment of TB-SEKs provides a reduction of the communication overhead, and together with the employment of TB-KEKs, it provides increased resistance against recently introduced generic attacks on a class of BE schemes. Accordingly, the proposed BE-TBK has the following two main advantages compared with a traditional BE: (i) it yields a significantly lower cumulative communication overhead in a number of scenarios; (ii) it yields increased resistance against the generic vulnerability of BE reported in [14].

On the other hand, the main disadvantage of BE-TBK is the following. The TB-SEKs can not be revoked in a simple manner because the expiration of the time-bound keys plays the role of revocation. Indeed certain revocation procedures could be established via appropriately changing TB-KEKs (i.e. the related public data) but they are out of the scope of this paper.

References

1. S. Berkovits, "How to broadcast a secret", EUROCRYPT '91, *Lecture Notes in Computer Science*, vol. 547, pp. 536-541, 1991.
2. H.-Y. Chien, "Efficient Time-Bound Hierarchical Key Assignment Scheme", *IEEE Trans. Knowledge and Data Eng.*, vol. 16, pp. 1301-1304, Oct. 2004.
3. A. Fiat and M. Naor, "Broadcast encryption", Advances in Cryptology - CRYPTO93, *Lecture Notes in Computer Science*, vol. 773, pp. 480-491, 1994.
4. D. Halevy and A. Shamir, "The LCD broadcast encryption scheme", CRYPTO 2002, *Lecture Notes in Computer Science*, vol. 2442, pp. 47-60, 2002.
5. N. Jho, J. Y. Hwang, J. H. Cheon, M-H. Kim, D. H. Lee, E. S. Yoo, "One-way chain based broadcast encryption scheme", EUROCRYPT 2005, *Lecture Notes in Computer Science*, vol. 3494, pp. 559-574, 2005.
6. Y. Kaji and R. Nojima, "A Management Scheme for Time-Limited Cryptographic Keys, *ACNS 2005 - The Third Int. Conf. on Applied Cryptography and Network Security*, New York, June 2005, Proceedings, Industrial and Short-Papers track, pp. 106-117.
7. J. Lotspiech, S. Nusser and F. Prestoni, "Broadcast encryption's bright future", *IEEE Computer*, vol. 35, pp. 57-63, Aug. 2002.
8. J. Lotspiech, S. Nusser and F. Prestoni, "Anonymous trust: Digital rights management using broadcast encryption", *Proc. IEEE*, vol. 92, pp. 898-909, June 2004.
9. A.J. Menezes, P.C. van Oorschot and S.A. Vanstone, *Handbook of Applied Cryptography*. Boca Roton: CRC Press, 1997.

10. M.J. Mihaljević, "Key management schemes for stateless receivers based on time varying heterogeneous logical key hierarchy", ASIACRYPT 2003, *Lecture Notes in Computer Science*, vol. 2894, pp. 137-154, Nov. 2003.
11. M.J. Mihaljević, "Reconfigurable key management for broadcast encryption", *IEEE Communications Letters*, vol. 8, pp. 440-442, July 2004.
12. M.J. Mihaljević, M.P.C. Fossorier and H. Imai, "Secret-public storage trade-off for broadcast encryption key management", ICICS 2004, *Lecture Notes in Computer Science* vol. 3269, pp. 375-387, October 2004.
13. M.J. Mihaljević, M.P.C. Fossorier and H. Imai, "Key management with minimized secret storage employing an erasure channel approach", *IEEE Communications Letters*, vol. 9, no. 8, pp. 741-743, Aug. 2005.
14. M.J. Mihaljević, M.P.C. Fossorier and H. Imai, "Security weaknesses of certain broadcast encryption schemes", DRMTICS 2005, *Lecture Notes in Computer Science*, this volume, 18 pages.
15. D. Naor, M. Naor and J. Lotspiech, "Revocation and tracing schemes for stateless receivers", CRYPTO 2001, *Lecture Notes in Computer Science*, vol. 2139, pp. 41-62, 2001.
16. D. Naor and M. Naor, "Protecting cryptographic keys: The trace-and-revoke approach", *IEEE Computer*, vol. 36, pp. 47-53, July 2003.
17. W.G. Tzeng, "A Time-Bound Cryptographic Key Assignment Scheme for Access Control in a Hierarchy", *IEEE Trans. Knowledge and Data Eng.*, vol. 14, pp. 182-188, Jan/Feb 2002.
18. X. Yi and Y. Ye, "Security of Tzengs Time-Bound Key Assignment Scheme for Access Control in a Hierarchy", *IEEE Trans. Knowledge and Data Eng.*, vol. 15, pp. 1054-1055, July/Aug 2003.
19. M. Yoshida, Y. Kaji and T. Fujiwara, "A Time-Limited Key Management Scheme Based on One-Way Permutation Tree", HISC 2005 - 2005 Hawaii, IEICE and SITA Joint Conference on Information Theory, Hawaii, USA, May 2005, Proceedings, pp. 165-170 (ISBN 4-902087-13-8).

A Vector Approach to Cryptography Implementation

Jacques J.A. Fournier[1,2] and Simon Moore[1]

[1] University of Cambridge, Computer Laboratory, UK
{Jacques.Fournier, Simon.Moore}@cl.cam.ac.uk
[2] Gemplus S.A, La Ciotat, France
jacques.fournier@gemplus.com

Abstract. The current deployment of Digital Right Management (DRM) schemes to distribute protected contents and rights is leading the way to massive use of sophisticated embedded cryptographic applications. Embedded microprocessors have been equipped with bulky and power-consuming co-processors designed to suit particular data sizes. However, flexible cryptographic platforms are more desirable than devices dedicated to a particular cryptographic algorithm as the increasing cost of fabrication chips favors large volume production. This paper proposes a novel approach to embedded cryptography whereby we propose a vector-based general purpose machine capable of implementing a range of cryptographic algorithms. We show that vector processing ideas can be used to perform cryptography in an efficient manner which we believe is appropriate for high performance, flexible and power efficient embedded systems.

Keywords: Cryptography, AES, Montgomery Modular Multiplication, RSA, vector architecture.

1 Introduction

Given the commercial value of digital contents, their management in mobile equipments (like PDAs, mobile phones or smart-cards) has become a critical issue for content issuers. Digital Right Management (DRM) schemes are being worked on. For example the Open Mobile Alliance (OMA) is working on a DRM architecture for the mobile industry [1]. In those DRM schemes, the distribution, management and protection of data rely on the use of complex cryptographic protocols and algorithms. In such a context, the processors used (in particular those in mobile equipments) face constraints of size, power, cost, performance and security.

During the past 15 years, we saw quite a few publications about hardware modules for cryptographic applications. Most of those proposals make use of processors which are very application specific. They are not only optimized for one particular algorithm but also for particular sizes to suit market requirements. For security, counter-measures have been proposed, most of which are

R. Safavi-Naini and M. Yung (Eds.): DRMTICS 2005, LNCS 3919, pp. 277–297, 2006.
© Springer-Verlag Berlin Heidelberg 2006

software-based leading to bulkier codes and slower programs. A hardware-software co-design approach is being undertaken by other researchers [2, 3, 4] in order to have a hardware that would reduce the cost of those software countermeasures.

Our approach uses Data Parallel techniques for cryptographic applications. We first describe how we chose the vector design space. We then illustrate how cryptographic algorithms can be vectorised by giving two examples. This then takes us to the design of the corresponding vector processing machine before finally presenting results obtained on the functional simulator. With this approach, we propose an architecture which can achieve high performance and flexibility with little increase in control logic compared to scalar processors. Those characteristics of performance and flexibility are particularly relevant to DRM applications where cryptographic applications are made to run on processors having different constraints, going from the 'computer terminal' of the Rights Issuer to the small embedded chip of the DRM Agent found in a mobile equipment.

2   Having a Quantitative Approach

Recently, there has been an explosion in the use of cryptographic processors for embedded applications. For *secret-key* algorithms those hardware implementations can be considered to be rather straight-forward. For *Public-Key* systems however, given the complexity of the computations involved, designers have been implementing systems for static lengths (like having long-precision number multipliers for example). Some have been integrating crypto-oriented instructions into the instruction set of General Purpose Processors (GPPs) [5, 6, 7]. Others had a more scalable approach as depicted in [8]. But none have had a systematic approach where hardware designers would look for a design which would be the 'best' trade-off between speed, security, chip area and power consumption.

Having identified this need, we went back to the architecture design space and look for the best architecture that would allow us to undertake such a quantitative study. Note that this paper focuses on the micro-architecture design of a cryptographic accelerator. Issues of security (and related countermeasures) are beyond the scope of this paper.

2.1   A Case for a Vector Architecture

According to [9], the architecture design space can be decomposed into a tree shown in Figure 1. From there, our approach was to parse through that tree and decide on the best design approach for our cryptographic algorithms.

Single Instruction Scheme. Processors are chosen in order to maintain compatibility with existing smart-card chips. Having a *Multiple Instruction Scheme* would imply having a multi-processor system which does not fit with actual power and size constraints on embedded chips. *Instruction Level Parallel* architectures were also put aside because having parallel instruction executions:

- requires complicated instruction decoding and scheduling units, which be against our motivation of reducing complexity.
- implies the use of very sophisticated instruction decoders and issuers, which consume a lot of power as illustrated in [10]. In the latter paper, the authors that in a superscalar microprocessor where instructions are issued in parallel, the instruction issue and queue logic accounts for nearly one quarter of the total energy consumed by the processor while another quarter is accounted for by the instructions' reorder buffers.
- is not well suited for those particular applications: most cryptographic algorithms involve the sequential use of precise instructions or operations leaving little room for parallelism at this level.

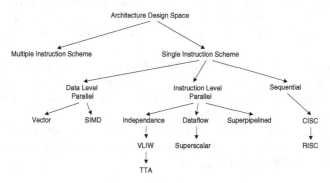

Fig. 1. Tree decomposition of the architecture design space

A *Data Level Parallel* approach was chosen because

- the data used by those cryptographic algorithms can be decomposed into a vector of shorter data onto which operations can be applied in parallel (or *partially-parallel*) as illustrated in this paper.
- The instruction decoding is simpler, i.e. no dedicated logic is required for dynamic instructions' schedule and reordering.
- In terms of security, working on data in parallel can in theory reduce the relative contribution of each data piece to the external power consumption as announced by [11].

Hence we used Data Level Parallel techniques to design our cryptographic processing unit. Our design's vector machine is controlled by a General Purpose Processor (GPP) which also allows the optimal execution of 'scalar' codes[1].

---

[1] In this paper, a *scalar code* is an algorithm's code implemented on a scalar machine (MIPS-I) and a *vector code* is an algorithm's code implemented on a vector machine (VeMICry).

3   Proposed Methodology for Vectorizing Cryptographic Algorithms

We chose two case studies to illustrate how cryptographic algorithms can be vectorised: the AES symmetric key algorithm and modular multiplication based on Montgomery's algorithm (used in both RSA or Elliptic Curves Public Key Cryptography). For each of those case studies we look at their performance on a scalar MIPS-I architecture ([12, 13]). We identify the most time-consuming operations. We then show how the latter can be improved by having a vector approach based on an instruction set defined in Appendix A. In section 5 we show how these algorithms perform on our functional simulator.

3.1   Vectorising the Advanced Encryption Standard

The AES algorithm is described in [14]. The algorithm is meant to work for key lengths namely 128, 192 or 256 bits. In this study, we will concentrate on the 128-bit version of the AES as it is very representative of what's happening.

Scalar Implementation on the MIPS. Our test implementation on the MIPS-IV is illustrated in Figure 2. The key schedule is done first and the sub-keys stored in RAM. The encryption process is then executed. No counter-measures are implemented. We focus on the encryption process.

Table 1 is an analysis of the time taken the different processes. This provides an indication of the most penalizing operations, in particular the KEY-SCHEDULE, SUBBYTE and MIXCOLUMNS operations.

Table 1. Decomposition of the AES-128 encryption

Sub-Process	♯ clock-cycles	♯ times called	Total	% of total encryption
KEY-SCHEDULE	508	1	508	16
ADDRNDKEY	16	11	176	6
SUBBYTE	68	10	680	22
SHIFTROWS	26	10	260	8.5
MIXCOLUMNS	143	9	1287	42

Vector Approach to AES. We applied a vector approach to the encryption. We propose to vectorise the different processes as follows (based on instructions from Appendix A).

The ADDRNDKEY is a byte-wise XOR between the data matrix and the corresponding sub-key matrix. This operation is applied to each column (which corresponds to a 32-bit word. With our vector ISA, the ADDRNDKEY can be implemented in just four instructions:

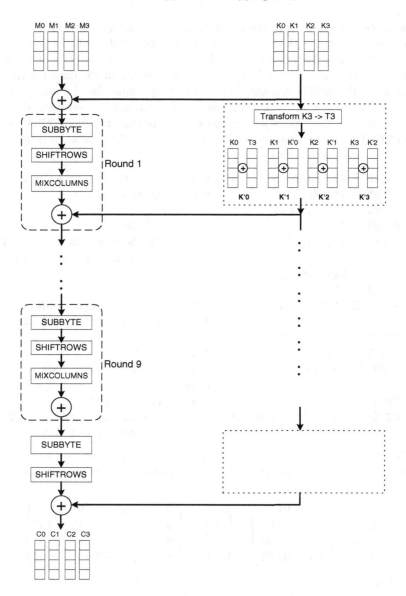

Fig. 2. AES structure

```
VLOAD    V0, (adr_key), 3     # loads 4 words into V0
                              # starting at address 'adr_key'
VLOAD    V1, (adr_data), 3
VXOR     V2, V0, V1
VSTORE   V2, (adr_data), 3
```

The SUBBYTE is a byte-wise look-up process. For this purpose we have a VBYTELD
Vx, Ry, m instruction as explained in Appendix A. Such an instruction can be

implemented given we have the memory organization described in Section 4.2. Note that this optimization is also useful for the KEY-SCHEDULE.

Originally the SHIFTROWS function is composed of left rotations on each row of the data matrix and if we had represented each row of the data matrix on a 32-bit word, the SHIFTROWS would have been very simple. But in our implementation, each 32-bit word is one column of the data matrix, hence the difficulty of implementing this operation. Suppose we have the operations VTRANSP and VBCROTR[2] (Vector-Bit-Conditional-Rotate-Right), the SHIFTROWS operations can be implemented as follows:

```
VLOAD   V0, (adr_data), 3    # loads 4 words of data into V0
VTRANSP V1, V0, 4            # V1 = V0 transposed
ADDIU   R11, 0x000E
MTVCR   R11                  # VCR = 1110b
VBCROTR V2, V1, 24           # V2 = V1 whose words indexed 1,
                             # 2,3 are rotated right by 24 bits
ADDIU   R11, 0x000C
MTVCR   R11                  # VCR = 1100b
VBCROTR V1, V2, 24           # V1 = V2 whose words indexed 2,3
                             # are rotated right by 24 bits
ADDIU   R11, 0x0008
MTVCR   R11                  # VCR = 1000b
VBCROTR V2, V1, 24           # V2 = V1 whose word indexed 3
                             # is rotated right by 24 bits
VMOVE   V0, V2, 4            # V0 = V2 transposed
VSTORE  (adr_data), V0, 3    # stored words indexed 0,1,2,3
                             # of V0 to address of data
```

The MIXCOLUMNS operation is the most time consuming one as shown in Table 1. It is a matrix multiplication working on each column as defined below:

$$\begin{pmatrix} a' \\ b' \\ c' \\ d' \end{pmatrix} = \begin{pmatrix} 02\ 03\ 01\ 01 \\ 01\ 02\ 03\ 01 \\ 01\ 01\ 02\ 03 \\ 03\ 01\ 01\ 02 \end{pmatrix} \bullet \begin{pmatrix} a \\ b \\ c \\ d \end{pmatrix} = \begin{pmatrix} x \cdot a + (x+1) \cdot b + c + d \\ a + x \cdot b + (x+1) \cdot c + d \\ a + b + x \cdot c + (x+1) \cdot d \\ (x+1) \cdot a + b + c + x \cdot d \end{pmatrix} \quad (1)$$

such that

$$\begin{pmatrix} a' \\ b' \\ c' \\ d' \end{pmatrix} = \begin{pmatrix} x(a \oplus b) \oplus b \oplus c \oplus d \\ x(b \oplus c) \oplus a \oplus c \oplus d \\ x(c \oplus d) \oplus a \oplus b \oplus d \\ x(a \oplus d) \oplus a \oplus b \oplus c \end{pmatrix} \quad (2)$$

Each of the individual byte multiplications is done in the field $GF(2^8)$, modulo the irreducible polynomial given by

$$m(x) = x^8 + x^4 + x^3 + x + 1 \quad (3)$$

---

[2] See Appendix A.

whose binary representation is 0x11B. The central operation is hence the multiplication operation by x modulo $m(x)$. Given the instructions in Appendix A, the MIXCOLUMNS operation can be implemented as follows:

```
VLOAD    V0, (adr_data), 3    # loads 4 words in V0.
                              # Suppose each word of V0
                              # is made up of bytes (a,b,c,d)
ADDIU    R11, R0, 0xFFFF
MTVCR    R11                  # VCR = 0xFFFF
VBCROTR  V1, V0, 8            # Each word of V1 = (d,a,b,c)
VBCROTR  V2, V0, 16           # Each word of V2 = (c,d,a,b)
VBCROTR  V3, V0, 24           # Each word of V3 = (b,c,d,a)
VXOR     V4, V0, V3           # Each word of V4 =
                              # (a+b,b+c,c+d,d+a)
ADDIU    R11, R0, 0x011B
MTVCR    R11                  # VCR = 0x011B
VMPMUL   V5, V4, R0           # Each byte of V4 is shifted
                              # by 1 bit left and XORed with
                              # last byte of VCR if outgoing
                              # bit is 1.
                              # Mult. by 'x' mod 0x011B.
                              # 1 word of V5 =
                              # (x(a+b),x(b+c),x(c+d),x(d+a))
VXOR     V0, V5, V1           # 1 word of V0 = (x(a+b)+d,
                              # x(b+c)+a,x(c+d)+b,x(d+a)+c)
VXOR     V0, V0, V2           # 1 word of V0 = (x(a+b)+d+c,
                              # x(b+c)+a+d,x(c+d)+b+a,x(d+a)+c+b)
VXOR     V0, V0, V3           # 1 word of V0 = (x(a+b)+d+c+b,
                              # x(b+c)+a+d+c,x(c+d)+b+a+d,
                              # x(d+a)+c+b+a)
VSTORE   V0, (adr_data), 3
```

3.2   Vectorizing Montgomery's Modular Multiplication

Two commonly used Public Key algorithms are RSA and ECC[3]. RSA is based on the modular exponentiation of large integers (typically between 1024 to 2048 bits or more). ECC is based on the scalar multiplication of a point on an elliptic curve in a finite field (either in $\mathbb{F}_p$ with p prime or $\mathbb{F}_{2^m}$). In both cases the most critical operation is the long precision modular multiplication. In [15], the author looks at different techniques for optimally implementing the modular multiplication operation. One technique that came out of the lot, both in terms of performance and code complexity, is based on the method originally proposed by Montgomery in [16].

For our study, we looked at Elliptic Curve Cryptography over binary fields [17]. The basic modular multiplication consists of multiplying the co-ordinates

---

[3] Elliptic Curve Cryptography.

of given points on the elliptic curve. Those co-ordinates have a polynomial representation and the multiplication is done modulo an irreducible polynomial in the same field. Modular multiplications have been thoroughly studied and optimized. Methods like those proposed in [18] based on Montgomery's method are quite rapid algorithms. As explained in [18], Montgomery's algorithm can be implemented to interleave the multiplication and the reduction phases. In the latter paper, the authors show that we can use Montgomery's algorithm to calculate $c(x) = a(x) \cdot b(x) \cdot r(x)^{-1} \bmod f(x)$ where $f(x)$ is an irreducible polynomial. Given that we are working in the field $\mathbb{F}_{2^m}$, the polynomials involved in this algorithm are of length m, the authors in [18] show that $r(x)$ can be chosen such that:

$$r(x) = x^k \text{ where } k = 32M \text{ and } M = \left\lceil \frac{m}{32} \right\rceil \tag{4}$$

If we suppose that the multiplicand a(x) can be decomposed into a linear combination of 32-bit polynomials denoted by $A_i(x)$ such that

$$a(x) = A_{M-1}(x).x^{32(M-1)} + A_{M-2}(x).x^{32(M-2)} + \ldots + A_0(x) \tag{5}$$

we have the algorithm in Figure 3 for a 32-bit architecture: $C_0(x)$ is the least significant 32-bit word of the polynomial $c(x)$ and $N_0(x)$ is the 'Montgomery's constant', which is pre-calculated, such that $N_0(x) \cdot F_0(x) \bmod x^{32} = 1$.

Input   : $a(x), b(x), f(x), M$ **and** $N_0(x)$
Output : $c(x) = a(x).b(x).x^{-32M} \bmod f(x)$

1. $c(x) \leftarrow 0$
2.   **for** $j = 0$ **to** $M - 1$ **do**
3. $c(x) \leftarrow c(x) + A_j(x) \cdot b(x)$
4. $M(x) \leftarrow C_0(x) \cdot N_0(x) \bmod x^{32}$
5. $c(x) \leftarrow c(x) + M(x) \cdot f(x)$
6. $c(x) \leftarrow c(x)/x^{32}$
7.   **endfor**

return $c(x)$

Fig. 3. 32-bit Montgomery Modular Multiplication

Scalar implementation on MIPS. On the scalar MIPS, the modular multiplication takes about 22300 clock-cycles. In this test program, we used test values from the field $\mathbb{F}_{2^{191}}$ with a modulus $f(x) = x^{191} + x^9 + 1$ allowing us to store all values in registers. We thus spare additional memory accesses.

Vector approach to modular multiplication. We looked at the vector instructions that can help to enhance the execution of this 'interleaved' Montgomery Modular Multiplication. As a result of which, we obtain the following assembly code (The comments refer to the algorithm in Figure 3):

```
        .global MultBinPoly
        .ent    MultBinPoly

MultBinPoly:
        lw        $24, 16($29)        # loading data size (M)
        lw        $2, 20($29)         # loading the value of N0
        vload     $v0, $5, 5          # v0 <= b(x) on 6 words
        vload     $v1, $6, 5          # v1 <= f(x) on 6 words
        vsmove    $v3, $0, 8          # v3 cleared; (v3 == c(x))
        addiu     $15, $0, 0          # 'j': loop init
        sll       $24, $24, 2         # $24 <= 4M

LoopBin:
        add       $8, $15, $4         # add. of j-th word of a(x)
        lw        $8, 0($8)           # j-th word of a(x)
        vspmult   $v5, $v0, $8        # v5 <= a[j]*v0;(v0=b(x))
        vxor      $v3, $v5, $v3       # v3 <= v5 + v3
        vextract  $9, $v3, 1          # $9 <= C_0
        vsmove    $v2, $9, 1          # v2[0] <= $9;($9=C_0)
        vspmult   $v4, $v2, $2        # v4 <= N0 * v2
        vextract  $9, $v4, 1          # $9 <= M(x)
        vspmult   $v5, $v1, $9        # v5 <= v4[0]*v1;(v1=f(x))
        vxor      $v3, $v3, $v5       # v3 <= v3 + v5
        vwshr     $v3, $v3, 1         # v3 <= v3 shifted right by 1
        addi      $15, $15, 4         # Increase index by 4
                                      # as we read 4 bytes

        bne       $15, $24, LoopBin
        nop
        vstore    $7, $v3, 5
        j         $31
        nop
        .end      MultBinPoly
```

4   Proposed Architecture

Vector Processor techniques have been widely used either in super-computers like the Cray machine [19] or in Digital Signal Processing applications like on Intel's MMX or the T0 architecture described in [20]. In the latter example, the authors already use a MIPS-like scalar processor. In this section we present the foundations for our vector architecture.

Our design aims at offering high performance for the parallel data cryptographic processes without penalizing the scalar executions. Because of this, we have an approach where we go from an already existing, highly performing, General Purpose Processor and 'plug' in the vectorial co-processor. This is particularly true with the MIPS architecture where co-processor interfaces are well defined, easing user Application Specific Extensions. The specification and definition of what we will call the Vectorial MIPS for Cryptography (VeMICry) has to be done on two levels:

- **Resource/Architectural Level:** definition of the resources present in that vectorial unit (register files, processing units, memory interface units ...).
- **Instruction scheduling and pipelining:** Specification of the vector instructions' execution with respect to the scalar pipeline in addition to the inner pipeline for each of the vector instruction.

4.1 Architectural Specification

Appendix A of [21] provides a comprehensive picture of the theory behind vector processing and its application to micro-processors. To suit the MIPS 'load-store' architecture and to avoid complex memory accesses, we chose a *Register-to-Register* vector architecture: we hence hope to reduce memory-register transfers, which are the privileged attack paths for side channel analysis. Note that in this paper we work only on code implemented directly in assembly language, which means that we will not be talking about compiler optimization techniques.

4.2 Vector Register File

The structure and architecture of the vector register file will be the determinant factor in defining the rest of the architecture. 6 factors will determine the structure of our vector register file:

- m: The size of each element of the vector elements ($m = 32$).
- q: The number of such vector registers.
- p: The number of elements in each vector register. This will be called the *depth* of each vector.
- r: The number of lanes into which the vector registers are organized. This notion is borrowed from [20] where it is associated to the number of VPUs[4] available to the VeMICry. We have as many lanes as there are VPUs. Ideally we would have $r = p$ allowing us to work on the p elements in parallel: the jth VPU for example would be 'associated' to a register file made of all the jth elements of all the vector registers. However, in some cases, for size and power constraints we will not be allowed p VPUs. We leave r as a parameter for our analysis as to what would be the best performance to size trade-off. As a result, the jth VPU will be associated not only to the jth elements across the register file but also $j + r^{th}$, $j + 2r^{th}$...
- l: The number of elements of the vector processor onto which the function is applied. Our analysis revealed that it would be interesting to work on vector lengths which are not necessarily equal to the depth of each vector register; specially in the case where $r \neq p$, both in terms of speed and power consumption. Setting the vector's length could done by setting a configuration register for example[5].

---

[4] Vector Processing Units.

[5] Note that this factor is relevant when pipeline issues come into consideration. For the functional simulator, we assume that we work on all p elements.

- The memory latency is also an important factor. This not only depends on the number of read and write ports per VPU but also on the definition of the interface with the memory or even how many 'memory banks' we could have in parallel. In our architecture, we propose to have a software managed memory bank *per* lane. Within each 'bank' we have 4 parallel concurrently accessible byte arrays of say 1 kilobytes each. Such a structure allows each VPU to smartly fetch four bytes in parallel, specially for the VBYTELD instruction.

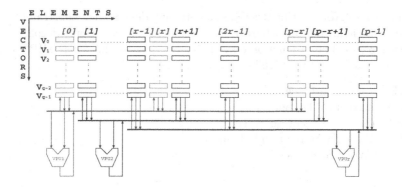

Fig. 4. Vector Register File

We obtain the register file architecture shown in Figure 4. We propose to study the influence of those 6 factors on performance and area. In addition to the Vector Registers, we identified the need for a Vector Conditional Register (VCR) which is a p bit register, a Scalar Buffer Interface (SBI) register to act as buffer from scalar values being shared between the scalar core and the vector processing unit and a CARry buffer (CAR) to store the most significant word or carry when doing addition or multiplication (in particular when $l = p$).

4.3 Vector Instruction Execution and Scheduling

In this section we briefly describe the schedule and execution of the vector instructions. A vector instruction is meant to replace what would be in software a loop; a loop where the data being operated on are independent from each other and where the calculation of each iteration of the loop is independent from the calculation of the neighboring iterations. However by looking at some of the instructions in Appendix A, we can see that operations like VADDU, do not obey to this basic requirement. For such instructions we will take advantage of the fact that the calculation on each element of the vector is only 'partially' independent from that on its neighbors.

From then on, we define three classes of vector instructions:

Definition 1. *A Genuinely Independent Vector Instruction (GIVI) is one where the transformation applied to every element of the operand vectors is independent from the application of that same transformation on this same element's neighbors.*

Definition 2. *A Partially Independent Vector Instruction (PIVI) is one where the transformation applied to every element of the operand vectors depends partially on the result of the same operation applied to one of its neighbors.*

Definition 3. *A Memory Accessing Vector Instruction (MAVI) is a vector register-memory instruction where a memory access is required for the application of the required transformation on every element of the operand vectors.*

Each of those groups of instructions has its own dependency constraints which lead to the definition of a characteristic sequence of execution's decomposition for each group. The instruction decoding is handled by the scalar MIPS as part of its 'normal' five stage pipeline:

- **IF**: Instruction Fetch.
- **ID**: Instruction Decode.
- **EX**: (Scalar) Execution Stage.
- **DC**: Data Cache read and alignment.
- **WB**: Write Back stage.

Upon the detection of a vector instruction, each VPU enters into its own four stage pipeline:

- **Data Fetch (DF)** stage where each VPU fetches the two (depending on the instruction) elements from the target vector registers. If a scalar register is involved, the value is fetched from the latter scalar register and written back into the SBI register.
- **Execute-Multiply (EXM)** stage where the VPU performs the corresponding multiplication or addition calculation for a PIVI. For a GIVI or a MAVI, nothing is done.
- **Execute-Carry (EXC)** stage where the 'carry' selection is done for the PIVIs and the latter's calculation is completed. For a GIVI or a MAVI, the corresponding calculation/manipulation is done onto the arguments fetched in stage DF.
- **Write Back (WB)** stage where the result from the VPU is written back to the corresponding element of the destination vector register.

It is left to the software to make sure the vector register length is properly set before doing any vector instruction when working on vectors of length $l < p$.

GIVI execution. Let's consider the general case where p is 'too' large and that we only have r VPUs where $r \leq p$ (could be specially true for embedded processors). This means each VPU will have to enter $\lceil \frac{p}{r} \rceil$ times in order to apply the required operation on all p elements of the targeted vector registers as shown in Figure 5. Hence the next vector instruction will only be issued $\lceil \frac{p}{r} \rceil$ cycles later.

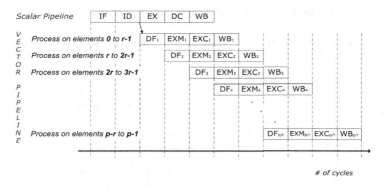

Fig. 5. Timing relationship between scalar & vector executions

PIVI execution. In a *Partially Independent Vector Instruction*, the calculation on every element of the vector register depends on the calculation of the neighboring elements: the functions concerned by this category are VADDU, VSPMULT, VSAMULT and VTRANSP. For the optimal schedule of the PIVI instructions we will assume that each VPU has an internal 'temporary' 32-bit register. Most the above mentioned instructions have to handle the addition of vector elements and to anticipate on the carry being propagated from the neighboring least significant element. To do so, we assume that each VPU has a 32-bit Carry Select Adder (CSA): at each addition step the addition is performed for both cases where 'incoming' carry is 0 or 1 and the 'correct' output is determined once the correct carry is known. Like this the PIVI instruction can be made to have the same instruction issue rate as the GIVI.

MAVI execution. Looking back at the Appendix, we have three MAVI instructions: VBYTELD, VLOAD and VSTORE. Each VPU has its own software managed memory which is the VPU can access by bytes (with 4 bytes in parallel) for the VBYTELD instruction and by 32-bit words for VLOAD and VSTORE. With such an arrangement the issue rate would be $\left\lceil \frac{p}{r} \right\rceil$.

Vector instructions' chaining and hazards. If we work on vector depths which are greater than the number of VPUs, an instruction may take several iterations as illustrated Figure 5 for a GIVI instruction. The main type of hazard we might be confronted which is data hazard. Data hazards occur when the instruction I has as operand the result from the preceding instruction $I-1$. With our vector operations, data hazards occur when an instruction takes only 1 or 2 iterations (i.e. $\frac{p}{r} \leq 2$). For instructions having a larger number of iterations, the latency incurred by the multi-iteration process diffuses the data dependency. The following table describes the different data hazards that might occur between an instruction $I-1$ and the instruction I and how, when this is possible, pipeline stalls can be avoided by using data feed-forward mechanisms.

Table 2. Data Dependencies on the vector instructions

I-1	I	Description	Stall?	Bypass Required
GIVI	GIVI	Calculation done at EXC stage	No stall	Data forwarded from the EXC stage of $I-1$ to the EXC stage of I
GIVI	PIVI	PIVI needs result at EXM stage	Pipeline stalls after ID stage	Data forwarded from the EXC stage of $I-1$ to the EXM stage of I
PIVI	GIVI	PIVI needs result at the EXM stage	No stall	Data forwarded from the EXC stage of $I-1$ to the EXC stage of I
PIVI	PIVI	PIVI needs result at the EXM stage	Pipeline stalls after ID stage	Data forwarded from the EXC stage of $I-1$ to the EXM stage of I

5   Functional Simulation

We started by building a functional simulator for our VeMICry architecture: a functional architecture allows us to test the vector code presented in Sections 3.1 and 3.2. Moreover, with such a simulator, we can perform performance studies in terms of instruction cycles and see the effect of the parameters from Section 4.2.

5.1   Use of the ArchC Simulation Tool

The ArchC tool is an architecture description language which is developed by the Computer Systems Laboratory of the Institute of Computing of the University of Campinas (www.archc.org). The tool allows to build an architectural instruction simulator which is composed on:

- A language description used to describe the target architecture including the memory hierarchy (**AC_ARCH**) and the instruction set architecture (**AC_ISA**).
- A simulator generator (**ACSIM**) which uses the above description language to generate a Makefile which is then used for building a **SystemC** model.

It is based on a widely used commercial tool like SystemC [22] and allows to build quite simple architectures which is sufficient for our immediate needs. Moreover, the simulation software builder is based on GCC (www.gnu.org). Hence it is easy to modify the instruction set. The idea behind this study is to build a simulator of our VeMICry architecture to test the vector instructions described in A and perform some preliminary performance studies in terms of instruction cycles.

5.2 Building the Functional Model

Our architecture is based on the 32-bit MIPS architecture with an instruction set fully compatible with the (basic) MIPS-I family. Moreover, we hacked GCC's Assembler to compile our vector codes.

The backbone of the VeMICry model is composed of the definition files of the MIPS-I model which we have upgraded to add our vector instructions. In our model model:

- We have 8 vector registers ($q = 8$).
- Each vector is composed of 8×32-bit elements ($p = 8$).
- We have 8 VPUs working in parallel ($r = 8$). Hence there are eight lanes where in the jth lanes the jth VPU works across the jth elements of the vector registers.
- We assume that each instruction is executed in 1 cycle (only a functional model).

The simulator generates a series of basic statistics like the sequence of instructions executed (vemicry.dasm), a trace of the Program Counter (vemicry.trace) and the occurrences of each instruction along with the number of cycle-counts (vemicry.stats).

5.3 Functional Simulation of Vectorised AES

As explained previously, the vector instructions are used to optimize the SHIFTROWS, MIXCOLUMNS, ADDROUNDKEY and SUBBYTE operations. The KEY_SCHEDULE is implemented as a separate routine.

We validated the results generated by our vector AES encryption code. Simulations show that encrypting 16 bytes (for an AES-128) takes 160 instruction cycles. In addition to this the KEY_SCHEDULE took 246 instruction cycles. Those figures represent a large gain in performance when compared to the same algorithms implemented the scalar MIPS. For the scalar code the key schedule took 519 instruction cycles and the encryption took 3283 cycles.

More performance gain is achieved when we encrypt larger data files. We ran simulations where we encrypted 32 bytes with one same key, i.e. we ran the KEY_SCHEDULE once and the encryption codes was modified to work on 8 words of each vector register. Encrypting 32 bytes took 182 instruction cycles. This illustrates a major advantage of our architecture: depending on the depth of vector registers, we are able to encrypt large data tables with little performance penalties.

Another big advantage with our approach is that robust software countermeasures (like those described in [2]) can be implemented to compensate for any side-channel information leakage.

5.4   Simulation of Vectorised Montgomery Multiplication in Binary Fields

On the VeMICry, the calculation of the Montgomery's constant is executed in 22 instruction cycles. The main part of the modular multiplication takes 97 instruction cycles. The same modular multiplication operation takes 22331 instruction cycles on the scalar MIPS.

Note that our test values are taken from the field $GF(2^{191})$, which means that the data values have a maximum length of 192 bits. Given that in the actual architecture each vector register has 8 elements, each vector register is used to hold the 192 bits of each variable. With a depth of 8, we could work on up to 256-bits ECC (with the same number of instruction cycles), which would be far from what would be required for the next 20 years or so.

Note that in the preceding example, we perform a reduction by 32 bits each time. However, one could envisage to perform a reduction by 64 bits as this would mean that we would have half as many loops. In the algorithm depicted in Figure 3, each word is on 64 bits, which means that the calculated N_0 is also on 64 bits and also the we shift by 64 bits in the end. We only perform half the number of loops.

We modified the vector code presented at the end of section 3.2 to emulate this reduction by 64 bits. The calculation of N_0 took 72 instruction cycles and the modular multiplication itself took 84 instruction cycles. Note that N_0 can be calculated only once at the beginning of the signature algorithm and hence for comparing performances, we focus only on the multiplication algorithm. Performance gain when doing a 64-bit reduction is of the order of 13% compared to the same algorithm implemented with a reduction by 32 bits. This gain is achieved at the expense of one additional vector register.

6   Ongoing Research

To have a significant quantitative study, it makes sense to study modular multiplications on larger values like in RSA. So the next phase of the study is to test the modular multiplication on 1024 to 2048 bit values and see how the number of instruction cycles changes by varying the different sizes of the vector architecture. Then we will be implementing a synthesisable Verilog model to add the 'gate count' parameter to our benchmark.

7   Conclusion

In this paper we proposed a vector architecture for embedded cryptography. We have shown how the vector approach is relevant to cryptography and how cryptographic algorithms can be efficiently vectorised. We built and validated a functional model of our vector architecture. The vector architecture combined with our proposed instructions have helped us to reduce the number of cycles taken for an AES encryption from 3283 on the MIPS-I to 160 on the VeMICry. Likewise, modular multiplication in the field $GF(2^{191})$ has been reduced from

22331 instruction cycles to 84 cycles. We can anticipate that each lane will be at least (if not less) complex than a scalar MIPS. This would mean that our vector approach is a sound one given the performance figures measured. Further research is currently being done to study the complexity of our vector architecture and find the best trade-off between performance, size and power consumption.

References

[1] Open Mobile Alliance, "DRM Specification V2.0 Candidate Version 2.0 - 26 April 2005," Tech. Rep. OMA-DRM-DRM-V2_0-20050426-C, Open Mobile Alliance (OMA), April 2005.

[2] M.-L. Akkar and C. Giraud, "An Implementation of DES and AES, Secure against Some Attacks," *Proceedings of the Workshop on Cryptographic Hardware and Embedded Systmes (CHES 2001)*, vol. LNCS 2162, pp. 309–318, 2001.

[3] J. Zambreno, A. Choudhary, R. Simha, and B. Narari, "Flexible Software Protection Using Hardware/Software Codesign Techniques," *Proceedings of Design, Automation and Test in Europe Conference and Exhibition (DATE'04)*, vol. 01, no. 1, p. 10636, 2004.

[4] J.-F. Dhem and N. Feyt, "Hardware and Software Symbiosis helps smart card evolution," *IEEE Micro*, vol. 21, no. 6, pp. 14–25, 2001.

[5] J. P. McGregor and R. Lee, "Architectural techniques for accelerating subword permutations with repetitions," *IEEE Transactions on Very Large Scale Integration (VLSI) systems*, vol. 11, pp. 325–335, June 2003.

[6] J. Groszschaedl and G. Kamendje, "Instruction Set Extension for Fast Elliptic Curve Cryptography over Binary Finite Fields GF(2^m)," *Proceedings of IEEE International Conference on Application Specific Systems Architectures and Processors (ASAP2003)*, pp. 455–468, June 2003.

[7] MIPS-Technologies, "SmartMIPS ASE," http://www.mips.com /content/Products/.

[8] A. F. Tenca and Çetin K. Koç, "A Scalable Architecture for Montgomery Multiplication," *Proceedings of CHES'99*, vol. LNCS, no. 1717, pp. 94–108, 1999.

[9] H. Corporaal, *MicroProcessor Architectures : from VLIW to TTA*.

[10] D. Folegnani and A. González, "Energy Effective Issue Logic," *Proceedings of 28th Annual International Symposium on Computer Architecture 2001 (ISCA'2001)*, pp. 230–239, June-July 2001.

[11] E. Brier, C. Clavier, and F. Olivier, "Optimal Statistical Power Analysis," *Cryptology ePrint Archive*, http://eprint.iacr.org/, vol. Report 2003, no. 152, 2003.

[12] "MIPS*pro^{TM}* Assembly Language – Programmer's Guide," Tech. Rep. 007-2418-001, Silicon Graphics Inc., 1996.

[13] "MIPS^{TM} Architecture For Programmers Volume II: The MIPS32^{TM} Instruction Set," Tech. Rep. MD00086, Revision 0.95, MIPS Technologies, 1225 Charleston Road, Mountain View, CA 94043-1353, March 2001.

[14] NIST, "Specification for the Advanced Encryption Standard," Tech. Rep. 197, Federal Information Processing Standards, November 26 2001.

[15] J.-F. Dhem, *Design of an efficient public-key cryptographic library for RISC-based smart-cards*. PhD thesis, Université Catholique de Louvain, Louvain-la-Neuve, Belgium, May 1998.

[16] P. Montgomery, "Modular Multiplication without Trial Division," *Mathematics of Computation*, vol. 44, pp. 519–521, April 1985.

[17] I. Blake, G. Seroussi, and N. Smart, *Elliptic Curves in Cryptography*, vol. 265 of *Lecture Note Series*. London Mathematical Society.

[18] C. Koç and T. Acar, "Montgomery Multiplication in GF(2^m)," *Designs, Codes and Cryptography*, vol. 14, pp. 57–69, 1998.

[19] R. M. Russell, "The CRAY-1 Computer System," *Communications of the ACM*, vol. 21, pp. 63–72, January 1978.

[20] K. Asanovič, *Vector Microprocessors*. PhD thesis, University of California, Berkeley, Spring 1998.

[21] J. L. Hennessy and D. A. Patterson, *Computer Architecture: A Quantitative Approach*. Morgan Kaufmann, 3 ed., 2003.

[22] T. A. Team, "The Archc Architecture Description Language - Reference Manual," Tech. Rep. v1.2, University of Campinas, http://www.archc.org/, December 2004.

A   Vector Instructions

The VeMICry processor is composed of two families of instructions: the *scalar* instructions which correspond to the conventional MIPS-I instruction set and the *vector* instructions tailored to suit cryptographic requirements.

Suppose we have a vector processor having q vector registers. Each vector register is a vector of p words of 32 bits each. We also have a Vector Condition register (VCR) which contains p bits and which is used for conditional vector instructions to show if the condition is applied to each of the individual words of the vector. Moreover, we have a second 'scalar' register called the Carry Register (CAR) which, for some instructions, 'carry bits/words' are written back. We also assume that we are able to work on an arbitrary vector length l with, of course, $l \leq p$.

V_i	corresponds to the ith vector register
R_j	corresponds to the jth scalar regsiter
n	16-bit immediate value

VADDU V_l, V_j, V_k performs the unsigned addition between the ith elements of V_j and V_k, writing the result as the ith element of V_l. The carry is propagated and added to the $i + 1^{st}$ element of V_l. The carry from the addition of the corresponding p^{th} words is added to the content of CAR if $l = p$.

VBYTELD V_l, R_i, n each word of V_l is treated as four bytes. Each byte is an offset which is added to the address stored in R_i and the byte stored at that address is read from the VPU's corresponding memory. The read byte is written to the same location as that of its original corresponding byte. This process is executed for n words of V_l.

VLOAD V_l, R_i, n loads in V_l the n consecutive 32-bit words from memory starting from address stored in R_i with a stride of 1 (*The notion of stride is introduced in Annexe A of [21]. A stride of '1' means that the words that are consecutively stored in the vector register are fetched by parsing the specified memory with a step of 1 word unit*) .

VBCROTR V_l, V_j, n The Vector-Bit-Conditional-Rotate-Right operates on each ith word of V_j. If VCR[i] is 1, then $V_j[i]$ is rotated by n bits to the right and the result is written to $V_l[i]$. If VCR[i] is 0, then $V_j[i]$ copied to $V_l[i]$ without transformation

VEXTRACT R_i, V_j, n copies the value of the $V_j[n-1]$ into R_i. If $n = 0$, then it is CAR which is written to scalar register

VTRANSP V_l, V_j, n copies vector in V_j to register V_l. If n is zero, there is a direct copy without transposition. If n is non-zero, V_j is viewed as a $4 \times p$ matrix which is transposed and written to vector register V_l with a stride of n

VMPMUL V_l, V_j The Vector Modular Polynomial Multiplication treats each ith word of V_j as four bytes: each byte is a polynomial in $GF(2^8)$ which is multiplied by x modular the polynomial represented in the 9 least significant bits in scalar register VCR. The result is written to V_l

VSADDU V_l, V_j, R_k Vector-Scalar-Addition does the unsigned arithmetic addition of value in R_k to every i^{th} word of V_j and writes the result to V_l. The carry is not propagated but is instead written as the ith bit of the register CAR

VSAMULT V_l, V_j, R_k Vector-Scalar-Arithmetic-Multiplication: multiplies R_k by $V_j[p] || V_j[p-1] || \ldots || V_j[0]$ with carry propagation and result is written to V_l. The most significant carry bits are written to register CAR

VSMOVE V_l, R_k, n copies the value in register R_k to the first n words of V_l. If n is *zero*, then R_k is copied to every word of V_l

VSTORE R_k, V_l, n stores the first n consecutive 32-bit words from register V_l to memory starting from address stored in R_k with a stride of 1

VSPMULT V_l, V_j, R_k Vector-Scalar-Polynomial-Multiplication: does the polynomial multiplication of R_k by $V_j[p] || V_j[p-1] || \ldots || V_j[0]$ and the result is written to V_l. The most significant $p+1^{st}$ word is written to the register CAR

VXOR V_l, V_j, V_k XORs corresponding words between V_j and V_k and stores the result in V_l

VWSHL V_l, V_j, n Vector-Word-Shift-Left shifts the contents of vector V_j by n positions to the left inserting *zeros* to the right. The resulting vector is written to V_l and the outgoing word to CAR

VWSHR V_l, V_j, n Vector-Word-Shift-Right shifts the contents of vector V_j by n word position to the right inserting the data stored in CAR to the left. The resulting vector is written to V_l.

MTVCR R_j Writes to VCR the value contained in the scalar register R_j.

MFVCR R_j Copies the value contained in VCR to the scalar register R_j.

A Novel Privacy and Copyright Protection Enforced Peer-to-Peer Network

Xiaoming Wang[1], Bin Zhu[2], and Shipeng Li[2]

[1] Dept. of Computer Science, Jinan Univ., Guangzhou, 510632, China
twxm@jnu.edu.cn
[2] Microsoft Research Asia, Beijing, 100080, China
{binzhu, spli}@microsoft.com

Abstract. Peer-to-peer (P2P) networks are widely used to share copyrighted contents and software illegally around the world. Development and applications of P2P technologies have faced strong legal and legislative challenges. A P2P network has to have built-in copyright protection to enable P2P technologies to advance on its own without court's and legislature's interference. In this paper, we propose a novel and practical P2P network with a strong privacy protection and reliable tracking mechanism to track the original uploader of any material in the P2P network. When a pirated material is found, its uploader is tracked down, and can be punished by revoking the access to the network, removing his or her uploaded materials, etc. The whole protection system is completely transparent to end users. The proposed scheme would effectively deter users from uploading illegally any copyrighted materials to and dramatically reduce copyrighted materials shared through our P2P network.

1 Introduction

Introduction and proliferation of peer-to-peer (P2P) software have facilitated a large-scale piracy among networked computer users. We have witnessed a dramatic increase in using P2P software such as Kazaa [1] and BitTorrent [2] to share files by hundreds of thousands of users throughout the world. In addition to legitimate usage, an individual can easily use the same P2P software to illegally exchange copyrighted digital commodities such as digital multimedia and software with another he or she has never known or met. This empowerment of large-scale piracy by P2P networks has seriously infringed the interests of copyright holders. Recording Industry Association of America (RIAA) has mounted an anti-piracy war against P2P networks. The first generation of P2P networks such as Napster and Scour that used centralized servers to list contents available among peers was a natural target for RIAA. Those P2P networks were successfully shut down by RIAA as a result of the lawsuits. A direct consequence is accelerated development and adoption of completely decentralized P2P networks such as Gnutella [3] and FreeNet [4], which are much more difficult to shut down by lawsuits since there is no centralized service provider for illegal sharing. Although P2P networks are widely used for legitimate purposes, a recent ruling on June 27, 2005 by the U. S. Supreme Court in MGM v. Grokster held that "one who distributes a device with the object of promoting its use to infringe copyright, as

R. Safavi-Naini and M. Yung (Eds.): DRMTICS 2005, LNCS 3919, pp. 298–310, 2006.

shown by clear expression or other affirmative steps taken to foster infringement, is liable for the resulting acts of infringement by third parties" [5]. According to this ruling, the providers of software that designed to enable "file-sharing" of copyrighted works may be held liable for the copyright infringement that takes place using that software. In addition to lawsuits against P2P software and service providers as well as file-swapping individuals, RIAA has also been lobbying the US legislation to act with tough bills aiming at P2P technologies and service providers.

US Congress responded with several unsuccessful tries to pass bills targeted at P2P networks. In July 2002, US Representative H. Berman introduced a controversial bill H. R. 5211 [6] granting copyright holders immunity for hacking into personal computers (PCs) and P2P networks in thwarting piracy on P2P networks. In June 2004, US Senator O. Hatch introduced a bill S. 2560 [7] that would hold technology companies liable for creating products that could be used to pirate digital content, and therefore would effectively ban all P2P networks. Those bills, while intending to cure the widespread piracy of copyrighted materials, would severely impair advances and applications of P2P technologies that can be used by law-abiding users for many legitimate purposes. The lawsuits against P2P networks and the US legislation anti-piracy bills have shown a clear pattern: technologists are held liable for the activities of their end-users. The brief but dramatic history of Napster and other file-sharing services and the current debating in Congress underscore an important issue that we have largely ignored so far in the development of P2P technologies: how to protect intellectual property (IP) from illegal distribution in a P2P network so that the technology can advance on its own without court's and legislature's interference.

A major effort in the past decade or so has been directed to develop copyright protection technologies such as digital rights management (DRM) and watermarking to fight against piracy of digital assets. These technologies have also been applied to develop law-abiding P2P networks. A typical example is the P2P network to share music proposed in [8] which uses watermarking, fingerprinting, etc. to prevent pirated digital music from entering and sharing through a P2P network, and to ensure that a user can access and play only those music files that he or she is entitled to. These a priori approaches are based on immature technologies and such a system is very complex to implement and operate. A viable alternative approach is the a posteriori technology which relies on a tracking mechanism in a P2P network to find out and punish uploaders of pirated materials. Bakker et al. [9] have used this approach to build a P2P network called globe distribution network (GDN) for efficient free-software distribution. The law-abiding P2P network we are going to propose in this paper also adopts this a posteriori approach. Our system is called the privacy- and copyright-protected peer-to-peer network (PCPN) which is based on proven and widely used cryptographic primitives and technologies, and is therefore a compromised and viable solution to the current debate whether to shut down all P2P networks by passing some harsh laws or to tolerate rampant piracy through P2P networks. PCPN uses a novel and secure hardware-bound tracking mechanism that can reliably trace back to uploaders of pirated materials yet protect uploaders' privacy. This is very different from GDN which sacrifices an uploader's privacy in tracking software uploaders. GDN requests an uploader to provide passport or other sensitive private information before gaining a permission to upload a copy of software to GDN. This scheme is intrusive and impractical. Unlike GDN, there is no need to provide any sensitive private information to upload anything to PCPN. Operations of the protection mechanism in PCPN are completely transparent to an end user and fully decentralized. Once a peer is convicted of uploading pirated, malicious, or illicit materials to PCPN, all the materials the peer has uploaded can be removed from the network, the peer's access to PCPN can be permanently revoked, and legal actions may be taken against the illegal user. We argue that PCPN will meet the anti-piracy requirements sought by RIAA and the legislation yet allow law-abiding users to use it transparently in any legitimate applications. We would like to emphasize that our goal is not to stop illegal sharing of pirated contents through *all* P2P networks, which is a mission impossible. Our goal is to incorporate an anti-piracy mechanism in our P2P network to deter users from using it for illegal applications so that our P2P network can be used for legitimate applications without any legislative or legal interference.

This paper is organized as follows. In Section 2 we first review the existing IP protection technologies and their inadequacy in fighting piracy in P2P networks. PCPN is then described in detail in Section 3. We conclude the paper in Section 4 with future research we plan to do.

2 Related Protection Technologies

In this section, we briefly review existing IP protection technologies and their inadequacies in preventing copyrighted materials from illegal distribution in P2P networks. One protection technology is conditional access used in satellite TV and other applications that imposes restriction on access to protected contents to only the users who have subscribed a premium service. Conditional access cannot stop a subscriber from uploading and distributing protected materials in a P2P network. A more sophisticated protection system is the DRM system that regulates a user's rights for a protected content and ensures that the rights are observed throughout the life of the content. A DRM system is typically based on encryption of the content. Such a DRM protection can be easily bypassed by recording a protected content digitally or through digital and analog conversions. The recorded content which is free of DRM-protection can then be uploaded to and distributed through P2P networks. Current consumer recording devices and coding technologies can deliver a high-fidelity recording and an efficiently compressed multimedia file very easily for Internet distribution. Both protection technologies fall into the "breaking once, breaking all" scenario that only one person with needed privilege, expertise, and equipment is needed to break the whole protection system when P2P networks enter the picture. Although the US law of the Digital Millennium Copyright Act (DMCA) [10] prohibits anybody from getting around a content protection mechanism, and the copyright law prohibits illegal sharing copyrighted materials with others. They are very difficult to enforce, not to mention that one country's laws may not be applicable to computer users in other countries.

Another type of protection technologies is robust watermarking. Robust watermarking is a technology to embed an imperceptible mark in the content that is difficult or impossible to remove or fake. Two types of watermarking can be used for copyright protection: global watermarking and individualized watermarking (also referred to as watermarking and fingerprinting, respectively). Global watermarking embeds a mark to content to indicate its copyright owner and allowed actions such as copy-once or no-copy. Typical efforts to apply this type of watermarking to content protection are the Secure Digital Music Initiative (SDMI) [11] for music protection and the Copy-Protection Technical Working Group (CPTWG) [12] for video protection. Individualized watermarking, on the other hand, embeds a unique ID for each sale or instance of content so any pirated copy of the content can be traced back to its original buyer. Both types of watermarking suffer from various vulnerabilities. The major vulnerability of a watermarking protection is its weakness against intentional attacks. We have yet seen a watermark embedding with reasonable detection complexity that can survive an intentional attack to strip off the embedded mark or to render the mark unreadable while maintaining acceptable quality. Both watermarking technologies have yet shown effectiveness in fighting against piracy in real life. Some researchers even argue that such a technology may remain to be a dream forever. Additional vulnerability for the individualized watermarking is the simple but very effective collusion attack that multiple copies of the same content with different marks are combined together by some methods such as simple averaging to fake a new mark or make the embedded mark undetectable. All proposed individualized-watermarking schemes can survive at most a small-scale collusion attack at the expense of a dramatically reduced payload. With all those known vulnerabilities and ineffectiveness, the entertainment industry and the legislation still advance the idea of mandatory checking of copyright-indicating watermarks on every incoming bit for copyright protection. The bill S. 2048 [13] proposed by US Senator F. Hollings is a recent step towards that direction. In addition to technology unreadiness, such a dramatic measure may also have unintended consequences such as an invasion of users' privacy, and dramatically slowing down data communications. We can similarly argue that the copyright-protected P2P systems such as the one described in [8] based on watermarking technologies may not be practical in quite a few years.

GDN proposed by Bakker et al. [9] uses a completely different approach to get rid of pirated materials from a P2P network. Instead of preventing pirated software from entering a P2P network, GDN uses a cryptographically signed certificate attached to uploaded software to track the original uploader of pirated software. When a GDN user wants to publish software in GDN, he or she has to contact one of the access-granting organizations (AGOs) to apply for a tracking certificate. An AGO verifies an applicant's passport or other means of identification and checks against a blacklist of banned users with all the AGOs. If this checking step is fine, the AGO issues the applicant an AGO-signed certificate linking the applicant's identity to the applicant-supplied public key. This certificate allows the candidate to upload software into GDN. Without a valid certificate issued by an AGO, a user cannot publish anything to GDN. The certificate is attached to the software. When pirated software is detected, the attached certificate is retrieved, and its uploader's publishing right is revoked by placing him or her to the list of banned users maintained by AGOs. All the software published by the uploader is also removed from GDN. The GDN's protection mechanism seems to be a good deterring tool to potential pirates who would like to use GDN to distribute pirated software, but the tracking mechanism is not very practical. It is very cumbersome for a user to publish software to GDN since he or she has to contact a server, i.e., an AGO, and provide his or her passport or other sensitive private information that the applicant may be unwilling to disclose. It is hard to imagine that a user is willing to surrender sensitive private information to a P2P network server in exchange for a right to publish something to the network. Checking authenticity of supplied passport or other means of identification is time-consuming and expensive. It is impractical for an AGO to check if the supplied passport is authentic and really matches the applicant for every GDN user who wants to start publishing software to GDN. In addition, the certificate signed by an AGO may contain sensitive personal information to identify the uploader, which is a severe invasion to the uploader's privacy since everybody can read the information. Even if the certificate does not contain any sensitive private information, a user can still collect statistics to find out who published what, which is also a privacy invasion. To address the privacy issue, AGOs have to store the supplied sensitive private information associated with each issued certificate so that an illegal uploader can be properly identified when a user applies for a tracking certificate, a big burden to AGOs.

3   Our Privacy- and Copyright-Protected P2P Network

Like GDN, we use the a posteriori approach in our PCPN to be described in this section. We believe that the a prior approach that prevents pirated materials from entering and distributing in a P2P network is too complicated and expensive, and is beyond what the current and near-future's technologies can deliver. Our system is based on robust and proven technologies, and is therefore easy to implement and operate. PCPN relies on a novel and secure hardware-bound tracking mechanism to find out uploaders of pirated or illicit materials in PCPN. Each digital asset uploaded to PCPN is attached with persistent metadata which contains an uploader-signed certificate used to track the original uploader. Authenticity and validity of the certificate and the associated material are verified when a digital material is uploaded to PCPN, or replicated from one client to another. A major design principle for PCPN is the assumption that an uploader is liable to whatever he or she uploads to PCPN. Every PCPN end user is entitled to publish anything in PCPN, and to remain anonymous until a pirated, illicit, or malicious material is found. The tracking mechanism is subsequently invoked to track down the original uploader of the material. Once convicted, the materials uploaded by an illegal uploader can be removed from PCPN, and the uploader is punished in several possible ways ranging from permanently revoking the access or publishing privilege to PCPN to legal actions. A revocation list contains a list of convicted illegal peers along with the action specifications taken by PCPN against these peers which ranges from banning access to or publishing in PCPN, removing materials uploaded, etc. The action specifications can be as fine as specific actions for each individual peer in the revocation list. We believe that such a severe punishment would deter any potentially illegal uploaders and dramatically reduce pirated digital assets, pornography, illicit or malicious materials distributed through our P2P network. Unlike GDN, no sensitive private information is needed in basic operations of PCPN. All the operations of the protected mechanism in PCPN are completely transparent to end users. There is no need to provide any sensitive private information or to obtain access permission from a server to publish anything to PCPN. We would like to point out that our proposed system can incorporate any a priori protection technologies such as watermarking, DRM, or access control to make the system even better in fighting against piracy.

In the following description, a copy of digital material such as multimedia content, software, a file, in PCPN is called an object. The metadata associated with an object to provide auxiliary information or to specify behaviors is called attributes of the object. For example, the certificate used for tracking an uploader is a tracking attribute. In PCPN, an object and its tracking attribute are treated as an atomic unit when uploaded to PCPN or transferred from one peer to another.

3.1 PCPN Architecture

PCPN adds a copyright protection part to a conventional decentralized P2P network. The protection part controls access to PCPN and whether an object can be uploaded to, downloaded from, or replicated in PCPN. Each PCPN peer has a tamper-proof security module called signing and verifying module (SVM) which enforces copyright protection and access control. SVM functions like a black box to a user or other P2P client modules. It is very similar to the client side DRM module in a DRM system. Its security plays a key role in the copyright and privacy protection of PCPN. This paper focuses on the protection part of PCPN. The rest of the proposed P2P network is the same as a conventional decentralized P2P network. Details of most popular P2P systems can be found in [14].

Fig. 1 shows the basic architecture of the PCPN's protection part. The system consists of a trustworthy access control server (ACS) which individualizes SVM at each peer during software installation by issuing a (root) certificate that binds the peer's public key to the hardware of the peer. ACS also issues an ACS-signed revocation list to peers from time to time. ACS plays a critical role in PCPN. Its security must be guaranteed to ensure our P2P network operational. Once compromised, all clients' SVM modules need to be updated along with ACS, and all materials in the P2P network can no longer be used and will need to be re-uploaded. SVM at a peer generates a peer-signed certificate which is attached as the tracking attribute to each object the peer uploads to PCPN. SVM also checks the revocation list, verifies authenticity and integrity of an object and its tracking attribute before the peer uploads an object to or downloads an object from PCPN, or replicates an object. Any objects failed in this verification are removed from PCPN.

A revocation list (RL) containing a list of revoked certificates issued by ACS along with specifications of actions is distributed to peers or made available at a central server. A peer caches RL in local storage for later usage so that it does not have to download RL every time its SVM needs to check revoked certificates. When a peer enters PCPN, it optionally checks and updates the local RL from another peer or from the central server. If a threshold of maximum non-updating period has been reached, a peer is forced to update its locally stored RL. Objects signed by a revoked certificate may be removed from PCPN, depending on the action specifications in the revocation list. The action specifications also specify if a user whose ACS-issued certificate is listed in RL is allowed to access, upload to or download from PCPN. The SVM may also inform other modules of the peer's P2P software to refuse any service requests by the peer.

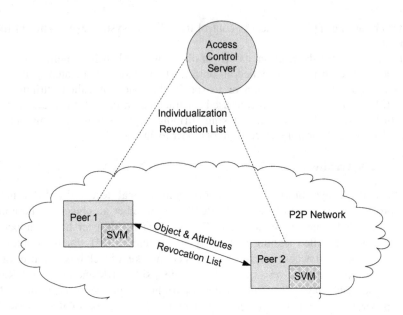

Fig. 1. Architecture of the PCPN's protection part

3.2 Peer Individualization

When the P2P software is first installed to a peer's PC, the peer's SVM is individualized. Individualization consists of several steps. A secure, tamper-proof individualization module (IM) at the client side executes these steps together with ACS. At the first step, IM retrieves the PC's hardware ID ID_p which is a combination of all the unique IDs of the PC's consisting components such as the hard drive(s), the network card, etc. IM also generates a private key k_p and a corresponding public key K_P, $D^a_{K_P}\{E^a_{k_p}\{x\}\} \equiv x, \forall x$, where $E^a_k\{\cdot\}$ and $D^a_k\{\cdot\}$ are respective asymmetric encryption and decryption operations with a key k. Symmetric encryption and decryption with a key k will be denoted by $E^s_k\{\cdot\}$ and $D^s_k\{\cdot\}$, respectively. This pair of private and public keys $\{k_p, K_P\}$ will be used to sign the objects uploaded by the peer and verify authenticity and integrity of objects in PCPN. IM then sends a request to acquire an ACS-signed certificate together with the peer's hardware ID ID_p and the generated public key K_P to ACS securely.

At the second step, ACS receives ID_p and K_P sent by a peer's IM, and calculates an message authentication code (MAC) or keyed hash of ID_p: $GUID = h_{k_h}(ID_p)$, with the key k_h known only to ACS. The generated $GUID$ is compared with those in revoked certificates. If the peer's $GUID$ appears in the list, the request is rejected. Otherwise ACS signs $GUID$ and K_P, $C_{ACS} = E^a_{k_{ACS}}\{GUID // K_P // T // Others\}$, where " $//$ " means concatenation, k_{ACS} is the ACS's private key used to sign certificates issued by ACS to peers, and T is the current time. In the basic form of the certificate C_{ACS} where the only action against an illegal peer is to remove the objects uploaded by the peer and to revoke the peer's access to PCPN, there is no other peer's information included in the certificate C_{ACS}, i.e., "Others" in C_{ACS} is empty. If the setting of PCPN requires the tracking mechanism to provide information for possible legal actions against an illegal user, personal information such as the peer's IP address, email address, etc. may be obtained from the peer, verified by ACS, encrypted by a symmetric encryption with the key known only to ACS, and inserted into "Others" which is signed together with $GUID$ by ACS. We note that the personal information is only known to ACS. A peer or its SVM cannot extract the personal information from the encrypted field in the certificate. Once a peer is convicted and the person is needed to be identified for legal actions, the personal information contained in C_{ACS} is decrypted by ACS and sent to law enforcement agencies to find out the perpetrator. At the end of this step, ACS sends C_{ACS} or rejection back to the peer.

At the third step, C_{ACS} received by the peer's IM is stored together with the public key K_P in the local secure storage. IM also stores securely the private key k_p. They will be used by the peer's SVM. IM then sends an acknowledgment to ACS which closes the individualization session. We note that the whole individualization process is completely transparent to an end user (except a user may possibly need to provide some personal information such as the email address in some setting of PCPN).

SVM consists of two components: the signing module (SM) and the verifying module (VM). SM is used to sign objects uploaded by the peer, and VM is used to verify authenticity and integrity of an object before the object is uploaded to, downloaded from, or replicated in PCPN. Both modules share a pair of secret keys k_1 and k_2. VM also contains the ACS's public key to verify ACS-signed certificates and revocation list.

3.3 Uploading Objects

To upload an object Obj to PCPN, the following steps are executed by a peer's SVM and P2P software. SM inside SVM first generates two random numbers α and β, and calculates the hash values $c = h_{k_1}(Obj//\alpha)$ and $\pi = h_{k_2}(\beta)$, where $h_k(\cdot)$ is a cryptographic keyed hash or MAC function using a key k. Then SM signs c to generate a peer signed certificate $C_p = E_{k_p}^a(c//T)$, where T is the current time, and encrypts its public key K_P and root certificate C_{ACS} with a symmetric cipher and the key π: $u = E_\pi^s\{K_P//C_{ACS}\}$. The set $\{ C_P, u, \alpha, \beta \}$ is then inserted by SM to the object's tracking attribute field which is treated as an integrated part of the object when moving into or out of PCPN or from one peer to another. SM sends the result to VM before finishing its task.

When VM receives an object, it first extracts the set $\{C_P, u, \alpha, \beta\}$ from the object tracking attribute field, calculates $\pi = h_{k_2}(\beta)$, and decrypts u to extract K_P and C_{ACS}: $K_P // C_{ACS} = D_\pi^s\{u\}$. VM checks C_{ACS} against the revocation list. If it is revoked, then VM returns the action specified in the revocation list, such as no uploading is allowed, and the client software executes corresponding action. Otherwise, VM verifies the root certificate C_{ACS} and the just decrypted K_P, the uploader's public key. If it is fine, VM decrypts C_p to extract the hash value c:

$c // T = D_{K_p}^a\{C_P\}$. This value c is compared with the hash value calculated from the object $h_{k_1}(Obj // \alpha)$. If they agree with each other, the authenticity and integrity of the object are verified and VM returns OK. The authenticity check verifies that the object is indeed signed by the claimed peer. This is done by first checking the client's public key against the ACS signed certificate and then using the public key to check the object integrity against the peer signed certificate C_p. Only the authentic peer who knows the peer's private key can pass these checks. The P2P software then uploads the object to PCPN. If any step in the authenticity and integrity verification fails, VM returns failure and the request to upload the object is rejected. When a peer uploads an object to PCPN, the peer does not need to contact any server. The whole process is completely transparent to an end user.

3.4 Other Operations

When a peer is going to download or replicate an object from another peer, the peer's VM checks authenticity and integrity of the object first. This checking is the same as the checking done by VM when a peer uploads an object, as described in Section 3.3. If the checking is OK, VM returns OK and the request is executed. Otherwise VM returns failure and the request is rejected. In the latter case, if the object fails authenticity and integrity verification or its uploader is in the revocation list and an action is required, the peer which stores the object that fails in the checking is contacted with the information of the problem, and the peer performs the corresponding checking. If the allegation is confirmed, the corresponding action is executed. For example, if the object fails the authenticity and integrity checking, then the alleged object is removed. If the uploader of the alleged object is in the revocation list, then the action specified in the revocation list is taken.

A peer also checks periodically the revocation list and the authenticity and integrity of all the objects stored at its side for PCPN. Any object that fails authenticity and integrity checking is removed from the peer's local storage, and actions on those objects uploaded by the peers in the revocation list are executed as specified by the revocation list. An example of actions is to remove all the objects uploaded by a peer in the revocation list. This checking usually occurs when the local revocation list is updated and new revoked certificates are found. This procedure ensures that PCPN functions as specified.

Depending on the policy set for PCPN and the actions specified in the revocation list, a peer in the revocation list may be denied to upload to or download from PCPN, or to access PCPN; confirmed pirated objects, if listed in the revocation list, are removed from PCPN; or even all the uploaded objects by the peers in the revocation list are removed. This can be implemented by requiring VM to check the revocation list and compare with the peer's public key.

It is also possible that a peer may be allowed to access or upload objects to PCPN when certain conditions are met. This can be realized simply by removing the peer from the revocation list or by modifying the specified actions. When VM rejects an a peer's request to upload or access PCPN due to the fact that the peer is in the revocation list, it usually updates its revocation list and checks if the peer's rights are recovered in the latest revocation list before returning failure.

3.5 Discussion

PCPN provides a strong protection of uploaders' privacy. What an end user of PCPN can see is the set $\{ C_P, u, \alpha, \beta \}$ associated with an object. Since the security module SVM appears like a black box to end users, a user cannot extract any information about the object's uploader from that set. In other words, PCPN provides anonymous uploading. In addition, there is no way for an end user to find out if two objects are uploaded by the same user or not. This prevents a user from using statistical analysis to find out how many objects a specific user, although the real identity of the user is unknown, has uploaded to PCPN. We note that the client side SVM knows only the uploader's GUID and public key. Any personal information such as the email address is known only to ACS. A user cannot access SVM or ACS by the design. This means that PCPN has a strong protection of the uploader's privacy against PCPN users. This strong privacy protection is very desirable in many applications.

In PCPN, the server ACS is lightly involved in routine operations of the P2P network. ACS is involved only when a peer installs the P2P software to a peer and when the revocation list needs to be updated. If our tracking mechanism can effectively deter most users from uploading pirated contents, then almost all users of PCPN are law-abiding. ACS would issue new revocation lists only occasionally. This light involvement of a server in using P2P networks is exactly what we sought for in designing PCPN: PCPN should be decentralized as much as possible, and the whole protection mechanism should be transparent to end users as much as possible. Otherwise users would not be willing to use the P2P network for legitimate applications.

In PCPN, before ACS issues a root certificate C_{ACS} to a peer, the hash value of the peer's hardware ID is checked against revoked peers. Once revoked, a user cannot regain access to PCPN by reinstalling the P2P software. This guarantees convicted peers are permanently revoked unless their access is recovered by ACS. In other words, ACS has a robust control on which peers cannot access PCPN.

When a user updates his or her PC's hardware containing a unique ID, for example, replacing a network card with a new one, there is no need in a typical setting of PCPN to update the peer's root certificate C_{ACS} to match the new hardware. This mismatch between C_{ACS} and the hardware is allowed in general, which will be corrected when the P2P software is reinstalled or updated. If needed, it is possible to set up PCPN to periodically check if C_{ACS} matches the corresponding hardware by requiring a peer's SVM to periodically report the peer's hardware IDs to ACS, either voluntarily or requested by ACS, and ACS responds with the checking result. If a mismatch is detected, the same steps executed in the individualization stage to acquire the root certificate C_{ACS} are executed between the ACS and the peer's SVM. In this case, IM is put as an integrated part of SVM. This change would dramatically increase the workload and bandwidth requirement for ACS. PCPN should not be set in this way unless an application really requires so.

A major issue we have not touched is how to find out and prove that an object is pirated, illicit, or malicious. This issue is very important in real applications of PCPN yet very tough to find a satisfactory solution for. Watermarking and fingerprinting can facilitate fulfillment of the task with automatic tools, but current technologies are far from delivering such tools. PCPN currently relies on manual or semi-manual methods to achieve the goal. Every peer is encouraged to report abnormal objects to the content owner or ACS. Content owners or law enforcement agencies can also set up listening posts to monitor traffic in PCPN and report to ACS pirated objects with the evidences to prove the allegation, and/or offer incentives to encourage end users to report pirated objects. ACS accepts orders from a court or makes a judgment by itself to determine if an alleged peer's certificate should be revoked.

3.6 Security

Many issues and components may have impact on PCPN's security. Since all the cryptographic primitives used in PCPN are well studied and widely used in real applications, we can assume that those cryptographic primitives are all secure, and it is very difficult for an opponent to break the built-in authenticity and integrity checking schemes. Then the major security issues are the security of SVM and IM, and the interaction between SVM and other components of the P2P software. Most of those issues are typical security engineering issues in designing security modules or systems used in hostile environments. For example, a DRM system faces similar security engineering problems. Many commercial DRM systems have already been widely used and accepted on the market. For example, the Windows Media Rights Manager [15] from Microsoft is widely used by hundreds of thousands of users around the world. Those successful security engineering experiences and skills can be applied to build secure PCPN software.

SVM at each peer contains the secret keys k_1 and k_2. It is possible that some user with necessary expertise can successfully compromise his or her PC's SVM and extract the secret keys k_1 and k_2. This would enable the opponent to read the content in the root certificate C_{ACS} and the public key K_P of the uploader of each object, which weakens the PCPN's strong privacy protection. It would not enable the opponent to get around the PCPN's copyright protection mechanism. Since the information about an uploader obtained by the opponent in such a compromise is very limited, the opponent cannot gain much personal advantage with the hacking activity. We argue that an opponent would not bother to take trouble to hack SVM to extract the secret keys k_1 and k_2, and the current simple design for privacy protection is good enough for most applications.

Another security issue we would like to discuss here is a revoked user may get around our hardware ID checking in peer individualization by changing some hardware components such as the hard drive, the network card, and reinstalling the

P2P software to regain access or uploading privilege. We argue that this is not really an issue. Most users are not willing to spend money to buy new hard drives or network cards and install to PCs simply to distribute pirated materials to people they have never met or known. There exist many more efficient means than P2P networks to distribute pirated materials to relatives and friends. Even some people are willing to spend their own money and take troubles to install new hardware for the sake of other unknown users of PCPN, they have to keeping spending and installing since PCPN will ban their access to PCPN every time their uploaded pirated contents are detected. This "loophole" can be tightened if ACS replaces *GUID* with an encrypted version of ID_p with the decryption known only to ACS when generating a root certificate C_{ACS} for a peer. When a peer sends its hardware ID ID_p which contains all the unique IDs of the consisting hardware components of the PC during the P2P software installation, all these hardware component IDs are compared with those of revoked peers. If any single submitted component ID matches with a hardware component ID of a revoked peer, the request to issue a root certificate is rejected. This forces a user to replace all the hardware components with unique IDs in a PC to regain access to PCPN, which dramatically increases the cost. A negative impact of this modification is that a legitimate user may buy some used hardware components from a convicted user, resulting in being unable to access PCPN if the P2P software is reinstalled to the modified PC.

4 Conclusion

We have described a novel law-abiding P2P network with strong protection of uploaders' privacy. The network relies on a secure, reliable, and user-transparent tracking mechanism to track the uploader of any material in the network for copyright protection. An illegal peer is punished with its access to the network permanently revoked. All the materials uploaded by an illegal peer are also removed from the network. The system may also provide information for law enforcement agencies to track down the actual person who uploaded the illegal materials to the network and take legal actions again him or her. The proposed tracking mechanism should effectively reduce pirated and illicit materials distributed through a P2P network, and would ensure P2P technologies to advance on their own without legal or legislative interference.

We are implementing and testing the proposed law-abiding P2P network. We also continue improving the anti-piracy and privacy protection mechanisms in the network. One of the major research efforts is to develop technologies to automatically or semi-automatically detect pirated or illicit multimedia materials.

References

1. Kazaa. http://www.kazaa.com/
2. BitTorrent. http://bittorrent.com/
3. Gnutella. http://gnutella.wego.com/
4. FreeNet. http://freenet.sourceforge.net/

5. Supreme Court Rules on June 27, 2005 in MGM v. Grokster. http:// www. copyright.gov/ docs/mgm/

6. Berman, H.: Peer to Peer Piracy Prevention Act (H.R. 5211). http://www.house.gov/berman/newsroom/piracy_prevention_act.html (July 2002)

7. Hatch, O.: Inducing Infringement of Copyrights Act (S. 2560). http://hatch.senate.gov/index.cfm?FuseAction=PressReleases.Print&PressRelease_id=1083&suppresslayouts=true (June 2004)

8. Kalker, T., Epema, D. H. J., Hartel, P. H., Lagendijk, R. L., van Steen, M.: Music2Share–Copyright-Compliant Music Sharing in P2P Systems. In: Proc. of IEEE. 92(6) (2004), pp. 961–970

9. Bakker, A., van Steen, M., Tanenbaum, A.: A Law-Abiding Peer-to-Peer Network for Free-Software Distribution. In: IEEE Proc. Intl. Symp. Network Computing and Applications (Oct. 2001) pp. 60–67

10. Digital Millennium Copyright Act. United States Public law (Oct. 1998)

11. Secure Digital Music Initiative (SDMI). http://www.sdmi.org/

12. Copy-protection Technical Working Group. http://www.cptwg.org

13. Hollings, F.: Consumer Broadband and Digital Television Promotion Act (CBDTPA) (S. 2048). http://thomas.loc.gov/cgi-bin/query/z?c107:S.2048: (March 2002)

14. Aberer K., Hauswirth, M.: An Overview on Peer-to-Peer Information Systems. In: Proc. Workshop Distributed Data and Structures (WDAS'2002) (2002)

15. Microsoft: Digital Rights Management (DRM) – Windows Media DRM 10. http://www.microsoft.com/windows/windowsmedia/drm/default.aspx

Design of a Secure Digital Contents Delivery System in P2P Networks

Youngho Park[1], Jung-Hwa Shin[2], and Kyung-Hyune Rhee[1,*]

[1] Division of Electronic, Computer and Telecommunication Engineering,
Pukyong National University, 599-1, Daeyon 3-Dong, Namgu,
Busan, 608-737, Republic of Korea
pyhoya@mail1.pknu.ac.kr, khrhee@pknu.ac.kr
[2] Tong Myung College, 505 Yongdang Dong Namgu,
Busan, 608-711, Republic of Korea
shinjh@tmc.ac.kr

Abstract. The growth of the Internet has created an electronic marketplace for digital goods, such as mp3, software, etc., and peer-to-peer(P2P) networks for distribution and sharing of files have enjoyed enormous popularity in recent. However, there is an essential problem related with trustiness and reliability in P2P, where untrustworthy parties may participate in financial transactions. One general solution to this problem is distributing the encrypted version of digital content so that a legitimate user can get the decryption key from key issuing server. In this paper, we propose a new approach to key issuing for designing a secure content distribution system. Each user can recovery the original digital content from the encrypted version of it by purchasing decryption key from key issuing server. However, instead of generating a random key, the key used for content encryption and decryption can be directly derived from the usage rules or transaction terms in our system. This approach allows to separate content encrypter and key issuer, and then it also enables to remove the need of secure key transfer between content provider and key issuing server in secure content distribution system.

Keyword: P2P, Escrow Service, Contents Distribution, Key Issuing.

1 Introduction

Peer-to-peer(P2P) network can be regarded as the sharing of computer resources by connecting peers directly[1]. In recent, advanced computing power of PC as well as various kind of network connections allow stand-alone clients to act as servers, called servant. For instance, a file sharing application using P2P networks provides massive virtual storage by enabling a peer to search all over the network for the intended file and to download it from other peers. This potential advantage of P2P system, as compared to server-based system which

---

* Corresponding author.

R. Safavi-Naini and M. Yung (Eds.): DRMTICS 2005, LNCS 3919, pp. 311–321, 2006.

has limited storage and single-point-of-failure problem, makes it possible for P2P to be used as a digital contents distribution network.

As P2P networks for distribution and sharing of files have enjoyed enormous popularity, one may argue that P2P file sharing of content has proven to be a killer application. Therefore, distribution of digital contents, such as mp3 files, becomes one of the main drivers of P2P development. However, some negative aspects of P2P are also addressed from the viewpoints of finance and security, such as copyright violation, free riding, fair-exchange etc., because of uncontrolled and thoughtless file sharing among P2P users. Some solutions to solve those problems faced in P2P services have been researched in the field of digital rights management(DRM)[2] for copyrights protection and payment-based escrow service[3] for fairness in P2P service.

1.1   Related Work

Some trends in P2P networks are the subscription-based and incentive-based file sharing service[4]. As early mentioned, one problem in P2P network is free riding of egoistic peers. Namely an egoistic peer just downloads some files from other peers without sharing its own files. Incentive-based service is a solution to stipulate peers voluntarily contributes their resources to P2P networks by compensating for their contribution with an actual money or bonus point. If we can make money in the P2P network in reward for our contribution, whoever does not share his files? Additionally, subscription-based services are also currently receiving a lot of attention from content industry as a viable business model for P2P content distribution for the purpose of keeping the content within the subscription community.

One of the problem in a P2P system where relatively unknown parties participate in financial transactions is a breakdown of trust. That is, how can Alice be sure that Bob will truly deliver a copy of the requested content? Similarly, how can Bob be assured that Alice will meet financial obligation for the delivered content? And finally, how can the original content provider get a piece of the transaction?

Escrow service in P2P networks is a solution to solve those problems[3]. The main operation of escrow service is to provide reliable and trustworthy mechanism by putting a trusted third party, named escrow server, for enabling payments in exchange for content among participants in a P2P network. In escrow service, party S prepares an encrypted version of the content, $E_K(C)$, namely encrypted content with a secret key K, and then provides the encrypted version to the party R who requested the content. At the preparing phase, S also sends the key K to escrow server together with a description of C. In order to obtain key K and recovery the content, R must send a payment and description for the purchased content to escrow server. Then, escrow server checks that the R's payment is valid. If it is, escrow server sends key K to R, and then R gets its desired content by decrypting with the received key K, i.e., $C = D_K(E_K(C))$.

Another issue is copyright violation caused by pirated file sharing. As digital media has become extremely popular, and consumers can get digital goods from the Internet at all times, secure distribution of digital goods is now a significantly important issue. As a solution to this concerns, contents distribution systems with DRM have been actively researched.

DRM refers to the administration of rights in a digital environment. This solution may include technologies to protect files from unauthorized use, as well as manage the financial transaction processing, while ensuring that rights holders are compensated for the use of their intellectual property[2]. In such system, a content publisher or package server prepares its packaged digital goods called secure container. This container consists of the encrypted content with a secret key K and some meta-data; this includes usage rules, trade conditions, distribution information, contract information and digital signature of publisher, etc. For example, the meta-data might say "This content must be purchased in order to be used and user is permitted to play this content according to the rules and conditions".

The content must be kept inside secure container that can only be available to specific user that enforce the rules, hence DRM systems typically employ tamper resistance techniques to prevent user from illegal manipulating the client-side system. Then, customer who wants to purchase and use the contents must make payment to content publisher in order to obtain a digital license. This license may contain the decryption key generated by the content publisher, usage rules, permission related information, and so on. The license enables the content publisher to permit the customer's privilege of accessing the content. According to the contents publisher's business model, the license does not need to be issued by the content provider but it can be issued at different points called license server or key issuing server in a transaction.

However, the main concerns of secure content distribution in DRM system is that it is not easy to independently set up a content publisher and a license server[5]. That is, a content publisher's secret encryption key must be corresponded to a license server's decryption key which will be requested by customer for recovering the encrypted content. Therefore, publisher and licence server have to cooperate with each other in order to generate the key or securely transfer the key from package server to license server. Furthermore, if an encryption key is randomly generated without relation to the specific container, the key is required to be explicitly bound with the rules and conditions of each container. For these facts, the flexibility must be considered when we implement secure content distribution system.

1.2   Our Contribution

In this paper, we design a secure content delivery system in P2P networks. Our main design considerations are as following: First, we give attention to P2P network because of its possibility of contents distribution network with a massive distributed virtual storage spaces. Second, we consider a secure content distribution system with DRM technology in order to protect a distributed contents from unauthorized use in P2P networks. In addition, we are aiming to incentivize users to contribute voluntarily to P2P file sharing service by rewarding their contribution with the form of money or bonus point.

Moreover, in order to make a secure container, we apply a new approach to generating secret key used in content encryption and decryption. In our system, the encryption key is not randomly chosen but can be directly derived from the rules or trade terms that govern the usage of the content as keeping the secrecy of the key to customer or user. Therefore, the binding of the key with the usage rules and conditions as well as secure key transfer from package server to license server are not required. Those are possible because license server also can derive decryption keying material from the rules and terms presented in payment and key issuance phase with customer. This is our main contribution in this paper.

The authors of [6] proposed similar key management protocol using some conditional terms for secure content distribution, but their scheme also need binding of key and conditional terms and secure key transfer. Therefore, this scheme does not satisfy our motivations.

The rest of this paper is organized as following: In section 2, we briefly describe our content distribution protocol with secure manner. In section section 2.3, we propose our new key issuance procedure. In section 3, we analyze the features of our system and conclude in section 4.

2   Proposed System

In this section, we define some notations and terms for describing our system model and protocols.

2.1   Assumptions and Notations

As shown in Figure1, we assume a service provider who acts as a trusted authority managing P2P service and billing server because subscription-based services are currently receiving a lot of attention. Moreover, accounting and authorization mechanisms are needed to assure financial transaction of subscribed users within the subscription community. The billing server is responsible for issuing keying material and settlement of the payment for digital goods.

In this service community, any peer can become a content publisher or act as a distributor who just serves the content of other publisher through the P2P network, otherwise end customer who wants to buy a content. In fact, the case of separated content publisher and distributor may be a general business model, for example, where the record companies or movie studios entrust their contents to the P2P service for sale instead of maintaining their own server system with high performance and massive storage. However, the other case that a publisher itself becomes a distributor is also possible where musicians provide their personal creations to the P2P network. If a peer acts as a distributor, then the peer will be compensated for his contribution with a commission realized money or bonus point useful in the P2P network.

Table 1 shows some notations used to describe our system and protocols. We assume that all parties have public key certificate and the parties agree on some cryptographic primitives for establishing a secure and authenticated channel between any two parties. These could be achieved by using symmetric

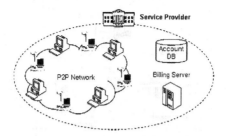

Fig. 1. Basic system composition

Table 1. Notations and terms

Notation	Description
CP	content publisher
SP	service provider
BS	billing server
$\mathcal{DC}$	digital content
C	customer
D	package distributor
$Sig_X()$	digital signature of X with private key SK_X
$Enc_X()$	encryption with public key PK_X of X
$E_K()$	encryption with secret key K
$D_K()$	decryption with secret key K
DK_{BS}	keying material issued by billing server
$Pack$	package of digital content for distribution
$Meta_{Pack}$	meta-data of the package $Pack$
P_{Pack}	public parameter for the $Pack$
$Desc_{Pack}$	description of the $Pack$

encryption scheme, such as AES[7], and public key cryptography just like used in SSL(Secure socket layer)[8]. We also assume that digital goods distributed in P2P network is a digitally formed package which contains encrypted version of original content and meta-data describing the rules and condition of its sale or usage such as price for use.

In addition, each package containing the same original content but with different meta-data is encrypted with different encryption key. That is, user who purchase one package cannot access another package with different usage rules and trade conditions due to different keying material even though the package contains the same digital content.

2.2 Content Distribution Protocol

Although a peer can become publisher and distributor simultaneously, we consider the scenario where content publisher and distributor are different entities as shown in Figure2. In this scenario, content publisher entrusts its original contents to service provider for the purpose of selling them. Service provider

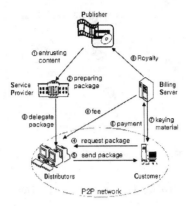

Fig. 2. Workflow of content distribution

prepares the digital package containing encrypted version of the content and its usage rules and trade conditions. The provider then distributes the package to peers. Customer can get a package from one distributor but he must pay to billing server in order to use the content.

When we assume the certified public key of each party is available in the network, the detailed protocols are performed as followings:

1. Publisher CP entrusts his content $\mathcal{DC}$ to the service provider SP.

2. SP prepares package $Pack$ as following:

$$Pack = E_K(\mathcal{DC}),\ P_{Pack},\ Meta_{Pack},\ Sig_{SP}(Meta_{Pack})$$

where the K is encryption key derived from the $Meta_{Pack}$ related to the usage rules and trade condition of the content, P_{Pack} is a public parameter to be used in decryption. We will describe the detailed key generation procedure in section 2.3.

3. SP distributes a copy of the $Pack$ to peers that are willing to serve it for a fee. Then, distributor D_i, which agreed on the contract of delivery the package, stores $Pack$ in its PC and serves it to the network.

4. Customer C who wants to purchase the $Pack$ searches P2P network, and then sends a purchasing request to D_i, if C finds desired one:

$$C \rightarrow D_i : Req_C = \{C, Desc_{Pack}\},\ Sig_C(Req_C)$$

5. D_i sends $Pack$ together with confirmation message:

$$D_i \rightarrow C : Pack,\ Conf_{D_i} = \{D_i,\ Req_C\},$$
$$Sig_{D_i}(Conf_{D_i})$$

6. C requests billing server, BS, to issue the keying value for decryption by sending obligation of the rules and condition of the traded package together with payment information:

$$C \rightarrow BS : Pay_C, \ D_i, \ Conf_{D_i}, \ Sig_{D_i}(Conf_{D_i}),$$
$$Meta_{Pack}, \ Sig_{SP}(Meta_{Pack})$$

$Sig_{SP}(Meta_{Pack})$ is the signature included in the package $Pack$. This step means that C wants to pay the price of the $Pack_P$ so that C plays the content observing the rules in $Meta_{Pack}$.

7. Billing server verifies $Conf_{D_i}$, Sig_{SP}, and the payment, and then sends key DK_B that will be used to decrypt the content by encrypting it with C's public key PK_C, if all the verifies are valid:

$$BS \rightarrow C : Enc_C(DK_{BS})$$

8. Fractions of the payment would be delivered to different parities, e.g., the content publisher P is paid for using the content and the specified distributor D_i is paid for delivering it:

$$BS \rightarrow D : fee$$
$$BS \rightarrow P : payment$$

9. Now, C decrypts $Enc_C(DK_{BS})$, then C can recovery the original content DC from the $Pack$ by using DK_{BS} according to the procedure for generating decryption key in section 2.3.

2.3   Key Generating Procedure

The main concerns of our proposed system is to generate encryption and decryption keying value independently by service provider and billing server, respectively. In order to achieve this purpose in our system, the secret keys for encryption and decryption are derived from meta-data included in the package. This concept was resulted from the ID-based encryption in which cryptographic key can be derived from unique and arbitrary identifier string of an entity[10]. In the case of digital package, because each package may be characterized by the meta-data contained in it, we can generate an encryption key from the meta-data at the phase of preparing package and billing server can generate keying value for decryption when it is given the meta-data by a customer at the phase of payment.

Our key issuing procedure uses bilinear pairings recently widely used in cryptography[9][10]. Assuming that discrete logarithm problem is hard[11] in both an additive cyclic group G_1 and a multiplicative cyclic group G_2 with the same prime order q, respectively, bilinear pairing $e : G_1 \times G_1 \rightarrow G_2$ satisfies the following properties from a cryptographic viewpoint:

1. Bilinearity: For $P, Q, R \in G_1$ and $a, b \in Z_q$, $e(aP, bQ) = e(P, Q)^{ab}$ and $e(P, Q + R) = e(P, Q)e(P, R)$.
2. Non-degeneracy: If P is a generator of G_1, then $e(P, P)$ is a generator in G_2.
3. Computable: There is an efficient algorithm to compute $e(P, Q)$ for all $P, Q \in G_1$.

In the next procedures, we assume the following notations:

- P : a generator of G_1 with prime order q.
- $x_i \in Z_q^*$: private key of entity i.
- $x_i P \in G_1$: public key of entity i.
- $H_1 : \{0, 1\}^* \to G_1$: cryptographic hash function.
- $kdf()$: key derivation function.

Encryption Key. Given meta-data $Meta_{Pack}$, key K for encryption can be derived from the $Meta_{Pack}$ by provider SP, according to the following procedure.

1. SP chooses a random value $r \in Z_q^*$ and computes,

$$P_{Pack} = rP \in G_1$$
$$k = e(x_b P, \ x_s H_1(Meta_{Pack}))^r$$

2. SP set key $K = kdf(k)$.
where $x_b P$ is public keys of billing server BS, and x_s is the private key of service provider SP. Note that $x_s H_1(Meta_{Pack})$ is the form of SP's signature for the meta-data using the BLS signature scheme[9], i.e. $Sig_{SP}(Meta_{Pack}) = x_s H_1(Meta_{Pack})$ in step 2.

Decryption Key. If a customer C is given the decryption keying value derived from $Meta_{Pack}$ by the billing server BS, C can compute decryption key as follows:

1. Given a $Meta_{Pack}$ to BS in step 7, BS computes DK_{BS} and sends it to C.

$$DK_{BS} = x_b \cdot Sig_{SP}(Meta_{Pack}) = x_b(x_s H_1(Meta_{Pack}))$$

2. C computes key k',

$$k' = e(P_{Pack}, \ DK_{BS})$$

3. C sets key $K' = kdf(k')$.

The correctness of key K generated by S and K' computed by C can be proven according to the following equations:

$$e(x_b P, \ x_s H_1(Meta_{Pack}))^r \tag{1}$$
$$= e(P, \ H_1(Meta_{Pack})^{x_b x_s r} \tag{2}$$
$$= e(rP, \ x_b x_s H_1(Meta_{Pack}) \tag{3}$$
$$= e(P_{Pack}, \ DK_{BS}) \tag{4}$$

3   Discussion

The purpose of the proposed system is to provide a content distribution network with a secure manner in P2P networks. However, the business scenario presented so far in this paper is not a new model in itself, and similar financial models where P2P service and digital content distribution mechanism are combined have been addressed in content distribution industry. Nevertheless, the main contribution of our system is a new approach to key issuance for content encryption and decryption. Therefore, we sketch the security and discuss some features of our proposed system.

3.1   Security and Reliability

The security of the system relies on the secret key for encryption and decryption. Although the decryption key K of $Pack$ is derived from the meta-data publicly known to customers, nobody can compute K due to the hardness of bilinear Diffie-Hellman problem[10] without knowing the private key of x_s of SP or x_b of BS at least. As shown in the equation (4), the customer C who wants to decrypt the content must obtain DK_{BS} from BS, but DK_{BS} can be obtained only after C's payment is verified as valid by BS. Consequently, without paying the price of the purchased package to BS any illegal customer cannot decrypt the $E_K(\mathcal{DC})$ in the $Pack$.

In addition, each package containing the same original content but with different meta-data is encrypted with different encryption key. That is, user who purchase one package cannot access another package with different usage rules and trade conditions due to different keying material even though the package contains the same digital content.

However, it is possible for a user who once obtains a decryption keying material from the BS to re-distribute recovered digital contents to others illegally. Unfortunately, it is rather difficult to protect this problem just by using cryptographic mechanism, hence, tamper resistant technology is required to protect digital goods from illegal manipulating.

The reliability of the system is based on the trustworthiness of billing server BS. In our system, the purpose of BS is to provide a escrow service in order to guarantee the property of content publisher for the distributed package in P2P networks. When we assume the secrecy of the decryption key for recover the content in the package, the customer C who wants to use the content must pay the price of the purchased package to BS. If BS is requested to issue keying material by C, it will check the payment according to the sales conditions in the meta-data for the package desired by the customer. Therefore, if BS is sure that C meets the financial obligation for the package, then it issues keying value for decryption. Otherwise, BS does not send anything.

Moreover, if the payment of C is valid, then BS settles the payment; the content publisher P is paid for sale of the package and the distributor D_i is paid a portion of the payment as a fee in reward for its contribution for package distribution.

3.2   Features of Deployment

As compared to a typical key issuance procedure for secure content distribution system, just our key issuing server has more computational efficiency by reducing public key cryptography operations related with secure key transfer from provider, but each entity except key issuing server in our system has little computational advantage because the overall protocols of both systems have no seeming difference. However, the proposed key issuing procedure makes it possible to implement the system with flexibility due to the following properties.

Implicit binding of key and rules. For example, suppose that a few of copies of a single content are sold to some customers with different usage rules and conditions. If we use randomly chosen key to encrypt each copy of the content independently according to its different rules and conditions, we need to maintain securely a lot of keys as the number of copies and require binding each key with the rules corresponded to its purpose. However, in the proposed system, because keys can be derived from the specific rules, we do not need to store a lot of keys and bind them with their usage rules. Furthermore, we do not need to keep them secure if BS's private key is securely maintained.

No interaction between provider and key issuance server. Key issuance procedure of our system also has the benefit of that secure key transfer is not required between the encrypter(or provider in our system) and the key issuance server(or billing server). In the case of that the encryption key is randomly generated by the encrypter, the encrypter must send the key to the server through a secure channel because the server does not know what the key was chosen by the encrypter. However, because the server can derive the key from the metadata and terms specified in transactions, our system does not require such key transfer protocol between the encrypter and the server. Moreover, these data do not need to be secret during the protocol. The need for key transfer protocol between encrypter and sever is not a critical problem for implementation, but it may be interesting if we can implement a more flexible system by removing the necessity of key transfer protocol.

Incentive in P2P network. One of concerns in P2P network free-riding problem that some peers cannot cooperate for maintaining P2P service, and one question of peer is that why they should contribute their resources for other peers. In our proposed system, because P2P network is assumed for contents distribution network contributions of peers are necessary. We intended to incentivize peers to store and distribute digital goods voluntarily by rewarding their contributions with a fee. As we mentioned earlier, the customer C can act as a distributor in order to distribute the purchased package to other peers. In this case, also C may be compensated with a fee by the BS for selling the package.

4   Conclusions

In this paper, we propose a new approach to key issuance procedure for secure digital content distribution in P2P networks. Since the proposed key generating procedure enables to separate content encryption and key issuance, and does not require for key issuance server to maintain decryption keys securely, it is possible to design more flexible digital contents distribution network where a lot of contents are encrypted with different keys and distributed with different usage rules and conditions. Our future work for continued research is to implement and experiment the system as part of a P2P network.

Acknowledgement

This research was supported by the MIC(Ministry of Information and Communication), Korea, under the ITRC(Information Technology Research Center) support program supervised by IITA(Institute of Information Technology Assessment).

References

1. D. S. Milojicic, V. Kalogeraki, R. Lukose, K. Nagaraja, J. Pruyne, B. Richard, S. Rollins and Z. Xu, Peer to Peer Computing, HP Laboratories Palo Alto HPL-2002-57, March, 2002.
2. J. Lee, S. Hwang, S. Jeong, K. Yoon, C. Park, J. Ryu. A DRM Framework for Distributing Digital Contents through the Internet, ETRI Journal, Vol. 25, No. 6, December 2003.
3. B. Horne, B. Pinkas, T. Sander. Escrow Service and Incentives in Peer-to-Peer Networks, *Proceedings of the 3rd ACM conference on Electronic Commerce*, 85–94, October 2001.
4. Market Management of Peer to Peer Services, http://www.mmapps.org
5. G. Hanaoka, K. Ogawa, I. Murota, G. Ohtake, K. Manima, K. Oyamada, S. Gohshi, S. Namba, H. Imai, Separating Encryption and Key Issuance in Digital Rights Management Systems, Proceeding of 8th Australasian Conference on Information Security and Privacy, Lecture Notes in Computer Science, Vol. 2727, 365–376, Springer, 2003.
6. Y. Watanabe, M. Numao, Conditional Cryptographic Delegation for P2P Data Sharing, In Proceedings of International Security Conference(ISC 2002), Lecture Notes in Computer Science 2433, 309–321, Springer, 2002.
7. The Advanced Encryption Standard, FIPS-197, http://csrc.nist.gov/CryptoToolkit/aes/
8. Secure Socket Layer, http://wp.netscape.com/eng/ssl3/
9. D. Boneh, B. Lynn, H. Shacham, Short Signatures from the Weil Pairing, Proceedings of Asiacrypt '01, Lecture Notes in Computer Science, Vol. 2248, 514–532, Springer, 2001.
10. D. Boneh, M. Franklin, Identity-based encryption from the Weil pairing, In Advances in Cryptology - CRYPTO '01, Lecture Notes in Computer Science 2139, 213–229, Springer, 2001.
11. A. J. Menezes, P. C.van Oorschot, S. A. Vanstone, Handbook of applied cryptography, CRC press, 1997.

Real-Time Implementation of Broadcast Switching System Using Audio Watermark

Jongweon Kim[1], Donghwan Shin[2], and Jonguk Choi[1]

[1] Copyright Protection Research Institute, Sangmyung University,
7, Hongji-dong, Jongno-gu, Seoul, 110-743, Korea
{jwkim, juchoi}@smu.ac.kr
[2] MarkTek Inc., 10F, Ssanglim Bldg.,
151-11, Ssanglim-dong, Jung-gu, Seoul, 100-400, Korea
dhshin@techonpalm.com

Abstract. The present study implemented a system to facilitate broadcast switching between a central broadcasting station and its local broadcasting stations using audio watermarking technology. Because extraction errors in synchronization system for broadcast switching cause broadcast accidents, audio watermark technology must be highly reliable. This research developed an audio watermarking algorithm efficiently applicable to broadcast synchronization system and implemented a broadcast switching system through the real-time application of the algorithm. SNR of broadcast signal with watermark inserted by the developed audio watermarking algorithm was 66.1dB, which is hardly distinguishable from broadcast signal before watermark insertion. In a robustness test, when MP3 compression of 96kbps and 128kbps was used, the extraction rate was 100%. In addition, the extraction rate was 100% for the addition of noise below -50dB. The implemented system was proved to be reliable as a broadcasting system, showing extraction rate of 100% and error rate of 0% for broadcast signal with watermark inserted in 240 hours' actual broadcasting situation.

1 Introduction

A broadcasting system with nationwide network is generally composed of a central broadcasting station and multiple local broadcasting stations. The central broadcasting station organizes overall broadcasting programs and provides them to local broadcasting stations, and they share most programs. However, local broadcasting stations organize their own programs for specific time frames and broadcast programs produced by the local stations. In a regular news show, after nationwide news are broadcasted, broadcasting program transmission should be switched from the central broadcasting station to each local broadcasting station in order to broadcast local news. In this way, when a local broadcasting station is going to transmit its own program after the completion of the program organized by the central broadcasting station, central broadcasting should be switched to local broadcasting and the process is called broadcast synchronization. Fig. 1 shows an example of broadcast synchronization system.

R. Safavi-Naini and M. Yung (Eds.): DRMTICS 2005, LNCS 3919, pp. 322–331, 2006.
© Springer-Verlag Berlin Heidelberg 2006

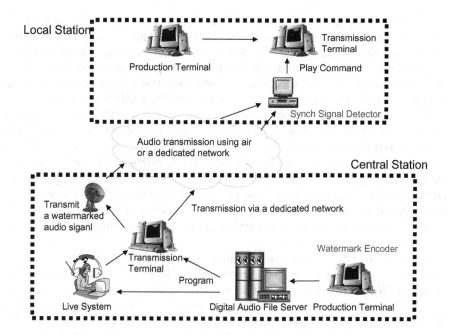

Fig. 1. Structure of broadcast synchronization system

Several systems have been proposed and used for automating broadcast synchronization. In early days, a person monitored broadcasting and switched it manually but, because of limitation in human concentration, it was highly possible to delay or omit broadcast switching, which could turn into a broadcast accident. Accordingly, broadcast synchronization system is used to reduce the waste of manpower and prevent broadcast accidents through automated equipment.

Currently available broadcast synchronization automation systems for broadcast switching transmit signals using voice recognition technology and dedicated lines. Specific audio is inserted at the point of broadcast switching, and the audio is recognized by voice recognition technology and broadcast switching is attempted. This method has a high rate of unexpected operation because the voice recognition technology cannot recognize voice 100%. If the broadcast contains the same content as the broadcast switching audio, the system may confuse it with the switching signal. In case a dedicated network is used in transmitting synchronization signals, the transmission condition of the dedicated network is an important factor. If there is a delay in transmission, it may be directly linked to a broadcast accident. In this way, delays and recognition errors are obstacles to the automation of broadcast synchronization system.

The present research attempted to apply audio watermarking technology to a synchronization system for broadcast switching. There have been a number of researches to use digital watermarking technology in broadcasting. In Europe, a technology called Musicode is used to insert watermark in music for broadcast monitoring, and a project [1][2] called VIVA (Visual Identity Verification Auditor) is used to insert watermark in video images for monitoring.

In order to build up an automatic broadcast synchronization system for broadcast switching using audio watermarking technology, the audio watermarking algorithm must be absolutely reliable. The algorithm should be able to extract broadcast switching signals 100% in any broadcasting environment. In particular, it must be free from wrong extraction of switching signals in broadcasts that do not contain broadcast switching signals. That is, its false positive error must be strictly restricted to 0%.

The present research proposed an audio watermarking algorithm robust in broadcasting environment as well as a method of inserting a broadcast switching signal into broadcast signals and extracting it. The proposed algorithm used a digital filter to generate broadcast signals indistinguishable from the original audio and secured robustness in noisy environment and for signals compressed for broadcasting. The proposed algorithm was implemented real-time using DSP (Digital Signal Processor) and was designed for broadcast switching by extracting 5 bits of information within 0.5 second. In particular, the manufactured system proved its usability through a test in actual broadcasting environment.

In this thesis, Chapter II introduced the proposed audio watermarking algorithm, and Chapter III explained how to implement the synchronization system for broadcast switching. We also carried out experiments with signals containing noise and those compressed for broadcasting to test the robustness of the audio watermarking algorithm, and tested the equipment implemented real-time in actual broadcasting. The results were discussed in Chapter IV. Chapter V presented the conclusions of this research.

2 Audio Watermarking Algorithm

The audio watermarking algorithm used in this research is a technology to insert and extract watermark by transforming the spectrum of original audio in a way of not affecting the audio system using digital filtering.

2.1 Watermark Insertion

Fig. 2 shows the module for inserting an audio signal into information. In the figure, Cover Signal is the original audio signal that does not contain watermark, and Stego Signal is a signal that contains watermark.

In the process of watermark insertion, the first step is to divide the input Cover Signal into band frequency to be filtered through wavelet transformation and band frequency not to be filtered. In the filtering step, Cover Signal is decomposed through wavelets and the only target frequency is filtered in order to avoid unnecessary change in neighboring frequencies in the digital filtering process. Even if an ideal digital filter is designed, it is impossible to prevent effects on surrounding signals in the process of digital filtering. Furthermore, because a high frequency band has relatively low energy, if this part is distorted, audio specialists can sense the change of the tone color. That is, wavelet [5] is used to separate signals from time-frequency area in order to prevent distortion as explained above.

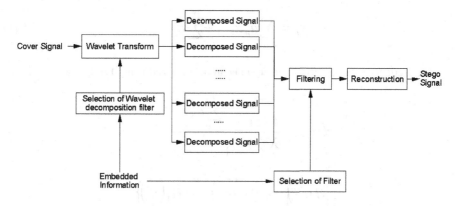

Fig. 2. Flow diagram of watermark insertion

The second step filters the target frequency signal using a filter designed in advance. Because the filter designed for filtering is IIR (Infinite Impulse Response) filter, a non-linear phase change occurs and the non-linear phase change can bring the change of the tone color. In order to solve the problem of phase change, we used zero-phase filtering [4,6] so that phase change does not happen during filtering. Fredrik [6] prevented phase change through forward and backward IIR filtering and calculated the initial value of filtering.

The last step restores the original audio signal, which is Stego Signal containing information, by reuniting the filtered signal with signals separated through wavelet.

The digital filter used in this research was designed in advance according to the volume of information and the properties of contents. The system to be implemented used a band stop digital filter with properties as presented in Table 1, considering that the system to be implemented would be used in broadcasting system and that watermark would be inserted mainly to voice signals.

Table 1. Digital filter (kHz)

No.	Pass band	Stop band	Change in passband (dB)	Stopband suppression rate (dB)
1	2.85~3.15	2.95~3.05	0.1	74
2	3.30~3.60	3.40~3.50	0.1	75
3	4.00~4.30	4.10~4.20	0.1	77
4	4.60~4.90	4.70~4.80	0.1	78
5	5.30~5.60	5.40~5.50	0.1	80

Considering the characteristics of the system, the present study attached greater importance to robustness. In addition, the band for watermark was set at 3~6kHz because target information was usually audio data. Filtering extracted only necessary signals by Eq. (1).

$$y_k = \sum_{m=0}^{M} a_m x_{k-m} + \sum_{n=0}^{N} a_n y_{k-n} \ulcorner \qquad (1)$$

The frequency characteristic of Eq. (1) can be analyzed using Eq. (2) [4].

$$H(z) = \frac{Y(z)}{X(z)} = \frac{\displaystyle\sum_{m=0}^{M} a_m z^{-m}}{1 - \displaystyle\sum_{n=0}^{N} b_n z^{-n}} \qquad (2)$$

$$\left| H(e^{\omega}) \right| = \sqrt{\left\{ H_R(e^{\omega}) \right\}^2 + \left\{ H_I(e^{\omega}) \right\}^2}$$

2.2 Watermark Extraction

Watermark can by extracted by analyzing the amplitude spectrum of audio. We set the length of frequency analysis to 1024 bits considering the sampling frequency of Stego Signal containing watermark information, the bandwidth of inserted information, etc.

Assuming that the frequency of signals other than watermark signals is random, we used the property that watermark signals get stronger and other signals get weaker if a watermarked broadcast signal is divided into 1024-bit samples and the samples are added up. In this research the number of iterations N was set at 85. Fig. 3 shows a block diagram for watermark extract in this system.

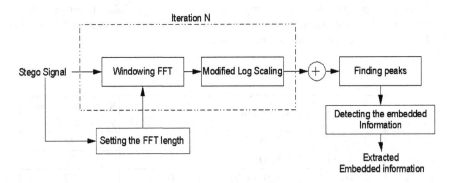

Fig. 3. Watermark extraction block diagram

In order to limit the maximum number, watermark information is emphasized using modified log scaling. Based on that, the positions of peaks are identified, and whether watermark has been inserted is determined using the identified location information.

3   System Implementation

We designed and implemented hardware in order to build up a stable system for real-time processing. Because of its characteristic, a broadcast synchronization system must detect a synchronization signal and switches to a control signal within a short time. It must extract a synchronization signal at least within 0.5 second. For this, a PC-based system can be implemented but it does not guarantee stability. Thus we implemented the system using a DSP chip, which is stable and fast in operation. The DSP chip used in this research was TMS320VC5410 - 100MIPS of TI (Texas Instruments). Fig. 4 shows the block diagram for the hardware of the implemented system.

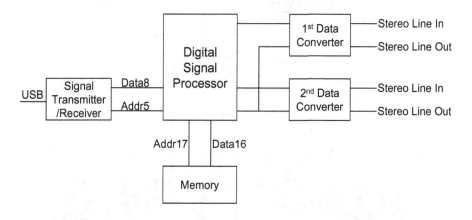

Fig. 4. Hardware block diagram

In the hardware block diagram, the 1st data converter and the 2nd converter are D/A and A/D converters respectively, converting input analog audio signals into digital signals in the form of 44.1kHz stereo 16-bit ADPCM and, at the same time, digital stereo audio signals into digital stereo audio signal.

In the present research, we generated and used loop back signals of input audio. This is to convert input audio signals into digital signals and again to output them as analog signals. By doing so, we can monitor the state of input signals. The memory is composed a 128-Kword flash memory, two broadcast signals can be processed simultaneously, and each broadcasting channel can process up to 40 MIPS.

Digital broadcast audio signals input through the digital signal processor are looked up real-time by the watermark detection algorithm. If watermark information inserted as a synchronization signal is extracted, the result is informed to the monitoring PC through the UBS port. The information sent to the monitoring PC is saved into log file together with the time when the synchronization signal was detected and the accumulated number of times that synchronization signals have been detected. Fig. 5 shows the structure diagram of the designed system, and Fig. 6 is a photograph of the manufactured system.

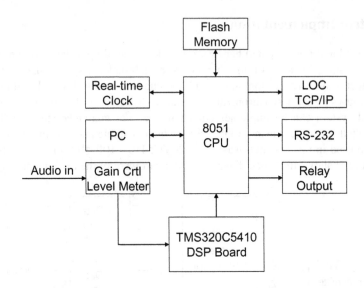

Fig. 5. System structure

Fig. 6. Implemented real-time broadcast synchronization system

4 Experiment Results and Analysis

In order to test the robustness of the implemented algorithm in two ways, this test carried out an experiment with changing noise and compression level to create restrictive conditions similar to actual broadcasting. Watermarking audio used in the experiment was a 0.7-second-long frame, and the audio signal is followed by a mute interval of over 0.5 second. The mute is a signal to inform the synchronization signal and to remove noise resulting from broadcast switching.

Fig. 7 shows the voice used in the experiment. This is a voice of a man announcer. The horizontal axis indicates time (unit: second) and the vertical axis indicates the size of waveform (unit: dB). –inf indicates a perfect mute and the largest amplitude possible to represent 0dB in 16 bits, and the smallest amplitude possible to represent is–90.3dB.

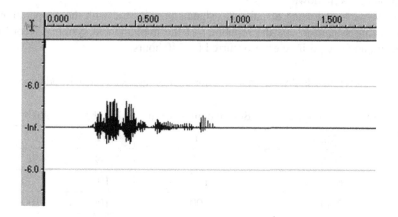

Fig. 7. Broadcast switching signal used in the experiment

4.1 Sound Quality Test

Among methods of evaluating sound quality quantitatively, the most common one is to find the signal to noise ratio (SNR). A signal is usually mixed with noise and SNR is the ratio of signal to noise.

$$SNR = 20\left(\log_{10} \frac{Signal}{Noise} \right)dB \qquad (3)$$

In case of audio, SNR is not so meaningful but it is known that noise is almost undetectable if SNR is over 60dB.

When watermark is inserted using the proposed algorithm, SNR measured 66.090dB. This means that the insertion of watermark caused almost no degradation of audio signal.

4.2 Robustness Test

In an experiment of noise addition to test the robustness of watermark in the implemented system, we added white noise of -70dB, -60dB and -50dB. To test by compression rate, we applied MP3 compression at 128kbps and 96kbps. Because broadcasted analog signals are converted to digital signals and then watermarks are extracted in the system, attacks by D/A and A/D conversion are contained basically.

Table 2 shows the result of the robust test in conditions as stated above. In the experiment, audio containing watermark was tested 100 samples per each SNR, and the result of watermark detection was presented.

According to the result of the experiment, watermark was always detected when added noise was up to -60dB noise. However, when added noise was intensified over 50dB, the number of detection errors increased. In compression at 128kbps, detection rate was almost the same as that before compression, but in compression at 96kbps, detection rate went down.

Lastly, we tested using actual radio signals broadcasted with the cooperation of a broadcasting system to test the reliability of the implemented system. According to the result, no false positive error occurred for 240 hours.

Table 2. Result of watermark detection after compression and noise addition

Intensity of noise	Before compression	128kbps	96kbps
-45dB	71	72	67
-50dB	97	99	96
-60dB	100	100	100
-70dB	100	100	100

5   Conclusions

The present study implemented a broadcast synchronization system that notifies the time of broadcast switching automatically using watermark. Particularly to meet high reliability required in broadcasting equipment, we designed the system to detect watermark within 0.5 second and inform the time of broadcast switching by processing broadcast signals real-time. In addition, we tested the reliability of the system in actual broadcasting environment for 240 hours. In the test, the system showed a watermark detection rate of 100% without detection error of no watermarked signal.

This research also confirmed that the implemented system is robust to white noise attacks of over −60dB and attacks against compression. Furthermore, in the sound quality test of watermarked audio, the sound containing information was almost indistinguishable from the original sound.

The watermarking technology used in this research is applicable to broadcasting advertisement monitoring systems or broadcast monitoring system for counting royalties for copyrights. Moreover, it can be used in equipment that controls multiple systems using a radio receiver.

Acknowledgement

Soli Deo Gloria. This work was supported by International Cooperation Research Project of Ministry of Science and Technology in Korea.

References

1. T. Kalker, G. Depovere, J. Haitsma, M.J. Maes, "Video watermarking system for broadcast monitoring" Proceedings of the Society and Watermarking of Multimedia Contents, 103-112, 19990125.
2. De Strycker, Pascale Termont, et al, "The VIVA project: Digital watermarking for broadcast monitoring", Proceedings of the 1999 International Conference on Image Processing, volume 2, 202-205, 19990124.
3. S. W. Shin, J. W. Kim, J. U. Choi, "Technology for Hiding the ID Code of Copyrighted Works for Internet Broadcasting Service of Digital Audio", Conference of Korea Broadcasting Engineering Society, November 2001
4. Oppenheim, A.V., and R.W. Schafer, Discrete-Time Signal Processing, Prentice-Hall, 1989, pp. 311-312
5. Yang Yan, Zhang Dong, "Enhancement of Angiograms via M-Band Wavelet Transform", Proceedings of SPIE Biomedical Photonics and Optoelectronic Imaging, 165-169, 2000.
6. Fredrik Gustafsson, "Determining the initial States in Forward-Backward Filtering", Transactions on Signal Processing, V.44 N.4, 1996. 4. 1.
7. M. Adinolfi et al., Nucl. Instrum. Methods A 329 (1993) 117.
8. Peter Weilhammer, private communicaton, The RD20 Collaboration, preprint CERN/DRDC 9439 (Geneva, 1994).
9. D. H. Shin, J. K. Ahn, Y. I. Shin, J. W. Kim, J. U. Kim, "Implementation of Broadcast Synchronization System Using Audio Watermark", Conference of Korea Broadcasting Engineering Society, 2002

Enforcing Regional DRM for Multimedia Broadcasts With and Without Trusted Computing

Ulrich Greveler

Horst Görtz Institute for IT Security,
Ruhr University Bochum, Germany
ulrich.greveler@nds.rub.de

Abstract. We present the problem of enforcing a Digital Rights Management (DRM) system that needs to consider location-dependent licensing policies and operates on top of existing conditional access standards. A major application for location-dependent DRM is Pay-TV broadcasting as rightsholders require different business models in different regions. A global provider's enduser equipment needs to validate the user location in some way in order to enforce DRM in this scenario. We will depict several solutions to the problem and compare their security qualities. The main result is that trusted computing hardware may not be the most appropriate solution given reasonable conditions.

1 Introduction

In this paper we focus on the problem of enforcing Digital Rights Management (DRM) with location-dependent licenses for multimedia broadcasts (i.e. Pay-per-View television). Today, a Pay-TV provider serves its customers in a dedicated region (e.g., a country). The program offering is tailored to the potential customers in this region (e.g., language, national interest). As the digital rights holders may require different terms regarding distribution and pricing depending on the region in which the content is distributed to the end-customers, every Pay-TV provider will deliver the multimedia content under terms valid for the region it serves. The content is generally scrambled (encrypted) so that only the paying customers can consume the content.

A customer trying to circumvent regional limitations might be able to buy Pay-TV services in a distant region (another country) and move all the equipment needed (smartcard, set-top terminal) to his home region and use it there if signal reception is possible (e.g., satellite coverage). However, the audio streams and subtitles are still tailored to the customers in the distant region so the content might lose some of its value for this traveling pirate customer. Due to this effect, regional Pay-TV providers establish a regional DRM system in the sense that licenses for specific regions are implicitly enforced.

As standard set-top terminals (STTs) and broadcast technologies are becoming a reality, a future Pay-TV provider might want to serve customers in several

R. Safavi-Naini and M. Yung (Eds.): DRMTICS 2005, LNCS 3919, pp. 332–340, 2006.
© Springer-Verlag Berlin Heidelberg 2006

regions or globally. The broadcast signal might already be received in a super-region when radio or satellite networks cover multiple countries or Internet multicast is used. In these cases, the offering quickly becomes global. Transmissions can incorporate several audio and subtitle streams so that each customer is enabled to choose and consume the content following his preferences.

The digital rights holders may welcome such a global Pay-TV provider when transmission costs are reduced significantly but they will most probably not accept the content being distributed in a way that infringes rules on regional licensing and eases piracy.

	Region 1	Region 2	Region 3
Transmission 1 (**date:** Jan 15) **audio:** E, F, DE **subtitle:** E1, E2, F	per-view 5\$ audio: all subtitle: all	per-view 3\$ audio: DE subtitle: E1, DE	black out
Transmission 2 (**date:** Feb 12) **audio:** E, F, DE, ES, IT, CH, JP **subtitle:** E1, E2, F, DE1, DE2, ...	per-view 3\$ audio: all subtitle: all	black out	per-view 5\$ audio: E, JP subtitle: all
Transmission 3 (**date:** Jun 19) **audio:** E, F, DE **subtitle:** E1, E2, F	free for subscribers audio: all subtitle: all	per-view 1\$ audio: DE subtitle: E1, DE	free for subscribers audio: E, JP subtitle: all

Fig. 1. Several transmissions of same content, example

We illustrate these different regional distribution or business models with Fig. 1. The rights holder of a certain multimedia content (e.g., a movie production) sells to regional Pay-TV providers. The pricing, release dates and supported languages (audio and subtitles) depend on the region. Each regional provider is able to diversify the digital content to meet the requirements and transmit the tailored content to his customers. However, if a global provider emerges that wants to serve all regions with *one* transmission covering all regional needs (and reducing transmissions costs) it has to ensure that the customers can only receive (i.e. descramble) the content they are entitled to. For instance, a customer living in *Region 1* of Fig. 1 shall not be able to buy the Pay-Per-View package for *Transmission 1* in *Region 2* and receive it at home for a lower price and with more language options than entitled. Loosely speaking, the equipment shall know where it is located and change its behavior when moved to another region and follow local rules regardless where it was bought.

2   Background and Definitions

Let us first fix what a license in our regional DRM context shall be. A user is entitled to certain content consumable under certain conditions that depend on the region once she bought a subscription and / or a Pay-Per-View product. This consumption right shall be her license and be expressed as a machine-readable license ticket shown in Fig. 2.

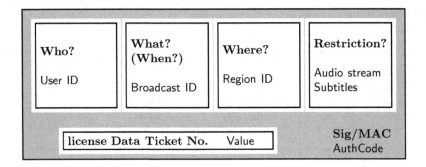

Fig. 2. License ticket

The license ticket is usually sent via the broadcast channel individually to each user and processed by the user equipment (here: smartcard). It carries the User ID so the STT or the smartcard knows whether it shall process the ticket, a Broadcast ID to map it to a transmission and a Region ID to specify the region in its regional licensing model. The restrictions are not necessarily a list of rules but could be a set of one-time keys which allow to decrypt certain parts of a transmission. This broad definition of restrictions allows us to be compatible with established technology standards. The Broadcast ID refers to a certain transmission and will change when a transmission is repeated. The time of the transmission is thus indirectly encoded with this ID. The ticket is authenticated by some cryptographic mechanism (e.g., a MAC function) and may carry a unique number for differentiation.

Multimedia Standards. In order to approach practical relevance for our proposed system, we briefly describe the relevant standards regarding Pay-TV and multimedia distribution. The goal is to operate on top of established technology so that security can be achieved without the need to roll out a new infrastructure based on a revised standard.

Our aim is to re-use conventional conditional access technology for securing multimedia transmissions. The content we refer to is coded in MPEG [1] format and encrypted by the DVB encryption standard. DVB can be broadcasted via satellite (DVB-s), terrestrial emitters (DVB-t) and cable (DVB-c).

Currently, most Pay-TV customers own an STT equipped with a *Common Interface* [2], an established standard used in digital video broadcasting. This Common Interface is connected with a *CI module* that is incorporating a smart card reader where the user will put in a smart card issued by his Pay-TV provider. Most currently available set-top boxes and DVB-cards for Personal Computers provide at least one or more than one Common Interface slot. Different CI modules facilitate different cryptographic protocols and algorithms that the Pay-TV service providers use and implement on the module. All STTs are applying the same content descrambler (specified by the *Common Scrambling Algorithm*). During a secured transmission the STTs continuously receive so-called *Control Words* via the Common Interface that they need to descramble the secured content. These Control Words are short-lived session keys only used for small parts of one transmission.

3 Enforcing Regional DRM

3.1 Appropriate Organizational Measures

The DRM enforcement could be based on organizational measures only – or be combined with technical measures described in the next sections.

Regional Smartcards. If the distribution of smartcards (as part of the Conditional Access system) could be linked to the regions defined by the DRM policy (and each card stays in a region), it is not a difficult task to enforce the license restrictions. The sender would send the management messages containing the descrambling information to the set of smartcards distributed to a region. Only these cards are then able to descramble the content according to the regional licensing model. This regional licensing approach is not new and was in particular set into practice for DVD media in the nineties (by applying *regional codes*) and did not prove to be successful.

The attacker's task in such a scenario would then be to move the smartcard from one region to another (e.g., from an *inexpensive* region to an expensive one) or to alter the card distribution process. The sender (in the role of the smartcard issuer) could prohibit that cards are moved across borders but this would probably not stop all potential attackers. Moreover, such a regulation might not even be enforceable by law as a violation of the subscription contract is not necessarily a breach of law in every region. In this case the sender is unable to prosecute traced pirates. Such a situation renders regulations useless.

3.2 Technical Measures: Tamper Resistance / Trusted Computing

In order to technically prevent unauthorized movement of the user's STT (including the CI module and the smartcard), either the network or at least one component has to validate the location when no other technical measures are in place. If the STT is forced to initiate a communication to the sender before a transmission there are several proposed ways to locate the equipment by letting the STT initiate a communication to the broadcast sender [3], but as we aim to operate on top of the established DVB and Conditional Access standards, we cannot expect the STT to have such a convenient call-out feature. The communication is one-way only, hence the sender does not know where the receiver is located.

As the STT itself is standard off-the-shelf hardware being sold across regions with no localization features, either the CI module or the smartcard may be augmented with extra-functionality to validate the user location.

Positioning Systems. The CI module delivered by the Pay-TV provider could incorporate a positioning module like a GPS or Galileo signal receiver. If the positioning unit operated in a secure (i.e., tamper resistant) environment it would be able to securely validate the location and check the license against geographical co-ordinates. If a confidential channel to the smartcard is established, the descrambling of content will only be initiated if the correct location is determined.

The positioning module would unlikely be incorporated in a smartcard as the restriction on size and computational power are much higher compared to the CI module. However, this option should be taken into consideration for completeness. Our findings regarding the CI module augmented with a localization module are also valid for smartcards with localization features, so we do not elaborate on an augmented smartcard approach further.

The tamper-resistant device in this scenario needs to validate the license ticket by checking the co-ordinates of the STT against the Region ID in the ticket. If the user (her equipment) is located in the specified region, then the descrambling process is initiated. This process is specified by Algorithm 1.

Algorithm 1. ticket processing and localization

---
repeat
   read ticket
until ticket on User ID is received
get STT co-ordinates
if Region ID matches co-ordinates **then**
   return keys from ticket restriction field
else
   return license violation error
end if

3.3   Technical Measures: 2nd Radio Network

For this scenario we apply an idea from [4] where an additional radio network for Pay-TV localization purposes is used. This 2nd radio network with low data throughput performance can send small amounts of key information (individually encrypted for a user) to a *radio cell*, which is a rather tiny area (compared to the rather big regions), so that this information would be missing in other regions where only the broadcast signal is available. In order to use established technology, the individual information could be transmitted via the GSM [5] mobile phone network using the service *cell broadcast* [6]. This radio interface does require the CI module device to incorporate a basic non-voice GSM terminal card so that these cell broadcast messages can be received. Regions without GSM coverage can also participate if another local radio network with cell addressability is available (e.g., pager networks or analogue mobile phone networks).

This enhanced CI module is called a *DRM device* (in [4]) to distinguish it from an ordinary CI module.

The localization is implicitly performed via the 2nd radio network and there is no need to use clients of positioning systems. In order to apply the second radio network scheme to our ticket based licenses approach each ticket is split up into two parts. The restrictions field containing the cryptographic keys are removed from the ticket that is sent via the broadcast channel. This part, which is represented by a rather small amount of data, is sent via the 2nd radio network to the user location's radio cell if the cell co-ordinates match the Region ID. Note that Algorithm 2. does not contain any conditional statements.

Algorithm 2. ticket assembling using 2nd radio network

---

repeat
    read ticket.part1 (broadcast channel)
until ticket.part1 on User ID is received
read ticket.part2 (2nd radio network)
assemble ticket from both parts
return keys from ticket restriction field

3.4   Security Analysis of Measures

Organizational measures. There is no obvious way to compare the strength of the organizational measures named in the preceding section to technical measures, but history shows that selling devices in a certain region and banning export to other regions is not a method to stop users from doing so. The Digital Versatile Disc (DVD) region codes [7] are an example for this strategy. The DVD world is divided into six regions and DVD players in one region shall only play media with the correct region code embedded. It has not been a successful security mechanism: one problem is that many software players need to be configured for region locking before first use but could be resetted later or patched to be *region-free* while the media are shipped to more regions by mail-order anyway. But apart from that license enforcement weakness, the DVD has been a commercial success.

Small-size devices like smartcards can easily be transported or shipped by mail and it does not require any expertise to remove the smartcard from the card reader and send it to somebody else in another region. Moreover, different national laws might not legally support the system supplier's export regulation and render it useless.

Trusted Computing. While the trusted computing property of the CI module (or a part of it) can be a significant line of defense for an attacker, the positioning radio signals are received outside the TC environment before the secure computation is initiated. A straightforward attack scenario would be to remove the antenna and record the signals at another location in order to replay it. The same result could be reached by generating fake signals and feed them to the positioning unit directly. Regarding the current de-facto standard positioning system (GPS), the latter task is feasible as the positioning satellites' signals are not cryptographically protected at all and fake signals can easily be generated.

A direct attack on the Trusted Computing hardware is generally regarded to be too costly for an average attacker, but it still needs to be considered here as the pivotal machine command executed by the secure hardware is the **if**-statement of Algorithm 1.. The attacker only needs to provoke a faulty system state at this computation step in order to circumvent the trusted hardware; he does not need to read any secret keys in the device. This kind of attack on tamper-resistant hardware could be rather inexpensive [8], and special protection concepts against these attacks have to be considered [9].

2nd radio network. Our first observation is that the second radio network (e.g. GSM network) is used as a trusted party in this scenario. A manipulation of a network that makes it possible to re-route a cell broadcast to a different region (in a different country) would threaten the system security as the DRM device could not securely determine the user location anymore. This kind of attack might unlikely be performed by a single Pay-TV pirate user, but it shall be regarded as an attack on the whole global DRM system that could be launched by a group of attackers being organized.

As the key information needed to descramble the content is not available in other regions (by the trusted 2nd radio network), an attacker can not gain anything from manipulating the STT, smartcard or DRM device hardware. If the information is not available in the region the attacker is located in, it could not be derived from other information stored by the user equipment at all.

An attacker might utilize a functional STT together with a license in one region for the purpose of intercepting the Control Words on the slot interface and use the intercepted data to run a STT in another region where the license is not valid. These Control Words are the secret information continuously issued by the DRM device via the Common Interface that is needed by the STT to descramble the content during a broadcast session.

If this type of attack is feasible (the Control Words need to be transmitted realtime to another region if the transmission there is to be descrambled in realtime as well) then it could be applied already today for regional Pay-TV systems where the data broadcast is covering a super-region (e.g., satellite Pay-TV, cable networks). The attack could also be applied for the trusted computing based solution sketched above, so it does not distinguish the measures from each other.

A possible counter-measure for this type of attack is to enforce a mutual authentication of the CI module and the STT. As the underlying standardized Pay-TV technology is the vulnerability in this case the proposed system is at most as secure as the content scrambling standard adopted by it. If the scrambling algorithm is broken, then new STTs have to be rolled out anyway and the system could operate on top of this new standard technology again.

Comparison of technical measures. In order to compare the measures it is reasonable to identify the differences first. The trusted computing solution of the problem does require a trusted hardware framework for the localization device that needs to be issued together with the STT to the enduser. Such a device would increase the cost for the enduser equipment considerably. Moreover it is limited in its suitability for solving the problem as current available positioning systems can be circumvented by feeding a fake signal to the antenna input. The trusted computing device would still store secret information that could be used by an attacker to descramble the content if a successful attack on the secure hardware could be launched. The 2nd radio network solution does not need additional trusted computing hardware (a smartcard would still be used, though) and it would not store secret information that could be used to descramble the content as this information is not available outside a target region. The major difference to the TC solution is that another (trusted) network is needed and the usage of the network services would also add cost to the global content distribution (and some extra hardware is needed as well). The security limitation here is the amount of trust towards the second radio network management. If the cost generated by both solutions is assumed to be comparable or negligible regarding the security considerations, the remaining differentiator is the security limitation of each solution. As the generation of fake positioning signals (or usage of copied signals) is a feasible task for an attacker, while the manipulation of a radio network is considered infeasible, and as the trusted computing hardware can also be subject to successful attacks, we would favor the latter solution under reasonable conditions. Note that this decision is based on theoretical analysis only and might not withstand real-life conditions regarding cost and availability of hardware and radio networks.

4   Conclusion and Outlook

Solutions to the problem of enforcing a DRM system that needs to consider location-dependent licensing policies can be based on very different technical or organizational measures. A global Pay-TV provider being forced to provide the enduser equipment for user location validation can choose between these different options. The options differ in cost and security properties. Trusted computing hardware that is often considered to be a standard instrument for DRM enforcement is not the only option to follow here, depending on the additional conditions to be considered, it might even be inferior to other solutions.

References

1. Jan Bormans, K.H.: Mpeg-21 overview v.5. Technical Report JTC1/SC29/WG11/N5231, ISO/IEC, Requirements Group (2002)
2. CENELEC: Common interface specification for conditional access and other digital video broadcasting decoder applications. Technical Report EN 50221, Technical Committee TC 206 (1997)
3. Gabber, E., Wool, A.: How to prove where you are. Proceedings of the 5th ACM Conference on Computer and Communications Security (1998) 142–149
4. Greveler, U.: How pay-TV becomes e-commerce. Proceedings of the 7th International IEEE Conference on E-Commerce Technology 2005 (2005) 508–511

5. Hillebrand, F.: GSM and UMTS - The Creation of Global Mobile Communication. First edn. Wiley (2002)
6. Harris, I.: Technical realization of short message service cell broadcast (smscb). Technical Report 3GPP TS 03.41, 3rd Generation Partnership Project (3GPP) (1996)
7. Taylor, J.: DVD Demystified. Second edn. McGraw-Hill Professional (2000)
8. Anderson, R., Kuhn, M.: Low cost attacks on tamper resistant devices. IWSP: 5th International Workshop on Security Protocols, LNCS 1361, Springer-Verlag (1997) 125–136
9. Kommerling, O., Kuhn, M.: Design principles for tamper resistant smartcard processors. Proceedings of the USENIX Workshop on Smartcard Technology (1999) 9–20

A DRM System Supporting What You See Is What You Pay

Bin B. Zhu[1], Yang Yang[2], and Tierui Chen[3]

[1] Microsoft Research Asia, Beijing 100080, China
binzhu@microsoft.com
[2] Dept. of Elec. Eng. & Info Sci., Univ. of Sci. & Technol. of China,
Hefei, Anhui 230027, China
wdscxsj@ustc.edu
[3] Inst. of Computing Technology, Chinese Academy of Sciences, Beijing 100080, China
chentierui@software.ict.ac.cn

Abstract. We present a Digital Rights Management (DRM) system that supports what you see is what you pay. In our system, multimedia is compressed with a scalable codec and encrypted preserving the scalable granularity and multi-access capability. This paper focuses on the DRM modules enabling efficient key generation and management. We employ a light license server which stores only the master keys of content publishers, which are used to regenerate decryption keys for clients during license acquisition. All the remaining information needed in key generation is efficiently packaged in a DRM header of protected content. The DRM header is sent to a license server during license acquisition to allow the license server to generate a single key for a requested access, which is sent to the client in a license along with the acquired rights. The key is used by the client to generate all the remaining keys of subordinate accesses.

1 Introduction

With advances of digital technologies, more and more multimedia contents are released in or converted to digital formats. Wide access to high speed Internet makes distribution of digital multimedia efficient and easy. At the same time, the same technologies and Internet create rampant piracy of digital multimedia, which causes dramatic financial damage to the content owners and prevents content owners from releasing more contents in digital formats through the Internet as an efficient and cheap distribution channel. There is a great demand for technologies to protect digital contents from illegal access, copy, or sharing. Digital Rights Management (DRM) is a system to address such a need. A DRM system provides persistent management of all rights ranging from description, identification, trading, and protection to monitoring and tracking for digital contents from creation to consumption [1][2]. Such a system consists of many core technologies and essential parts such as rights expression language to describe rights to be managed, encryption and key generation and management to protect the content from unauthorized access and usage, and tamper-proof trusted DRM modules on the client side to ensure and manage the rights exactly as acquired.

R. Safavi-Naini and M. Yung (Eds.): DRMTICS 2005, LNCS 3919, pp. 341–355, 2006.

We have seen in recent years an increasing interest in DRM from both academia and the industry. Standardization of DRM systems has also been actively pursued. The Moving Picture Experts Group (MPEG) has adopted recently a DRM framework, eXtensions to the Intellectual Property Management and Protection (IPMP-X), for both MPEG-2 and 4 [3][4]. The Open Mobile Alliance (OMA) has also adopted a DRM system recently for mobile environments [5]. There are also several proprietary DRM systems available on the market. Typical commercial DRM systems include the Windows Media Rights Manager (WMRM) from Microsoft [6], Commerce and Rights|System from InterTrust [7], Electronic Media Management System (EMMS) from IBM [8], Helix DRM from RealNetworks [9], and the EBooks from Adobe [10]. A typical DRM system encrypts multimedia content which is distributed to consumers via distribution channels such as superdistribution. Superdistribution is a powerful distribution mechanism that treats ease of replication of digital content as an asset rather than a liability. Superdistribution actively encourages free distribution of digital content via any distribution mechanism imaginable to reach the maximum number of potential consumers. A DRM system enforces acquired rights of multimedia content through the trusted DRM modules on the client side and a license which contains the decryption key along with specifications of the rights a user has acquired. A license is usually individualized, typically encrypted with a key that is bound to the hardware of a user's player, so the license cannot be illegally shared with others. Control of content consumption rather than distribution is much more efficient in protecting digital assets in the digital world since modern networks, storage, and compression technologies have made it trivial to transfer digital content from one device or person to another.

The same multimedia content can be consumed with devices of a variation of characteristics and capacities such as mobile devices or PC. To enable different devices to play the same content, the traditional DRM approach is to compress and encrypt a single multimedia content into multiple copies, with each copy targeted at a specific application scenario such as a PC with high resolution display and computing power and storage, a 3G cellular phone with a small display and limited computing power and storage, etc. These multiple copies are all stored in a server to make them available for each individual user to select a copy that best fits his or her need. Another approach is to apply a transcoder at some node of the multimedia delivery path to generate a lower resolution or quality bitstream to fit in the targeted network condition or device capability. Decryption and re-encryption are typically used in performing such transcoding. A more elegant solution is to encode multimedia contents with a fine granularity scalability (FGS) codec. A scalable codec encodes a signal into a single codestream which is partitioned and organized according to certain scalable parameters or importance. Based on scalabilities offered by a codestream, each individual user can extract from the same codestream the best representation that fits his or her application. An FGS scalable codec offers near continuously optimal tradeoff between quality and rates over a large range. Unlike traditional approaches, a single scalable codestream is stored and used for all different applications, with possible simple adaptation manipulations such as truncations on the codestream. This capability of one-compression-to–meet–the–needs–of–all–applications is very desira-ble in many multimedia applications. Many scalable codecs have been proposed. Some have already been adopted by standard bodies. MPEG has adopted a scalable video coding format called *Fine Granularity Scalability (FGS)* into its MPEG-4 standard [11]. The Joint Photographic Experts Group (JPEG) has adopted a wavelet-based scalable image coding format called *JPEG 2000* [12] and *motion JPEG 2000* [13]. Many schemes have been proposed in recent years to encrypt scalable codestreams such that fine granularity scalability is preserved in the encrypted codestream to enable direct truncations without decryption. Most of those schemes are described in the review paper [14].

One of the unique features offered by an FGS codec is multiple access types in a single scalable codestream. For example, a PC can show a high-fidelity full resolution video from a scalable video codestream, while a mobile phone can show a low quality video at a reduced resolution from the same codestream. Different accesses should be charged differently. It is natural to require a PC user to pay more for a high-fidelity full resolution video than a mobile phone user. A DRM system for FGS codestreams should preserve the property of multiple access types in a single DRM-protected codestream to enable the business model that charges different accesses differently. This means that a scalable codestream should be encrypted with multiple keys. Generation and management of multiple keys for different accesses of a scalable codestream are a challenge in the design of a DRM system.

We have been building a research prototype of a DRM system on top of the Microsoft Windows DRM system [15] to support scalable codestreams, esp. scalable encryption to enable direct truncations of encrypted codestreams and multiple accesses to support what you see is what you pay, as well as content and license roaming among devices of different characteristics in a digital home (eHome). An example application is to view multimedia at reduced quality and resolution, either free or at a small cost. If the content is good and a better version is desired, then the user can acquire a new license, and download the enhanced portion (i.e., the difference) of the encrypted content if needed. A typical case for content roaming is that a full version is downloaded to a PC, and then truncated to appropriate representations to fit other eHome devices. Appropriate licenses are also roamed to those devices. In this paper, we concentrate on the part of our DRM system related to the management of multiple keys to support multiple accesses with a single protected scalable codestream. The major contribution of this paper is that we propose and implement a DRM system to support a new business model of what you see if what you pay. In addition, we present an efficient key generation and management scheme to facilitate a light license server used in our DRM system. A license server does not need to remember the decryption keys for individual protected contents. Instead, only the publisher-specific master key is remembered by the license server, which is then used to generate content decryption keys. In typical DRM applications, the number of publishers is much less than the number of protected contents, therefore our license server is much cheaper to run and simpler to maintain. The system has a very small overhead on the file size. This design is very desirable in many DRM applications since license server is a single point of failure in a DRM system. To play a protected content, a player has to acquire a license from a license server if the license has not been acquired previously or has expired. Reliability and availability of the license server is essential in a DRM system. A light and simple license server enables deployment of many cheap yet secure servers to provide license granting servers for a DRM system, therefore increases reliability, scalability, and availability of the license granting service. In addition, some of the low quality levels in a codestream can be unencrypted in our DRM system to enable free preview and content-based search with a single DRM-protected codestream.

This paper is organized as follows: In Section 2 the background of Microsoft's WMRM, JPEG 2000 and motion JPEG 2000 are briefly described. They are the basis in describing our DRM system. In Section 3 the detail of our DRM system is described. Experimental results are reported in Section 4 and the paper concludes with Section 5.

2   Background

2.1   Microsoft's Windows Media Rights Manager

Microsoft has developed a Windows based DRM system called *Windows Media Rights Manager* (WMRM). A developer can download the WMRM and format SDKs to build his or her own DRM applications. Fig. 1 shows the work flow of Microsoft's WMRM. The basic WMRM process is described as follows. More details can be found in [15].

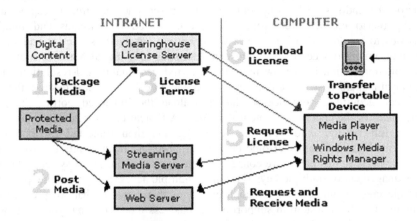

Fig. 1. Microsoft's windows media rights manager flow (from [15])

i. **Packaging.** The rights manager encrypts the digital media and then packages the content into a digital media file. The decryption key is stored in an encrypted license which is distributed separately from the media file. Other information such as a link to the license is added to the media file to facilitate license acquisition.

ii. **Distribution.** The packaged file is distributed to users through some distribution channels such as downloading, streaming, and CD/DVD. Superdistribution is a convenient distribution mechanism. There is no restriction on distribution of the packaged content.

iii. **Establishing a license server.** The content provider (referred to as the publisher in the following) chooses a license clearing house that stores the specific rights or rules of the license and runs a license server which is used to authenticate the consumer's request for a license. Licenses and protected media files are distributed and stored separately to make it easier to manage the entire system.

iv. **License acquisition.** To play the protected content, a consumer first acquires a license which contains the decryption key and the rights the consumer has with the content. This process can be done in a transparent way to the consumer or with minimal involvement of the consumer (such as when payment or information is required).

v. **Playing the content.** A player that supports the DRM system is needed to play the protected content. The DRM system ensures that the content is consumed according to the rights or rules included inside the license. Licenses can have different rights, such as start times and dates, duration, and counted operations. Licenses, however, are typically not transferable. Each consumer has to acquire his or her own license to play the protected content.

Microsoft's WMRM is a complex and complete DRM system with a lot of advanced features such as revocation, license backup and restoration, obfuscation and other tamper-resistant mechanisms. By building our research DRM system on top of Microsoft's WMRM, we are able to leverage the existing modules and building blocks in WMRM and focus on the key DRM modules under studies. We believe that this approach is the easiest way to build a real and working DRM system for research purpose.

2.2 JPEG 2000/Motion JPEG 2000 and Scalable Encryption

For convenience, we use motion JPEG 2000 as the scalable codec to demonstrate our DRM system in this paper. Our DRM system is also applicable to other scalable codecs. JPEG 2000 [12] is the newest image coding standard based on the wavelet transform. In JPEG 2000, an image can be partitioned into smaller rectangular regions called tiles. Each tile is encoded independently. Data in a tile is divided into one or more components in a color space. A wavelet transform is applied to each tile-component to decompose it into different resolution levels. The lowest frequency subband is referred to as the resolution level 0 subband, which is also resolution 0. The image at resolution r (r>0) consists of the data of the image at resolution (r-1) and the subbands at resolution level r. Each subband is partitioned into smaller non-overlapping rectangular blocks called code-blocks. Each code-block is independently entropy-encoded. Bitstreams from code-blocks are distributed across one or more layers in the codestream. Each layer represents a quality increment. A layer consists of a number of consecutive bit-plane coding passes from each code-block in the tile, including all subbands of all components for that tile. JPEG 2000 also provides an intermediate space-frequency structure known as the precinct. A precinct is a collection of spatially contiguous code-blocks from all subbands at a particular resolution level. The fundamental building block in a JPEG 2000 codestream is called the packet, which is simply a continuous segment in the compressed codestream that consists of a number of bit-plane coding passes from each code-block in a precinct. Each packet is uniquely identified by the five scalable parameters: tile, component, resolution level, layer, and precinct. In motion JPEG 2000, each frame is independently encoded as an image with JPEG 2000. Details on JPEG 2000 and motion JPEG 2000 can be found in [12][13].

Many scalable encryption schemes have been proposed for JPEG 2000 [16-20]. They can be used as a building block in our DRM system to encrypt motion JPEG 2000 codestreams. Multiple access control for a scalable codestream is equivalent to the access control of a partially ordered hierarchic set (poset). An efficient key scheme for a poset was proposed in [21], which is the basis of the key scheme of multiple accesses in our DRM system. Fig. 2 shows the key generation scheme in [21] that a parent node such as n_1 derives the key of its child node n_2 by using the parent's key k_1, the unique label l_2 of the node n_2, and the value $v_{1,2}$ of the edge linking the parent node n_1 to the child node n_2 : $k_2 = v_{1,2} + H(k_1, l_2)$, where $H(\cdot)$ is a cryptographic hash function.

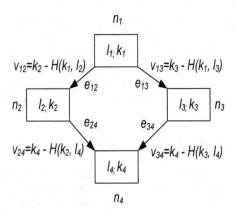

Fig. 2. Key scheme proposed in [21] which is the basis for the multiple access control of our DRM system. The arithmetic is modulo ρ which is a proper number.

3 Our Multi-access DRM System

In our DRM system, content is packed by the content owner or a publisher. The license terms of the content is then sent to a license server in a secure channel. Each publisher uses a publisher-specific master key in generating encryption keys to encrypt all the contents packed by the publisher. This master key has to be shared with the license server to enable the latter to generate decryption keys for clients. Symmetric encryption is used to encrypt the content so that the same key is used for both encryption and decryption. When a player plays a protected content, the DRM header packed with the content is extracted and the local license store and possibly the local secure storage of play statistics such as the number of times the content has been played are searched for a valid license of the content. If the search returns positive, the access key in the local license store is extracted along with the access node which is the subroot of all the accessible types and levels. The keys of all the lower access levels that the user has the right to access are derived and used by the client DRM module to decrypt the corresponding data of the protected content. The decrypted data is then decoded and rendered to show to the user. The associated DRM parameters in a secure local storage such as the count of playing times are adjusted accordingly. If no valid license can be found from the local license store, the user is prompted to select a proper access type(s) and level(s) with possible payment, depending on the setting of the content owner. The information is sent to the license server along with the key generation information included in a DRM header packed with the protected content. The license server generates the key for the specific access type(s) and level(s) and returns to the client in a license which also contains the acquired rights by the user. The client receives the license and stores it in the local license store. The aforementioned process when a valid license is found in the local license store is repeated to play the protected content. The detail of the processes is described in the subsequent sections.

3.1 Content Packaging

A publisher must first generate a pair of public and private keys called content publisher public key $K_{P,Pub}$ and private key $K_{P,Priv}$ and a publisher-specific master key $K_{P,M}$ before performing any content packaging. The publisher has also to obtain a certificate $C_{P,pub}$ for the public key $K_{P,Pub}$ from a certificate authority. The certificate will be used by a client to verify the publisher's public key in a DRM protected codestream. Armed with the above keys and the certificate, the publisher is ready to pack contents into DRM-protected codestreams.

To pack an individual piece of content, the publisher first generates a unique ID denoted as *KeyID* for the content. This *KeyID* is used to identify the license associated with the protected content in a local license store as well as to generate encryption keys. Since content is encrypted with a symmetric encryption primitive in our DRM system, decryption and encryption keys are the same. As we mentioned previously, multiple access control of a scalable codestream such as motion JPEG 2000 is equivalent to the access control of a poset with a single root node. The key of the root node is generated with the following equation in our DRM system:

$$k_{root} = MAC_{K_{P,M}} (KeyID), \tag{1}$$

where $MAC(\cdot)$ is a Message Authentication Code (MAC) which can be implemented with a secure keyed hash function. This equation means that the root key k_{root} of the multiple access control is a MAC of the *KeyID* with the master key as the key in generating the MAC.

To generate other encryption keys, the Hasse diagram representing the multiple access poset is first generated. Each node n_i except the root node $n_0 \equiv n_{root}$ is assigned a random key k_i. Those keys are used to encrypt the corresponding data for each frame. To avoid repetitively applying the same encryption parameters to encrypt different frames, each frame is inserted with a random initialization vector IV_{frame} which is used together with the above keys in encrypting the data for the corresponding frame. A proper scalable encryption scheme is used in the encryption process. For motion JPEG 2000, any scheme described in [17-19] can be used.

To enable a node to derive all the keys of its descendants, the key scheme proposed in [21] for a poset is used in our DRM system. Each node n_i in the Hasse diagram is assigned a unique label l_i. Since an encrypted scalable codestream may be truncated to fit a certain application scenario, care has to be taken in generating the node labels. We want to ensure that the nodes generated by a truncated codestream match the original nodes without any truncation. This implies that the node labels should be invariant to truncations. In other words, truncation-invariant parameters that uniquely identify each node should be used in generating the node labels. For JPEG 2000 and motion JPEG 2000, canvas coordinates are such parameters and are used in our DRM system to generate truncation invariant node labels { l_i }. The labels generated in this way are unique and therefore valid. A major advantage in generating the labels { l_i } in such a way is that the labels are not stored in a DRM-protected codestream. They can be regenerated once the Hasse diagram is generated. The file size overhead is therefore reduced. The value $v_{i,j}$ for each edge $e_{i,j}$ in the Hasse diagram that links a parent node n_i to its child node n_j is then calculated as:

$$v_{i,j} = k_j - H(k_i, l_j) . \tag{2}$$

A publisher packages the following information into a DRM-protected codestream:

- **KeyID:** This allows the proper license to be looked up in a local license store and requested from a license server. It is also used by a license server to generate the root key of the codestream. KeyID also contains information to identify the publisher.
- **License Server URL:** This allows a client to request a license from a proper license server.
- **Information of access types and levels:** This contains the information for the supported multiple access types and number of access levels for each type of the protected codestream packaged by the publisher.
- **Key generation information:** This contains the edge values of the Hasse diagram ordered in a certain order, and the information on how the edges are ordered and how the nodes are labeled. The information will be used to generate decryption keys by both the license server and the client.
- **Other DRM information:** This contains additional information about the DRM protection of the codestream such as DRM version, encryption scheme, etc.
- **Publisher's signature:** Everything above is signed with the publisher's private key $K_{P,Priv}$.
- **Publisher's public key $K_{P,Pub}$ and certificate $C_{P,pub}$:** This part allows a client to check whether the DRM header has been tampered or not before requesting a license. This is important in preventing hackers from modifying

DRM header to point to a malicious server that a client machine might get viruses or other attacks when requesting license from the server.

3.2 Content Playing

Fig. 3 shows the sequence of steps a player executes in playing a codestream. In the first step, a player opens the codestream and checks whether the codestream is DRM-protected or not. If a DRM header is found, the DRM subsystem on the client side is called, and the DRM header is sent to the subsystem along with the requested action such as playing. When first launched, the DRM subsystem performs sanity checks to ensure that the subsystem is functioning well and there is no tampering to the system. It then extracts the publisher's public key and corresponding certificate from the DRM header and checks whether the DRM header has been tampered or not. If the checking is passed, *KeyID* is extracted from the DRM header and used to search the local license store to find any matching licenses. Our DRM system allows multiple licenses on a client side for the same protected content. Each license is assigned a priority level. All found matching licenses are ordered and checked for validity and to find out if there is any valid license that matches the requested action. Any invalid licenses are removed from the license store. If multiple valid and matching licenses are found, the default action is that the one that matches the client's characteristics and has the highest priority is used. For example, if the client is a powerful PC, the license containing the key of the highest access priority in the Hasse diagram, e.g., in case of motion JPEG 2000 the one with the highest resolution and best quality is used by default. A user can also set the DRM system to prompt the user to select from the set of licenses. If no valid license can be found from the license store, the user is asked to select the access type(s) and level(s) of which the decryption key is requested. An alternative approach is to select the access type(s) and level(s) automatically that best fits the client's hardware without user's input. A user can set up the DRM system to behave in either mode. A user may be requested to pay in this process, depending on the setting of the publisher. Once a license is acquired from a license server, the license is inserted into the local license store, and is used to address the current requested action. The detail of license acquisition is described in the next subsection.

In the next step, the DRM system extracts the information on access types and levels from the DRM header to generate the corresponding Hasse diagram of the multiple access control supported by the encrypted scalable codestream. The key generation information is also extracted from the DRM header to regenerate the unique label for each node and to assign the value for each edge in the Hasse diagram. The decryption key and the information of the corresponding node of the key are extracted from the license. The keys of all the descendants of the node are then derived in the following way: if node n_i is a parent of node n_j, and the edge linking the two nodes has a value $v_{i,j}$, then the key k_j of node n_j can be derived from the key k_i of the parent node n_i and the label l_j of the child node k_j:

$$k_j = v_{i,j} + H(k_i, l_j).$$ (3)

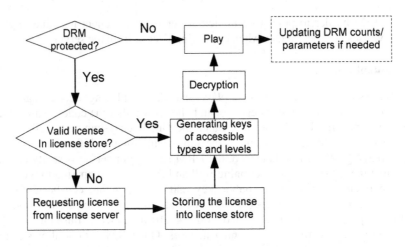

Fig. 3. Content playing flowchart

Eq. (3) is applied repetitively until the keys of all the descendants have been derived. Once the decryption keys that the user has rights to access are available, they are used to decrypt the encrypted data for each frame, together with the frame initialization vector IV_{frame}. Decrypted data is then decompressed and rendered for the user to view the content. At the last stage for DRM-protected content, the DRM parameters in the local secure storage such as playing counts are updated if needed to reflect the accomplished action requested by the user.

3.3 License and License Acquisition

License has to be acquired before the DRM-protected content can be played. Each license is individualized that only the targeted client can use it. This is achieved by generating a pair of public key $K_{C,Pub}$ and private key $K_{C,Priv}$ for the client with a DRM key generation module at the DRM system installation phase. The private key $K_{C,Priv}$ is tied with the hardware's unique IDs of the client's machine while the public key $K_{C,Pub}$ is signed by a trusted certificate authority. The certificate $C_{C,pub}$ of the client's public key $K_{C,Priv}$ is stored at a local store, which will be used in communication with a license server during license acquisition time.

To acquire a license, the client DRM subsystem first extracts the license server's URL from the DRM header, and uses the client's public and private keys to authenticate with the license server through a public key based challenge and response protocol. In our DRM system, the license server also has a pair of public and private keys, with the public key signed by a certificate authority. After the mutual authentication, the client's DRM subsystem sends to the license server securely the *KeyID*, the information of access types and levels, the key generation information extracted from the DRM header along with the requested access type(s) and level(s) selected by the user or automatically by the DRM subsystem that best fits the characteristics of the client's hardware, depending on the setting of the DRM subsystem by the user. The license server identifies the publisher from the received *KeyID* (recall that *KeyID* contains the unique identifier of the publisher), and extracts the publisher's master key $K_{P,M}$. The received information of access types and levels as well as the key generation information are used by the license server to regenerate the Hasse diagram and node labels { l_i }, and assign the edge values $v_{i,j}$. The root key k_{root} of the Hasse diagram is generated with Eq. (1), which is used in turn to generate the key $k_{req.\,node}$ of the node corresponding to the requested type(s) and level(s). The node is in fact the subroot of all the accessible types and levels the requesting user is entitled to access. This key is then packed into a license and sent to the requesting client. We note that in our DRM system, only a single key is sent in a license to a client. The remaining keys associated with the types and levels that are accessible to the client are generated by the client's DRM module based on the received node key $k_{req.\,node}$ and the information obtained from the DRM header of the protected content. Fig. 4 shows the process that a license server generates the key of the requested node.

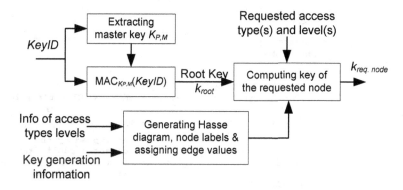

Fig. 4. Key generation by the license server

The rights a client requested and the info about the node of the key generated by a license server are also packed into the license to a client. A license is written in XML for flexibility and extensibility. Fig. 5 shows an example of a license. In the license, the node key $k_{req.\,node}$ is encrypted with the client's public key so that only the client with the corresponding private key can recover the node key. A client's private key is only available to the client DRM subsystem. This effectively prevents a client from sharing the content decryption keys with other clients. The data part of the license is signed by the license server and the chain of certificates is also provided in the license so that a client's DRM subsystem can check whether the license has been tampered or not. When a received license passes the checking, it is inserted into the local license store for future usage.

4   Experimental Results

Without loss of generality, we have implemented our DRM system for motion JPEG 2000 to test functionalities of the system and to conduct feasibility studies. Motion JPEG 2000 provides nice scalabilities ideal to test our DRM system. We should emphasize here that our DRM system is equally applicable to other scalable codecs and formats.

```
<?xml version="1.0" ?>
    <LICENSE version="1.0.0.0">
        <LICENSCONTENT>
            <DATA>
                <KID>...</KID>
                <ISSUEDATA>...</ISSUEDATA>
                <PRIORITY>...</PRIORITY>


                <ONSTORE>
                    <ACTION>
                        secstate.playcount = 5;
                    </ACTION>
                </ONSTORE>

                <ONACTION type="Play">
                    <CONDITION>
                        secstate.playcount > 0
                    </CONDITION>
                    <ACTION>
                        secstate.playcount --
                    </ACTION>
                </ONACTION>

                <KEYDATA>
                    <KEYALGORITHM type="SCALABLEDRM" />
                    <PUBKEY type="client">...</PUBKEY>    ← Client's public
                                                              key.

                    <VALUE>...</VALUE>           ← The node key k_{req., node}

                                                    encrypted by the
                                                    client's public key.
                    <NODEINFO>...</NODEINFO>    ← The node info associated
                                                    with the node key.

                </KEYDATA>
            </DATA>

        <SIGNATURE>
            <HASHALGORITHM type="SHA" />
            <SIGNALGORITHM type="SCALABLEDRM" />  ← Signature signed by
                                                      the license server.

            <VALUE>...</VALUE>
        </SIGNATURE>

        <CERTIFICATECHAIN type="SCALABLEDRM">
            <CERTIFICATE>...</CERTIFICATE>        ← The certificates for
                                                      the license server.
        </CERTIFICATECHAIN>
        <CONTENTPUBKEY>...</CONTENTPUBKEY>

    </LICENSCONTENT>
</LICENSE>
```

Fig. 5. Example of a license to a client

As we mentioned previously, our DRM system was built on top of Microsoft's WMRM. We maximized reuse of the DRM modules offered by the SDKs of Microsoft's WMRM so that we could focus on the core parts we wanted to develop in our DRM system. In our experiments, Kakadu [22] was used as the frame encoder and JasPer 23was used as the frame decoder. A set of standard CIF sequences of first 100 frames were used in our experiments. Each frame was of the size 352 by 288 pixels. Each frame of the experimental sequences was encoded with 5 layers, 3 resolutions, 2 tiles, and 2 precincts. Layers were determined in such a way that each layer shows visible improvement in perceptual quality over the next lower layer. The nominal frame rate was set to 30 frames per second.

Table 1 shows the experimental results of the file size overheads and PSNR values for different layers for four MPEG standard CIF sequences. It can be seen that the file size overheads due to the DRM header for key generation is small, around 0.209% to 0.294%. Since the DRM header does not change with increasing number of frames, we would expect that the actual overhead for a typical length of video should be negligible. The sequence "foreman" at different accesses of resolutions and layers are shown in Fig. 6.

Table 1. Experimental results of file size overheads and PSNR values (in dB) for different layers. Each sequence consists of 100 frames.

Sequence (cif)	Bitrate (kbps)	Overhead (%)	PSNR Layer 5	PSNR Layer 4	PSNR Layer 3	PSNR Layer 2	PSNR Layer 1
crew	6436.16	0.260	42.110	38.328	31.219	28.175	23.901
foreman	7000.18	0.239	42.082	38.222	30.937	27.867	21.695
irene	5682.90	0.294	42.197	39.033	31.604	27.846	23.114
soccer	7975.84	0.209	42.124	37.359	30.081	27.145	22.592

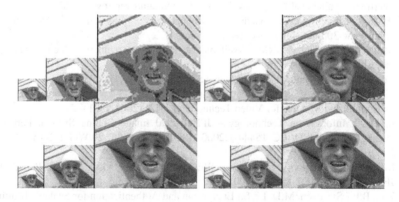

Fig. 6. The sequence "foreman" at resolutions 1, 2, and 3 and layers 1 (top left), 2 (top right), 3 (bottom left), and 4 (bottom right)

5   Conclusion

We have described a DRM system that provides what you see is what you pay, where multimedia content is encoded and encrypted to enable multiple access types and multiple access levels for each type with a single DRM-protected codestream. Different users can share the same protected content or download the codestream truncated to best fit the device. Different keys are acquired for different accesses. We presented in detail the parts of the DRM system that enables a light license server which stores only the publisher's master key. Such a system allows a wide deployment of cheap yet secure servers for license granting services, and therefore improves license service's reliability and availability, and the system's performance since license service is a single point of failure in a DRM system.

References

1. Iannella, R.: Digital Rights Management (DRM) Architectures. D-Lib Magazine, 7(6) (June 2001)
2. Eskicioglu, A.M., Town, J., Delp, E.J.: Security of Digital Entertainment Content from Creation to Consumption. Signal Processing: Image Communication, Special Issue on Image Security. 18(4) (2003) 237 – 262
3. ISO/IEC JTC1/SC29/WG11 13818-11:2003(E). Information Technology – Generic Coding of Moving Pictures and Associated Audio Information – Part 11: IPMP on MPEG-2 Systems (2003)
4. ISO/IEC JTC1/SC29/WG11 14496-13:2004(E). Information Technology – Coding of Audio-Visual Object – Part 13: Intellectual Property Management and Protection (IPMP) Extensions (2004)
5. Open Mobile Alliance. OMA DRM Specification Draft Version 2.0. http://www.openmobilealliance.org (March 2004)
6. Microsoft Windows Media Digital Rights Management. Available at http://www.microsoft.com/windows/windowsmedia/drm/default.aspx
7. Intertrust. Available at http://www.intertrust.com/main/overview/drm.html
8. IBM: Electronic Media Management System. Available at http://www-306.ibm.com/software/data/emms/
9. RealNetworks: Helix DRM. Available at http://www.realnetworks.com/products/drm/index.html
10. Adobe EBooks. Available at http://www.adobe.com/epaper/ebooks
11. Li, W.: Overview of Fine Granularity Scalability in MPEG-4 Video Standard. IEEE Trans. on Circuits and Systems for Video Technology. 11(3) (2001) 301 – 317
12. ISO/IEC: Information Technology – JPEG 2000 Image Coding System, Part 1: Core Coding System. ISO/IEC 15444-1:2000 (ISO/IEC JTC/SC 29/WG 1 N1646R) (March 2000)
13. ISO/IEC: Information Technology – JPEG 2000 Image Coding System, Part 3: Motion JPEG 2000. ISO/IEC 15444-3:2002
14. Zhu, B.B., Swanson, M.D. Li, S.: Encryption and Authentication for Scalable Multimedia: Current State of the Art and Challenges. Proc. of SPIE Internet Multimedia Management Systems V, Vol. 5601, Philadelphia PA (Oct. 2004) 157-170
15. Microsoft: Architecture of Windows Media Rights Manager. Available at http://www.microsoft.com/windows/windowsmedia/howto/articles/drmarchitecture.aspx.
16. Wee, S.J. Apostolopoulos, J.G.: Secure Scalable Streaming and Secure Transcoding with JPEG-2000. IEEE Int. Image Processing, 1 (Sept. 2003) I-205-208
17. Wu, H., Ma, D.: Efficient and Secure Encryption Schemes for JPEG2000. IEEE Int. Conf. on Acoustics, Speech, and Signal Processing, 2004 (ICASSP '04). 5 (May 2004) V869 — 872

18. Wu, Y., Deng, R. H.: Compliant Encryption of JPEG2000 Codestreams. IEEE. Int. Conf. on Image Processing 2004 (ICIP'04), Singapore (Oct. 2004) 3447-3450

19. Zhu, B.B., Yang, Y., Li, S.: JPEG 2000 Encryption Enabling Fine Granularity Scalability without Decryption. IEEE Int. Symp. Circuits and Systems 2005. (May 2005) 6304 – 6307

20. Zhu, B.B., Feng, M., Li, S.: A Framework of Scalable Layered Access Control for Multimedia. IEEE Int. Symp. Circuits and Systems 2005. (May 2005) 2703-2706

21. Zhong, S.: A Practical Key Management Scheme for Access Control in a User Hierarchy. Computer & Security. 21(8) (2002) 750-759

22. Kakadu. Available from http://www.kakadusoftware.com/welcome.html

23. JasPer. Available from http://www.ece.uvic.ca/~mdadams/jasper/

Author Index

Lecture Notes in Computer Science

For information about Vols. 1–3975

please contact your bookseller or Springer

Vol. 4019: M. Johnson, V. Vene (Eds.), Algebraic Methodology and Software Technology. XI, 389 pages. 2006.

Vol. 4018: V. Wade, H. Ashman, B. Smyth (Eds.), Adaptive Hypermedia and Adaptive Web-Based Systems. XVI, 474 pages. 2006.

Vol. 4016: J.X. Yu, M. Kitsuregawa, H.V. Leong (Eds.), Advances in Web-Age Information Management. XVII, 606 pages. 2006.

Vol. 4014: T. Uustalu (Ed.), Mathematics of Program Construction. X, 455 pages. 2006.

Vol. 4013: L. Lamontagne, M. Marchand (Eds.), Advances in Artificial Intelligence. XIII, 564 pages. 2006. (Sublibrary LNAI).

Vol. 4012: T. Washio, A. Sakurai, K. Nakajima, H. Takeda, S. Tojo, M. Yokoo (Eds.), New Frontiers in Artificial Intelligence. XIII, 484 pages. 2006. (Sublibrary LNAI).

Vol. 4011: Y. Sure, J. Domingue (Eds.), The Semantic Web: Research and Applications. XIX, 726 pages. 2006.

Vol. 4010: S. Dunne, B. Stoddart (Eds.), Unifying Theories of Programming. VIII, 257 pages. 2006.

Vol. 4009: M. Lewenstein, G. Valiente (Eds.), Combinatorial Pattern Matching. XII, 414 pages. 2006.

Vol. 4008: J.C. Augusto, C.D. Nugent (Eds.), Designing Smart Homes. XI, 183 pages. 2006. (Sublibrary LNAI).

Vol. 4007: C. Àlvarez, M. Serna (Eds.), Experimental Algorithms. XI, 329 pages. 2006.

Vol. 4006: L.M. Pinho, M. González Harbour (Eds.), Reliable Software Technologies – Ada-Europe 2006. XII, 241 pages. 2006.

Vol. 4005: G. Lugosi, H.U. Simon (Eds.), Learning Theory. XI, 656 pages. 2006. (Sublibrary LNAI).

Vol. 4004: S. Vaudenay (Ed.), Advances in Cryptology - EUROCRYPT 2006. XIV, 613 pages. 2006.

Vol. 4003: Y. Koucheryavy, J. Harju, V.B. Iversen (Eds.), Next Generation Teletraffic and Wired/Wireless Advanced Networking. XVI, 582 pages. 2006.

Vol. 4001: E. Dubois, K. Pohl (Eds.), Advanced Information Systems Engineering. XVI, 560 pages. 2006.

Vol. 3999: C. Kop, G. Fliedl, H.C. Mayr, E. Métais (Eds.), Natural Language Processing and Information Systems. XIII, 227 pages. 2006.

Vol. 3998: T. Calamoneri, I. Finocchi, G.F. Italiano (Eds.), Algorithms and Complexity. XII, 394 pages. 2006.

Vol. 3997: W. Grieskamp, C. Weise (Eds.), Formal Approaches to Software Testing. XII, 219 pages. 2006.

Vol. 3996: A. Keller, J.-P. Martin-Flatin (Eds.), Self-Managed Networks, Systems, and Services. X, 185 pages. 2006.

Vol. 3995: G. Müller (Ed.), Emerging Trends in Information and Communication Security. XX, 524 pages. 2006.

Vol. 3994: V.N. Alexandrov, G.D. van Albada, P.M.A. Sloot, J. Dongarra (Eds.), Computational Science – ICCS 2006, Part IV. XXXV, 1096 pages. 2006.

Vol. 3993: V.N. Alexandrov, G.D. van Albada, P.M.A. Sloot, J. Dongarra (Eds.), Computational Science – ICCS 2006, Part III. XXXVI, 1136 pages. 2006.

Vol. 3992: V.N. Alexandrov, G.D. van Albada, P.M.A. Sloot, J. Dongarra (Eds.), Computational Science – ICCS 2006, Part II. XXXV, 1122 pages. 2006.

Vol. 3991: V.N. Alexandrov, G.D. van Albada, P.M.A. Sloot, J. Dongarra (Eds.), Computational Science – ICCS 2006, Part I. LXXXI, 1096 pages. 2006.

Vol. 3990: J. C. Beck, B.M. Smith (Eds.), Integration of AI and OR Techniques in Constraint Programming for Combinatorial Optimization Problems. X, 301 pages. 2006.

Vol. 3989: J. Zhou, M. Yung, F. Bao, Applied Cryptography and Network Security. XIV, 488 pages. 2006.

Vol. 3988: A. Beckmann, U. Berger, B. Löwe, J.V. Tucker (Eds.), Logical Approaches to Computational Barriers. XV, 608 pages. 2006.

Vol. 3987: M. Hazas, J. Krumm, T. Strang (Eds.), Location- and Context-Awareness. X, 289 pages. 2006.

Vol. 3986: K. Stølen, W.H. Winsborough, F. Martinelli, F. Massacci (Eds.), Trust Management. XIV, 474 pages. 2006.

Vol. 3984: M. Gavrilova, O. Gervasi, V. Kumar, C.J. K. Tan, D. Taniar, A. Laganà, Y. Mun, H. Choo (Eds.), Computational Science and Its Applications - ICCSA 2006, Part V. XXV, 1045 pages. 2006.

Vol. 3983: M. Gavrilova, O. Gervasi, V. Kumar, C.J. K. Tan, D. Taniar, A. Laganà, Y. Mun, H. Choo (Eds.), Computational Science and Its Applications - ICCSA 2006, Part IV. XXVI, 1191 pages. 2006.

Vol. 3982: M. Gavrilova, O. Gervasi, V. Kumar, C.J. K. Tan, D. Taniar, A. Laganà, Y. Mun, H. Choo (Eds.), Computational Science and Its Applications - ICCSA 2006, Part III. XXV, 1243 pages. 2006.

Vol. 3981: M. Gavrilova, O. Gervasi, V. Kumar, C.J. K. Tan, D. Taniar, A. Laganà, Y. Mun, H. Choo (Eds.), Computational Science and Its Applications - ICCSA 2006, Part II. XXVI, 1255 pages. 2006.

Vol. 3980: M. Gavrilova, O. Gervasi, V. Kumar, C.J. K. Tan, D. Taniar, A. Laganà, Y. Mun, H. Choo (Eds.), Computational Science and Its Applications - ICCSA 2006, Part I. LXXV, 1199 pages. 2006.

Vol. 3979: T.S. Huang, N. Sebe, M.S. Lew, V. Pavlović, M. Kölsch, A. Galata, B. Kisačanin (Eds.), Computer Vision in Human-Computer Interaction. XII, 121 pages. 2006.

Vol. 3978: B. Hnich, M. Carlsson, F. Fages, F. Rossi (Eds.), Recent Advances in Constraints. VIII, 179 pages. 2006. (Sublibrary LNAI).

Vol. 3977: N. Fuhr, M. Lalmas, S. Malik, G. Kazai (Eds.), Advances in XML Information Retrieval and Evaluation. XII, 556 pages. 2006.

Vol. 3976: F. Boavida, T. Plagemann, B. Stiller, C. Westphal, E. Monteiro (Eds.), NETWORKING 2006. Networking Technologies, Services, and Protocols; Performance of Computer and Communication Networks; Mobile and Wireless Communications Systems. XXVI, 1276 pages. 2006.